PHILOSOPHERS

Contents

World map and timeline

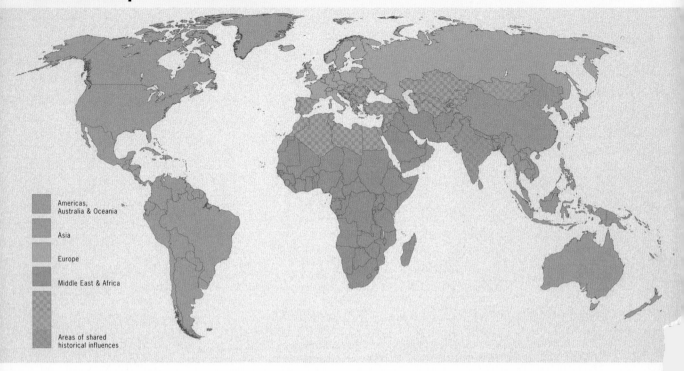

Americas,
Australia & Oceania

Asia

Europe

Middle East & Africa

Areas of shared
historical influences

This history of philosophers and their world-changing endeavors begins with a map and timeline. These are intended to help locate philosophers both geographically and within a general temporal framework.

World map

The map is divided into four major areas: the Americas, Australia, Oceania (all colored purple); Asia (blue); Europe (green); and the Middle East and Africa (brown). The demarcations provide a rough guide to each person's birth place and sphere of influence and the same color-coded theme is carried through the rest of the book. Of course divisions of this nature must reflect a certain arbitrariness, and cultural influences are rarely so geographically bound. It will be noted that some areas on the map overlap, representing approximate

regions of shared historical influence. For example, the Iberian Peninsula – now modern Spain and Portugal, and part of Europe – is shown to overlap with North Africa to indicate the spread of Arab culture during the Golden Age of Islam. Likewise, classical Greek philosophers born in what is now modern Turkey, part of the Middle East, are located in an area sharing historical links with Europe, indicating the vast reach of Greek culture during ancient times.

Timeline

The timeline highlights periods of intense philosophical activity, and locates philosophers in a stream of time running from the seventh century BCE to the present day. The numbers in the colored dots refer to the list of philosophers on the page opposite; their positions on the timeline are determined according to birth dates.

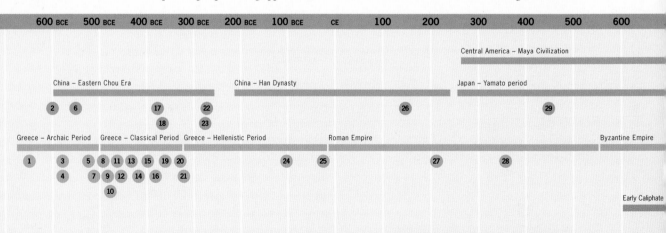

| 600 BCE | 500 BCE | 400 BCE | 300 BCE | 200 BCE | 100 BCE | CE | 100 | 200 | 300 | 400 | 500 | 600 |

Central America – Maya Civilization

China – Eastern Chou Era   China – Han Dynasty   Japan – Yamato period

2   6   17   22   26   29

18   23

Greece – Archaic Period   Greece – Classical Period   Greece – Hellenistic Period   Roman Empire   Byzantine Empire

1   3   5   8   11   13   15   19   20   24   25   27   28

4   7   9   12   14   16   21

10

Early Caliphate

Americas, Australia, & Oceania

70 Charles Peirce 1839–1914
71 William James 1842–1910
76 John Dewey 1859–1952
90 Nelson Goodman 1906–98
93 William Van Orman
   Quine 1908–2000
96 John Rawls 1921–2002
98 Noam Chomsky b.1928
101 Richard Rorty 1931–2007
102 John Searle b.1932
103 Robert Nozick 1938–2002
104 Peter Singer b.1946

Asia

2 Laozi c.605–c.530 BCE
6 Confucius c.551–479 BCE
17 Mencius c.372–289 BCE
18 Zhuangzi c.370–c.301 BCE
22 Li Si c.280–208 BCE
23 Traditional Indian
   philosophy c.300 BCE–c.1200 CE
26 Nagarjuna c.150–c.250
29 Zen Masters From the fifth century
30 Kukai 774–835
77 Nishida Kitaro 1870–1945
81 Sarvepalli
   Radhakrishnan 1888–1975

Europe

1 Thales of Miletus c.640–c.651/c.549 BCE
3 Pythagoras c.570–c.500 BCE
4 Xenophanes
   of Colophon c.570–c.475 BCE
5 Heraclitus of Ephesus c.535–c.475 BCE
7 Parmenides of Elea c.510–c.450 BCE
8 Anaxagoras c.500–428 BCE
9 Empedocles c.493–c.433 BCE
10 Zeno of Elea c.490–c.425 BCE

11 Protagoras c.490–420 BCE
12 Socrates c.470–399 BCE
13 Democritus c.460–c.370 BCE
14 Plato c.428–347 BCE
15 Diogenes the Cynic c.404–323 BCE
16 Aristotle 384–322 BCE
19 Pyrrho of Elis c.360–c.270 BCE
20 Epicurus 341–270 BCE
21 Zeno of Citium 335–263 BCE
24 Cicero 106–43 BCE
25 Philo of Alexandria c.20 BCE–c.50 CE
27 Plotinus 205–270
28 Saint Augustine of Hippo 354–430
34 Saint Anselm
   of Canterbury 1033–1109
36 Peter Abelard 1079–1142
39 Saint Albert the Great c.1206–80
40 Saint Thomas Aquinas c.1225–74
41 John Duns Scotus c.1266–1308
42 William of Ockham c.1287–1347
43 Niccolò Machiavelli 1469–1527
44 Francis Bacon 1561–1626
45 Thomas Hobbes 1588–1679
46 René Descartes 1596–1650
47 Baruch Spinoza 1632–77
48 John Locke 1632–1704
49 Gottfried Leibniz 1646–1716
50 George Berkeley 1685–1753
51 Joseph Butler 1692–1752
52 Voltaire 1694–1778
53 David Hume 1711–76
54 Jean-Jacques
   Rousseau 1712–78
55 Adam Smith 1723–90
56 Immanuel Kant 1724–1804
57 Moses Mendelssohn 1729–86
58 Edmund Burke 1729–97
59 Thomas Paine 1737–1809
60 Jeremy Bentham 1748–1832
61 Mary Wollstonecraft 1759–97
62 Georg Wilhelm
   Friedrich Hegel 1770–1831

63 Arthur Schopenhauer 1788–1860
64 Auguste Comte 1798–1857
65 John Stuart Mill 1806–73
66 Alexander Herzen 1812–70
67 Søren Kierkegaard 1813–55
68 Karl Marx 1818–83
69 Friedrich Engels 1820–95
72 Friedrich Nietzsche 1844–1900
73 Gottlob Frege 1848–1925
74 Edmund Husserl 1859–1938
75 Henri Bergson 1859–1941
78 Bertrand Russell 1872–1970
79 George Edward Moore 1873–1958
80 José Ortega y Gasset 1883–1955
82 Ludwig Wittgenstein 1889–1951
83 Martin Heidegger 1889–1976
84 Rudolf Carnap 1891–1970
85 Gilbert Ryle 1900–76
86 Karl Popper 1902–94
88 Jean-Paul Sartre 1905–80
89 Kurt Gödel 1906–78
91 Maurice
   Merleau-Ponty 1908–61
92 Simone de Beauvoir 1908–86
94 Isaiah Berlin 1909–97
95 Alfred Jules Ayer 1910–89
97 Michel Foucault 1926–84
99 Bernard Williams 1929–2003
100 Jacques Derrida 1930–2004

Middle East & Africa

31 Al-Kindi
   (Alkindus) c.801–c.873
32 Avicenna (Ibn Sina) c.980–1037
33 Solomon ibn Gabirol
   (Avicebrol) c.1022–c.1058
35 Al-Ghazali (Algazel) 1058–1111
37 Averroës (Ibn Rushd) 1126–98
38 Moses Maimonides 1135–1204
87 Sayyid Abul
   Ala Maududi 1903–79

	800	900	1000	1100	1200	1300	1400	1500	1600	1700	1800	1900	2000

North America – Hohokam Civilization
South America – Inca Empire
Age of Revolutions   World War I & World War II

70 76 | 93 98 104
71 | 90 96 102

Japan – Heian period
China – Ming Dynasty
77 81 | 101 103

30

European Renaissance
Enlightenment

85 91

34 36 | 39 40 41 | 43 | 44 46 47 50 53 58 61 64 67 72 78 86 94
42 | 45 | 48 51 54 59 62 65 68 73 80 100
49 52 55 60 63 66 69 79 84 95

Islamic Renaissance
Mughal Empire
56 | 75 83 88 97

31 | 32 33 35 37 | 57 | 74 82 89 99
38 | 87 92

7

Introduction

Immanuel Kant, one of the most influential thinkers of the eighteenth century, once said that philosophy explores three questions: "What can I know?", "What should I do?", and "What may I hope?" And all of these add up to one great question: "What is a human being?" Fundamental questions such as these − essentially questions that every person reflecting on the world is prone to ask − are the sort of questions addressed by philosophers.

Although the word "philosophy" originates in the Western intellectual tradition (it means "love of wisdom" in Greek), many figures from Eastern cultures have pondered over the same seemingly insoluble questions, sometimes with strikingly different results. The corpus of work of philosophers from the Far East, including China, India, and Japan, and the general area, makes up what is known as Eastern philosophy, while the philosophers of North Africa and the Near East, because of their strong interactions with Europe, contribute to Western philosophy.

Philosophical thought was born when the Greek philosopher Thales, in c.600 BCE, began to employ reason in his quest to explain the natural forces of the world around him. This marked him out from others who were offering supernatural accounts of phenomena, or from religious thinkers who used revelation and dogma to support their answers to fundamental questions of right and wrong, and life and death. Thales' final conclusion may have been wrong (he claimed that everything is made out of water), but his method of thinking was philosophical. Similarly, Confucius in the East, around 100 years after Thales, began looking for rational answers, this time to questions about how people should live and be governed. His ideas would provide the basic structure of Chinese culture and society, and underpin government elsewhere in Asia, for hundreds of years.

Until the Renaissance in Europe, philosophy and science were considered to be the same discipline. The works of Aristotle and other philosophers from ancient Greece played a large part in forming the foundations for the natural sciences, and then later the social sciences. But although science, like philosophy, searches for answers to difficult questions, philosophy and science are essentially distinct by virtue of the methods they employ. Philosophers look for answers through rational argument, logic, and linguistic analysis, and not primarily through experimental data collected from the world, the basic method of scientists.

The Enlightenment philosopher John Locke famously said that philosophy is a sort of intellectual "underlaborer" to the sciences. Others prefer to think of philosophy not as something "useful" to other disciplines, but as a discipline that opens up possibilities in thought, that leads to new ways to understand human nature and the human experience. What is certain is that philosophers through the ages have influenced countless generations to adopt certain behavior, to forge new programs of research, even, in the most negative example, to provide a foundation of belief that could underpin something so terrible as the Holocaust, as Nietzsche's philosophy was misappropriated by the Nazis to do.

Although the selection of philosophers in this book is, by its nature, somewhat arbitrary, as so many influential philosophers have lived and could have been included, those chosen are generally acknowledged as leaders in their field or representative of a particular movement. All can be said to have left indelible marks on the world.

On using the book

■ The entries on each philosopher are arranged chronologically, roughly according to birth dates. Entries are color-coded to match the geographical regions described on pages 6–7.

■ Each entry includes a short description of the life and work of the philosopher, essential points about their philosophy, key dates in their biography, and an analysis of their legacy and contribution.

■ Cross-references to other philosophers in this book are given in grey bold type (e.g. **Réne Descartes**) on their first appearance in an entry. These cross-references allow the reader to track philosophical developments by turning to all the pages that are linked in this way.

■ Philosophical terms are in dark bold type (e.g. **existentialism**) the first time they appear in each entry, and are explained in the glossary on pages 198–205.

■ Generally, philosophers are referred to by their names in common usage, although full and alternative names are also given.

■ Arabic names are used unless a Latinized version is more well known in the West.

■ Chinese names − with the surname first − are given in the modern Pinyin transliteration, although the older Wade-Giles version is also mentioned.

Thales of Miletus

Thales is recognized as the first sage of the Western world to engage in genuinely philosophical thought. Rather than offer supernatural accounts of phenomena, he employed reason in his quest to uncover the natural forces at work. Sometimes known as the "father of science", he is best remembered for his claim that everything is ultimately made out of water.

There is little we know for certain of Thales' life and since none of his writings survive what we know comes to us through later writers. He was a citizen of the trading port of Miletus in Ionia (now part of modern Turkey) where Eastern and Egyptian ideas mingled with Greek thought. According to Greek historian Herodotus (c.484–c.425 BCE), he successfully predicted an eclipse of the sun which took place in 585 BCE, a skill he probably acquired from the Egyptians. **Aristotle** tells the story that Thales was able to foresee a good olive crop by studying the stars. He bought up all the olive presses in Miletus, and then made a profit by renting them out, thus showing the practical value of his learning. **Plato** says that Thales fell into a well while looking up at the sky. When a young girl answered his cries she asked how he expected to learn about the stars when he didn't even know what was beneath his feet.

> ### *Time is the wisest of things, for it finds out everything.*
>
> Thales, quoted in Diogenes Laertius, *The Lives and Opinions of Eminent Philosophers* (third century CE)

Essential philosophy

The water theory

Thales' claim that everything is made of water is often regarded as the first of many scientific hypotheses concerning the ultimate nature of physical reality. The theory states that throughout all processes of physical change there remains some underlying substance – water – which remains constant. It seems probable that observations of how water mutates through distinct states – solid, liquid, and vapor – may well have inspired the conjecture. He also noted that all living things consume water. Coming from a seafaring culture it would have been natural for him to see water as the source of sustenance and life.

Cosmology

Whatever the origins of the water theory, it was closely allied to his cosmological view that the earth floats in a vast ocean and that it originally came from the sea by a process of solidification. The theory also provided Thales with an explanation of earthquakes: that they are produced when the earth is rocked by waves. The particular

Legacy, truth, consequence

■ Thales was the first of three philosophers – the other two were Anaximander (who flourished c.550 BCE and may have been a pupil of Thales) and Anaximines (*fl.* c.550 BCE) – who together formed the Milesian school.
■ The importance of the Milesians lies in their preparedness to search for naturalistic explanations of phenomena and for the ultimate substance from which all things are composed. This project still informs modern physics with its efforts to find a unified theory that will explain everything.

Key dates

c.640 BCE	In one report, according to the biographer of the Greek philosophers **Diogenes Laertius**, Thales is born on this date. As a young man he may have traveled to Egypt and Babylon where he learned geometry and astronomy. Sources say he wrote two astronomical works *On the Solstice* and *On the Equinox* but if so neither have survived.
585 BCE	Successfully predicts an eclipse of the sun. According to Diogenes Laertius there are two versions of his domestic life, one that he marries and has a son, and another that he never becomes a father.
c.561/ c.549 BCE	Possible date of death. He dies while watching a gymnastic contest aged either 78 or 90.

significance of this theory for the history of science is that it gives an account of the origin of the universe and of natural phenomena which is not couched in the religious language of fable and myth.

Science

Alongside his cosmological speculations it is Thales' knowledge of astronomy and geometry that appear to have earned him his reputation. He is said to have been able to calculate the distance of ships at sea from the shore as well as measure the height of the pyramids from the ground.

Laozi

A semi-legendary mystic, Laozi is traditionally held to be the author of the main text of Daoism, a Chinese path offering an approach to harmony with nature. Its precepts affected Chinese art, religions, and other philosophies, and merged with folk traditions to become an essential part of traditional Chinese culture.

All our knowledge of the ancient Chinese sage Laozi (Lao Tsu or Lao Tzu) comes from legend and anecdote. In a way this is oddly appropriate, for the philosophy he pioneered, **Daoism** (Taoism), is best approached through story and symbolism, through parable and **paradox**, or through poetry and art.

With the suffix -zi meaning the honorific "Master", Laozi's name just means "Old Master". Writing centuries later, the historian Suma Qian (c.145–90 BCE) recorded that Laozi lived in the state of Chu (now located in modern Henan province) during the Zhou dynasty, and worked as a state archivist. He gained a reputation for wisdom, and, when an old man, decided to spend the rest of his life in seclusion as a hermit. Disgusted by the state of the world, he headed west to the "barbarian" lands outside China, and it was the warden guarding the western approaches who asked Laozi to write down his wisdom before he left China. The result was the classic book the *Dao de Jing* or *The Book of Dao and Virtue*, recording Laozi's observations on the Dao (Tao). Although some scholars say it was actually compiled over a couple of hundred years, it was nevertheless the most important Daoist text, laying out the essence of the philosophy's approach to life and politics.

The Dao is usually somewhat simplistically interpreted as the "Way", but it encompasses not only a way of life, but also the way of the universe. Mystical and unseen, the Dao is the "life force" or "flow of nature" which underlies all existence, and at its very heart is movement, as seen in the seasons, the flow of time, the turning of the earth, and the cycle of life and death. While most of the natural world spontaneously follows the way of Dao, human beings strive against nature by seeking to control every aspect of their lives, including the natural cycle.

Using allegories and parables, Laozi suggests ways for ordinary people and rulers to live happier lives and create a happier society by harmonizing with the Dao and by understanding its virtue.

Zhuangzi, writing in the fourth century BCE, is considered to be the spiritual and intellectual successor of Laozi.

> **Dao is the softest thing in the world, but it can overcome the hardest thing in the world.**
>
> Dao de Jing
> (sixth century BCE)

Essential philosophy

Definition
Partly in deliberate contrast to the other main Chinese school of thought at the time, the highly analytical **Confucianism** (see pages 16–17), and partly because the concept of the Dao is in itself intangible and cannot be easily broken down, Laozi avoided drawing up any clear-cut, logical outline of his philosophy. He wrote in metaphor and poetic imagery, inviting readers to contemplate for themselves, rather than instructing them: "*Looked at but cannot be seen – it is beneath form … These depthless things evade definition …*"

Harmony
One of the main observations in the *Dao de Jing* is "*Cultivate harmony within yourself, and harmony becomes real.*" Laozi believed that if people aligned themselves with the Dao, they were aligning with the natural order, so would feel the positive benefits of harmony in their lives. He wrote: "*The best of man is like water, Which*

benefits all things, and does not contend with them, Which flows in places that others disdain, Where it is in harmony with the Way.*"

Non-action
Nature does not try to control, it simply acts spontaneously. Therefore humans should not try to force events or nature to conform to their desires, but should simply "*go with the flow*" and let events take their course without agonizing over mundane desires. Laozi's views on politics particularly reflected non-action: his advice to rulers was to conquer people with inaction, to make no laws or taboos, but to allow people to harmonize with each other naturally. "*Manage a great nation as you would cook a delicate fish*", i.e. with as little disturbance as possible.

The best rulers are hardly known by their subjects, he wrote, and he advised against being greedy or tyrannical by pointing out, "*When people have nothing more to lose, Then revolution will result.*" He highlighted very practical reasons for people to follow the Dao.

■ True to its own principles, Daoism "bent in the wind" and adapted itself to other philosophies, absorbing some **Buddhist** ideas, and giving some of its concepts to other schools such as Confucianism and traditional folk religion.

■ Traditional Chinese arts – painting, sculpture, calligraphy – all attempted to express Laozi's ideal of harmony with nature.

■ Laozi's ideas of harmonizing with the flow, of not offering resistance but yielding to force until it loses its momentum, and of cultivating inner strength, had a major impact on the development of martial arts in China. In addition, the famous strategist Sunzi (Sun Tzu) who wrote the sixth-century BCE military manual, *The Art of War*, was influenced by Laozi.

■ Laozi and his followers provided the philosophical basis for the later development of a Daoist religious tradition, merging his ideas with ancient folk religion, talismanic and magical practices, and worship of immortals. Traditions such as the fortune-telling system Yi Jing (I Ching) and the **geomantic** art of Feng Shui survived partly because of the philosophical underpinning he provided.

■ In 440 CE Daoism was adopted as an official state religion, and Laozi was declared to be a saint. He was given grandiose titles as a mark of respect, including "Supreme Emperor of the Mysterious Origin" and "Heavenly Lord of Dao and its Virtue".

■ Laozi began the convention that Daoist sages, or indeed all wise men, went into the wilderness to become solitary hermits. It is reported that during the Tang dynasty (618–907 CE) beco-ming a hermit was the only way to shortcut the examination system for entry into lucrative government service. Men would retreat into the mountains for long enough to gain a reputation for wisdom, then jump at the first job offer they got from those who sought out the sages to ask advice.

■ There was a resurgence of interest in Laozi's ideas when twentieth-century discoveries in quantum mechanics showed how similar some of his descriptions of underlying reality are to modern scientific views of the wave-particle duality of matter.

Non-violence

Laozi pointed out that if powerful men resort to violence, it has a habit of returning to them. He also said that a wise man will not join an army, for the purpose of a sage is creation, not destruction.

Yin/yang

Although Laozi did not go into details, his writings hint at the concept of **yin** and **yang**. These are two opposite yet complementary forces whose constant movement as they flow around each other, seeking balance and harmony, is one of the ways in which the Dao functions. Yin is the passive, accepting force in the universe, while yang is the dynamic, active force, and as they move in constant counter-balance, they give rise to movement in the universe: life and death, the seasonal cycle, growth and withdrawal.

■ The *Dao de jing* is the second most translated book in the world after the Bible.

> *There is a whole formed and born earlier than heaven and earth. Silent and empty, it relies on nothing, in constant movement. We can consider it the mother of all things. I do not know its name, so I call it the Way, and I further call it the Great.*
>
> Dao de Jing (sixth century BCE)

The traditional representation of the concept of yin and yang describes two opposing but complementary aspects of one phenomenon.

Key dates

c.605 BCE	Born in modern Henan province, China.
c.580–540 BCE	Period during which it is thought he formulated his philosophy.
c.530 BCE	Dies in the western lands outside China.

Pythagoras

Credited with discovering the deductive method in mathematics and the geometric theorem that bears his name, Pythagoras was the first to recognize the potential of mathematics for unlocking the secret workings of the universe. He was also the leader of a secretive religious cult committed to the mystical significance of numbers.

Born on the Greek island of Samos not far from the ancient port of Miletus (in present-day Turkey), Pythagoras may first have studied under Thales before continuing to develop his mathematical genius in Egypt. Whether his passion for numbers was first kindled by Thales or some other teacher, it was to be a life-long obsession. Pythagoras settled in Croton in southern Italy, where he set up a religious society that welcomed women on equal footing with men and was devoted to the study of mathematics. Initiates were required to keep their possessions in common and follow a diet of raw food and little meat as well as strict codes of practice, including a vow of silence. Pythagoras himself appears to have cut an austere figure. He commanded devotion from his followers and was regarded by the community as semi-divine. It is said he never drank or ate to excess, always dressed in white, and abstained from laughter.

The Pythagoreans were privy to esoteric knowledge and their behavior was governed by a set of cryptic precepts including avoiding stirring the ashes of a fire with a sword or looking back when traveling abroad. The latter, seemingly superstitious injunction is interpreted by **Diogenes Laertius** as meaning that when dying one should not yearn for the pleasures of this life. The interpretation accords with Pythagoras' belief in reincarnation and his practice, so we are told, of recalling many past lives. According to **Xenophanes** he could also recognize the voices of friends' souls in the calls of animals, which may account for his vegetarianism. However, his concern for animal life appears not to have been consistent. According to Diogenes Laertius, when Pythagoras discovered his famous theorem he marked the moment by sacrificing 100 oxen.

Essential philosophy

The immortality of the soul

It is not possible to separate clearly the teachings of Pythagoras from those of his followers, the Pythagoreans, who continued to teach well after his death; and in modern times scepticism has arisen over the various philosophical positions and mathematical achievements attributed to him. Nonetheless, one point upon which the sources are agreed is that he believed that physical death was not the end and that the soul is reborn in a continuous cycle. Reincarnation could be into the body of another human being, some other animal, or even into a plant. Through adherence to a life dedicated to speculative study, as practiced by the Pythagoreans, the human soul may become purified and escape the cycle of rebirth to join the "world soul".

Scientific and geometric discoveries

There are various key discoveries accredited to Pythagoras, most notable is the theorem that bears his name: that the square of the hypotenuse of a right-angled triangle is equal to the sum of the squares of the other two sides. As a rule of thumb this fact had been known by the Egyptians for some time before Pythagoras' day, but it may well be that he was the first to produce the mathematical proof, thereby establishing it as a timeless truth. He is also credited with being the first to recognize that the morning star and evening star are the same planet, namely Venus. Pythagoras was interested in music and is said to have played the lyre as a means to cure the sick. He observed that the lengths of vibrating strings producing harmonious musical intervals could be expressed in terms of ratios between whole numbers. This discovery appears to have inspired him to surmise that the workings of the whole universe might be reducible to arithmetical relations in a similar way. Thus he came to regard the structure of the world in terms of a harmonic scale expressible in numbers, and gave the study of mathematics not just a scientific, but a deeply religious and occult significance. Numbers were also believed by the Pythagoreans to exemplify moral and social concepts equating, for example, justice with the number four.

Pythagoras' reverence for mathematics has its roots in the timeless and universal nature of its discoveries. Having established a theorem in geometry it is recognizable as **necessarily true** for all times, all places and all people; and so confers upon the mathematician a

> ### *Reason is immortal, all else mortal.*
>
> Pythagoras, quoted in Diogenes Laertius, *The Lives and Opinions of Eminent Philosophers* (third century CE)

PHILOSOPHERS

EXTRAORDINARY PEOPLE WHO ALTERED THE COURSE OF HISTORY

HUGH BARKER, JOHN BRATHERTON, DAN CARDINAL,
GARETH FITZGERALD, MEREDITH MACARDLE, ROBERT TEED

EDITOR:
NICOLA CHALTON

METRO BOOKS
NEW YORK

Text and design © 2008 by Basement Press, London

This 2008 edition published by Metro Books,
by arrangement with Basement Press.

Designed and produced by Basement Press
61 Ivydale Road
London SE15 3DS, United Kingdom
www.basementpress.com
Design & picture research: Pascal Thivillon
Editorial: Nicola Chalton
Philosophy consultant: Gareth Fitzgerald
Glossary: Simon Riches

Metro Books
122 Fifth Avenue
New York, NY 10011

ISBN-13: 978-1-4351-1017-5

Printed and bound in Malaysia

10 9 8 7 6 5 4 3 2 1

Picture credits Heritage Image Partnership/Art Media Cover. Book Builder All portraits. Visipix.com pages 25, 31, 33, 41, 49, 51, 61, 67, 75, 83, 109, 113. 177, 189. Library of Congress, Prints & Photographs Division pages 47, 59, 87, 105, 119, 127, 137, 143, 165, 179, 185. Basement Press pages 19 (bottom), 151. History of Science Collections, University of Oklahoma Libraries; © the Board of Regents of the University of Oklahoma pages 77, 81. Yorck Project pages 63, 69, 71, 169. Photo © Spoon - Creative Commons page 13. Photo © AlMare - Creative Commons page 19. NASA Jet Propulsion Laboratory (NASA-JPL) page 27. Photo © rosemanios - Creative Commons page 45. Photo © Immanuel Giel page 57. Photo © Dano - Creative Commons page 73. Photo © Ctsnow - creative commons page 89. Photo © Jondavidoakley - creative commons page 91. Photo © Christian Bickel - creative commons page 95. Architect of the Capitol page 101. Photo © Andrea Fregnani - creative commons page 115. Photo © Moja - GNU Free Documentation License page 141. Photo © Andrew Dunn - Creative commons page 145. Photo © Deepak - Creative commons page 149. Photo © G. Naharro - creative commons page 153. Photo © Jeff Ooi page 159. Photo © Géry Parent page 167. Photo © Jesse Gardner - Creative commons page 173. National Archives and Records Administration page 175. Department of Defense. Department of the Navy. U.S. Marine Corps - National Archives and Records Administration page 183. Dr. Leon Kaufman. University Of California, San Francisco page 191. NASA Marshall Space Flight Center (NASA-MSFC) page 195.

Publisher's note Every effort has been made to ensure the accuracy of the information presented in this book. The publisher will not assume liability for damages caused by inaccuracies in the data and makes no warranty whatsoever expressed or implied. The publisher welcomes comments and corrections from readers, emailed to info@basementpress.com, which will be considered for incorporation in future editions. Likewise, every effort has been made to trace copyright holders and seek permission to use illustrative and other material. The publisher wishes to apologize for any inadvertent errors or omissions and would be glad to rectify these in future editions.

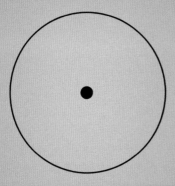

Symbolic representation of the *Monad*, a term for God or the first being, or the totality of all beings, according to the Pythagoreans.

Key dates

c.570 BCE Born on Greek island of Samos.
c.550 BCE Possible that he studies in Miletus under Thales and Anaximander (*fl.* c.550 BCE). Soon after travels in Egypt and Babylon.
c.520 BCE Returns briefly to Samos but leaves to avoid the tyranny of Polycrates.
c.515 BCE Settles in Croton, southern Italy, and founds the Pythagorean school.
c.500 BCE The circumstances of Pythagoras' death are equally shrouded in legend as the events of the rest of his life. Most are agreed he left Croton for Metapontium (northern Italy), where he died, possibly fleeing after having his house burned down by disaffected followers. However, other sources suggest he returned to Croton where he is reported to have lived to at least 90, and that he taught **Empedocles**.

Legacy, truth, consequence

■ Pythagoras was the most important of the **pre-Socratic** philosophers. His significance to philosophy, mathematics, and science led **Bertrand Russell** to assert that he knew of no other man who has had more influence on modern thought.

■ His influence on **Plato** is particularly noteworthy. From him Plato acquired the key distinction between the world as conceived by the mind and the world perceived by the senses.

■ Also due to Pythagoreans is the idea that the philosophical life of speculation is the route to the salvation of the soul.

■ Ultimately his greatest significance lies in being the first to apply mathematics within science and philosophy, the fruitfulness of which is hard to overestimate.

Pythagoras was one of the first to realize that the morning star and evening star are the same planet, namely Venus.

vision of the eternal. Ordinary beliefs about the physical world around us contrast unfavorably with such knowledge in that they lack certainty, are prone to error, and subject to change. Mathematical objects such as numbers and geometric shapes also appear to transcend the mundane world of ordinary sense experience. A circle as contemplated by the mind is perfect and incorruptible, while all the actual circles appearing in physical reality are mere approximations to this ideal and inevitably decay and die. From here it is a short step to the view that the realm of mathematics apprehended by the intellect is more real than the shifting world of appearances perceived by the senses.

The Pythagorean ... having been brought up in the study of mathematics, thought that things are numbers ... and that the whole cosmos is a scale and a number.

Aristotole discusses the Pythagoreans, in *Metaphysics* (fourth century BCE)

Xenophanes of Colophon

What we know of Xenophanes' thought comes in fragments of his poetry quoted by later Greek writers. These include satires of Greek polytheistic religious beliefs alongside what are often regarded as the first philosophical arguments for monotheism. A sceptic about the possibility of acquiring genuine knowledge he regarded scientific hypotheses as conjectures which should remain open to refutation.

Although later writers say he was the teacher of **Parmenides**, and **Plato** identifies him as the founder of the **Eleatic school**, both today are thought unlikely. What is clear, though, is the influence of the Milesian thinkers (from Miletus, in present-day Turkey) on his explanations of natural phenomena. Xenophanes was born in the small Ionian town of Colophon (in Turkey) but fled his homeland when it was invaded by the Persians. He settled for a time in Sicily, where he made his living from reciting his philosophical poems. He continued to travel around the Greek world producing poetry on a range of topics: principally satirizing popular religious beliefs, but also outlining what he regarded as the true divine nature, exploring the extent and possibility of human knowledge, as well as putting forward his own cosmology and natural philosophy. Some say he was sold into slavery for a time, but otherwise we know very little of note from his life.

Essential philosophy

The critique of traditional religion

Xenophanes' critique of popular religion focuses on the tendency to see the gods in human terms. He draws our attention to the fact that different races portray their gods in their own image and remarks that if horses had hands to draw they would depict their gods with hooves and manes. In projecting our own nature and limitations we not only misunderstand the nature of the divine, but we also stray into impiety. For this reason he also criticized traditional mythology in which the gods are depicted as performing all manner of immoral actions and displaying all-too-human emotions. Such stories do not show proper reverence for the divine and are morally corrupting. In place of polytheism he argued for one eternal and spiritual God, and so was the first to offer philosophical arguments in defense of a view which would come to dominate religious and philosophical thought in Europe during the Christian era.

Clouds

The dismissal of anthropomorphic gods is closely allied to his rejection of supernatural explanations of phenomena. He argued that the clouds are formed by vapor from the sea under the heat of the sun, and he apparently tried to account for all the heavenly bodies in terms of transformations of clouds, so that the sun, for example, is a great burning cloud and the moon a compressed cloud. He appears to have believed that everything is made either from earth or water, or a mixture of the two, and explained the existence of fossilized sea creatures found inland by supposing that there were alternating periods of drought and flood in a grand cosmic cycle. However, he does not seem to have claimed certain knowledge of such speculations, treating **perception** as an unreliable basis for **knowledge** and regarding all human theories as mere conjectures.

Legacy, truth, consequence

■ **Karl Popper** looked to Xenophanes as a forerunner of his "critical rationalism" (see page 158), the view that we cannot expect our hypotheses about the world to be true, but that it is reasonable to hold them so long as they remain unrefuted.

■ His critique of religious belief prefigures Ludwig Andreas Feuerbach (1804–72), **Karl Marx**, and Sigmund Freud (1856–1939), all of whom regarded religion as a human construct.

Key dates

c.570 BCE	Born in Colophon, Ionia (now part of modern Turkey).
c.546 BCE	Flees the Persian invasion for Sicily aged 25. Subsequently travels around Magna Graecia (area in Southern Italy and Sicily) reciting his poetry and teaching philosophy.
c.475 BCE	Dies in old age, probably at least 90.

> *But mortals suppose gods are born, wear their own clothes and have a voice and body.*
>
> Xenophanes, quoted in H. Diels and W. Kranz, *Die Fragmente der Vorsokratiker* (1952)

Heraclitus of Ephesus

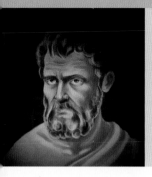

Sometimes referred to as the weeping philosopher, Heraclitus was renowned in antiquity for his melancholy disposition and for the obscurity of his writings. He believed reality to be in a continual state of change or strife governed by a law of tension between opposites, which he identified with fire. Wisdom, he held, comes from apprehending this law – the *logos* – which governs all things.

Heraclitus came from an aristocratic family from Ephesus not far from Miletus (in present-day Turkey) but apart from this we have no certain details of his life. He appears to have been a disagreeable character and had disparaging words to say both about his compatriots and other philosophers. He turned down a request to write a constitution for Ephesus because he said the people were too corrupt, and he dismissed the learning of **Pythagoras** and **Xenophanes**, among others, as giving no genuine understanding.

His thought was known in the ancient world through his book *On Nature*, which was very popular but is now lost so that we know of his ideas only through fragments that survive in the writings of others.

According to the third-century Greek biographer Diogenes Laertius, in later years Heraclitus became increasingly misanthropic and went to live in the mountains, where he survived on grasses and plants. He became ill and returned to the town, where he died.

> **We both step and do not step into the same rivers. We both are and are not.**
>
> Heraclitus, quoted in J. E. Barnes, *The Pre-Socratic Philosophers* (1982)

Legacy, truth, consequence

■ The idea that there is a cosmic order underlying apparent change was influential on **Plato**.

■ To regard the universe as governed by an organizing principle became important in Greek thought and was to have an impact on Christianity and the identification of the *logos* with God, e.g. in the opening passage of St John –"*In the beginning was the Word [logos] and the Word was with God, and the Word was God*" (*New American Standard Bible*, John 1: 1).

■ Nineteenth-century thinkers became interested once again in Heraclitus: **G. W. F. Hegel** claimed the doctrine of the harmony of opposites as a precursor to his **dialectical** view of historical change, which operates through a synthesis of conflicting doctrines; **Friedrich Nietzsche** hailed Heraclitus as one of the few thinkers to embrace "becoming" rather than "being".

Key dates

c.535 BCE	Born in Ephesus, Anatolia (in present-day Turkey). He writes *On Nature*, which is now lost. Details of other events in Heraclitus' life are unknown.
c.475 BCE	Dies at Ephesus; interred in the marketplace.

Essential philosophy

Everything is fire

Heraclitus is the first of the **pre-Socratic** philosophers to produce a unified and systematic philosophical vision and the fragments of his writings that survive allow us to reconstruct a reasonably coherent picture of his system. At the center lies the claim that everything is in a state of flux driven by the tension between opposites. War or strife is identified as the dynamic principle governing the universe. **Plato** quotes him as saying that you cannot step into the same river twice, meaning that nothing remains the same and that the universe is continually flowing: that "becoming", rather than "being", is the one true reality. For Heraclitus fire is the primordial element, underscoring the claim that stability is illusory and that all things are forever changing, caught in a continuous process of transformation.

The harmony of opposites

But significantly, any conflict between opposites is subject to a more fundamental cosmic principle, or *logos*, which functions to reconcile them. "*Logos*" is the Greek word for "law" or "rationale", and Heraclitus is saying that there is a unity and interdependence that obtains between opposites and by which they are attuned to each other. He appears to have believed that a true grasp of the *logos* was not available to ordinary mortals and the notion of harmony between opposites is perhaps inherently **paradoxical**, which may explain why his sayings are often cast in apparently contradictory language.

Confucius

Concerned with questions of morality and social order, Confucius' ideas provided the basic structure of Chinese culture and society for hundreds of years. Not until Chairman Mao did any other individual have such an influence on the country.

Born in the Spring and Autumn Period, a time of chaos and brutal civil war, Confucius, the Latinized name for Master Kong (Kong Fuzi or Kung Fu Tzu), belonged to an era called the Period of the Hundred Philosophers when many important schools of thought developed. Like most of the scholars of the time, the misery he saw around him concentrated his thoughts on how to restore law and order and create a peaceful society.

The reason his times were so violent, he concluded, was that people had lost the virtue that had been shown by China's semi-legendary ancient empires in what he considered a peaceful and prosperous "Golden Age", when sovereigns ruled with benevolent justice and the people responded with "proper" behavior.

Formulating rational theories of how to improve individual and social morality, he decided that moral standards must be set by a ruler, and the state should be administered by **ethically**-trained officials. Wandering from state to state offering his advice, he failed to convince a single ruler to put his views into practice, so settled down to teaching. He is thought to have spent the last years of his life editing five classical books which, with his own teachings and those of his followers, became the official Confucian canon. As well as writings on history, poetry, and rites, they included the *Yi Jing* (*I Ching*), more widely known in the West as a manual of divination.

Although he had no social impact during his lifetime, he gathered a few devoted followers and his ideas were eventually adopted by the government, making him probably the single most influential figure in Chinese history. With Confucianism coming to govern personal, family, social, and bureaucratic life in the pre-**communist** empire, many foreigners erroneously take his philosophy to be a religion.

Essential philosophy

Human kindness

In one way, Confucius was close to **Daoism** (see page 10): he felt that humans were born in harmony with the natural order, but allowed themselves to indulge in selfish behavior that led them away from natural harmony with their fellows and with society. He expressed this natural impulse towards harmony as human kindness or human-heartedness: the feeling of love, kindness, and respect a person feels towards others. Expressing this in proper and compassionate behavior allowed the individual to develop themselves as a morally correct person.

Social duties

In a principle he called "the rectification of names", Confucius believed that every social position carried a natural responsibility to fulfil the duties of that role, particularly in relation to other positions. A superior position carried duties of firm but kind control, and people in inferior positions were responsible for immediate obedience.

"*Let the ruler be ruler, the minister minister, the father father and the son son.*" (*Analects*, 479 BCE)

Society

If everyone behaved in the morally appropriate manner their position required, i.e. either obediently or with strong but loving

rule, society would function smoothly and in accordance with natural moral principles. A strong legal framework was seen as a failure, since morally correct individuals were self-regulating.

The ruler

A particular responsibility lay with the ruler, who had to set a correct ethical example for other levels of society to follow.

"*Your job is to govern, not to kill.*" (*Analects*, 479 BCE)

Ritual and religion

As well as obedience, correct moral behavior involved good manners, etiquette, and the practice of rites and ceremonies. To Confucius, these rituals were to do with expressing social cohesion and confirming the natural

To practice five things under all circumstances constitutes perfect virtue; these five are gravity, generosity of soul, sincerity, earnestness, and kindness.

Analects (479 BCE)

Legacy

- Confucius' teachings were spread by his followers until they became an essential guide to individual moral aspirations and to the structure of society.
- Adopted by the first Han emperor as the official ideology, Confucian principles were used to maintain the bureaucracy that administered China's vast empire for hundreds of years.
- His theories became the basis of governments and social culture elsewhere in Asia: Japan, Korea, Vietnam.
- His acceptance of a strict social hierarchy bound together by ritual and etiquette formed the basis of China's later rigid, stultifying social stratification. The resultant intellectual stagnation contributed to China's industrial inferiority compared to Europe and the downfall of empire in the twentieth century.
- Vilified by the communists, Confucian ideas have made a comeback in post-Maoist China and are now considered as making a valuable contribution to the study of ethics.

Confucius as an administrator.

Key dates

c.551 BCE Born to a poor noble family in Qufu, in the state of Lu, now part of modern Shandong province.

520 BCE By now he is, like many philosophers of his time, a wanderering scholar, taking temporary government posts and gaining respect.

c.501 BCE Although acknowledged as a wise scholar, he abandons hope of finding a ruler who will adopt his principles, and returns to Lu to teach.

479 BCE Dies, after which his small but committed band of followers collate his major sayings into the text known as the *Analects* of Confucius.

202 BCE Emperor Wu of the Han dynasty adopts **Confucianism** as the official state ideology since it is the perfect way to regulate his government ministers.

c.1180 CE During the Song dynasty, the scholar Zhu Xi develops Neo-Confucianism, restricting culture to the orthodox Confucian texts.

order of heaven and earth. Although he accepted that there was an impersonal force in heaven he opposed superstition and empty rites: he considered traditional ancestor veneration or sacrificing to the emperor of heaven as simply showing proper respect for family and the universe.

Education
Confucius believed that through education and the example of proper standards, the virtuous qualities which lead man and society back into the natural order could be cultivated so that any individual could become morally correct. Education in the proper customs of life had to be available to everyone.

The sage
A person who behaved correctly could become what Confucius called a "superior man" or "sage". A sage showed his superiority in every area of life, from artistic tastes to respecting the ancestors, and spread virtue to others because of his example.

The family
Crucial to Confucius, and to all Chinese before and after, was the ideal of the family as the most important social unit and the basis of all moral behavior. For example, a son might love a particular girl, but would be expected to marry whomever his father chose as being most likely to advance the family. Confucius held that if children were taught human kindness within the family circle, they would be able to spread that feeling to wider human relationships.

Role of women
Like most schools of thought at the time, women were relegated to the position of second-class citizen, with no individual rights. They could win respect only by behaving with proper obedience towards their father/husband/master.

The golden rule
Confucius taught a version of the near-universal "golden rule": "*Do unto others as you would have them do unto you.*" See also **Immanuel Kant**'s **categorical imperative**, page 101.

Neo-Confucianism
Although Confucius' views were based on compassion and equal opportunity, the impulse towards venerating the past and respecting one's superiors later hardened into a rigid culture actually suppressing new thought in art, science, or philosophy. The Confucian Classics, or books which represented orthodox Confucian thought, became the sole basis of knowledge and education.

Parmenides of Elea

Parmenides is significant for constructing the first sustained attempt to deduce metaphysical conclusions using abstract reasoning from fundamental principles. In so doing he shaped the future course of Greek philosophy as subsequent generations were forced either to take on board his highly paradoxical conclusion that all multiplicity and change are illusory, or to engage with the rigor of his arguments.

Little is known of Parmenides' life other than that he hailed from the Greek colony of Elea, on the southern coast of Italy. This is where he founded the **Eleatic school**, the major defender of which was to be **Zeno of Elea**. Parmenides wrote a successful and popular constitution for Elea and according to legend lived a morally praiseworthy life. Some sources say he was a student of **Xenophanes**, and it is certainly true that he knew the work of his contemporary **Heraclitus** as his ideas appear to be framed in conscious opposition to Heraclitus' philosophy of multiplicity and change. **Plato**'s dialogue, *Parmenides*, has him meet the youthful **Socrates** on a visit to Athens aged about 65 years. Some claim that he was associated with the Pythagoreans (see pages 12–13) and this may have influenced the **mystical** tone of his writing, although he rejects their cosmological views as illusory.

His epic poem *On Nature* (c.480 BCE), probably written when he was still a young man, is preserved in fragmentary form in the writings of Sextus Empiricus (*fl.* second century CE) and Simplicius (c.490–c.560 CE), among others, and represents one of the greatest bodies of surviving writings of any **pre-Socratic** philosopher. The introductory section details Parmenides' journey from darkness into light where he encounters an unnamed goddess who invites him to consider both the truth and the erroneous opinions of humans. In the first part of the poem, the "Way of Truth", the goddess offers a series of **deductive** arguments to conclusions which are generally thought to be Parmenides' own concerning the ultimate nature of reality. In the second part, the "Way of Opinion", he outlines how the world appears to the senses of ordinary mortals and produces a cosmology inspired by **Pythagoras**. There is some dispute as to the status of this cosmology in Parmenides' mind, but it is most likely that he regarded it as an account satisfactory for human purposes, but which falls short of the truth.

Essential philosophy

The "Way of Truth"

The argument of the "Way of Truth" begins by contrasting "what is" or "being" with "what is not" or "not-being". Only "what is" is thinkable, for we cannot think about "what is not" since it is nothing. Parmeminides concludes that only "what is" has any reality and that since "not-being" is impossible the true account of the nature of the world cannot make any reference to it. It follows firstly that "what is" cannot be created or destroyed since it is impossible for it either to come from or become "what is not", as "what is not" does not exist. Thus "what is" has always been and always will be. Moreover, "being" cannot admit of any change, since doing so would involve ceasing to be what it was, and taking on a property it doesn't yet have, and both would involve "not-being". He generalizes these temporal conclusions to space, arguing that there can be nothing other than "what is", meaning that "being" must exist everywhere. Also "what is" cannot admit of degrees but must be as much in one place as in any other, and so "being" must be one and undifferentiated. Movement within "being" is also impossible since it would involve moving into empty space or the void, but empty space is nothing which, as we have seen, cannot exist. Finally, since "what is" cannot exist more in one place than any other it must be evenly extended in all directions, and so the universe is a perfect sphere.

The "Way of Opinion"

So far Parmenides has used reason to demonstrate that all that can truly exist is a motionless, unchanging, invariable "one". But how does he account for our ordinary experience of movement, change, and plurality? The second part of the poem appears to give an answer to this question, although little of this section has survived. Here Parmenides outlines the deceptive world as it appears to the

> *How could what-is perish? How could it have come to be? For if it came into being it is not; nor is it if ever it is going to be. Thus coming into being is extinguished, and destruction unknown.*
>
> On Nature (c.480 BCE)

Archeological remains of Elea, the place of the Eleatic school. The medieval tower in the background was built on the ruins of the Greek temple.

Legacy, truth, consequence

■ Parmenides' abstract logical approach was a departure from those philosophers who preceded him and had a profound impact on the path philosophy was to take so that he may be called the father of **"metaphysics"**, though his writings precede the invention of the term.

■ The **atomists** Leucippus (*fl.* c.440 BCE) and **Democritus** (see pages 26–7) conceived of their atoms in terms of the Parmenidean unchanging "one", but against Parmenides they reintroduced the void and allowed for a multiplicity. The question of whether there could be a void or vacuum remained a live philosophical and scientific issue into modern times.

■ His influence on the young Socrates is noted by Plato. The contrast between the use of reason as the unique route to knowledge of reality as opposed to the deceptive route of **sense perception** is a dominant theme of Plato's own philosophy.

Key dates

c.510 BCE	Born in Elea, on the southern coast of Italy.
c.490 BCE	Studies under Xenophanes and becomes familiar with Pythagorean and Heraclitean philosophies.
c.480 BCE	Writes *On Nature*.
c.445 BCE	Travels through Athens and meets with the young Socrates.
c.450 BCE	Dies of unknown causes.

Schematic diagram of Parmenides' structure of the cosmos.

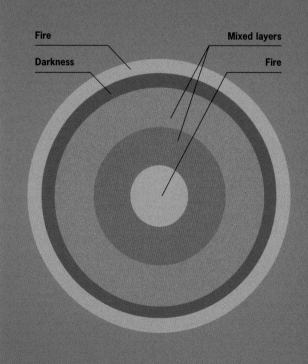

Fire

Darkness

Mixed layers

Fire

Helplessness guides the wandering thought in their breasts; they are carried along deaf and blind alike, dazed, beasts without judgement, convinced that to be and not to be are the same and not the same, and that the road of all things is a backward-turning one.

On Nature (c.480 BCE)

senses and puts forward a systematic cosmology, which appears to have been inspired by the Pythagoreans. In the apparent world there are two primary elements, fire and darkness, and it is from these that the earth and heavenly bodies are generated and into which they will decay once again. The universe consists of concentric circles of differing mixtures of these elements. Included in the "Way of Opinion" are accounts of the generation of animals as well as a **psychology**, but the surviving details are sketchy.

Reality and appearance

Through the contrast between the "Way of Truth" and the "Way of Opinion" Parmenides draws the influential distinction between the way things really are as discovered through the application of reason, and the way things appear within ordinary experience. Since reason reveals reality to be one and unchanging, the temporal world of change and multiplicity is essentially misleading. This is not to say that it is completely worthless; he appears to have thought that our understanding of the apparent world may be useful for everyday purposes even while it does not constitute genuine knowledge.

Anaxagoras

Anaxagoras accounted for the movements of the heavens in terms of vortices propelled by a cosmic intelligence and in so doing was the first to introduce mind as a way of explaining the natural world. He denied the divinity of the heavenly bodies claiming them to be great burning rocks, the view for which a prosecution for impiety was brought against him by the Athenians.

Anaxagoras was from the port of Clazomenae in Ionia (now Turkey), where he is said to have given up any political aspirations in order to devote himself to the quest for knowledge. He made his way to Athens, which had embarked on a golden age of wealth under the democratic leadership of Pericles. Anaxagoras arrived around 462 and proceeded to introduce philosophy to a culture brimming with invention and self-confidence. He remained in Athens for 30 years, becoming teacher and ally to the powerful Pericles. However, sentenced to death for impiety by Pericles' enemies, he eventually escaped to Lampsacus in Asia Minor. He wrote one work of **natural philosophy**, which now survives only in fragments.

> *In everything there is a portion of everything except mind.*
>
> Anaxagoras, quoted in G. S. Kirk, J. E. Raven & M. Schofield, *The Pre-Socratic Philosophers* (1957)

Essential philosophy

Infinitely many substances

Anaxagoras was familiar with his predecessor **Parmenides'** arguments which purported to demonstrate that nothing can come into or go out of being and consequently that the cosmos is a static, undifferentiated "one". However, while accepting that "being" cannot be created or destroyed, he hoped to find a way to allow room for the reality of movement and change. To this end he rejected Parmenides' claim that there is just one kind of "being". Rather, there are infinitely many different elements or substances, each infinitely divisible and each occupying all portions of space but in different concentrations. The substance that predominates in any given place is what determines the nature of the thing occupying that space. For example, what we call water is the stuff in which the element water predominates over all other substances, such as air and fire. In this way Anaxagoras is able to assert that nothing is created or destroyed, but rather all change consists in the separation and mixing of substances. For instance, water when evaporating doesn't turn into a new substance, but rather the air already mixed in the water separates from it. Similarly a plant can turn earth into leaves and wood by extracting these latter substances already existing diluted in the earth.

Legacy, truth, consequence

- Anaxagoras is important for his attempt to marry Parmenides' arguments about the impossibility of creating or destroying "what is" or "being" with the possibility of change.
- His firmly **materialist** explanations of phenomena such as rainbows, eclipses, and meteorites furthered the scientific spirit begun among the philosophers of Miletus, Anatolia (in what is now Turkey). He is credited for certain key scientific discoveries, such as that the moon shines by reflecting light and has mountains.
- **Socrates**, **Plato**, and **Aristotle** were attracted by his use of mind as an explanatory principle, but disappointed by his mechanistic (and not purpose-driven) explanations of natural phenomena, which could not explain why the universe came into being.

Key dates

c.500 BCE	Born in Ionia, in the ancient Greek city of Clazomenae (in present-day Turkey).
c.462–432 BCE	Settles in Athens, where he writes his one work of philosophy.
c.432 BCE	Charged with impiety and sentenced to death. Pericles probably helps his friend to escape into exile.
c.434 BCE	Returns to Ionia and founds a school in Lampsacus.
428 BCE	Dies in Lampsacus.

Cosmology

In the beginning, according to Anaxagoras' cosmology, there was a chaotic mixture of substances and a cosmic mind that governed their movement. Mind then induced matter to rotate, causing heavy things to gravitate to the center and lighter things to rise to the edges, and in so doing separated out the elements, producing the earth and the heavenly bodies. The cosmic mind is also the source of minds in humans and animals, which is what animates them.

Empedocles

A miracle worker, religious mystic, politician, poet as well as a scientist, Empedocles was the first to posit the existence of independent forces of nature, and his theory of the four elements eventually became the established view of medieval chemistry. He is also remembered for prefiguring Charles Darwin by producing a theory of the origin of species through natural selection.

Empedocles was a citizen of Acragas, Sicily. Although a champion of **democracy**, by all accounts he cut a regal figure, dressing in purple robes, gold girdle, and bronze sandals. He was renowned for his magical powers, which included the ability to control the winds, end plagues, and bring people back from the dead. Like **Parmenides** he wrote in verse but only fragments remain of two works: *On Nature*, which outlines his philosophical system, and *Purifications*, which gives a mythical account of the origins of the universe.

According to **Diogenes Laertius** he died after leaping into the crater of Mount Etna, so that his body would be consumed and his followers would believe he had become immortal. However, the deception was exposed when the volcano threw back one of his bronze sandals.

Essential philosophy

Four primary elements

Accepting Paremenides' argument that nothing can be created or destroyed, Empedocles tried to account for the possibility of change and multiplicity by positing the existence of four primary elements – earth, water, fire, and air. Out of these indestructible "roots" grow all the things we see around us, including living creatures, as the elements are mixed in different proportions. Forces of repulsion, or "strife", and attraction, "love", govern the processes of combination and separation of the elements and explain how change can occur while the ultimate substances remain simple and unchanging.

Empedocles is credited with being the first to give an **empirical** demonstration of the existence of one of his elements – air – by observing that by covering one end of a pipe and immersing the other in water there remains something in the pipe preventing the water from entering. When the other end is uncovered the air can escape and water rushes in.

Origin and evolution of species

In order to explain how it is that animals are well suited to survival in their environments, he put forward the theory that originally limbs and organs grew out of the earth and entered into chance combinations, producing all kinds of chimerical creatures. Most of these arrangements would not be conducive to the creatures' survival or reproduction, and many died out leaving only the best adapted.

Legacy, truth, consequence

- Empedocles' significance lies principally in his theory of the four classical elements. His idea that all the substances we observe are compounds of unchanging elements remains the basis of modern chemistry.
- He prefigured Darwin's theory of natural selection (*On the Origin of Species*, 1859) by recognizing that the creatures which now exist are those that have survived and so are best suited to their environment.

Key dates

c.493 BCE Born to a wealthy family. Among those credited with being his teacher are **Parmenides, Anaxagoras, Xenophanes,** and **Pythagoras.** Takes up politics and helps institute democracy in Acragas. By some accounts he is exiled and becomes an itinerant sage and healer in Sicily.

c.433 BCE His death is the topic of several competing stories. He is said to have died in the fires of Etna; by falling from a ship and drowning; in an accident driving his carriage; and according to Lucian of Samasota (c.125–180 CE) by propulsion into space by a volcanic eruption.

Many creatures arose with double faces and double breasts, offspring of oxen with human faces, and again there sprang up children of men with oxen's heads ...

Empedocles, quoted in Arthur Fairbanks, *The First Philosophers of Greece* (1898)

Reincarnation

He accepted the Pythagorean belief in reincarnation (see **Pythagoras,** pages 12–13), recommended vegetarianism, and saw the pursuit of philosophy as the path the soul must follow to escape the endless cycle of rebirth and take its place in the divine order for eternity.

Zeno of Elea

Zeno was a follower of Parmenides and is remembered for his paradoxes that attempt to demonstrate the impossibility of motion, change, and plurality and so establish his teacher's bold and counterintuitive claim that the universe is static, unchanging, and undifferentiated. Aristotle credits him with inventing the dialectical method of reasoning by which he was able to reduce his opponents' arguments to absurdity.

From Elea in southern Italy, Zeno was the student of **Parmenides** and the foremost defender of the **Eleatic school**. Zeno is said to have produced more than 40 **paradoxes** contained in a book, which is now lost, each designed to demonstrate the incoherence of the common-sense view of the nature of reality. **Aristotle**'s key work *Physics* is our best source for those that have survived.

We know most about his life from **Plato**'s dialogue *Parmenides* where Zeno, "nearly forty", meets the young **Socrates** and deploys the **dialectical** method of question and answer, which Socrates came to exploit himself. Plato reports that Zeno had written the work containing his paradoxes as a young man and that it had been stolen and circulated widely without his permission, so that his arguments were already known in Athens when he visited.

> *... the quickest runner can never catch the slowest, since the pursuer must first reach the point whence the pursued started, so that the slower must always hold the lead.*
>
> Zeno's argument, recorded in Aristotle's *Physics* (c.330 BCE)

Essential philosophy

Reality is one

Zeno accepted the view of his master, Parmenides, that reality is simple and unchanging and therefore the appearance of plurality and change is an illusion of the senses. His paradoxes were designed to demonstrate the unreliability of **sense experience** as a basis for coming to a genuine understanding of reality.

No plurality

Zeno claimed there must be an error in the view that there exists more than one thing, on the grounds that it leads to contradictory conclusions. For if there are many things then, on the one hand, they must total a definite and therefore a finite number; but on the other hand, if you take any two adjacent things there must, he claims, be some space between them which separates the two. And so there must be another thing between them. And between these three, there must be another two, and so on ad infinitum. This leads to the

Legacy, truth, consequence

■ Zeno's paradoxes have continued to exercise the minds of philosophers over the many centuries since he produced them. They were not effectively solved until the development of certain mathematical tools dealing with infinity in the nineteenth and twentieth centuries.

■ His arguments on the impossibility of infinite divisibility appear to have influenced the **atomists Democritus** and Leucippus (*fl.* c.440 BCE) in postulating indivisible units of matter.

Key dates

c.490 BCE	Born in the Greek colony of Elea (now Velia), in southern Italy. As a young man he becomes a student of Parmenides and (according to Plato) his lover, and writes his book of paradoxes.
c.450 BCE	Visits Athens with Parmenides and meets the young Socrates. Possibly remains in Athens for some years before returning to Elea, where he becomes involved in a political struggle with the tyrant of Elea, Nearchos.
c.425 BCE	Dies a heroic death at the hands of Nearchos, as recorded by **Diogenes Laertius**.

conclusions *both* that there is a finite number of things, *and* that there is an infinite number of things, which is absurd. Zeno concludes that the universe must be one and undifferentiated.

No movement

His best-known paradox attempts to demonstrate the impossibility of movement. Imagine that Achilles races against a tortoise and gives it a ten-yard (or meter) head start. By the time he has covered the ten yards the tortoise will have moved on. And by the time he has caught up with the beast a second time, again it will have moved on, and so on ad infinitum. Achilles can never catch the tortoise. The conclusion is that the appearance of movement to our senses is an illusion.

Protagoras

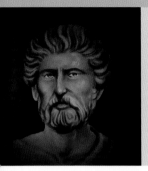

Protagoras was the principal figure of a group of itinerant teachers known as the Sophists, or wise ones, who, for a fee, would teach the art of rhetoric. He is best known for the sceptical view that "man is the measure of all things", which is standardly interpreted as meaning that all claims to knowledge are relative to the person making them and so have no objective validity.

Protagoras was from Abdera, Thrace, and traveled around Greece earning his living as a teacher to wealthy young men. Although he appears to have produced at least two works, *Truth* and *On the Gods*, only a few quotations from them survive in other writers, and most of what we know of Protagoras' life and thought comes from **Plato**. One visit to Athens around 432 BCE is recorded in Plato's *Protagoras*, while his philosophical doctrines are discussed in some detail in the *Theaetetus*. A famous anecdote has it that Protagoras taught a young man, Euathlos, the art of rhetoric for use in courts of law, agreeing to waive his fee if his pupil lost his first case. To evade payment, Euathlos avoided taking any cases until Protagoras himself brought a suit in order to recover his fee. The situation is known as Protagoras' **paradox**, for, on the one hand, in order to recover his fee Protagoras would have to win, but on the other hand, since Euathlos would then have lost his first case, the fee should be waived.

Essential philosophy

No objective truth

Protagoras' assertion that man is the measure of all things seems to be saying that because individual judgements are inherently subjective, we cannot hope to achieve **objective knowledge**. If human nature determines any judgement then there is no universal truth on any subject. This **sceptical** position appears to have been based on observations about the subjective character of **perception**. For example, while one person may find a room too hot, another may find it too cold. Since each judgement seems equally well justified, there cannot be an objective truth of the matter. One **inference** Protagoras appears to have drawn from this is that both sides in any dispute can be made to appear equally strong. Moreover, since certain knowledge is impossible we should remain agnostic on all matters, including, for example, whether or not the gods exist.

Moral scepticism

Such scepticism can be extended to moral judgements, for if what appears to me to be morally praiseworthy can appear to someone else as reprehensible, then all moral judgements become a matter of convention or opinion. Many detected in such arguments the threat of a slide into moral anarchy, something Plato for one was concerned to resist. The idea that human reason cannot discover

Legacy, truth, consequence

- Plato's efforts to defeat Protagorean scepticism are what led to his positing the real existence of ideal objects, the "Forms", of which genuine knowledge is possible.
- The recognition that subjective human perception of things determines their appearance is an important insight and one that continues to be discussed today.

Key dates

c.490 BCE	Born in Abdera, Thrace (in modern Greece). Goes on to study with his compatriot **Democritus**.
432 BCE	Having left Abdera to earn his living as a teacher, makes one of at least two visits to Athens. Becomes associated with the democratic ruler Pericles and the Sophists. Meets the young **Socrates**.
444 BCE	Asked by Pericles to write a constitution for the Athenian colony of Thurii.
420 BCE	Dies (place unknown).

Concerning the gods, I have no means of knowing whether they exist or not ... Many things prevent knowledge including the obscurity of the subject and the brevity of human life.

Protagoras, quoted in Arthur Fairbanks, *The First Philosophers of Greece* (1898)

the truth was seen by some to imply that persuasion is the only art worth learning, and that moral scruples are in vain. Such views became associated with the **Sophists** who acquired a reputation for verbal trickery and the manipulative use of rhetoric to achieve unscrupulous ends. There is a story that he was prosecuted for impiety, and had to flee Athens while his books were burned, although this is generally thought to be unlikely.

Socrates

Socrates was primarily a critic of received opinion. He claimed no knowledge for himself, but by engaging the young aristocrats of Athens in conversation, he exposed their ignorance about matters of essential moral concern. Among his positive doctrines are the notion that no one willingly does wrong and that living virtuously is its own reward.

Socrates' mother was a midwife and his father a sculptor and it may be that he made his living as a stonemason. It is well documented that he cared little for his physical appearance, going everywhere barefoot; that he was rather ugly but possessed great physical fortitude; and that on occasion when absorbed in thought he would stand motionless for hours apparently oblivious to his surroundings. Except for his military service in the Peloponnesian wars as a young man, Socrates spent his whole life in his native city of Athens. He is said to have preferred to remain in the city because he wanted to learn from people, and there are more people in the city than the country.

His initial philosophical interest appears to have been in **natural philosophy** and he was attracted to the work of **Anaxagoras**. However, he soon became disillusioned with Anaxagoras' failure to explain the purpose for which the universe is made and turned his attention instead to **ethical** matters. Like his contemporaries, the **Sophists**, Socrates would engage the young men of Athens in discussion of moral issues, but unlike them denied he had any special knowledge to impart and refused payment. Possibly under the influence of **Zeno of Elea**, Socrates deployed the **dialectical** method of question and answer by which he would try to discover what knowledge his interlocutors possessed. Unfortunately, he repeatedly found that they knew as little as he did. While Socrates claimed they ought to be pleased to have their ignorance exposed, many Athenians did not see it this way, and during his career Socrates succeeded in making many powerful enemies. When the oracle at Delphi proclaimed that there was no one wiser than Socrates, he professed surprise. His own explanation was that he was the one person who was not under the illusion that he knew what he did not.

After Athens' defeat to Sparta in 404 BCE, Socrates lived through the brief regime of the thirty tyrants, a period where many were executed by being forced to drink hemlock. During this time he remained true to his principles in the face of personal risk and defied the authorities by refusing to take part in the arrest of an innocent man. On that occasion he escaped punishment, but, as a thorn in the side of the restored democratic regime, he was tried and executed a few years later. Socrates faced his death with equanimity, secure in the knowledge that his personal integrity was intact and apparently confident of the immortality of his soul.

Essential philosophy

Socrates the gadfly

Because Socrates wrote nothing himself what we know of his philosophical outlook comes to us through the writings of his followers, most eminent among these, **Plato**. How faithful the Platonic portrait of Socrates is to the historical figure is a matter of debate. However, what seems fairly certain is that Socrates saw it as his divinely given mission to expose the muddled thinking of his contemporaries on the important matters affecting how we live. He likened himself to a gadfly: an irritant that would not allow people to become complacent in their attitudes, but constantly reminded them of the need to question and critically reflect on their assumptions. The dialectical method he employed was designed in the first instance to expose the hidden confusions in people's thinking. Typically he would pose questions such as "What is justice?" or "What is courage?" and encourage his interlocutors to propose definitions that would capture the essential nature of such moral virtues. When the definitions were shown to be wanting, usually because they failed to identify the single feature shared by all just individuals or all courageous acts, Socrates would conclude that he and his companion clearly had no knowledge of the virtue in question.

Socrates the midwife

But Socrates appears not to have been a **sceptic** about the possibility of knowledge and saw the recognition of one's own ignorance not as an end, but as the necessary spur to further inquiry. By continuing the dialectical process of question and answer Socrates hoped to reveal the knowledge hidden within the minds of others. This process, the dialectic or *elenchus*, he likened to giving birth and himself to a midwife, who helped others bring forth understanding.

Legacy, truth, consequence

- Socrates, as well as his contemporaries the Sophists, oversaw a shift of philosophical focus from the natural world to human conduct which profoundly influenced the future development of philosophical inquiry.
- Socrates' commitment to the unwavering search for truth and his willingness to die rather than compromise his moral integrity or philosophical principles set the standard for future philosophers.
- His influence on Plato is of particular significance and is fundamental to the whole development of **Western philosophy**. Plato appears to have accepted from Socrates that a virtuous character is of greater worth than material and social success, and much of his philosophical work is devoted to showing that it is in one's best interests to be moral.

Key dates

c.470 BCE   Born in Athens, in Greece. Remains in Athens his whole life where he marries Xanthippe and has several children. According to **Diogenes Laertius**, Socrates helps to sculpt the figures of the Graces on the Acropolis. He avoids involving himself in public life, regarding it as too risky to a lover of truth.

c.450 BCE   Meets **Parmenides** and **Zeno of Elea** on their visit to Athens.

c.432 BCE   **Protagoras**, the most eminent of the Sophists, arrives in Athens.

399 BCE   Just a few years after the restoration of democracy in Athens, Socrates is condemned to death on vague charges of impiety and corrupting the young. Although, according to Plato he has the opportunity to escape, he refuses, electing instead to accept his punishment and drink the poison hemlock.

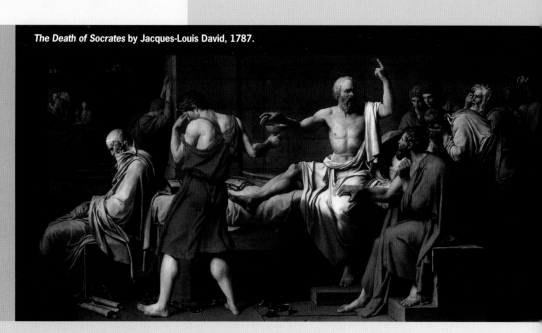

The Death of Socrates by Jacques-Louis David, 1787.

> **. . . it is never right to do a wrong or return a wrong or defend one's self against injury by retaliation**
>
> Socrates in Plato's
> *Crito* (c.360 BCE)

The Socratic paradox

Although Socrates himself never claimed to have knowledge, he does appear to have held certain positive doctrines. Principal among these is the Socratic **paradox**, that no one willingly chooses to act immorally. On the face of it this appears clearly false. After all, there are all kinds of action one recognizes as wrong but which one may choose to perform if one judges that they will bring benefit to oneself. For example, someone may choose to lie, cheat, or steal if they believe they can get away with it and gain some advantage. Socrates, however, held that this betrays some confused thinking. For in acting immorally they actually harm their own character far more than they harm their victim. While they may succeed in stripping others of material possessions and other trappings of worldly accomplishment, genuine human happiness is a matter of inner harmony and self-mastery rather than material success. To come to this realization, however, requires some careful reflection on the true nature of virtue; reflection which will show, according to Socrates, that acting morally is the true route to personal flourishing. Hence another of his paradoxical claims, that virtue is knowledge, or, in other words, that if one truly knows what is good one cannot but choose to do it.

Whatever the details of Socrates' views on **ethics**, it is his philosophical method and the position he gives it in human life which is his important legacy. He believed that the unexamined life is not worth living and that only by subjecting our common beliefs to critical scrutiny can we hope to discover how best to live. Thus he placed the unswerving use of critical reason at the heart not just of the philosophical enterprise, but of the good life.

Democritus

Known as the laughing philosopher because his ethical system regarded cheerfulness as the highest good, Democritus elaborated the theory that all that exist are indivisible corpuscles of matter – "atoms" – moving in empty space. Atomism committed Democritus to the view that the soul is purely material and therefore that there is no afterlife.

Atomism, the theory most associated with Democritus' name, appears to have first originated with the rather shadowy figure of Leucippus (*fl.* c.440 BCE). So little is known of Leucippus that **Epicurus** (341–270 BCE) even suggested he may be purely mythical. However, it seems likely that he did exist and possibly came from the ancient Greek city of Miletus (in what is now Turkey), continuing the tradition of seeking naturalistic explanations of phenomena that began with **Thales** (*fl.* c.580 BCE). Democritus refined and elaborated the fundamental theory in great detail but exactly which ideas he inherited from his teacher and which are due to him is impossible to determine.

We know far more of Democritus than Leucippus. He was born into wealthy nobility in Abdera in Thrace (in modern Greece). He may have studied with Leucippus and possibly **Anaxagoras**. His father is said to have entertained Xerxes' troops as they passed through during the Greco-Persian war, for which service Democritus was educated by Magi serving in the Persian court. Upon his father's death he took his considerable inheritance and left his home town in search of learning. He is said to have gone to Egypt and Persia, where he studied mathematics and **natural philosophy**. After some years, having exhausted his funds, he returned to Abdera where he had to make a living by giving public lectures. According to the third century CE biographer Diogenes Laertius he wrote 72 works on a great range of subjects, including biology, **ethics**, mathematics, music, and **sense perception**, all working out the details of the atomic theory. None of these survive so that we must rely on over 300 preserved fragments and later discussions of his ideas, principally by **Aristotle**.

Democritus was a contemporary of the **Sophists**, renowned teachers of oratory and the nature of virtue based in Athens, and of **Socrates**, and according to some sources he did visit Athens on his travels. **Plato** records Socrates meeting with other traveling sages, such as **Parmenides**, so it is perhaps surprising that there is no mention of Democritus in any of Plato's writings. One explanation is that Plato simply knew nothing of Democritus, although according to Diogenes Laertius the truth is that Plato hated his mechanistic philosophy and wished his books to be burned.

The great Roman thinker and statesman, Seneca (4 BCE–65 CE) reports that Democritus was continually laughing at the follies of human kind and so was considered by many to be mad. He went to see the physician Hippocrates (c.460–c.370 BCE) who told him he was perfectly sane, just lucky to have a happy disposition. He is also said to have blinded himself so as to put an end to his desire for women and so preserve his happiness.

Essential philosophy

The Eleatics

Atomism developed in response to the arguments of the **Eleatic school**, many of which Leucippus and Democritus accepted. For example, they agreed that movement is impossible unless there is empty space for a body to move into. They also accepted that nothing can arise from nothing, and nothing can be destroyed. However, like Anaxagoras and **Empedocles**, the atomists wanted to resist the conclusion that "being" is one, unchanging and undifferentiated, instead finding a place for the reality of movement and **pluralism**.

The void

To this end they posited the existence of "the void", that is, of empty space. In so doing they were rejecting what to many of their contemporaries had appeared an unassailable piece of logic from Parmenides, namely, that what is not cannot be, implying that a vacuum, which is nothing, cannot exist. On what basis, if any, they were able to deal with this argument is not known. But in any case, by allowing the reality of the void, motion is restored to the universe, since it allows for some space into which a thing can move.

Atoms

On the basis that an end to space is unthinkable, Democritus reckoned it must extend infinitely in all directions. Within this infinite space, as the evidence of the senses would suggest, there are beings of a great variety of kinds, and while all these beings can be divided, it is impossible, Democritus argued, to divide them *ad infinitum*. There must, therefore, be a point where division ends and

Legacy, truth, consequence

■ The claim that all that exists is matter in motion involves the rejection of a spiritual dimension to the universe, a position that fell from favor and was viewed with considerable hostility in Europe throughout the Christian era. Not until the eighteenth century did **materialism**'s fortunes begin to revive, and today it is the orthodox view among philosophers.

■ The rejection of teleological or purpose-driven explanations of natural phenomena chimes with the approach of modern science, but from the time of Plato and Aristotle this approach was viewed with suspicion.

■ Of all the ancient Greek natural philosophies, atomism is closest to the modern physicists' view of reality.

■ Democritus' materialism and ethics had an important influence on **Epicurus**. Epicurean social and **political philosophy** became, after **stoicism**, the most influential and enduring of the **Hellenistic philosophies**.

■ Democritus anticipates **John Locke**'s distinction between primary and secondary qualities in arguing that hot and cold, tastes, colors, and other perceptions are caused in us by the impact of different types of atoms on our sensory apparatus and the soul, and so depend on the observer, and that the real world consists exclusively of matter in motion.

Key dates

c.460 BCE   Born in Abdera in Thrace (in modern Greece).
c.480 BCE   Encounters Magi serving with Xerxes' army with whom he studies astrology and theology. Later travels in the East to study further, returning to make his living teaching and writing in Abdera.
c.370 BCE   Dies in Abdera aged about 90 years.

By convention are sweet and bitter, hot and cold, by convention is color; in truth are atoms and the void ... In reality we apprehend nothing for certain, but only as it changes according to the condition of our body and of the things that impinge on or offer resistance to it.

Democritus, quoted in G. S. Kirk, J. E. Raven, & M. Schofield, *The Pre-Socratic Philosophers* (1957)

Infrared image of the center of the Milky Way galaxy. Democritus was the first to understand that the Milky Way was made up of a large amount of distant stars.

we reach the smallest possible particles of matter: particles too minute to be detected by the senses. Since these particles cannot be divided he called them "atoms" which means "uncuttable". They are indivisible because they contain no void or pores and so no space by which to divide one part from another, in other words they are perfectly hard and indestructible. Consequently they always have existed and always will.

Atoms are unlimited in number, perpetually moving, and everything is composed of them. Differing only in respect of their shape, size, and (possibly) weight their movements are governed by strict **deterministic** laws, causing them to collide and form themselves into vortices that eventually coalesce into physical bodies and create worlds. There are and have been infinitely many worlds all created and destroyed according to

unthinking mechanical forces, a view which stands in contrast to notions of providence or the work of any intelligence in the scheme of things. There is no account in Democritus of how or why the universe came into existence in the first place and he eschews the notion that purpose can explain anything in the natural world.

For Democritus, life too develops by purely mechanical means. Perception and thought are physical processes, no more than movements of matter, meaning that the human soul is made of atoms, albeit particularly fine spherical ones, akin to those that compose fire. This means that when they dissipate at death, that is the end of us. By the same logic, the gods must be purely physical and like everything else are subject to natural processes of decay, and so are mortal.

Plato

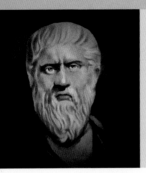

Alongside his student Aristotle, Plato has had the profoundest impact on the development of Western thought of any thinker. He is the first philosopher whose works survive in significant numbers and his systematic, rigorous explorations of a great range of subjects have such profundity and are written with such literary genius that they remain the subject of intellectual fascination to this day.

From an aristocratic Athenian family, Plato is thought to have had political ambitions in his youth, but, under the influence of his teacher **Socrates**, appears to have given them up fairly early in life. A key event leading to his disillusionment with the Athenian democracy was its implication in the trial and execution of Socrates in 399 BCE. Plato, then aged 30, left Athens and traveled extensively in the Greek world, and possibly as far afield as Egypt. He spent some time in Sicily teaching Dion, the brother-in-law of the tyrant of Syracuse, Dionysius I. After his return to Athens he founded the first institution of higher education, the Academy, which survived until it was closed down by the Roman Emperor Justinian in 529 CE.

With the death of Dionysius I, Plato returned to Sicily to tutor the young Prince Dionysius II in the hope of transforming the tyrant into a philosophically enlightened ruler. However, it appears Dionysius did not have the requisite qualities, and is even said to have made Plato his prisoner. Plato eventually escaped back to Athens, where he spent the rest of his days teaching at the Academy.

Socrates was the most significant influence on Plato's career. Because of him Plato devoted himself to the philosophical life, and the manner of his teacher's death seems to have prompted Plato to defend his memory by making records of his philosophical discussions. Plato's early dialogues are clearly not verbatim transcriptions, but they are generally accepted as being fairly accurate in their portrayal of Socrates and his approach to philosophy. These works involve Socrates exploring **ethical** concepts in search of proper definitions but are largely inconclusive, so that it is not until the middle period dialogues that Plato begins to develop his own doctrines. Socrates remains the main speaker but is now the mouthpiece for Plato's views. In the later dialogues Plato begins to question some of the central doctrines elaborated in the middle period, once again making the matter of identifying Plato's own position problematic.

> *If no pure knowledge is possible in the company of the body, then either it is totally impossible to acquire knowledge, or it is only possible after death ....*
>
> Phaedo (fourth century BCE)

Essential philosophy

The Ideas

The central theory of Plato's entire philosophical system is the so-called "theory of **Ideas**" or "Forms". To understand the theory we need to return to Socrates' project as pursued in the early dialogues. There Plato describes Socrates' unsuccessful endeavors to discover definitions for moral qualities such as courage or virtue. The problem that Socrates draws attention to is that no particular courageous act or person is totally or perfectly courageous, but only to some degree or in some respects. Courage itself, in other words, is not the same as any particular acts of courage, rather, the general term appears to refer to what all courageous acts have in common, and which makes them courageous. This is not any particular thing in the physical world, but rather what philosophers nowadays call a "**universal**". Since universals are not identifiable with particular acts or objects that we observe with the senses, Plato reckoned that they must exist independently of them and so that they are apprehended by the intellect alone. They are, in other words, "Ideas" – *eidos* in Greek. Platonic Ideas are perfect or ideal versions of the particular things that exist in the physical world. So an act of courage is akin to an imitation of, or approximation to, the Idea of courage.

In the same way, Plato figured that there was an ideal realm of geometric and mathematical objects which we recognize with the mind rather than the senses. Perfect circles and exactly straight lines are Ideas we grasp intuitively with the mind in order to do geometry, and yet we never encounter such things in the physical world. All circular objects are only approximately circular – they fall short of the ideal. It is unclear how far Plato was prepared to extend the theory of Ideas, but it appears he may have believed that there are Ideas corresponding to all general terms. This would mean, for example, that there is an Idea of the "bed", a perfect exemplar perceived in the mind's eye of a carpenter, which functions as a model when fashioning an actual bed.

Legacy, truth, consequence

- Along with **Aristotle**, Plato is the most influential philosopher in the development of Western thought. So significant is he, that the mathematician and philosopher Alfred North Whitehead (1861–1947) called the whole of **Western philosophy** a series of footnotes to Plato.
- Indirectly he influenced the development of Christianity: **Neo-Platonism**, as developed by thinkers such as Plotinus (204/5–270 CE), came to inform Christian theology. This process was so successful that in the nineteenth century **Friedrich Nietzsche** was able to call Christianity "*Platonism for the masses*".
- One of his key works, *The Republic*, represents the first attempt in the Western tradition to describe an ideal state or utopia. Other examples include **Saint Augustine's** "City of God" (413–26 CE) and Thomas Moore's *Utopia* (1516).

Papyrus fragment of Plato's *Alcibiades*, c.131 CE.

Key dates

c.428 BCE	Born in Athens, Greece.
399 BCE	Socrates is executed and Plato leaves Athens. Where he travels is unknown, although legend has him visit Egypt.
387 BCE	Arrives in Sicily where he encounters the Pythagorean school (see **Pythagoras,** pages 12–13) and becomes involved with the rulers of Syracuse.
c.385 BCE	Returns to Athens and, with the mathematician Theaetetus (c.417–369 BCE), co-founds the Academy, often considered the first European university.
367 BCE	Visits Sicily, and again in 361 BCE; otherwise remains in Athens.
347 BCE	Dies in Athens.

The society we have described can never grow into a reality or see the light of day, and there will be no end to the troubles of states, or indeed … of humanity itself, till philosophers become kings in this world, or till those we now call kings and rulers really and truly become philosophers, and political power and philosophy thus come into the same hands.

Republic (fourth century BCE)

The Good

Through the use of the **dialectical** method of cooperative inquiry, philosophers can hope to analyze concepts and eventually acquire knowledge of the Ideas. This process reaches its apogee in knowledge of the ultimate Idea, the Good. Knowledge of the Good enables us to know all other things because we can then understand the ultimate purpose or reason for all things. Genuine knowledge must concern what is unchanging and eternal, namely the Ideas; by contrast, since the physical world is subject to change Plato held that it can only be an object of belief. In this way he draws a distinction between the real world of Ideas and the apparent world which is perceived by the senses.

The soul

Since it is the mind which apprehends the unchanging Ideas, it must, like them, be incorruptible. In other words, the soul is immortal and must exist before birth. Learning in this life is in reality recollecting what we knew before we were born, and when we die the soul will be reborn into a new body. Philosophers, in their pursuit of the eternal Ideas, prepare their souls for a return to the eternal realm and in so doing may escape the cycle of rebirth and live forever among the Ideas.

Politics

Plato's philosophy is not purely speculative and he never lost his concern for the politics of this world, writing extensively on how an ideal state might be realized. He opposed **democracy** principally because he believed governing was a skill requiring specialized knowledge and extended training. The *Republic* (c.360 BCE) provides a detailed blueprint of the ideal of political organization in which an elite class of philosophers rules.

Diogenes the Cynic

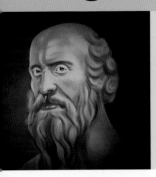

The founder of cynicism, from the Greek "*kynikos*" meaning "dog-like", Diogenes and his followers turned their backs on what they regarded as the illusory trappings of social life and espoused a philosophy of self-reliance and mastery over one's desires. Genuine happiness is achieved by shamelessly living a simple, animal existence.

Diogenes was born in Sinope (in modern-day Turkey), according to some legends on the day of **Socrates'** execution. The story goes that his father, who was a money changer, was prosecuted for defacing the Sinope coinage, forcing Diogenes to flee to Athens. There he came across Antisthenes (c.445–c.360 BCE), a former student of Socrates, and pestered him to allow him to become his disciple. When Antisthenes raised a stick to discourage him, Diogenes' great respect for the philosopher led him to say that there was no stick hard enough to drive him away so long as Antisthenes was still speaking. Antisthenes finally gave in to his persistence, teaching him a form of asceticism and **scepticism** about the value of social customs. However, Diogenes soon outdid his master in degree of commitment to these ideas. He abandoned possessions and even gave up his feeding bowl when he saw a boy eating from cupped hands. Following the example of a mouse in finding shelter where it could, he made his home in a barrel. His disdain for convention is perhaps best illustrated in the story of his masturbating in the market place, responding to rebukes by saying "*if only I could relieve my hunger as easily by rubbing my belly*".

Diogenes was a contemporary of **Plato** who called him "*a Socrates gone mad*", and many anecdotes have Plato as a foil to Diogenes' wit. One such episode, recounted by **Diogenes Laertius**, concerns Plato's definition of a human being as a featherless biped (in Plato's dialogue, *Statesman*), which proposed to show that we should not regard ourselves as particularly special within the animal kingdom. Diogenes refuted the definition in dramatic fashion, by taking a plucked chicken to where Plato was lecturing at the Academy and declaring it to be Plato's human. Diogenes Laertius says that after this the definition had to be amended to include "*with broad flat nails*".

It is said that Diogenes would carry a lantern around the central assembly and market square in broad daylight, and when asked what he was doing announced that he was searching for an honest man, clearly regarding such a thing as a rarity in the center of the civilized world. Alexander the Great visited Athens only once, but is reported to have met the famous philosopher in his barrel. When he asked Diogenes whether there was anything he could do for him, Diogenes answered he could step out of his light, a remark which was presumably to be taken metaphorically as well as literally. Diogenes had no need of the material assistance the most powerful man in the world might offer, and the prospect of worldly success that Alexander presented could serve only to obscure the philosopher's view of the good life as revealed by the light of reason. Apparently impressed, Alexander is said to have responded that if he were not Alexander he would want to be Diogenes.

Essential philosophy

Although no writings of Diogenes survive, if indeed he wrote any, it is the manner in which he is reputed to have lived his life which is the most eloquent expression of his philosophy. The central message, the rejection of social convention, required living at the margins of society, but within view in order to be its conspicuous critic. Hence so many of the anecdotes involve Diogenes exposing, by his example, the moral bankruptcy of civilized living.

Diogenes taught that conventional morality and customs are artificial and misguided, and that reason reveals the route to genuine virtue requires a return to a simple and more natural way of life. Happiness is to be found by abandoning all conventional responsibilities and ties, as well as the false idols of social status and material success. So he rejected as irrational those values that depend on the judgements of society, such as honor and reputation, and replaced them with those of self-sufficiency and austerity, which impact only on the character of the individual, thereby taking charge of the realm which truly matters, one's own soul. He lived like a tramp, making his livelihood by begging for the minimum needed to survive, rejecting all accepted codes of conduct, from the manner of his dress to where and how he ate and slept; ignoring taboos, he insisted that any behavior which is generally done in private may as well be done in public without shame. Unsurprisingly, many regarded him as mad, but for Diogenes it was conventional attitudes and one's slavish adherence to them that were truly without rational foundation; the dictates and mores of particular societies he regarded as unnecessary and local. One implication is that he did not consider

- Diogenes' uncompromising example and his scathing wit – the weapons in his battle with the forces of convention – won him many converts and over the next several centuries there continued to flourish a succession of followers, the **cynics**, consciously emulating Diogenes' way of life right up to the fall of the Roman Empire.

- Diogenes' follower, Crates, became in turn the teacher of **Zeno of Citium**, the founder of **stoicism**, which, alongside cynicism, became the most influential philosophy of the Roman Empire. Zeno inherited from Diogenes the rejection of social convention.

- The modern sense of the term "cynicism" as showing contempt for any apparently selfless and virtuous behavior, involves a misunderstanding of the cynics' central message. They were not sceptical about morality, but rather devoted to debunking the superficial mores of social existence in favor of true or natural virtue.

Diogenes seeks a true man, painting by Caesar Van Everdingen, 1652.

> *He claimed that to fortune he could oppose courage, to convention nature, to passion reason.*
>
> Diogenes, quoted in
> Diogenes Laertius' *Lives of Eminent Philosophers*
> (third century CE)

Another well-known anecdote informs us that he was captured by pirates and sold into slavery. At the slave market he gave his trade as governing men, saying he should be sold to someone who needed a master. He was bought by a Corinthian to bring up and tutor his children in the tenets of Diogenes' philosophy, in this way demonstrating that Diogenes, although a slave, was free, while the master was subject to his tuition.

> *Everything belongs to the gods; and wise men are the friends of the gods. All things are in common among friends; therefore everything belongs to wise men.*
>
> Diogenes, quoted in Diogenes Laertius'
> *Lives of Eminent Philosophers* (third century CE)

himself the subject of any particular city or culture, declaring himself instead a citizen of the world.

For Diogenes, contrary to received opinion the way to happiness is not through the satisfaction of one's desires, for it is desire itself which is the source of dissatisfaction. The more one strives to satiate one's appetites, the more powerful they become, in the process enslaving their owner. Thus the pursuit of wealth and luxury can serve only to increase desire and so must lead to more frustration. The only solution is to bring one's desires under control. Reining in our needs to the absolute minimum strips them of all that is unnatural, freeing us from the tethers of hollow convention, so that, like the beasts, we may find true happiness.

Key dates

c.404 BCE	Born in Sinope (in modern-day Turkey), but is forced into exile and goes to Athens. There are numerous anecdotes from his life in Athens, but no reliable dates for any of these, bar his meeting with Alexander (later "the Great"), which may have taken place in 338 BCE.
c.323 BCE	Dies at Corinth in Greece. He is said to have died from eating a raw octopus to make a point about the unnaturalness of preparing food.

Aristotle

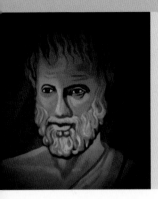

The sheer depth and breadth of Aristotle's investigations are astonishing. He was the first to define many of the disciplines that are studied to this day, including logic, physics, metaphysics, biology, psychology, and ethics. His work had a profound and ultimately restraining influence on European thought up to the Enlightenment when finally thinkers began consciously to extricate themselves from his orbit.

Aristotle arrived in Athens to join **Plato**'s Academy aged just 17 and quickly made his name as an exceptional student. He had left his home in Stagira in northern Greece on the death of his father, the last in a long line of court physicians to the royal family of Macedon. Aristotle went on to teach at the Academy for some years, only leaving on Plato's death in 347 BCE. Why he was prompted to leave is not known. It may be that he was angered at having been passed over for leadership of the Academy, which went to Plato's nephew, Speusippus. The divergence between the views of the younger man and those of his teacher, Plato, may explain why he didn't get the appointment. Or it may be that he had stayed out of loyalty to Plato and was eager to find new intellectual challenges. Whatever his reasons, under the patronage of a one-time fellow student of the Academy and current King of Atarneus, Hermias, he settled in Assos (in modern Turkey). During this time he conducted extensive research into natural history, notably on the nearby isle of Lesbos, and married Hermias' daughter, Pythias. With the Persian invasion three years later, Aristotle escaped to the city of Mytilene on Lesbos, and not long after became tutor to the son of Philip of Macedon, Alexander – later to become "the Great". The Macedonian court is said to have funded Aristotle's research, helping him to produce the first great collection of biological specimens.

When Alexander acceded to the thrown on his father's death, Aristotle left Macedon and returned to Athens, where he founded his own school, the Lyceum, also known as the peripatetic school, probably after Aristotle's habit of walking up and down as he lectured. He is said to have produced two types of work during this period: lecture notes for the inner circle of advanced students; and the popular works, including dialogues for a broader audience. The latter are said to have been written in beautiful prose – Cicero described them as a "a river of gold" – but unfortunately they have been lost. The remaining works,

Essential philosophy

Logic and metaphysics

Aristotle wrote on a great range of topics and many of his works represent the first forays into fields of inquiry that have grown over the last 2,500 years into major disciplines. He was the first to produce a formal **logic**, which examined the principles underlying correct reasoning and identified different forms of **deductive inference**. The rules he established were considered the final word on the matter until the nineteenth century. His *Metaphysics* is concerned with "being", that is, with the categories of things there are that exist. In a departure from the teaching of Plato, Aristotle argued that general terms like "bed" or "goat" – referring to what philosophers now call "**universals**" – do not have any real existence independently of actual beds and goats. So there is no such thing as the "Platonic **Idea**" (see pages 28–9) of a goat, only the many goats in the physical world. What makes something a goat is that the matter of which it is composed is organized in a certain way, in other words it has a certain form which is not substantially distinct from matter. Significantly this means that our souls, which for Aristotle are the forms of the body, cannot persist after physical death, apparently meaning that we cannot hope for any afterlife.

His opposition to Plato on these subjects is symptomatic of his more down-to-earth concern with observation of this world as the proper starting point for scientific as well as philo- sophical investigations. For Aristotle, knowledge begins with **sense experience** rather than abstract reasoning, and a meticulous observation of the great variety of phe- nomena in the physical world characterized much of his work, in particular in the realm of biology.

> *Now it is evident that that form of government is best in which every man, whoever he is, can act best and live happily.*
>
> Politics (fourth century CE)

Aristotle's pupil, Alexander the Great (*Alexander Mosaic*, Pompei, c.200 BCE).

■ What influence the teachings of Aristotle may have had on the young Alexander of Macedon has been the source of much speculation. Plutarch in the first century CE recorded that Alexander learned important lessons in **ethics** and **politics**, and was initiated into esoteric doctrines that Aristotle never wrote down. **Bertrand Russell**, however, argues it more likely that Alexander regarded him as a "*prosy old pedant*". What does seem clear is that Alexander provided his tutor with the means to collect a vast array of scientific observational data, and through his conquests and the library in Alexandria ensured his ideas spread and endured.

■ The fall of the Roman Empire around the fifth century CE saw the loss of Aristotle's works to European scholars but he continued to be studied in the Islamic world. Not until the Middle Ages was Aristotle rediscovered in Europe and a new era of philosophical endeavor began as attempts were made to square his ideas with Christian teaching. Known during this time as "The Philosopher" his ideas came to dominate **medieval philosophy**.

The good for man is an activity of soul in accordance with virtue ... in a complete lifetime. One swallow does not make a summer; neither can one day, or a brief space of time, make a man blessed and happy.

Nicomachean Ethics (fourth century CE)

while relatively turgid in style, make up for this in philosophical richness. They include, *Physics*, *Metaphysics*, *Nicomachean Ethics*, *Politics*, *On the Soul*, and *Poetics*.

While Aristotle had been establishing the Lyceum, Alexander had been busy conquering the known world and establishing Macedon as the dominant military and political power. With Alexander's early death in 323 BCE, a wave of anti-Macedonian sentiment led to a prosecution against Aristotle for impiety. Rather than allow the Athenians to "*sin twice against philosophy*", a reference to the execution of **Socrates**, Aristotle fled to Chalcis on the Greek island of Euboea, where he died a year later.

Ethics

Aristotle observed that human beings are social animals and saw the role of government as helping to produce the conditions in which we can flourish. But, rather than rule by an enlightened elite, as recommended by Plato, he believed **democracy** was best suited to promoting human happiness. The good life consists in our fulfilling our function as human beings, and given our rational nature we should allow a central role to the exercise of reason in choosing how to live. Based on this reasoning Aristotle regarded contemplation as an essential component of the good life. Reason dictates we should avoid extremes and so to live virtuously is to follow the "golden mean" between vices. Thus, for example, to be courageous is to avoid the extremes of cowardice on the one side and foolhardiness on the other; to be generous is to avoid the extremes of extravagance and meanness. In this way, a balanced life will lead to human well-being. Aristotle outlines what is now called his "**virtue ethics**" in his treatise *Nicomachean Ethics*.

Key dates

384 BCE	Born in Stagira, northern Greece.
c.367 BCE	Moves to Athens to study at the Academy, where he stays until Plato's death in 347 BCE. He becomes tutor to thirteen-year-old son of Philip of Macedon, the future Alexander the Great.
335 BCE	With Alexander's accession to the throne, Aristotle returns to Athens and founds the Lyceum. It is in this period he is thought to have produced his major works.
323 BCE	Alexander dies and Aristotle is forced to flee Athens because of anti-Macedonian feeling.
322 BCE	Dies in Chalcis on the Greek island of Euboea.

c.372–289 BCE

Mencius

Mencius, the Latinized name for Master Meng (Mengzi or Meng-tzu), was the second most important Confucian after Confucius himself. Sometimes called the "Second Sage", Mencius played a major role in shaping the philosophy of Confucius and ensuring its survival as an essential part of Chinese culture and society.

Born in the **Warring States period**, Mencius was a wealthy man who enjoyed the luxuries of life, but nevertheless admired **Confucius'** simple way of living and search for the truth. More doctrinaire than his exemplar, he became so attached to Confucius' teachings that he began to preach them as truth, and ensured that they would be passed down through history.

He traveled from state to state, looking for a ruler who would attend to his moral preaching but, like Confucius, in the end gave up and settled down to teaching. More idealistic and also lighter-hearted than Confucius, he developed and expanded the themes of the *Analects* (479 BCE), but used wit and humor and stories to illustrate points.

> **There is no man who is not good, just as there is no water that does not flow downward.**
>
> Attributed to Mencius

Essential philosophy

Human nature
According to Mencius, humans are fundamentally good and moral, so everyone has within themselves the ability to become a Confucian sage or superior man. Humans are born with four virtues: human kindness, righteousness (a sense of the right thing to do), courteousness, wisdom. These virtues arise spontaneously if not deliberately suppressed by selfish desires, so can be cultivated in everyone through education and discipline.

Compassion
Mencius believed the human virtues are expressed through compassion. He used the example of a child about to fall into a well: people will naturally feel compassion for the child and for its parents, so will rush to try to rescue the child.

Society
The goal of the Confucian sage was to live well, Mencius said, not just to govern well, as Confucius thought. If there are many individuals in society who are living an ideal life, then society will naturally be improved. If many people behave negatively, then society will reflect this lack of virtue.

Legacy, truth, consequence

- Mencius ensured that Confucius' teachings survived and spread.
- He strengthened Confucian politics by providing them with a foundation in moral **psychology**.
- His interpretation of Confucius became accepted as the orthodox view, and the *Mencius* (289 BCE) became one of the classic Confucian texts.
- Although Chinese emperors expressed admiration for Mencius' views they generally failed to live up to his ideals of moral behavior.
- Mencius had a revolutionary idea of sharing land into cooperatives. This was never popular until **communist** theories took hold centuries later.

Key dates

c.372 BCE Born in the state of Zhou (now modern Shandong province), just 18 miles (29 km) from the birthplace of Confucius. Studies under Zisi, a grandson of Confucius, then becomes a wandering philosopher.

319–312 BCE Works as an official in the state of Qi. Later becomes a teacher.

289 BCE After his death his ideas are gathered by his followers into the influential book, the *Mencius*.

Government
A ruler's main aim is to ensure the welfare of his people. If a ruler becomes unjust and oppressive he should be removed, by violent revolution if necessary. This view reinforced the traditional idea that a ruler has the "Mandate of Heaven", which is withdrawn if they lose virtue.

Mysticism
Unlike Confucius, Mencius held a vein of **mysticism** in his philosophy, arguing that the cultivation of virtue within oneself leads to the ultimate bliss of union with heaven.

Zhuangzi

The author of one of the classic Daoist texts, Zhuangzi articulated many of the core Daoist concepts in a witty, entertaining way and helped ensure that the philosophy would survive to permeate Chinese culture. The stories in the text that bears his name, the *Zhuangzi*, reveal a life-loving man who enjoyed simple pleasures and rejected the stresses and strains of politics.

We have few definite dates and details of the life of Zhuangzi (Chuang Tzu). It is thought that he was born in the state of Song (modern Henan province), and worked for a company making lacquer or varnish from trees before withdrawing from everyday life to become a hermit. He refused public office, preferring to remain poor but happy, and, according to later legend, became an immortal, one of the perfect human beings who can ascend to heaven but also return to earth to help other people.

Zhuangzi, or Master Zhuang, was the second most important **Daoist** philosopher after **Laozi**. He seems to have lived harmoniously with nature in a rural retreat, epitomizing the Daoist hermit-sage. However, unlike most Daoist authors, his individuality – spontaneous and slightly cheeky – emerges from his texts.

Essential philosophy

Harmony
Zhuangzi's stories stress the ultimate harmony of nature: in particular death is not to be feared but is simply part of the natural process of transformation.

Respect for others
Although many of his stories poke gentle fun at **Confucian** officials, in some stories it is the Confucian who reveals the Daoist wisdom. Zhuangzi typified the Chinese ability to draw from other disciplines when appropriate.

Equality
From the perspective of Dao, people are neither noble nor humble, he argued.

Society
In an ideal society everyone would conform to Dao by clearing their minds of self-centered desires, meditating, or perhaps receiving sudden enlightenment. These concepts closely mirror those of **Zen Buddhism**. Unlike Laozi, however, Zhuangzi did not write about politics.

Living a full life
When the envoys of the King of Chu went to offer Zhuangzi the post of prime minister, he was fishing in a river. He said to them: "*I have heard that in the king's temple in Chu there is kept the body of a huge tortoise that lived so long that when it was 3,000 years old it was killed and worshipped. What would the old tortoise want – to be dead and worshipped, or alive and crawling around in mud?*" The envoys replied instantly: "*To be alive and crawling around in mud.*" Zhuangzi answered: "*I'll be the tortoise in the mud.*"

Legacy, truth, consequence

- The *Zhuangzi* was revered as a sacred text in itself, not just for its elaboration of Laozi's original Daoist vision.
- Zhuangzi was called the "Perfect Man of Nanhua" by Emperor Xuan Zong of the Tang dynasty (reigned 712–56 CE), and was given the title "Perfect Sovereign of Numinous Subtlety and Mysterious Pervasion" by Emperor Hui of the Song dynasty (reigned 1100–25 CE).
- During the Tang dynasty his writings became an official field of study.

Key dates

c.370 BCE	Born in what is now Henan province, China.
c.350–301 BCE	Period during which he probably formulated his philosophy.
c.301 BCE	Dies in China.

Once Zhuangzi dreamed he was a butterfly ... Then he woke up, and was in his own solid body ... But he didn't know if he was Zhuangzi dreaming that he was a butterfly, or a butterfly dreaming that he was Zhuangzi.

Zhuangzi (fourth century BCE)

Pyrrho of Elis

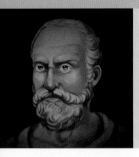

Known as "the sceptic", Pyrrho argued that we should suspend belief about how things really are and confine ourselves to appearances alone. By refusing to assert anything for sure we would free ourselves from worry and so attain complete peace of mind. Pyrrhonian scepticism burgeoned into one of the major schools of thought of the Roman Empire.

At a young age Pyrrho left his home town of Elis in southern Greece and, accompanied by his teacher Anaxarchus of Abdera, joined the train of Alexander the Great's army in its lengthy campaigns across the Middle East to northern India. There he is said to have encountered naked fakirs, the "gymnosophists", from whom he learned his detachment from worldly concerns and a solitary lifestyle.

After his return from India, Pyrrho remained in Elis for the rest of his life. He appears not to have written down any of his ideas, leaving his disciple, Timon of Phlius (c.320–230 BCE), to disseminate them. However, it is principally Sextus Empiricus' (c.140–225 CE) *Outlines of Pyrrhonism* that established the accepted picture of Pyrrho's philosophy, although it should be noted that it is a matter of some scholarly controversy how far the views of later **sceptics** accurately reflect those of the historical Pyrrho.

> *The chief good is the suspension of the judgement, which tranquillity of mind follows like its shadow.*
>
> Pyrrho, quoted in Diogenes Laertius' *Lives of Eminent Philosophers* (third century CE)

Essential philosophy

Living by appearances

Like the **Sophists** before him, and in particular **Protagoras**, Pyrrho argued that there are always arguments that are equally strong which can be marshaled both for and against any claim so that no definitive judgement can be made. Rather than accept any belief that falls short of certainty, he argued that it was wiser to withhold assent from them all. The practical implications of this are that it is equally rational to perform any action as it is not to, meaning we must give up our vain efforts to discover any universally valid answer to the question of how we ought to conduct ourselves. The conclusion drawn is that we must make do with living according to what appears best, which means following the customs of the land in which we find ourselves. By this method he claimed we might achieve peace of mind.

Scepticism about the senses

Pyrrho's commitment to withholding judgement about all things was such that there sprung up numerous anecdotes, doubtless

Legacy, truth, consequence

■ No group of Pyrrhonist philosophers emerged either during or immediately after Pyrrho's lifetime, although scepticism came to have an important influence on **Plato**'s Academy in Athens, firstly under Arcesilaus (c.316–241 BCE) and throughout its middle period (at least up until 155 BCE).

■ It was not until some 200 years later that a school of thought self-consciously heralding Pyrrho as its progenitor appeared: the school founded by Aenesidemus in the first century BCE.

■ Scepticism once again exerted an important influence during the modern period, most notably in the philosophies of **René Descartes** and **David Hume**.

Key dates

c.360 BCE	Born in Elis in southern Greece.
336–325 BCE	Accompanies Alexander the Great's army as far as India, then returns to Elis.
c.270 BCE	Dies in Elis. A statue is erected in Athens in his honor.

apocryphal, about his refusal to accept the evidence of his senses. For example, it is said that when he saw his teacher Anaxarchus stuck in a bog, he didn't offer any aid because he was unable to recognize Anaxarchus with certainty. Equally, unable to accept evidence of danger to his own person, it is said he would happily walk over a cliff if his friends did not prevent him. During a storm at sea, unlike his fellow passengers, he remained unperturbed by the danger and, emulating a pig that was also on board, he continued calmly to enjoy his meal. Despite such dedication to his philosophical outlook he was once seen to flinch before a barking dog, which suggested that he did after all believe in the existence of its sharp teeth. When confronted with this he confessed that our instincts are hard to overcome.

Epicurus

A follower of Democritus, Epicurus was committed to materialism and the view that the gods have no interest in human affairs, and that physical death is the end of us. The hedonistic conclusions he drew from this concerning how we should live had a great impact on the philosophical outlook of Rome and continue to exercise an appeal to this day.

Epicurus was from the island of Samos, an Athenian colony. His family was of modest means. His most significant philosophical influence was his teacher, Nausiphanes, who introduced him to the **natural philosophy** of Democritus, which remained the basis of Epicurus' own philosophical teachings. He left Samos and set up his own schools, firstly in Lampascus (now in modern Turkey) and later in Athens, from where his ideas were disseminated. The school was run from the garden of Epicurus' house and was scandalous in so far as it admitted slaves and women on an equal footing with the male citizens. "The Garden", as it became known, was the first of many Epicurean communities that spread through the Hellenic and later Roman worlds.

We know Epicurus' thought principally through **Diogenes Laertius**, who preserved various of his works including his *Letter to Herodotus* on natural philosophy and the *Letter to Menoeceus* on **ethics**, as well as through the writings of Lucretius (c.99–c.52 BCE) and the Roman statesman and orator **Cicero**.

> ## ... a correct understanding that death is nothing to us makes the mortality of life enjoyable ...
>
> Letter to Menoeceus

Legacy, truth, consequence

- In the centuries after his death Epicurean communities appeared and flourished throughout the **Hellenic** world.
- It was the poet Lucretius who introduced Epicurus' thought to the Roman world in *On the Nature of Things*, and Epicureanism became second only to **stoicism** in terms of its influence.
- Cicero disliked Epicureanism and is largely responsible for sullying its reputation in the popular imagination by suggesting it recommended the pursuit of base pleasures such as food, drink, and sex.
- The Christian Church violently disapproved of both its hedonism and opposition to religious practice, and with the Christianization of Rome Epicureanism went into decline.

Key dates

341 BCE	Born on the Greek island of Samos.
327–324 BCE	Studies under Nausiphanes for three years in the Ionian city of Teos (in present-day Turkey).
323–321 BCE	Completes two years of military service in Athens.
306 BCE	Founds his school, "the Garden", in Athens.
270 BCE	Dies in Athens from kidney stones.

Essential philosophy

Epicurus was a student of the **atomism** of Democritus and accepted the view that the universe consists exclusively of innumerable microscopic particles moving according to natural laws through infinite space. He did not deny the existence of the gods, but argued that they have no interest in human affairs and so can safely be ignored. However, it is the ethical implications of his atomism which are the centerpiece of the **Epicurean philosophy**. The soul, like everything else, is composed of material atoms and death will mean the dispersal of these atoms and so the demise of the self. But this should not be a source of concern to us. On the contrary, as purely material creatures the only good that we can aspire to is pleasure in this life, and since death will be the end of all experience our demise can mean nothing to us.

The conclusion is that the best way to live is to avoid irrational fear of the gods and death and live to maximize pleasure and minimize pain. Epicurus' **hedonism** did not, as his detractors often supposed, license the unfettered pursuit of base physical pleasure. On the contrary, he argued that an intemperate lifestyle would actually be counterproductive since it would tend to lead to increased disturbance of mind and an escalation of frustrated desire. To live the good life, it is necessary to reduce desire, live simply, and achieve a state of serenity and peace of mind. True happiness is found not through pleasures of the flesh, but through higher pleasures such as friendship, good conversation, and philosophical speculation. He advised avoiding involvement in political and family life since these could only serve to disturb the mind.

Zeno of Citium

Zeno was the founder of stoicism, a philosophy which came to dominate the Hellenistic and Roman worlds, even counting the Emperor Marcus Aurelius among its exponents. The stoics argued that virtue and tranquillity of mind are achieved through control of the passions, conformity to the natural order, and a passive acceptance of fate.

Zeno was from the Athenian colony of Citium, Cyprus, and is said as a young man to have been a merchant. However his life was radically changed when, aged about 30, he was shipwrecked and made his way to Athens. There he discovered philosophy and – eager to learn more – attached himself to the cynic philosopher Crates. Crates taught that social conventions were worthless and he worked hard to rid Zeno of his attachment to propriety. The story goes that he made Zeno carry a bowl of soup and then smashed it with his staff covering the hapless disciple with lentils.

Zeno's new life in Athens appears to have been a frugal one as befitting his philosophy, although he is said to have enjoyed a drink, saying it is better to slip with the feet than with the tongue. It was not until quite late in life that he began himself to teach, lecturing in front of the decorated colonnades or "stoa" in the market place, for which reason he and his followers became known as stoics. According to **Diogenes Laertius**, as an old man Zeno took a fall and, believing he was being called to death, strangled himself. All his works, including his political utopia, *The Republic*, are lost.

Essential philosophy

Natural philosophy

Against **Plato**'s **dualism**, Zeno argued that the universe is one and therefore that there is no division between ideas and material things. As there is just one kind of stuff, both the gods and the human soul must be reducible matter. However, despite his **materialism**, he argued that the universe is governed by one creative force, identified with fire, and that all physical processes unfold according to strictly determined yet rational principles. The souls of humans are also composed of fire, and just as the cosmic fire controls and permeates all things, so too the souls of humans infuse and rule over the body.

Ethics

The practical implications are that virtue consists in submitting oneself to the governance of reason and so to conformity with the natural order. Control over the passions involves an indifference to pleasure and pain, which is to be achieved through meditation and the acceptance that what will be will be. Nothing is to be gained

Legacy, truth, consequence

- Stoicism became the dominant philosophy of **Hellenic** and Roman times and had an important influence on the development of early Christianity and the view that the universe is divinely ordered.
- The term "stoical" has survived into modern times with the meaning of being impassive in the face of hardship or misfortune and resigning oneself to fate.

Key dates

335 BCE   Born in Citium, Cyprus. Spends his early life based in Citium as a successful merchant.

c.312 BCE   Shipwrecked and makes his way to Athens, where he discovers philosophy and becomes a disciple of Crates the Cynic. Late in life he begins lecturing and founds the stoic school.

263 BCE   Dies in Athens.

Steel your sensibilities, so that life shall hurt you as little as possible.

Attributed to Zeno

by railing against personal misfortune, and so peace of mind becomes possible for those with the wisdom to embrace the divine providence.

Political philosophy

His *Republic* described an ideal state run on rational principles that emphasized the importance of the rule of law. Because its citizens were perfectly rational there would be no need of private property, money, law courts, marriage, or religious temples. He preached equality between the sexes and argued against sexual taboos such as against masturbation, prostitution, and homosexuality.

Li Si

As an important exponent of the short-lived Chinese philosophy of legalism, Li Si had a major influence on the country's future development. He was prime minister to the tyrannical king of the state of Qin – later emperor of all China – and his totalitarian theories, which were imposed on all of China, had subtly long-lasting results.

Born in the turbulent **Warring States period**, Li Si (Li Ssu or Li Szu) studied under the well-known teacher Xunzi (Hsun Tzu) who, although a **Confucian**, believed that human nature is essentially evil, not moral. With his fellow student Hanfeizi (Han Fei Tzu), Li was drawn to the emerging ideas of **legalism**, which proposed strict laws to produce an ordered state.

Working for the king of Qin, Li was committed to creating a strong central government, although the king and his brutal policies were widely hated.

> *Today, however, the whole empire is at peace, all laws and order come from one single source, the common people support themselves ... while students study the laws and prohibitions.*
>
> Li Si, quoted in Sima Qian, *The Records of the Grand Historian* (91 BCE)

Essential philosophy

Human nature
Like most Chinese philosophers, Li and Hanfeizi applied their theories to the problem of society. They concluded that since people are basically selfish, they have to be strictly controlled in order for the state to function and grow in power.

The State
Instead of Confucian or **Daoist** views that an ordered society should be based on morality, legalists held that good government is achieved simply by laying down strict laws and demanding obedience to the law. Any action that strengthens the state is moral in itself.

The ruler
The ruler has absolute authority to enforce the law, yet the law applies to all.

Education
Ordinary people have to be trained to obey the ruler, and need no other education than the legal code.

Punishment
If minor crimes are eradicated, there will be no major crimes. This stance justifies harsh punishments and brutal executions.

Legacy, truth, consequence

- Li Si encouraged the First Emperor to treat people as nothing but tools of the state, conscripting millions for war or for projects such as the first Great Wall and the emperor's massive tomb containing the "terracotta army".
- He was responsible for the centralization of China.
- His policies resulted in the destruction of many sources of ancient knowledge.
- He influenced the Confucians who later introduced strict hierarchies into society.

Key dates

c.280 BCE — Born in the state of Zhou in China's Yangtze River valley.

247 BCE — Becomes a government official in the powerful state of Qin. His authoritarian philosophy appeals to the aggressive, despotic king, Ying Zheng.

233 BCE — Now minister of justice, Li engineers the death of colleague Hanfeizi.

221 BCE — King Ying Zheng completes the conquest of China, becoming "First Emperor". He follows Li's advice to end the feudal system, and instead directly rules all China.

219–213 BCE — Promoted to prime minister.

213 BCE — Following an argument with a Confucian, Li persuades the First Emperor to burn historical and philosophical texts, and kill traditionalist scholars by burying them alive.

208 BCE — Accused of treason, Li is executed by being cut in half at the waist.

Traditional Indian philosophy

Shankara

Indian philosophy has always been multi-faceted, tangled, and changing. From the Vedas originated Hinduism, as well as Buddhism and Jainism – two religious philosophies that borrowed freely from and gave back to Hinduism and each other. Then, in what is called the Classical Hindu Period from about 300 BCE to 1200 CE, the six classical systems of Indian philosophy flowered in Hindu thought.

We know very little about the lives of most of the "classic" Indian philosophers, but they might have continued the ancient tradition of propounding their views to a circle of listeners, who would gather around them somewhere in the open air.

Gautama (no relation to the Buddha) chose to write his *Nyaya Sutras* in a series of very brief **aphorisms**. He may have been a contemporary of the **Buddhist** thinker **Nagarjuna**.

Shankara, the **Vedanta** philosopher, was only 32 when he died but he was accepted as a great teacher while still young. He determined to become a monk during a crocodile attack, by renouncing the world so he would be pure at the time of death. Upon this, so says the tradition, the crocodile let him go, and he became a wandering ascetic, teaching, debating, and founding four monasteries. He was only 16 when, having won a debate against a famous philosopher, the philosopher's wife challenged him to demonstrate that if he had mastered everything that was important, he was also a master of sexual skills. He demanded a month's time-out, went into a trance and, leaving his body behind, entered the body of a well-known lover, from whom he learnt everything there was to know about the "science of sex".

Essential philosophy

By about 1200 BCE the **Vedic** religion, the forerunner of **Hinduism**, was established in India. Using the revealed Vedas (the oldest Hindu sacred texts), which literally means "knowledge", the religion showed how to invoke the Vedic gods, who were seen as arising from the basic essence of the universe. Centuries later commentaries on the Vedas were written (the *Upanishads*), questioning some Vedic rituals and sacrifices, and introducing new concepts such as meditation as a means of self-knowledge and a step towards directly approaching the universal essence or Brahman.

Most philosophers accepted that the essence of the individual self, or Atman, was a reflection of the Brahman, and that by understanding the true nature of self or consciousness humans could achieve a state of pure bliss, or enlightenment. This would therefore liberate them from re-birth and the pains of the physical world.

The **sceptical** trend in philosophy, about 600 BCE, contributed to the development of **Jainism** and Buddhism. Consolidated by the ascetic Vardhamana Mahavira, "The Great Hero" (599–527 BCE), Jainism teaches right faith, right knowledge, and right conduct as a way to understand the universe. A young prince, Gautama Siddhartha, born about 566 BCE, sought a middle way between asceticism and **hedonism**, and through meditation reached Buddhahood, or enlightenment, in turn teaching others his way of escaping the bonds of existence.

Buddhism and Jainism are considered to be heterodox schools or *darshanas* (meaning that they incorporate unorthodox beliefs), whereas the six classic *darshanas* (ways of seeing the divine) of Indian philosophy are all orthodox, in that they all accept the authority of the Vedas, and just vary in their interpretations. The classic *darshanas* are as follows:

Samkhya
Meaning "counting" or "enumeration", Samkhya or Sankhya is probably the oldest school. It offers an explanation of human nature by proposing a **dualism** between spirit or individual consciousness (*purusha*) and primordial matter (*prakriti*). From the interactions between spirit and matter, the world is made manifest in an enumerated order such as intellect, ego, mind, senses, powers of action, material elements. Matter consists of three qualities or *gunas* – activity, pureness or steadiness, and dullness – a doctrine that was later accepted by other philosophical traditions. The Samkhya way to enlightenment or liberation is through knowledge of the essential dualism of the universe.

Yoga
Literally meaning "union" or "yoking", Yoga is also considered the "discipline school" in the sense of the discipline of achieving liberation. There is little intellectual discussion in Yoga, because its goal is union with pure consciousness, a reflection of the universal spirit, and neither pure consciousness or spirit can be approached through mere thoughts. Instead, practical disciplines show the way to separate matter and spirit. Although ancient in origin, the sage Patanjali drew the philosophy together into an eight-limbed system, including principles such as restraint and concentration, as well as posture and breath control. Yogic disciplines also include

- The six classic schools of Indian philosophy between them forged the philosophy behind modern Hinduism, a religion and a way of life.
- Some of their practices, particularly spiritual meditation and physical yoga, have become popular around the world.
- On the whole the schools of philosophy were for philosophers. Most ordinary people were more involved in devotional religious activity.

A standing Shiva sculpture, date unknown. In some Hindu traditions, Shankara is regarded as an incarnation of Shiva.

Key dates

200–100 BCE	Gautama writes the *Nyaya Sutras*, founding the Nyaya school.
200–100 BCE	Patanjali writes the *Yoga Sutras*.
c.788–820 CE	Life of the Vedanta philosopher Shankara.

When true knowledge is attained, wrong notions disappear; on the disappearance of wrong notions the six defects disappear; the disappearance of defects is followed by the disappearance of activity [leading to cessation of pain], followed by final release, which is the highest good.

Gautama, *Nyaya Sutras* (200–100 BCE)

chanting, sexual practices, and even the use of some drugs. Overall, Yoga means much more than the physical exercises of hatha yoga, the form that is most commonly seen in the West. Patanjali's treatise on Yoga, the *Yoga Sutras*, dates from 200–100 BCE.

Nyaya

Based on the *Nyaya Sutras* of Aksapada Gautama, probably written in the second century BCE, this is the school of logic, literally meaning "analysis", which used intellectual reason to uncover the true nature of reality and thereby reach enlightenment. Gautama tested how knowledge can be acquired, and how its validity can be identified, producing a system of logic and methodology that was adopted by most of the other schools.

Nyaya logic had five parts: hypothesis, reason, example, application, conclusion. The methods of gaining knowledge were: **perception** or intuition, **inference** (including logic), comparison, and testimony from a trustworthy source.

Vaisheshika

This was an "**atomist**" school, and has been called the school of pluralistic **metaphysics**. Meaning "particular", it proposes that everything in the physical world can be reduced to separate atoms – mind, space, self, as well as the four elements of water, earth, fire, and air. The spiritual essence of the universe is a force, giving consciousness or soul to these atoms.

Vaisheshika was very close to Nyaya, and eventually the two systems merged.

Mimamsa

Meaning "interpretation", the Mimamsa or Purva Mimamsa school believed simply that the Vedas supplied the only true source of knowledge, and that proper performance of Vedic rituals – sacrifices, chants, priestly prayers – was the way to liberation. Mimamsa philosophers originally felt that the other schools might have useful logical ideas, but all focused too much on individual desire for freedom, whereas the correct approach was to put aside personal desires and concentrate solely on the Vedas. This school actually had a major influence because it laid down widely accepted rules for interpreting the Vedas.

Vedanta

Literally meaning "end of the Vedas", Vedanta focused on interpreting the spiritual and philosophical ideas of the later or second part of the Vedas, sometimes called the knowledge part, especially the *Upanishads* but also the epic *Bhagavad Gita*. It had little time for rituals and prayers, instead stressing **mystical** methods of understanding such as meditation and self-discipline. Most Vedanta philosophers asserted nonduality, that everything in the universe is one, and that belief in the existence of individual things is due to ignorance or illusion. If this illusion is removed, one sees the truth, that individual consciousness is the same as the universal spirit.

Different sub-schools arose, but Advaita Vedanta, consolidated by Shankara (c.788–820 CE), became the central theme in Hindu thought. Advaita Vedanta is firmly nondualistic.

Cicero

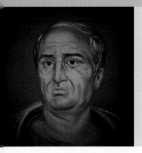

Roman statesman, orator, and writer of a great many philosophical works, Cicero is an important source for our knowledge of the Greek philosophical traditions of antiquity. Adopting stoic ideas in his political philosophy, he argued for universal rights and equality of all based on a common human nature.

Cicero studied philosophy as a young man and pursued a career in law. He was a brilliant orator and rose quickly to become an influential political figure, winning the position of consul, the highest office in the Roman government, at the age of 43. In 60 BCE Julius Caesar, Pompey, and Crassus – known as the triumvirate – took power, but as an influential member of the Senate and supporter of the Republic, Cicero refused to join them. In so doing he made enemies, which eventually led to a brief exile in 58 BCE, giving him the opportunity to write philosophy. After a year and a half he was allowed to return, and between 55 BCE and 51 BCE he wrote discussions of the Roman constitution, *On the Republic* and *On the Laws*. In 49 BCE civil war broke out between Caesar and Pompey, and Caesar, the victor, had his reign cut short when he was assassinated in 44 BCE. Cicero gave a series of speeches to the Senate in support of Octavian, Caesar's heir and adopted son, in the power struggle with Mark Antony. When Antony and Octavian joined forces, Antony insisted Cicero be put to death and Cicero was killed as he fled Rome. His head and hands were nailed to the speaker's podium at the Senate to discourage anyone else from opposing the new regime.

> *To be ignorant of what occurred before you were born is to remain always a child.*
>
> De Oratore
> (On the Orator, 55 BCE)

Essential philosophy

Cicero's greatest philosophical influence was Academic **Scepticism**, the philosophy of the heirs to **Plato**'s Academy in Athens. The Academic Sceptics would demonstrate how either side of a dispute could be equally well defended, either in order to undermine faith in any positive belief or as an exercise to determine where the stronger arguments lay. Many of Cicero's philosophical works are in dialogue form, allowing him the flexibility to explore arguments without the need to reach a definitive conclusion. Against the **Epicureans** he argued that we are social animals and, as such, duty bound to engage in political life. For Cicero, the techniques of the Academy were an essential weapon in pursuit of his political ambitions. Concerned to unite philosophical inquiry with the art of **rhetoric**, he hoped to persuade the Roman political elite to accept

Legacy, truth, consequence

■ Cicero is important for disseminating Greek ideas within the Roman world. His translations of Greek philosophy created much of the Latin philosophical terminology still in use today.

■ He had a significant influence on the Renaissance and Enlightenment and in particular on **David Hume**, who argued against Cicero's statement of the **Argument from Design** in the *Dialogues Concerning Natural Religion* (1750–76, published posthumously in 1779).

Key dates

106 BCE	Born in Arpinum (present-day Arpino), a town south of Rome, Italy. A talented student and lover of Greek culture and philosophy, he studies law in Rome.
87 BCE	Philo of Larrissa, head of the Academy in Athens, visits Rome and the young Cicero attends his public lectures, discovering the philosophy of Plato and Academic Scepticism.
79 BCE	Marries Terentia by whom he has a son, Marcus, and daughter, Tullia. In this same year he visits Athens and the Academy.
58 BCE	Exiled to Greece; returns to Rome the following year and rises quickly to the principal offices of state, namely, quaestor (75 BCE), curule aedile (69 BCE), praetor (66 BCE), finally consul (63 BCE).
45 BCE	Divorces Terentia, the same year that their daughter, Tullia, dies after giving birth. Cicero is plunged into a deep depression.
43 BCE	Decapitated trying to flee Rome.

universal reason as the basis for proper governance. He argued that the divinely ordained natural law determines what the laws of particular societies should be, and since we all share in human reason we have the means to discover the universal principles of justice upon which all states should be founded. So any tyrannical laws not grounded in natural justice are not genuine laws at all.

Philo of Alexandria

Philo was a Jewish philosopher from Alexandria in Egypt. His writing brought a deep knowledge of Greek philosophy, especially Plato, to bear on Judaism, often starting from an allegorical interpretation of the scriptures. He was one of the most prominent representatives of Hellenistic thought to influence the early Christian thinkers.

Reliable facts on Philo's life are scarce. The one event which we can date with certainty is his participation in an embassy to the Roman Emperor Gaius Caligula in 40 CE, when he was about 60 years old. There had been civil strife between the Greeks and Jews in Alexandria. Fighting had escalated and leaders were despatched to talk to the emperor. That Philo was chosen shows that this man, who had spent most of his life writing on philosophy, was a respected member of the Jewish community. The embassy to the emperor failed, and Philo later wrote of how the Jewish population continued to be abused under the rule of the Roman governor Flaccus.

> [God] is the one ... to whom alone it is lawful to govern and regulate everything.
>
> On the Eternity of the World
> (first century CE)

Essential philosophy

Philo's philosophical writing focused on a detailed, allegorical interpretation of Jewish scripture. But many of the strongest influences on his thought were Greek thinkers, especially **Socrates** (via **Plato**), **Pythagoras**, and the **stoics**. Philo identifies the biblical God with the "Form of the Good" in Plato, as the ultimate source of all being and knowledge. We cannot directly know this **Idea**, or Form, so we use reason to examine our conceptions and to come to understand our own souls.

Allegorical thinking

Philo tended to reject ideas that couldn't be adapted to his religious ends, and in the allegorical approach he had a tool that allowed him some flexibility in his use of the ideas of earlier thinkers.

From Pythagoras and his followers he took the use of number-symbolism. For instance he treated one as the number of God, three as the number of the body, and ten as the number of perfection.

He distinguished between the literal and allegorical meaning of biblical texts, and in many cases he would ignore the literal meaning.

Finally, he had a set of rules to indicate to the reader the biblical passages which demanded an allegorical interpretation. Thus, passages that contain, for example, a repetition of a statement previously made or a play upon words must be analyzed to find a special allegorical sense.

Legacy, truth, consequence

- Philo had a strong influence on early Latin Christianity.
- Unlike the stoics, Philo believed that man cannot attain virtue alone, only through contemplation of God. While **Saint Augustine** identified flaws in Philo's allegory, other Christian thinkers adopted his method.
- In his book *De Opificio Mundi*, Philo described five doctrines that one must learn as part of the religious life. These were: that God exists, that he is One, that he formed the cosmos, that this cosmos is unique, and that God exercises providence on the cosmos. He also described God as an exalted being, known only to himself. It was this version of **Platonism** that would be so influential on early Christian thinkers.

Key dates

c.20 BCE	Born in Alexandria, Egypt. His key works (dates unknown) are: *On the Creation* (*De Opificio Mundi*), *On the Life of Moses* (*De Vita Mosis*), *The Special Laws* (*De Specialibus Legibus*), *On the Virtues* (*De Virtutibus*), *On the Eternity of the World* (*De Aeternitate Mundi*).
40 CE	He is part of the embassy to Gaius Caligula.
c.50 CE	Dies in Alexandria.

Man and God

Philo saw God as the architect of the world, moulding matter that he discovered into our universe. Because matter was essentially evil in nature for Philo, God's interaction with the world is an indirect affair, where he creates our world according to an ideal pattern, using the *Logos* ("the word of God") as an intermediary. Man, being made of matter, is essentially imperfect. As physical beings we can never fully overcome this imperfection, but we can strive towards knowledge of the Good. When sensual and worldly desires take over, we sink into ignorance and lose the ability to seek for truth. In this condition, man seeks to usurp God, making himself a ruler (rather than a leader of men) in order to achieve his desires.

Nagarjuna

The founder of the Madhyamika or Middle Path tradition of Buddhism, Nagarjuna was the most significant Buddhist thinker after the Buddha himself, and is often referred to as "the second Buddha". He introduced the concept of "emptiness", which influenced the later development of many other Asian philosophies as well as Buddhism.

The historical facts of Nagarjuna's life, like for so many early Asian philosophers, are clouded by legend. It is thought that he was born in the Andhra Pradesh region of southern India, probably into an upper-caste **Brahmin** Hindu family, and, according to one story, he converted to **Buddhism** after a youthful misadventure. He and some friends sneaked into the local king's harem to seduce the women. They were discovered, and Nagarjuna was the only one to escape and survive. This experience showed him the pointlessness of physical desires, after which he renounced the world and found a path to enlightenment in Buddhism.

It is thought that he became a monk/scholar at a famous Buddhist monastery in northeastern India, the University of Nalanada. His story then descends again into mythology. He won the name Nagarjuna, partly meaning "noble serpent", because he was invited to visit the ocean-bed home of the wise, magical serpents, the Nagas, and was given Buddha's wisdom writings, the *Prajnaparamita (Perfection of Wisdom) Sutras*, which he brought back with him to share with humanity.

We can only roughly date Nagarjuna's adulthood because of letters that he wrote to a king in the region he was born, thought by many scholars to have been Gautamiputra Satakarni, who is known to have reigned about 166–196 CE. A rather war-like king, he ignored Nagarjuna's advice to live a peaceful Buddhist life. The topics that Nagarjuna discussed in his writings – the self and suffering, the nature of **causality** and **conditionality**, individuality, **metaphysics**, **ethics** – also indicate that he lived in the second century, during the period that Indian philosophers from the traditional Brahminical path and from the newer Buddhist schools began to engage in intense intellectual discussion on these topics.

Nagarjuna's greatest work is *Mulamadhyamaka-Karika (Fundamental Verses on the Middle Way)*, but he wrote many other important texts, none of which can be dated accurately. He claimed that his theories were not radical, but were firmly rooted in the original teachings of the Buddha, who, having become enlightened himself, showed the way for everyone to escape the suffering of existence by reaching enlightenment. Also, despite his own incisive logic and methodology, Nagarjuna argued that intellectualizing was not the most important thing in life – only the *practice* of Buddhism reveals the ultimate truth.

Essential philosophy

The Middle Path

Nagarjuna applied Buddha's advice to take the "middle way" to the then current philosophical debates on **dualities** such as subject versus object, or observer versus the observed world. He drove a path right through the very impulse to conceptualize and intellectualize, claiming that these impulses are themselves empty and lead to the illusions of dualities. His Middle Path is a way of avoiding extremist positions by going above and beyond all positions, and through it he **deconstructed** all the philosophical assumptions of the time, such as the existence of stable substances, direct and linear causality, fixed identity, and ethics.

Emptiness

Nagarjuna's concept of emptiness, called the Doctrine of Sunyata (literally "zero"), is a doctrine of relativity. He argued that nothing exists on its own or has any underlying essence (termed "self-existence"), but exists only in relation to something else, so everything is empty of independent self-existence. Nothing has a fixed essence, so the physical and **empirical** forms of things are built not upon an **absolute** being, but upon the fact that their emptiness allows them to relate to other phenomena, giving rise to constant change in the universe. When one realizes that the universe is essentially empty, Nagarjuna said, one realizes that all things are connected. So, it is not a **nihilist** philosophy, but instead is ultimately liberating.

Doctrine of dependent arising

Nagarjuna's theory that everything exists only because its emptiness means it depends on its relationships with other things for expression is called the doctrine of dependent arising. He argued that it is an illusion that anything is separate from other things or conditions. An example is a cup of coffee. The coffee plant is dependent upon earth to set root in, on sunshine and rain to grow, on people to pick and process it, and on a cup to fill. It is dependent on many other dependent arisings, and it exists because it has dependently arisen. This concept can be applied to the self: since it is empty, it is subject to change depending upon other arisings which might affect it.

Legacy, truth, consequence

■ Nagarjuna's *Mulamadhyamaka-Karika* became one of the key texts of the emerging Mahayana (Great Raft) Buddhist tradition and contributed to the split between this and the more conservative Theravada or Little Raft school. Along with Vajrayana, these are the three main Buddhist traditions today.

■ Most Buddhists agree that Nagarjuna's teachings expanded upon Buddha's original teachings to such an extent that he renewed the philosophy and practice of Buddhism. His thought is often compared to the turning of a wheel: while Buddha provided the first turn of the wheel, Nagarjuna contributed the second.

■ Some traditions consider that he was an actual manifestation of the Buddha. Even those Buddhists who follow a different path agree that he was the greatest Buddhist intellectual.

■ The concept of emptiness became a central concept for many schools and Buddhist sects. His theories also had a major influence on other Asian philosophies, particularly Hinduism and **Daoism**, and traditional Indian philosophical models of existence, ethics, **epistemology**, salvation, causation, and substantiality were all affected.

■ Nagarjuna's influence extended to schools of thought with which he once fiercely disputed. Because the concept of emptiness provided such a revolution in thought, it was later misappropriated by some traditions in ways which Nagarjuna might not necessarily have approved, e.g. schools which use doctrines of metaphysics and fixed knowledge as their philosophical bases.

> *Things derive their being and nature by mutual dependence and are nothing in themselves.*
>
> Mulamadhyamaka-Karika
> (second century)

Key dates

c.150	Born in southern India.
c.150–200	Period during which it is thought he develops his philosophy.
166–96	Writes letters of advice to a king in the region of modern Andhra Pradesh.
c.250	Dies near modern Nagarjunakonda, Andhra Pradesh (he is held in legend to have had an exceptionally long life).

Chinese Buddha of the Mahayana (Great Raft) tradition, c.650.

Two truths

Nagarjuna used and developed the two-truths doctrine, which argues that there are two different levels of truth, one which is only conventionally or empirically true, and another which is ultimately true. An example would be one's reflection in a mirror: the reflection is handy for putting on make-up and combing hair, but it has no independent self-existence. It is experienced by the senses, but does not really exist. Nagarjuna said that the whole world is like the reflection, and to realize this is to realize the ultimate truth.

Logic

Western philosophy often uses **Aristotle**'s two-value **logic** system where **propositions** are either true or false, discussing questions in terms of dualities, for example "Is suffering caused by the self or not?" As a tool, Nagarjuna used a concept first discussed by the Buddha: a four-value logic system suggesting that propositions can be true, false, true and false, or neither true nor false. Instead of a dilemma, this leads to a tetralemma, such as his example:

No suffering is self-caused.
Nothing causes itself.
If another is not self-made,
How could suffering be caused by another?

If suffering were caused by each,
Suffering could be caused by both.
Not caused by self or by other,
How could suffering be uncaused?

(*Mulamadhyamaka-Karika*, second century)

Achieving nirvana

Nagarjuna took the revolutionary step of extending emptiness to the basic Buddhist distinction between the cycle of rebirth into the universe of suffering (*samsara*) and the peace of enlightenment (*nirvana*). He declared that since both concepts were empty, there was no distinction between them. The changes which eventually lead to enlightenment only come about because of interdependent causality.

Plotinus

The last of the ancient philosophers writing in Greek, Plotinus is the originator of "Neo-Platonism", the name given to the mystical or religious brand of Platonism that was dominant between the year 250 and the closure of Plato's Academy in 529 and which had a great influence on early Christian theology.

It is said that Plotinus' **Platonic** distrust of the physical realm extended to a refusal ever to discuss the contingencies of his physical existence, such as the particulars of his biographical history. Yet, thanks to the biography written by his disciple, Porphyry (c.232–305 CE), as a preface to Plotinus' *Enneads*, we do know the principal events of his life. Plotinus lived during a difficult period for the Roman Empire. In the course of his lifetime war and disease reduced its population by a third and Plotinus' philosophy can be seen as an attempt to turn away from the vicissitudes and misfortunes of mundane affairs. For eleven years he studied the philosophy of the Greeks while living in Alexandria, which at that time was the center of the intellectual world. It was **Plato's** philosophy that would become the guiding influence of his subsequent development. His teacher Ammonius Saccus (c.185–250 CE) is sometimes credited with having established the basic tenets of the "**Neo-Platonism**" later developed by Plotinus.

When the Roman Emperor Gordian III set out against the Persians, Plotinus elected to accompany his army, hoping to learn more of the philosophies of the East. However, Gordian was assassinated in 244 in Mesopotamia and Plotinus made his way to Rome. At one time he had plans to found a city near Rome based upon Plato's *Republic*, to be called Platonopolis. However, the Emperor Gallienus withdrew his support and the project foundered.

His student Porphyry encouraged him to commit his ideas to writing and is responsible for collecting and systematizing them after Plotinus' death into the *Enneads* (from the Greek *ennea*, nine), so called because the six books are all divided into nine sections. The *First Ennead* concerns ethics; the *Second* and *Third* are on **natural philosophy** and **cosmology**; the *Fourth* is on the "Soul"; the *Fifth* contains his **theory of knowledge**; and finally the *Sixth* turns attention to the ultimate nature of reality and to discussion of the first principle of his system, "The One".

Essential philosophy

By his own account Plotinus was prone to intense religious experiences, which had a profound influence on his philosophical outlook. He turned away from things secular, and it was his distaste for the mundane and hope for redemption through the soul's reunion with God that fuelled his philosophical endeavors.

Plotinus' philosophy is essentially an attempt to give systematic form to Plato's **metaphysics**, although the influences of **Pythagorean mysticism** and that of **Parmenides** are also evident.

"The One"
Plato's "**Idea** of the Good" plays the central role: what Plotinus also terms "The One" or "God". Like Parmenides' "One", "He" as Plotinus has it, is eternal and unchanging. "He" is the ultimate reality and object of worship, and, while the source of knowledge of all other things, is Himself unknowable and ineffable. "The One" is conceived as perfectly free and fully good. Not being subject to differentiation or change, "He" transcends the material realm and so is immaterial; and although self-sustaining and self-causing, "He" is also that from which all other being derives. And herein lies a difficulty for Plotinus' system. For although perfectly self-contained, "The One" has also to be the source of all other being. To address the difficulty Plontinus is clear that "The One" does not make the world in an act of creation, since this would detract from His perfection. Rather the being of the universe is projected by "The One" through a process of "emanation", just as, using a Platonic metaphor, the light from the sun illuminates and sustains living things. "The One" becomes the highest of three levels of reality or *hypostases*: producing and sustaining; Mind or Intellect (*nous*); and lastly Soul.

Mind or Intellect
The realm of "Intellect" is that of Plato's "Ideas" contained in the mind of "The One" and is the proper object of philosophical speculation. So it is that through philosophy we can approach closer to "The One". Human souls are caught within the material realm, and our embodied condition is characterized by striving and desire for sexual gratification, food, and so forth. But the Soul is immortal and when released from the body is usually reincarnated. The condition into which one is reborn in the next life is determined by one's moral character in this.

Legacy, truth, consequence

- Plotinus' work heralded three centuries of renewed interest in Plato's philosophy and by the middle of the fifth century CE there were two main Neo-Platonic schools, one based in Alexandria and the other being the Academy in Athens. Among the best-known Neo-Platonists after Porphyry are Proclus (c.410–85) in Athens, and Hypatia (c.370–415) in Alexandria.

- Although both Plotinus and Porphyry rejected the personal God of Christianity, Neo-Platonism had a profound influence on early Christian theology and became the philosophical underpinning of the faith, largely through the work of the school in Alexandria, which converted to Christianity.

- Neo-Platonism remained the dominant philosophy in the West until the Middle Ages and also had an important influence on Renaissance thinkers.

Many times it has happened: Lifted out of the body into myself; becoming external to all other things and self-encentered; beholding a marvellous beauty; then, more than ever, assured of community with the loftiest order; enacting the noblest life, acquiring identity with the divine.

Enneads (253–70)

The Colosseum, symbol of Imperial Rome. Plotinus lived during a difficult period for the Roman Empire.

Matter and Soul

Matter is the lowest level of the system, a phantasmagorical image of reality, and, insofar as it is removed from "The One", the origin of evil. Yet the mind is able to glimpse the Platonic "Ideas" through the physical and in so doing thought can ascend through the levels of reality to mystical speculation of "The One". The individual's "Soul" is divided between a higher part, which contemplates the eternal, and a lower, which is the part constituting the individual personality. Through philosophy the Soul turns attention away from the physical realm and from the particulars of the individual person in order to achieve mystical union with "The One" and ultimately to escape from the cycle of rebirth. Plotinus himself claims to have experienced the Soul's momentary escape from the body and it is such **mystical** experiences as much as philosophical argumentation that give support to his system.

Key dates

205	Born in Lycopolis, an ancient town located in the eastern Nile delta, Egypt.
From 232	Studies under Ammonius Saccus in Alexandria.
243	Accompanies the Roman Emperor Gordian's military expedition to the East.
244	After Gordian's assassination flees to Antioch and on to Rome.
245–68	Founds his school in Rome where he teaches.
253–70	Writes the *Enneads*.
270	Dies in Campagnia, southern Italy.

Saint Augustine of Hippo

One of the four original Doctors of the Western Church (along with Ambrose, Jerome, and Pope Gregory I), and the first great Christian philosopher, Saint Augustine saw reason as subordinate to the revealed truth as found in the Scriptures. On this view, the worth of philosophical inquiry consists in helping us comprehend what we already accept on faith, a position summed up in the phrase *"I believe so that I may understand"*.

Born in the Roman city of Tagaste in North Africa, Augustine's father was a pagan; but his mother, Monica, a devout Christian, brought the young Augustine up in the faith. However, Augustine's reading of **Cicero**'s dialogue *Hortensius* (now lost) kindled in him an interest in philosophy and **scepticism**, and he decided to devote his life to the search for truth. He soon came to find the Scriptures intellectually unsatisfying and turned instead to Manichaeism, a popular religious movement of the day. Its founder Mani, who had been crucified in Persia in 277 CE, had taught that there are two Gods, one the source of good, the other of evil. Aged 17, Augustine moved to Carthage to study (and later teach) **rhetoric** where, by his own account, he pursued a life of **hedonistic** excess, enslaved by the "wretched sin" of lust. Although during this period he set up home with a woman and had a son, they were never married. One explanation is that she may have been an ex-slave and so forbidden under Roman law from marrying a citizen.

By now living and teaching in Rome, Augustine became increasingly interested in the sceptical philosophy of the later Academy (founded c.387 BCE by **Plato**) in Athens, and he abandoned Manichaeism. Then, aged just 30, he landed the prestigious professorship of rhetoric in Milan, where he came under the influence of the **Neo-Platonist** Christian and bishop of Milan, Ambrose (c.338–97 CE). Soon after Augustine's appointment, however, his life was to change direction dramatically. He reconverted to Christianity, left his post, and returned to Africa to join the priesthood and live a life of celibacy in the service of God. He eventually became bishop of Hippo Regius (now Annaba, Algeria), where he died during the siege of Hippo by the Vandals, the East Germanic tribe that would go on to sack Rome in 455.

By dictating to a team of secretaries, Augustine was able to produce some 230 works, many of which survive. Most concern theological disputes of the day, but the best known are firstly his *Confessions*, often considered the first autobiography, which describes his intellectual and spiritual journey to embrace the Christian faith. The other, *The City of God*, outlines the ideal spiritual community founded on love, which contrasts starkly with the decaying Roman Empire of his day.

Essential philosophy

The problem of evil

Augustine's mother had been a Christian, but he turned away from the faith of his childhood primarily because of its inability to explain the existence of evil in the world. If God is indeed all-loving and all-powerful, why would he allow suffering to occur within his creation? Manichaeism, with its commitment to two original forces one good the other evil, engaged in a vast cosmic battle, appeared to be more in keeping with the facts than Christianity. However, under the influence of Neo-Platonism, Augustine began to develop a distinctive solution to the difficulty; one which would allow him to reconvert. Evil, he argued, is not a substantive thing in its own right, but rather the absence of good; just as darkness is nothing more than the absence of light. Thus the act of creation produces only what is wholly good, and so is consistent with the omni-benevolence of the creator. Actions and persons are only evil to the extent that they fall short of and become distanced from God. And it is the possession of the divine gift of **free will** that allows finite beings, such as ourselves, to commit evil deeds. Thus it is us, rather than God, who are responsible for introducing evil into creation.

In this account the original sin of Adam and Eve is of particular significance, not just as the prime example of the abuse of our freedom, but also as the root cause of natural evils such as earthquakes, floods, and disease. The sin of Adam is inherited by the whole human race, and as such it is just for God to punish us by the natural evils we must endure.

Combating heresy

Augustine also devoted much of his intellectual energy to defending the Catholic orthodoxy against heresies of various kinds including, of course, Manichaeism. Another dispute of this kind stands out, namely his arguments against Pelagianism, the heresy that claims we can achieve communion with God by freely choosing the righteous path without the need for divine assistance.

Legacy, truth, consequence

■ Augustine represents the transition from pagan to Christian philosophy and his work is important for bringing together Neo-Platonism and Christianity. He is responsible for establishing the foundations for medieval Christian thought, which comes to fruition in the work of **Thomas Aquinas**.

■ He is also an important forefather of Calvinist teaching on grace with the claim that original sin means we cannot by our own free will be saved.

■ Augustine's defence against scepticism, in which he points out that if one doubts it is at least certain that one exists – "*If I am wrong, I exist*" (*City of God*, 11.26) – is often cited as an important antecedent to **René Descartes**' famous "*I think therefore I am*".

■ **Ludwig Wittgenstein** reintroduced Augustine's speculations on language and time to the mainstream of philosophy in his discussions of them in the *Philosophical Investigations* (published 1953).

Key dates

354	Born in Tagaste, North Africa.
371–3	Studies rhetoric in Carthage.
373–4	Teaches in Tagaste.
374	Returns to Carthage, where he sets up a school to teach rhetoric.
383	Moves to Rome and subsequently takes up a professorship in Milan.
386	Reconverts to Christianity and abandons his teaching post. Returns to Africa and becomes a priest (391), and later bishop of Hippo (in 396).
397–400	Writes the *Confessions*.
412–27	Writes the *City of God*.
430	Dies in the siege of Hippo (now Annaba, Algeria).

The Triumph of Saint Augustine, the defender of orthodoxy against heresy (taking here the form of a dragon) in a 1664 painting by Claudio Coello.

Augustine insists on the import of the original sin and fall from grace, arguing that to be redeemed we require God's help. He asserted that God's omniscience implies he must have foreknowledge of those who will be saved, meaning that the elect are predestined for salvation. Augustine's speculations on this issue and its implication for human free will have been of enduring interest.

Time

Augustine's reflections on the nature of time are also of interest. He argued that time is not infinite, but rather that God created it with the universe, so that it makes no sense to ask when the creation took place or what happened before. God stands outside of time and from his point of view it is an "eternal present". Thus our subjective **perception** of temporal succession must be a function of our limited perspective on things. Time, in other words, is a product of our perception, not an aspect of reality.

> *All things that exist, therefore, seeing that the Creator of them all is supremely good, are themselves good ... but their good may be diminished.*
>
> Enchiridion (c.420)

The soul

Augustine rejected the idea that the soul might be a material thing, arguing instead that humans are a composite of spirit and matter. At death the soul is separated from the body and must wait to be reunited with it at the general resurrection.

The Zen Masters

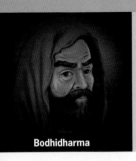

Bodhidharma

The school of meditative, contemplative Buddhism known as Zen arose in China, but three of the figures who were most instrumental in bringing about the Zen traditions we know today were Bodhidharma, originally from India, and the two Japanese philosophers Eisai and Dogen. Together they formulated a system that is continuing to thrive all over the world.

Early in the sixth century, the Buddhist monk Bodhidharma, known in Chinese as Damo (Tamo), traveled to China to spread Buddhist doctrines. There are many legends about him. Most accounts say he was from a southern Indian royal family, although some historians believe he was actually an Iranian, who journeyed along the Silk Road. Certainly he is usually shown in paintings as a barbaric-looking foreigner, sometimes with blue eyes. In China, he is supposed to have had an audience with the Liang emperor, during which he baffled the court with a conundrum, and then went on to join the Shaolin Temple in what is now Henan province.

Bodhidharma (c.440/60–c.528) fused several threads of **Buddhism** with the Chinese philosophy of **Daoism** (see pages 10–11) and developed a new way of realizing the Buddhist aim – escaping worldly suffering by reaching enlightenment. He argued that people do not need reason or logic, symbol or ritual, or philosophical argument, but can spontaneously become enlightened through meditation and direct experience.

The Japanese word "**Zen**" comes from the Chinese word "*Chan*", which in turn is a mispronunciation of the Indian word "*Dhyana*", meaning meditation. A simple, practical philosophy that can be followed by anyone, Bodhidharma's Chan Buddhism soon became popular in China, eventually splintering into different schools.

Emphasizing "a healthy mind in a healthy body", Bodhidharma is also traditionally thought to have invented the physical exercises that form the foundation of disciplined fighting skills such as gongfu (kung fu) and tai chi chuan. His Shaolin Temple became the home of Chinese martial arts.

Centuries later, Buddhism in Japan had become isolated and degenerate, until the young monk Eisai (1141–1215) decided to revive an old tradition and travel to China to receive new wisdoms. His first journey in 1168 was short, but he heard about the strange meditation practices, and returned in 1187 to study Chan at a monastery of the Linji (*Lin-chi* or *Rinzai* in Japanese) school, becoming the first Japanese to be recognized as a Zen teacher. Back in Japan he faced opposition from conservative Buddhist groups, but found that the military warlords were more receptive to his new teachings, and he set up the first Rinzai Zen temple in Japan at Kamakura.

One of Eisai's students was Dogen (1200–53), who came from an aristocratic family but who had learnt the Buddhist lesson of "impermanence" as a child when his parents died. A giant in Japanese philosophy, Dogen also went to China to learn Zen at first hand, studying the Caodong (Ts'ao-tung) school that became Soto in Japanese. During a meditation he reached enlightenment, exclaiming, "*There is no mind, there is no body!*"

Dogen founded his first Soto temple in Kyoto, and went on to teach and write extensively on spiritual and practical matters.

Essential philosophy

Meditation

Bodhidharma stressed that the Buddha gained enlightenment through his meditation, not by quoting scripture or discussing philosophy. He taught that others may also awaken their own "Buddha nature" very simply, without ritual or philosophy, just by meditating on the present moment, on breathing, or on emptiness. His original vision called for meditation or "mindfulness" to be carried out all the time, so that a practitioner might gain enlightenment even during everyday activities such as weeding or washing clothes, but over time the practice of meditating while sitting still became dominant. The Japanese term "*Zazen*", meaning "sitting in Zen", describes Zen meditation in which the practitioner sits silently, thinking about nothing. It was particularly emphasized by Dogen and his Soto school, and should be carried out in the approved posture of sitting cross-legged or in the lotus position with the hands loosely linked and the eyes always open.

Zen masters

Bodhidharma believed in personal experience, but he accepted that teachers would be needed to help guide students and directly communicate the ideas they had themselves been shown. Because of this, the lineage of a Zen master and school is important, and all modern sects trace their heritage through Chinese patriarchs to Bodhidharma and beyond him, to the Buddha himself.

Koans

Zen is known for jokes, illogical or playful stories and debates, and **paradoxical** riddles known as *koans*, the Japanese word for the

A special transmission outside the scriptures,
No dependence upon words and letters,
By pointing directly to the human mind,
It lets one see into one's own nature and attain Buddhahood.

Attributed to Bodhidharma (early sixth century)

Eisai

Legacy, truth, consequence

■ Chan become the largest Buddhist sect in China. Stressing a simple, spontaneous, natural way of life, it influenced Chinese art and calligraphy. Its founder, Bodhidharma, is traditionally held to have inspired the development of Chinese martial arts.

■ Bodhidharma's stress on developing the body as well as the spirit attracted the Japanese military samurai class (the aristocratic warrior class of pre-industrial Japan), who adapted Zen into their warrior philosophy of Bushido (the code of the Japanese samurai warriors).

■ Zen eventually permeated nearly every aspect of Japanese culture, from the tea ceremony to garden designs, and to the military nationalism of World War II – even though it was originally a pacifist philosophy.

The *enso* (circle), symbol of Zen Buddhism, one of the most common subjects of Japanese calligraphy.

Key dates

c.440/60	Bodhidharma born, probably in southern India.
c.517	Bodhidharma arrives in China.
c.528	Possible death of Bodhidharma.
1141	Eisai is born in modern Okayama, Japan.
1168	Eisai's first visit to China.
1187–91	Eisai's second visit to China, during which he studies Chan intensively.
1200	Dogen is born in Kyoto, Japan.
1215	Eisai dies.
1223–7	Dogen visits China to study.
1231	Dogen begins to compile his sermons into his masterpiece, *Shobogenzo (Treasury of the Eye of the True Doctrine).*
1253	Dogen falls ill and dies in Kyoto.

Chinese *gongan*, meaning "legal case". One well-known *koan* is "*What is the sound of one hand clapping?*" A puzzle like this does not have a straightforward correct answer, but aims to jolt the student out of conventional logical thinking and into spontaneous insight, which might lead to spiritual awakening. *Koans* are common in the Rinzai school introduced into Japan by Eisai.

Lack of scripture

Zen argues that the truth is not transmitted by reading scripture or by struggling with complicated philosophical concepts, but by enlightenment through Zen paradoxes. Chinese Buddhists wrote more books about this tradition than about any other Buddhist school. There is also a large body of literature from Japan, and Dogen himself was a keen wordsmith who wrote prolifically.

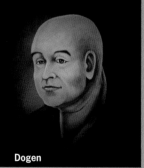

Dogen

Without looking forward to tomorrow every moment, you must think only of this day and hour ... You must concentrate on Zen practice ... thinking that there is only this day and this hour. After that it becomes truly easy.

Dogen, *Shobogenzo* (1231–53)

Kukai

A poet, artist, calligrapher, and scholar, as well as a Japanese Buddhist monk, Kukai was an intellectual giant who founded the Shingon or True Word school of Buddhism in Japan and who had a major influence on Japanese culture.

A member of a minor aristocratic family, the young Kukai studied **Confucianism**, then the official political doctrine, but he converted to **Buddhism** when he was taught an Indian mantra (a repetitive sacred chant).

By 804 he was part of an official governmental mission to China. Also in the party was the monk Saicho (767–822), who later founded the Tendai school of Buddhism in Japan.

Kukai learnt Sanskrit to read original Indian texts, and studied under the great master of esoteric Buddhism, Huiguo, who not only initiated Kukai, but also transmitted the line of teaching to him, making Kukai the next patriarch of the school. Kukai called his Japanese version "Shingon" (True Word), from a translation of the Sanskrit "mantra".

He found a sponsor in Emperor Saga, and Shingon began to permeate the Japanese court. At the same time, Kukai was writing, painting, producing beautiful calligraphy, and carrying out charitable or civil works, all of which gave him a powerful national reputation.

> ## Awakening in this very embodied existence!
>
> Attributed to Kukai

Essential philosophy

Esoteric Buddhism

Sometimes called Tantric Buddhism, this relies on mantras and pictorial mandalas, symbols, visualizations, and ceremonial rituals to allow people to have a bodily experience of the meaning of doctrine; Kukai himself carried out rituals for the health of the emperor, to protect the nation, and even for rain. His school held that the great mysteries in Buddhism – of the mind, the body, and speech – should not be written down, but must be transmitted orally directly from a teacher, and Kukai particularly disliked the dry, abstract writings of exoteric schools that made their teachings available to anybody.

Sound

Kukai taught that all sound and words can be sacred, but that mantras in particular can express the ultimate truth. He argued that the phonetic and syllabic Sanskrit writing was better at conveying the meaning of words than Chinese ideograms, and he worked for the adoption of a phonetic writing system.

Legacy, truth, consequence

- According to legend, Kukai is not dead, but only in a state of deep meditation, and one day he will arise again.
- In 1921 the emperor posthumously awarded Kukai the title Kobe Daishi, or Great Teacher Who Spread the Dharma, a name he is often known by.
- Mainly through his efforts, Buddhism replaced Confucianism as the state religion in Japan. His Shingon became the dominant form of Buddhism for centuries.
- Kukai paved the way for the Japanese phonetic writing, the *kana*.

Key dates

774	Born on Shikoku island, Japan.
804–6	Visits China. Studies esoteric Buddhism.
812	Begins to form Shingon, a new esoteric Buddhist order.
816	Founds the first Shingon monastery at Kongobuji on Mount Koya, near Kyoto.
817	Writes the major texts of Shingon.
823	Takes over the Toji temple in Kyoto.
830	Writes his great work, *Treatise on the Ten Stages of the Development of Mind*.
835	Dies on Mount Koya.

He added that the True Words transcend speech, and that Buddha's truth is embodied in all phenomena, so he encouraged all creative, artistic expression, incidentally contributing to the development of Japanese art.

Synthesis

Although he stressed the value of direct experience over abstract theory, Kukai wrote an important theoretical work, *Treatise on the Ten Stages of the Development of Mind*, describing and classifying all Buddhist philosophies and several other **ethical** systems. Naturally, he concluded that Shingon is the best approach to truth.

Al-Kindi (Alkindus)

A true polymath, al-Kindi was a musician and meteorologist, a chemist and cryptographer, a physician and psychologist, an astronomer and astrologer, as well as a philosopher. He was the first of the great Muslim philosophers to develop Aristotle's ideas, and he helped to introduce ancient Greek philosophy to Arab scholars, keeping the knowledge alive through centuries.

Known in the West as Alkindus, his Latinized name, Abu-Yusuf Ya'qoub ibn Ishaq ibn al-Sabbah ibn Omran ibn Ism'il al-Kindi lived during the Golden Age of Islam, the period of a few hundred years from the mid-eighth century when the Muslim world encouraged learning and scholarship. In particular, around the year 800 the Abbasid caliphs set up the library and intellectual center, the House of Wisdom, in Baghdad to preserve Islamic wisdom and to translate ancient Greek and Roman scientific and philosophical texts into Arabic.

Intellectually inclined, al-Kindi was born at the right time. The son of the governor of the city of Kufa, now in modern Iraq, he received a good early education, and showed so much promise that he was sent to Bagdad for further studies. There he soon gravitated towards the House of Wisdom. He led one of the groups of translators, and it was then that he was drawn towards the thinking of **Aristotle**.

He enjoyed intellectual freedom under the caliphs al-Ma'mun and al-Mu'tasim, but later caliphs persecuted anyone who strayed from a narrow orthodox line, especially philosophers like al-Kindi who, while still strongly religious, questioned some points of dogma. At one point al-Kindi's library was temporarily confiscated (although this may have been a case of professional rivals gaining the caliph's ear).

Interested in everything that came his way, al-Kindi wrote many papers on subjects as diverse as weather forecasting and the precursor to modern cryptology. He was also famous for beautiful calligraphy.

Essential philosophy

Al-Kindi adapted the ideas he found in Aristotle and the **Neo-Platonists** to create his own original arguments. His central theme was that philosophy and other "scientific" subjects were fully compatible with Islamic theology, and therefore topics such as the soul or the nature of God could be fruitfully addressed by secular philosophers as well as religious elders.

His most famous work, *On First Philosophy*, contained an appeal to readers to tolerate foreign or ancient wisdom, and introduced his basic ideas that the world is not eternal and that there is a unique "true One", the source of unity in the rest of existence. He saw that God was the cause of all being and therefore the cause of

Legacy, truth, consequence

■ Al-Kindi and his colleagues produced translations of Greek writings that became the authoritative texts in the Islamic world. From there they were later transmitted to Europe. He himself ensured that works by Aristotle and **Plotinus** survived.

■ He started the Arab tradition of synthesizing Islamic theology with philosophical ideas from external disciplines. He also introduced many of the standard Arabic philosophical constructs.

■ Al-Kindi's personal philosophy had only a minor impact on other Arab thinkers, and probably he had a greater influence among Jewish and Christian writers. But overall, one of his major achievements was to smooth the path for ancient works to survive in both Arab and Christian lands. Soon after his death he was called the "Philosopher of the Arabs".

> *... there is ... nothing more important than the truth, nor is the truth demeaned or diminished by the one who states or conveys it ...*
> On First Philosophy (ninth century)

Key dates

c.801	Born in Kufa (now in modern Iraq).
c.820	Studies in Baghdad, later becomes an important figure in the House of Wisdom.
833–42	Connected to the court of the caliph, al-Mu'tasim. Tutors the caliph's son, Ahmad.
c.873	Dies in Baghdad.

all truth – the subject of the first philosophy. Al-Kindi's "One" has no other attributes apart from its unity.

Al-Kindi wrote many other texts, including the first Arab treatise on the intellect – which he saw as beginning as just a potential, only becoming actual once it took hold of an intellectual form or idea.

Avicenna (Ibn Sina)

The Iranian/Persian polymath Avicenna was probably the most famous of all the great philosopher–scientists of the medieval Islamic world. His *Canon of Medicine* became the standard medical textbook for centuries, and his ideas influenced the future development of philosophy in both Christian Europe and the Islamic world.

Abu Ali al-Husayn ibn Abd Allah ibn Sina was known in Europe by his Latinized name, Avicenna. A natural scholar, he had memorized the Qur'an and other classic Islamic texts by the time he was ten.

He then began to study Islamic law, philosophy, and medicine all on his own. He was humble enough to admit that he struggled to understand **Aristotle's** *Metaphysics* (fourth century BCE) when he first read it at the age of 14.

In 999 Avicenna's peaceful development as a scholar was interrupted by unrest in the whole central Asian region. He spent the next 25 years as an unsettled wanderer.

Despite all, Avicenna formulated and set out his philosophy, and wrote his many texts on medicine and science. He finally settled down in Isfahan in about 1024 as the doctor and advisor to the local ruler, Ala al-Dawla, whom he served until his death.

> *Those who deny the first principle should be ... burned until they admit that it is not the same thing to be burned and not burned ...*
>
> Avicenna's eleventh-century comment on Aristotle's *Metaphysics*

Essential philosophy

Existence

Avicenna's intellectual proof for the existence of God drew from Aristotle and from the Arab philosopher Al-Farabi (c.872–950/1). Things exist, but we observe that some things come into existence and pass out of existence, therefore existence itself is not absolutely necessary. So, something else must cause things to come into being. However, Aristotle showed that it is not possible to have an infinite regress of causes, so the causal chain must end in a sole, necessary existent, which is God.

Avicenna made a distinction between essence and existence, arguing that the existence of something is not determined by what it is. This distinction applies to everything except God, who is both essence and existence in one.

Avicennian logic

Avicenna was the first to identify different methods within **inductive** logic such as the **method of agreement** and **concomitant variation**. To him logic was a crucial foundation for any science – "*And the way to these two is science. And no science which cannot be examined by the balance of logic is certain and exact.*"

Avicenna was particularly concerned with definitions, often relying on **hypothetical** (or **modal**) **syllogism** to establish them.

Emanation

Avicenna took the **Neo-Platonist** stance that the universe emanated from God as the sustaining cause. God is perfect and unchanging, so He could not have taken action to create the universe, for that would imply a change in His essence. This point of view directly clashed with theological **creationist beliefs**.

Legacy, truth, consequence

- Some of Avicenna's ideas were strongly opposed by orthodox theologians, and he was particularly targeted by the **mystic** philosopher **Al-Ghazali** (1058–1111), who felt that Avicenna was misguided in praising the philosophical method above traditional theology. Avicenna was also attacked by **Averroës** (Ibn Rushd), who disagreed with his interpretation of Aristotle.
- His theory of the soul and his **metaphysics** had a major influence on the **scholastics** such as **Thomas Aquinas**, while his **theory of knowledge** was studied by **Albert the Great** (Albertus Magnus).
- Avicenna had widespread influence through his major work, *The Canon of Medicine*, which was studied in the Middle East as well as in Christian Europe.

Key dates

c.980	Born near Bukhara, then in Iran (Persia), now in Uzbekistan.
c.1001	Writes his major medical work, *The Canon of Medicine*.
1027	Finishes writing his major book on philosophy, *The Cure*.
1037	Dies at Hamadan, northern Iran.

Solomon ibn Gabirol (Avicebrol)

The major religious poet of medieval Spanish Jewry, ibn Gabirol was also a philosopher who incorporated Neo-Platonism into his work to present a discussion of matter and form in existence, with matter emanating directly from God throughout creation. He had a major influence on the development of scholasticism in Europe.

Solomon ben Judah ibn Gabirol was also known in Christian Europe by his Latinized name, Avicebrol (or Avicebron). Living in Al-Andalus – Arab Spain – he was one of the first Jews to write frequently in Hebrew, which had up till then been used only for religious purposes in Judaism.

Ibn Gabirol's father died when he was a child, and his mother died when he was 23, after which he wrote pitifully: "*I am motherless and fatherless, young and lonely and oppressed …*" He was already famous by the time he was 16, when he wrote "*Though I am but sixteen, I have the wisdom of a man of eighty.*"

When he was 17 he found a patron at the court of Sargossa in the Jewish statesman Yekutiel ibn Hasan, who was later killed in a political plot. Ibn Gabirol wrote a 200-verse elegy for him, before beginning to wander round Spain.

Ibn Gabirol the poet, and Avicebrol, Avicebron or Avencebrol the scholastic philosopher, whose work survived only in Latin translations, were only matched as the same person in the mid-nineteenth century. Up until then, most philosophers had thought that Avicebron had been a Christian scholastic thinker.

Essential philosophy

Matter and form

Ibn Gabirol's major work, *Fons Vitae* (*Fountain of Life*), takes the form of a dialogue between philosopher and student, a common Arab format at the time. It is known in full only through its Latin translation, which is subtitled *De Materia et Forma* (*On Matter and Forms*).

His main contention is that all created beings are made up of two things, form and matter. This matter "emanates" directly from God, the prime matter that supports all substances. Therefore all beings or substances, whether grossly physical – humans, for example – or sublimely spiritual, such as the "intelligent" substances of angels and sphere-moving powers, contain the same matter.

In his system everything that exists fits into one of three categories: God, the first substance; the world, which is matter and form; or the will, an aspect of God's nature, which is intermediary. The divine will, or wisdom, is an expression of the creative aspect of divinity. The form that beings take proceeds from this divine will.

While *Fons Vitae* is thought to be mainly **Neo-Platonic** in outlook, it also includes elements of **Aristotelian logic** and **metaphysics**.

Legacy, truth, consequence

■ Ibn Gabirol's philosophy made little impact upon mainstream Jews. However the elements of his thinking influenced the development of the medieval Kabbalah, the **mystical** and occult strand of Judaism.

■ He did, however, influence Christian **scholastics**, particularly those of the Franciscan Order such as **John Duns Scotus**. He made enough of an impact on **Thomas Aquinas** for the Christian saint to feel it necessary to challenge ibn Gabirol's view that spiritual substances were material.

Sitting among everybody crooked and foolish his [the poet's] heart only was wise.

Song of Strife (eleventh century)

Key dates

c.1022	Born in Malaga (in Muslim Spain).
1045	Writes ethical treatise, *The Improvement of the Moral Qualities*.
c.1058	Dies in Valencia, Spain.
1150	His text *Fons Vitae* (*Fountain of Life*) is translated into Latin and spreads through Europe.

Ethics

His approach to **ethics** in his treatise *The Improvement of the Moral Qualities* was unique for the time since he argued that ethical conduct depends on the relationship between the physical and the psychological. He thought that the soul expressed its qualities through the five physical senses, and that virtues and vices were linked to different senses. For example, he said that pride, impudence, modesty, and meekness are all connected with the sense of sight.

He proposed that the soul can be cultivated by self-awareness. If people examine their habits and character, they can become aware of bad habits, and learn to abandon them.

1033–1109
Saint Anselm of Canterbury

A medieval Christian thinker, Anselm is most remembered in philosophy for his ontological argument for the existence of God, which holds that it is implicit in the very concept of God that he must exist. Unlike his contemporaries, his work shows comparative independence of thought from Christian doctrine and Scripture. His use of reason and analysis to provide an understanding of the Christian faith helped the development of scholasticism.

Born in Burgundy, now part of northern Italy, the young Anselm wanted to become a monk but was turned away by the local monastery. Partly to escape his tyrannical father, he traveled to Normandy in France, where he studied under the renowned Prior Lanfranc at the Benedictine Abbey of Bec. It was at Bec that Anselm regained his leanings to a monastic life and took his monastic orders in 1060.

He became known for his teaching and thinking on matters of human nature and moral and religious life, and in 1070 he began writing philosophical treatises, first the *Monologion* (meaning "Soliloquy"), followed by the *Proslogion* ("Discourse"), containing his *a priori* proof for the existence of God. Advancing from the office of novice, he became prior after Lanfranc was made abbot of Caen, and in 1078, the same year he completed the *Proslogion*, he was elected abbot.

In the aftermath of the Norman Conquest of England (1066) Bec, now with an enviable reputation in Europe as a seat of learning, had become wealthy, acquiring substantial property in England. One of Anselm's duties as abbot was to visit these properties. He became known in England and eventually was recognized as the natural successor of Lanfranc, who had become Archbishop of Canterbury. However, when Lanfranc died the English King William II (Rufus) kept the episcopal seat vacant, so he could collect the income. When forced to appoint Anselm in 1093, he made life so difficult for the new archbishop that Anselm went into exile. His request to be relieved of his office was refused by the pope, so he took the opportunity while away from the troubles in England to finish writing several religious treatises. Anselm returned to his seat after William Rufus' death, but conflict between him and the new English king, Henry I, once again forced Anselm to Rome, though a reconciliation was eventually made.

The influences for Anselm's work are not entirely clear. Without doubt, the pervading atmosphere was the tradition of **Saint Augustine**, but Anselm's contributions, although of the Augustinian, **Neo-Platonic** tradition, were original and paved the way for later **scholasticism**. His writings were designed to give his fellow Benedictine monks a greater understanding of the Christian faith through a completely new approach. Instead of relying on citation and interpretation of Scripture, he sought to develop arguments illuminating aspects of the Christian faith through reasoning. The scholastics of the twelfth century would seek to synthesize the works of **Aristotle** and **Plato** with medieval theology. Anselm's attempt to provide a rational proof of the existence of God was a preview of their work, and it has continued to attract numerous critics and advocates to this day.

> **Therefore, lord ... we believe that you are something than which nothing greater can be thought.**
>
> *Proslogion (1078)*

Essential philosophy

Of Anselm's two major philosophical works, the *Monologion* (1077) is by far the longest. The *Proslogion* (1078) was intended to reexamine and rearticulate many of the interconnected arguments contained in the earlier work to produce a "single argument". His aim was to employ reason to explain central aspects of the Christian faith, namely, as he said in the preface to the *Proslogion*:

> *"that God truly is, and that he is the supreme good needing no other, and that he is what all things need so that they are and so that they are well, and whatever else we believe about the divine substance."*

Anselm's ontological argument
In chapter two of the *Proslogion*, Anselm notes that God is believed to be something *"than which nothing greater can be thought"* (*quo maius cogitari non potest*), and he asks whether such a thing exists, since the non-believers, the "Fools" of the Christian Bible's Psalm 14, say *"There is no God"*.

> *"And certainly that than which a greater cannot be thought cannot exist in the understanding alone. For if it is in the intellect alone, it can be thought to also be in reality, which is something greater. If,*

Legacy, truth, consequence

- Anselm's work, in particular his **ontological** argument, has influenced philosophers and theologians through the ages. Variations of his argument appear in the philosophy of **René Descartes**, **Gottfried Leibniz**, and **Kurt Gödel**, among others.

- His rational investigations of the foundations of Christian belief influenced later scholastics including **Thomas Aquinas**, **John Duns Scotus**, and **William of Ockham**.

- Gaunilo, a Benedictine monk and contemporary of Anselm, was the first to argue that there must be something wrong with Anselm's argument. He famously contended that the argument could be applied to things other than God, such as an imaginary perfect island, proving it to exist in reality – clearly an absurd conclusion so Anselm's argument must be invalid. Anselm replied that his argument applies only to God, as only God satisfies, without incoherence, the description of a being "*that than which nothing greater can be thought*", so it may not be used to prove the existence of an imaginary perfect island.

- The ontological argument was criticized by **Immanuel Kant**, who held that existence is not a property of objects, so the concept of God that exists is identical in qualitative terms to the concept of a God that does not exist: both are concepts of perfect beings. Therefore, Anselm's claim that an existent God is greater than a non-existent God is false – one isn't any greater than the other – the result being that the ontological argument fails. Kant's criticism is widely accepted, although there are still supporters of some variants of Anselm's argument.

1033	Born in Aosta, in the kingdom of Burgundy (northern Italy).
1060	Takes his monastic orders at the Benedictine Abbey of Bec in Normandy, France.
1063	Elected prior of the Abbey of Bec.
1077	Writes the *Monologion*.
1078	Completes the *Proslogion* the same year he is elected abbot. Bec gains a reputation as a seat of learning. Anselm, during his time at Bec, writes *De Veritate* (*On Truth*), *De Libertate Arbitrii* (*On Freedom of Choice*), and *De Casu Diaboli* (*On the Fall of the Devil*).
1093	Takes up office of Archbishop of Canterbury.
1097	After disputes between Anselm and King William Rufus over investiture, Anselm seeks counsel of Pope Urban II in Rome.
1100	King William is killed and his successor, Henry I, invites Anselm to return to England, but conflict remains between Anselm and the king, who refuses to submit to papal rule.
1103	Anselm returns to Rome.
1105	Pope Pascal II excommunicates King Henry, but reconciliation is made.
1109	Dies in England. He is considered a saint by the Roman Catholic Church.

Canterbury Cathedral, the seat of Saint Anselm at the end of the eleventh century.

> *Nor do I seek to understand that I may believe, but I believe that I may understand. For this too I believe, that unless I first believe, I shall not understand.*
>
> Attributed to Saint Anselm

therefore, that than which a greater cannot be thought is in the intellect alone, that very thing than which a greater cannot be thought is that than which a greater can be thought. But surely that cannot be. Therefore, without a doubt, something than which a greater cannot be thought exists both in the understanding and in reality."

One way to summarize Anselm's argument is as follows:

(1) God is defined as that than which no greater can be conceived.

(2) If God is that than which no greater can be conceived then there is nothing greater than God that can be imagined.

Therefore it follows that:

(3) There is nothing greater than God that can be imagined.

(4) If God does not exist in reality then there is something greater than God that can be imagined, namely an existent God (this follows, argues Anselm, because an existent God is greater than a non-existent God, and if God were non-existent then we could imagine a God greater than he, namely an existent God).

But (4) is a logical absurdity, therefore:

(5) God exists both in the understanding and in reality.

Al-Ghazali (Algazel)

Known in the West as Algazel, Abu Hamid al-Ghazali was one of the greatest medieval Islamic philosophers. A mystic who wrote in depth about his own spiritual journey, he also studied the ancient Greek philosophers and explored the relationship between reason and religion. He helped ensure that Sufism, the mystical wing of Islam, was accepted by orthodox Muslims.

Al-Ghazali was a young boy when his father, a **Sufi**, died, but a family friend took him and his younger brother in, and ensured the boys had a good education. He concentrated on Islamic law or jurisprudence, and soon gained such a reputation for scholarship that he was brought to the camp court of the vizier of Iran. This was a traveling capital city that moved around the country, as big as a static city but consisting only of tents and temporary structures.

The vizier became al-Ghazali's patron and secured for him the appointment of a professor at the Nizamiyah University of Baghdad, one of the leading centers of learning at the time.

After only a few years of teaching, however, al-Ghazali went through a spiritual crisis, following which he gave up his academic pursuits and worldly interests. He sorted out his finances to ensure his family would not suffer, then became a wandering ascetic, making the pilgrimage to Mecca that every devout Muslim is supposed to make at least once in their lifetime, and roaming around the Middle East. He visited Jerusalem in Palestine (modern Israel)

and Damascus in Syria, before returning to Tus and living as a monastic Sufi, isolated from the material world and spending his time contemplating his philosophical ideas or writing them down.

Eventually he was persuaded to go back to the academic world, and he taught for a few years in Nishapur before withdrawing again into solitary **mysticism**. He also became associated with superstition and magic. Exploring the patterns made by religious symbols, he created a magic square out of the numbers representing the opening letters of the verses or *suras* 19 and 23 of the Islamic holy book, the Qur'an. In a magic square each line whether across or down adds up to the same figure, in this case 15. Al-Ghazali never expected it, but this magic square was named after him and was adopted for amulets and magical talismans.

Al-Ghazali was a popular lecturer, drawing more than 300 students to a talk, and his many books – at least 70 on philosophy, science, religion, mysticism, psychology, and even etiquette – also gave him a powerful reputation as a scholar as well as a magician.

Essential philosophy

Sufism

By the time al-Ghazali became a scholar the mystical Sufi movement was so extreme that its followers were neglecting the basic observances of Islam. He returned the movement to its religious roots, established a rigorous discipline, and showed all Muslims how Sufism could be the spiritual culmination of a devout life. Al-Ghazali explained his own spiritual journey away from rationalist explanations of religion and towards mystical experience in his autobiographical work, *The Deliverance From Error*. This book showed his passionate belief that a human being could approach God in his or her heart.

Opposition to philosophy

Al-Ghazali was adamantly opposed to excessively **rationalist** philosophers whose speculations ran contrary to established Islamic theology. **Avicenna** was one of those whom he particularly singled out for criticism, arguing that he had reached wrong conclusions such as believing that the universe was eternal, just as God is eternal. Al-Ghazali also rejected the view that God only has knowledge of abstract **universals**, not of particular things.

He was particularly sceptical of the ancient Greeks, and he attacked in his writings those people who slavishly followed old viewpoints.

His main work opposing these sorts of scholars was *Incoherence of the Philosophers*, in which he rejected the view that prophetic visions could be received by every purified person, rather than just by God's selected prophets. He therefore put forward a **sceptical** view that would not be seen again for centuries, but at the same time his opposition to rationalists led him to insist that the will of God is acted out in human interactions. Ironically, many of al-Ghazali's own works used the philosophical methods he had previously abhorred.

The Revival of Religious Sciences

In his book of this name al-Ghazali examines a wide range of subjects, from his own knowledge of Islamic law to the unique reflective power owned by human beings. In a later text he points out that the human self contains two qualities that without doubt separate humanity from animals – intellect and will. He also distinguished between animal will, driven by basic instincts such as

Legacy

- Al-Ghazali affected the course of Islamic philosophy. In his attack on thinkers who drew more on the ancient Greeks than on Islam he denounced them as corrupt non-believers, and his arguments laid out in *The Incoherence of the Philosophers* were so powerful that it was a turning point in Islamic development. He helped move Islamic thinkers away from non-religious philosophical constructs towards an idea of cause-and-effect determined by God.
- His systematic explanation of the mystical and spiritual elements of Sufism helped mainstream Muslims understand and accept it as part of orthodox religion.
- Al-Ghazali's theological arguments were taken up by several Jewish and Christian **scholastic** thinkers such as **Thomas Aquinas**, who used some of al-Ghazali's ideas to assert the authority of orthodox Christianity in Europe.

Al-Ghazali visited Damascus in Syria during his travels in the Middle East.

Do not believe that this corpse you see is myself
In the name of God, I tell you, it is not I,
I am a spirit, and this is naught but flesh ...

Poem on Death (eleventh century)

hunger or anger, and human will, which is controlled by the intellect. Overall, he said, the heart rules.

The Deliverance From Error

A significant work of scholarship, the autobiographical work *The Deliverance From Error* contains a description of al-Ghazali's personal spiritual feelings that led him to extol the insights gained by the mystical path of Sufism. He argued that this sort of experience is actually superior to a systematic and logical description of religion. This is one of the few works outside Asia at the time that records an individual's non-Christian response to spirituality.

Senses

Al-Ghazali was one of the first philosophers to categorize five separate external senses: sight, sound, smell, touch, and taste. He also distinguished between imagination, which he defined as the memory retaining a mental image of something that had actually happened; reflection, the ability to bring established ideas together; and recollection, the memory of the meaning and outer form of an object.

Key dates

1058	Born in Tus in the Khorasan province of eastern Iran.
1085	Invited to join the traveling court of the vizier of Iran.
1091	Appointed senior teacher in the Nizamiyal University in Baghdad.
1095	After a spiritual crisis begins a period of wandering as an ascetic.
1106	Returns to teaching, at the Nizamiyah University, Nishapur, northeastern Iran.
1111	Dies in Tus.

The true way of happiness is knowing what is right and doing it.

The Ten Articles (eleventh century)

Peter Abelard

The pre-eminent philosopher–theologian of the twelfth century, Peter Abelard is perhaps best known in modern times for his tragic love affair with Héloïse. In his day he was hugely influential as a controversialist and teacher, a logician, and a leading force in the development of the rationalistic element of scholasticism. He was condemned for heresy when his rational approach to theological matters and his extravagant claims became too much for the established religious order.

Born near Nantes, in Brittany, France, to a lesser noble family, Peter Abelard excelled early on at the art of **dialectic**, a branch of philosophy concerned with finding truths through the exchange of logical arguments. In Abelard's time this involved the application of the **logic** of **Aristotle** to a range of Christian theological questions and other concerns of the day.

He became a wandering scholar after renouncing his inheritance, traveling through France seeking instruction from teachers such as the monk Roscelin of Compiègne (c.1050–c.1125). In Paris he entered the cathedral school of Notre-Dame, where he attended lectures by William of Champeaux (c.1070–1122), a leading proponent of metaphysical **realism**, a dominant philosophical theory at the time. The young Abelard, who opposed the theory, challenged William in debate and his victory won him a reputation as a dialectician. With mounting confidence, he set up his own rival school.

Around 1113 he turned to theological studies as a student of the venerable Anselm of Laon (*d*. 1117), but again the quick-witted

Abelard courted controversy by upstaging his master in debate. He returned to Paris where the force of his personality and his brilliant lectures began to draw students from countries around Europe. It was here that his love affair with Héloïse began. One of the most literate women of her time, she became a student of Abelard, though she remained under the care of her uncle, the Canon Fulbert. When their affair was discovered, the lovers were married in secret. Héloïse became pregnant, which led to worsening relations with Fulbert: in his revenge he had Abelard castrated. Héloïse became a nun and Abelard retreated to the life of a Benedictine monk.

Though heartbroken, Abelard found enough courage to return to teaching, and his lectures once again attracted many followers. But his method of philosophical analysis was seen as a threat to the orthodox Christian Church, and his enemies plotted against him. On the publication of his *Theologia "Summi Boni"*, containing his rationalistic discussion of the Christian Trinity, he was

Essential philosophy

Dialectic and logic

Abelard defined dialectic as the art of discerning the true from the false through a discussion of apparently contradictory arguments and authorities. He applied this method to issues in logic, **metaphysics**, **philosophy of language**, and **philosophy of mind**, and in particular in his *Dialectica* (written before 1125). In this work, he provides an elucidation of the problems presented by the **Aristotelian logic** inherited from antiquity and the associated commentaries of Porphyry (c.232–c.305) and Boethius (c.480–c.526). Abelard's influential rational approach to philosophical and religious thought helped to establish Aristotle's authority in medieval Europe.

Nominalism

As an early example of a **nominalist** in the **Western tradition**, Abelard held that **universals** (general descriptive terms such as "blue" or "rough") are words or mental terms, and not things with independent existence in the world. The things in the real world are the concrete individual objects and that is all, on his view. He

was responding to the prevailing metaphysical **realist** view, ultimately grounded in the doctrines of **Plato**, that universals are "**Ideas**", or "Forms" – abstract entities present in the world – a theory he held to be incoherent. A universal, he argued, has universality because it is a characteristic or state present in many objects at once, so as to constitute their substance (make the individual what it is). Therefore a universal cannot be a thing existing in the world but instead is a feature of language.

The universal has no existence apart from the individual.

Dialectica (before 1125)

Ethics

In the realm of moral philosophy, his major works included *Ethics*, or, *Know Yourself* (before 1140), an analysis of moral value, and *Conversations* or *The Dialogue of a Philosopher with a Jew and a Christian* (1136–9), which follows two debates between characters who appeared to Abelard in a dream, about the nature of goodness and what it is to be happy.

Legacy, truth, consequence

- Despite his intellectual achievements, in modern times Abelard is popularly known for his connection with Héloïse.
- He had a seminal influence on philosophers and theologians in the thirteenth century, exercised chiefly through his pupil Peter Lombard (c.1100–60). His own resolution of the debate between the nominalists and the realists prefigured that of **Thomas Aquinas**.
- One of the most important dialecticians of the age, his method of reflection was to become a mark of Western culture, distinguishing it from other world cultures such as Islam and **Confucianism**.
- His strongly rationalistic form of **scholasticism** helped the re-establishment of the authority of Aristotle. He achieved more in **ethics** than many other scholastic philosophers.

Constant and frequent questioning is the first key to wisdom ...

Sic et Non ("Yes and No", twelfth century)

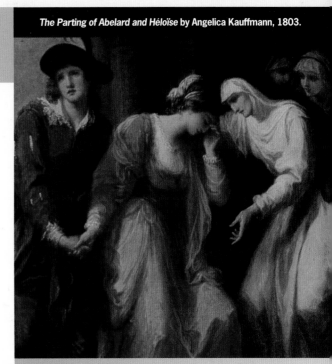

The Parting of Abelard and Héloïse by Angelica Kauffmann, 1803.

summoned to the council of Soissons in 1121. Charged with heresy, he was forced to burn his book on the Trinity and make a public avowal of faith. After this incident he sought solace in the desert, living as a hermit for some years, but even in the wilderness his students came to him. Perhaps to avoid further persecution he accepted an invitation to become abbot of the monastery of Saint Gildas de Rhuys in Brittany, but by 1136 he was once again lecturing in Paris, much to the consternation of Bernard of Clairvaux (1090–1153), who saw Abelard's **rationalistic** approach as an act of rebellion. The council at Sens set up to review Abelard's work (in 1140) condemned nineteen propositions it claimed to find in his works. Abelard was allowed to remain at the monastery of Cluny under the protection of Peter the Venerable (c.1092–1156) for the last two years of his life. His remains, which were moved more than once, are now said to lie with those of Héloïse in the much visited tomb at Père Lachaise cemetery in Paris.

He laid much stress on the morality of the intention of a person in judging the moral value of an act: the physical action itself is morally indifferent, and it is the subjective intention (for example, the intention of sinning) that determines the moral value of their action – whether it is good or evil.

God looks not to the deed, but to the intention, and He punishes the intention rather than the act.

Ethics, or, *Know Yourself* (before 1140)

Philosophical theology

His main works on systematic theology include his books *Theologia "Summi Boni"*, condemned at the Council of Sens, and *Theologia "Scholarium"*, condemned at the Council of Soissons. Abelard emphasized that faith is based on reason, and was inclined to remove the distinctions between philosophy and theology. His strongly rationalistic approach, in particular his comparison of the Holy Trinity to a **syllogism** (a form of **deductive reasoning**), offended religious thinkers and led to his condemnation by the Church.

Key dates

1079	Born near Nantes, Brittany, in France.
c.1097	Enters cathedral school of Notre Dame, Paris, and is taught by William of Champeaux.
1120–40	Writes his main works on philosophical theology, *Theologia "Summi Boni"* and *Theologia "Scholarium"*.
1121	Summoned to the council of Soissons, charged with heresy. He spends several years as a hermit.
Before 1125	Writes *Dialectica*.
c.1126	Accepts an invitation to become abbot of the monastery of Saint Gildas de Rhuys in Brittany.
1136–9	Writes *Dialogue of a Philosopher with a Jew and a Christian*.
Before 1140	Writes *Ethics* or *Know Yourself* and *Historia Calammitatum*, his autobiography, a remarkably frank self-portrait.
1140	Condemned by the council at Sens.
1142	Dies after spending the last two years of his life at the monastery of Cluny.

Averroës (Ibn Rushd)

A medieval Spanish Arab judge and doctor as well as a philosopher, Averroës (ibn Rushd) played an important part in transmitting the ideas of Aristotle down through the ages. He has been called "the Commentator" for his multi-leveled discussions of Aristotle's works, and his reconciliation of reason with religious faith was influential in the development of Christian scholasticism.

Abdul Walid Muhammad ibn Ahmad ibn Rushd, known to the West as Averroës, came from a family of well-known legal scholars in Muslim Spain. Both his grandfather and father were chief judges in Córdoba, and Averroës followed in their footsteps as a scholar and jurist.

He had a thorough traditional education, studying Islamic law, mathematics, linguistics, and philosophy as well as medicine. An all-rounder, he wrote an important medical book as well as many papers on medicine and law. He practiced as a doctor, was consulted on educational matters, became a judge, and wrote influential philosophical texts. In later years he was often called back from his legal positions in Spain to serve the caliph at his court in Marrakech, in either a legal or a medical role.

The patronage of Caliph Abu Yaqub Yusuf led Averroës to become a specialist in **Aristotle**. The prevailing attitudes in Islam at the time rejected both foreign influences and secular philosophy. Abu Yaqub Yusuf, however, was interested in Greek philosophy and was gradually liberalizing his regime, so he commissioned Averroës to produce commentaries on Aristotle to help explain the great Greek's thought.

Religious conservatives bitterly opposed Averroës' **rationalist** approach. Tensions grew until towards the end of his life there was a purge of liberal freethinkers, and although Averroës was only briefly exiled his philosophy never regained much of a following in the Islamic world. It did, however, soon find a great deal of interest from Jews and Christians.

Essential philosophy

Although he is best known for his detailed commentaries on Aristotle, Averroës made many philosophical contributions of his own. As a lawyer and judge, he was particularly interested in exploring logical arguments and rational thinking.

Defense of philosophy

Not long before Averroës was born, the **Sufi** mystic Abu Hamid **al-Ghazali** wrote *The Incoherence of the Philosophers*, a diatribe against philosophers who he thought were being led away from Islam by ancient Greek writers. In turn, Averroës attacked this in his *The Incoherence of the Incoherence*, in which he tried to show that the philosophical method of inquiry had real value to religious understanding, and should not be dismissed out of hand. He also pointed out that al-Ghazali had mainly been criticizing **Avicenna**'s interpretations of **Aristotelianism**. But, he said, Avicenna's ideas were a distortion of the real doctrines of the Greek, so al-Ghazali had not shown that Aristotelian reasoning was un-Islamic.

Averroës really did not like most of Avicenna's work. His sneering comment on one of the Iranian's books was that it was only useful for scrap paper.

Religion and philosophy

Averroës argued that religion and philosophy are simply different ways of approaching God. All human beings strive to know God, but there are two ways to do so, through religious revelation, or

> *Abu Bakr ibn Tufayl ... told me that he had heard the Commander of the Faithful complaining about the disjointedness of Aristotle's mode of expression – or that of the translators – and the resultant obscurity of his intentions. He said that if someone took on these books who could summarize them and clarify their aims after first thoroughly understanding them himself, people would have an easier time comprehending them.*
>
> Averroës, quoted in *History of Islamic Philosophy* by Seyyed Hossein Nasr and Oliver Leaman (1996)

Legacy, truth, consequence

- Averroës' commentaries were mainly responsible for reintroducing Aristotle's work to Europe. Before they were translated into Latin in the early twelfth century there had only been a few, scattered Aristotelian works available, as well as interpretations such as those by Avicenna. Averroës' versions quickly became the standard texts, intensively studied in monasteries and in the new universities that were appearing. To the **scholastic** philosophers he was simply known as "The Commentator".

- His personal philosophy on the distinction between religion and reason – and the supremacy of reason – offended many religious thinkers. As the Islamic world moved towards more theological systems of thought, Averroës' ideas gradually lost significance in the Middle East.

- His writings inspired a group of controversial Christian philosophers, led by Siger de Brabant, at the University of Paris, France, to develop the doctrine of "double truth", that there are two separate kinds of truths, one religious and one philosophical. Many Jewish thinkers also found his ideas a source of inspiration.

- However, a century after Averroës, scholastic Christian philosopher **Thomas Aquinas** fought hard to stamp out the Averroistic reading of Aristotle he and others considered to be heretical.

- Averroës has been described as the founding father of secularism for his division of reason and religion, which is held to be a justification for the separation of state and religion.

through pure reason. Revelation is the source of religious doctrine, but a true interpretation of it is only gained through reason. This is a true Muslim viewpoint, he argued, because the Qur'an contains some verses that have obvious, fixed meanings, but other verses have always been open to a range of interpretations.

He confirmed that Islam is the ultimate truth, and since philosophy is the search for truth, they are clearly compatible. If religious teachings do seem to clash with demonstrative truth, this apparent conflict can easily be resolved by viewing scripture as allegorical. Averroës argued that this approach is also traditional, since early Muslim communities accepted that some Qur'anic verses could have esoteric as well as surface meanings.

In *The Decisive Treatise* he wrote that a full interpretation of the Qur'an relies on analytical thinking, but his main point was that religion is concerned with one level of truth whereas philosophy is concerned with truth itself. The religious level unveils knowledge through symbols and stories, which is the only way uneducated people can approach truth, but philosophical reasoning, a superior way of inquiring into truth, is only available to the educated. Therefore, he argued, faith and reason do not need to be reconciled: there is no conflict because they deal with different levels.

In his view, religion was mainly useful for giving rules to ordinary people.

Key dates

1126	Born in Córdoba (now in modern Spain).
1160s	Writes short commentaries on some of Aristotle's books.
By 1169	Commissioned by Caliph Abu Yaqub Yusuf I to write fuller commentaries on Aristotle.
1171	Serves as a judge in Córdoba. During this period writes commentary on Aristotle's *Metaphysics* (fourth century BCE).
1179–80	Writes three original philosophical works, including his defense of philosophy, *The Incoherence of the Incoherence*.
c.1184	Returns to Córdoba as chief judge.
1195	Banished from Córdoba to the village of Lucena during an official backlash against perceived **liberalism**. His writings are banned and his books burned.
1197	Allowed to return to Córdoba.
1198	Dies in Marrakech (in Morocco).

Averroës' philosophy was later opposed by many Christian thinkers, as shown in this detail from *The Triumph of Saint Thomas Aquinas over Averroës*, 1471.

Other ideas

Averroës believed that humans had two souls, an individual one that did not survive after death, and a shared, single universal soul that was immortal and divine. He also followed Aristotle's argument that the universe had not come into being through an act of creation. Although he thought he could reconcile these ideas with religious orthodoxy, they were not popular with conservative Muslims.

Commentaries

Averroës also wrote commentaries on other great Greek books, such as **Plato**'s *Republic* and **Ptolemy**'s *Almagest*. His usual practice was to supply three different levels of commentary, meant for readers of differing abilities: he would write a short, simplified summary; a medium-sized commentary with some criticism; and a long, thorough, detailed study of the material. Overall, Averroës wanted to make available a pure version of Aristotle's ideas, since he felt that the prevailing interpretations had drifted too far from the original.

Moses Maimonides

The rabbi Maimonides was the leading intellectual figure of Spanish Judaism, whose *Guide for the Perplexed* was one of the great works of medieval philosophy. He was deeply devout, and his ideas on religion and articles of faith were later incorporated into orthodox Jewish traditions. At the same time, his inquiring, Aristotelian approach to religious truths also had a profound intellectual influence on philosophers from within the Islamic and Christian traditions.

Maimonides is often called the Rambam, an acronym from the initials of "rabbi" and his full name, Moshe ben Maimon (Moses son of Maimon). In Arabic he was called Abu Imran Musa ibn Maymun ibn Ubayd Allah al-Qurtubi al-Israili, and the Greek version of his name was Moses Maimonides. He was the "Rabbi Moses" referred to by **Thomas Aquinas**.

Maimonides was born into a rabbinical Jewish family in Muslim Spain, which had once tolerated all religions and had proven to be a haven of scholarship for centuries. However, within a few years of Maimonides' birth, the fanatical Almohad dynasty took power and demanded that non-Muslims should convert or leave.

For 11 years his family practiced their faith in secret, while Maimonides studied secular subjects such as Greek philosophy, as well as traditional Jewish lore. Eventually they feared they would be exposed as secret Jews, so moved to Morocco, where Maimonides also began to study medicine at the University of al-Karaouine. This career stood him in good stead when the family was forced to move again, eventually settling in Egypt, a country that tolerated other

faiths. He obtained a position as doctor to the sultan Saladin and his son. Some sources say that he also treated the English king Richard the Lionheart during the Crusades.

While he was attending court he also found time to teach at a public hospital in Cairo, become the head of the Jewish community, and begin writing in earnest. At age 33 he finished a ten-year project, a complete index of the Mishna (oral Jewish law) and important commentaries on it. This was written in Hebrew, but he produced many other papers on medicine, religion, and philosophy in both Hebrew and Arabic. His major work took him about 15 years to complete. This was *The Guide for the Perplexed*, written in Arabic, originally just as a private document for a student.

As his reputation grew Maimonides was frequently consulted by other Jewish communities or scholars on points of Jewish law, and as a result many of his letters, as well as his books, have survived. There were so many demands on his time that in one letter he wrote a long complaint about how tired he was at the end of another grueling day.

Essential philosophy

A clever, subtle, **rationalist** who was also whole-heartedly devout, Maimonides tried to show how **Aristotelian** science or philosophy could confirm religious statements and prove the existence of God.

The Guide for the Perplexed

Maimonides wrote several texts on the specifics of Jewish law, but while his major work of philosophy, *The Guide for the Perplexed*, reconciles Aristotelian philosophy with traditional Jewish religion, its principles and approach are relevant to all belief systems. He wrote this book as a response to the times. Aristotelian philosophy had become more and more influential in Islamic and Jewish societies across the Middle East, threatening the power of traditional theologians. Like his near-contemporaries in the Islamic world, **Avicenna** and **Averroës**, Maimonides was anxious to show that the investigative **logic** of philosophy could be used to confirm religious truths.

Allegory

Maimonides was to some extent an elitist who felt that the more knowledge a person gains, the closer they get to God, and he wrote *The Guide for the Perplexed* not for everybody, but for other intellectuals: "*The object of this treatise is to enlighten a religious man who … at the same time has been successful in his philosophical studies.*"

He also argued that religious writings sometimes appear in the form of allegory, because that approach is the only one that most uneducated people can follow. So, scripture is not necessarily to be looked at as literal truth, for example, when a biblical prophet "saw" God, it meant that the prophet became aware of truths about God. Maimonides claimed that a literal interpretation can sometimes reduce God to a material conception.

Nature of God

In particular, one of Maimonides' central points was **apophatic (or negative) theology**, that God's essence cannot be literally

Legacy, truth, consequence

■ Within Judaism, Maimonides was originally somewhat controversial. Traditionalists rejected his **metaphysics**, his reasoned conclusions, and his 13 Articles of Faith. A synagogue in southern France went so far as to burn his *Guide for the Perplexed*. Nowadays, however, he is considered to be one of the greatest of all Jewish thinkers, and his code and 13 Articles are an accepted part of orthodox Judaism. Literalists, of course, reject his allegorical approach.

■ His ability to reconcile philosophy with religion and successfully resolve **paradoxes** inspired European **scholastics** and even later thinkers such as **Baruch Spinoza**.

■ Having studied Muslim scholars as well as Greek philosophers, and made an impact on Jewish and Christian thinkers, Maimonides was one of the few people to have touched upon four different systems of thought.

Key dates

1135	Born in Córdoba (now in modern Spain).
c.1151	Only 16, writes his first paper, discussing logic.
1159	Moves with his family to Fez (now in modern Morocco) to avoid religious persecution.
1165	Forced to move again, to Palestine then finally Egypt.
1168	Publishes his *Commentary on the Mishna* (oral Jewish law), including his list of 13 Articles of Faith.
1177	Becomes head of the Jewish community in Egypt.
c.1178	Publishes the *Mishne Torah* (*Second Torah*), an influential code or index of the Mishna and important commentaries on it.
1190	After about 15 years' work, finishes his major philosophical work, *Guide for the Perplexed*.
1204	Dies in Fostat, Old Cairo, Egypt. His body is taken for burial to Tiberias, Palestine (now Israel).

> *When a man reflects on these things, studies all these created beings, from the angels and spheres down to human beings and so on, and realizes the divine wisdom manifested in them all, his love for God will increase, his soul will thirst, his very flesh will yearn to love God.*
>
> Mishne Torah (*Second Torah*, twelfth century)

Detail of a manuscript by Maimonides.

described by human beings, so any attempt to do so will be inadequate and false, or reduce God to the human level. God can therefore only be described in terms of what He is not, or by negative statements. It is possible to say that "God is not divided" or "God is not evil", but not correct to say "God is one" or "God is good". This argument was particularly relevant during Maimonides' time because there had been a recent tendency to anthropomorphize God.

Maimonides pointed out that it is still possible to praise God with positive statements as long as it is accepted that God's essence is unknowable, and that the praise is not a direct description. He wrote:

> "*Know that when you make an affirmation ascribing another thing to Him, you become more remote from Him in two respects: one of them is that everything you affirm is a perfection only with reference to us, and the other is that He does not possess a thing other than His essence …*"

Creation

Maimonides concurred with **Aristotle** in most areas, but differed on the creation of matter, which Aristotle had argued was eternal and "necessary". Maimonides showed that the two standard arguments for that view – that God is perfect and unchanging so could not change by creating the universe, or that the nature of the world is such that something new cannot emerge from nothing – do not conclusively prove creation could not have happened. In the first place God might always have intended an act of creation as part of His nature, and in the second place we cannot project our experience of the world as it is now onto the world at the moment of creation. In order to prove a creator, Maimonides claimed that there is no "necessary" reason for the irregular behavior of stars and planets, so there are no grounds for arguing that the cosmos is necessary and eternal. The alternative is that God created the universe in his own chosen manner.

Saint Albert the Great

Also known as Albertus Magnus, Albert the Great was a Dominican friar and became known as "Doctor Universalis" because of his extensive knowledge: he made contributions to a wide range of subjects from logic and metaphysics to psychology and nature. He realized the importance of squaring Aristotle's works, which had recently been rediscovered in the Christian West, with Christianity – an enterprise taken up by his famous student, Saint Thomas Aquinas.

Born in the town of Lauingen, in Germany, the eldest son of the Count of Bollstädt, he showed an early interest in the liberal arts and was sent to the University of Padua to pursue his studies. Around 1223, against the wishes of his family, he joined the Dominican Order, and after completing his training taught theology in several German cities, including Cologne. He was sent to Paris in 1245, where he received his doctorate and began lecturing in theology. Around this time he became acquainted with one of his most gifted students, **Thomas Aquinas**, marking the beginning of a friendship that would last a lifetime.

Albert was made provincial of the Dominican Order in 1254, a role he fulfilled with great care and perseverance, his characteristic approach to all the various ecclesiastical tasks he was appointed to do through his working life.

In 1270 he sent a memoir to help his friend Aquinas in an ongoing struggle against the Averroist movement among Parisian philosophers, led by Siger de Brabant (c.1240–c.1280). The Averroist reading of Aristotle's work, after the Muslim philosopher **Averroës**, was seen to be at odds with Christian doctrine. Albert had completed a refutation of Averroistic psychology in 1256 (entilted *De Unitate Intellectus Contra Averroistas*), which now helped Aquinas to oppose their line of thought and find a solution that was acceptable to the Church while upholding the authority of **Aristotelian logic**.

Albert was much saddened by the sudden death of Aquinas in 1274 and took pains in later years to defend his teaching, which came under attack in Parisian intellectual circles. There is a legend which says that Albert discovered the philosopher's stone (a legendary substance, supposedly capable of turning inexpensive metals into gold, or believed to be an elixir of life), and that he passed it to Aquinas, though there is no confirmation of this in his writings.

Essential philosophy

Albert was heavily influenced by the works of **Aristotle**, which had recently been reintroduced to the West accompanied by notes from several outstanding Arab philosophers. Some of these Arab commentaries, for example those of the eleventh-century Persian scholar **Avicenna**, would come to influence Albert's own philosophical doctrines.

Albert's great task arose when he realized that many people would need to be shown how they could accept Aristotle's highly persuasive arguments without refuting their own Christian religion. This became a central objective of his philosophical writings, which consist primarily of commentaries and paraphrases of Aristotle's works. For the most part, Albert was a devoted follower of Aristotle, but occasionally he made a challenge to the opinion of "The Philosopher" (as Aristotle was referred to by the medievals) based on his own observations and studies.

In addition, Albert wrote commentaries on the works of other thinkers such as Porphyry (c.232–c.305), Boethius (c.480–c.526), and Peter Lombard (c.1100–60). His writings taken together, over 40 volumes, resemble a kind of philosophical encyclopedia, they

> *Natural science does not consist in ratifying what others have said, but in seeking the causes of phenomena.*
>
> Attributed to Saint Albert the Great

are so broad in subject matter. Ultimately, what marks them out is their exact knowledge of science, the **rationalist** approach, and his philosophical-scientific-theological vision.

Natural philosophy and theology

Albert's systematic study of Aristotle helped form his considerable knowledge of **natural philosophy**, and develop his own vision of philosophy, nature, and theology in works such as *Tractatus de Natura Boni Summa Theologica* (c.1245). Albert found Aristotle's method in natural philosophy to be experientially based, forming conclusions through both **inductive** and **deductive reasoning**.

The Alchemist, by Pieter Bruegel the Elder, c.1558. The legend says that Albert the Great, as an alchemist and magician, discovered the philosopher's stone.

■ Albert the Great's immense contribution to scholastic philosophy and to the learning of his age is evident by the fact that his contemporaries, such as Roger Bacon (c.1214–c.1294), gave to his name the term "Magnus" during his lifetime. He advised and influenced popes, bishops, kings, and figures of state.

■ His systematized writings on Aristotle's works, along with those of Thomas Aquinas, succeeded in incorporating **Aristotelianism** and its scientific approach into the Christian West. They are also the basis for most modern knowledge of Aristotle.

■ Taking on the principles of scientific inquiry found in Aristotle, Albert carried out experiments of his own and built up a collection of plants and insects. He gained a reputation as a natural philosopher (or, anachronistically, a scientist) long before the age of science had begun, with interests in biology, chemistry, physics, astronomy, anthropology, psychology, **metaphysics**, and mathematics. Some of his students, and the generation who followed him, carried on his interests, for example Ulrich of Strasburg (c.1225–77), Hugh Ripelin of Strasburg (c.1200–68), and Dietrich of Freiberg (c.1250–c.1310).

Key dates

c.1206	Born in the German town of Lauingen.
c.1223	Joins the Dominican Order.
1245	Begins lecturing in theology at the University of Paris.
c.1245	Writes his first major work, *Tractatus de Natura Boni Summa Theologica.*
1248	Travels to Cologne to set up a house of studies for the Order, accompanied by his gifted pupil, Thomas Aquinas.
1254	Elected provincial of the Dominican Order.
1256	Completes *De Unitate Intellectus Contra Averroistas,* refuting Averroistic psychology.
1257	Returns to Cologne as regent of studies.
1258	Consecrated a bishop and sent to Ratisbon (modern Regensburg).
1263–4	Preaches the Crusade on the command of Pope Urban IV.
c.1267–75	Travels around Germany fulfilling various ecclesiastical tasks.
1274	Receives news of the death of Thomas Aquinas.
1280	Dies and is buried in Cologne.
1931	Declared a saint and a doctor of the Church.
1941	Pope Pius XII declares Albert the patron saint of the natural sciences.

On the other hand, Christian theology at the time was founded upon truths known through revelation and traditional doctrine. The two domains and their methodologies were quite separate and were not a threat to each other, he argued.

Universals

Like many of the **scholastic** philosophers, Albert addressed Porphyry's famous problem of **universals** (general descriptive terms) – namely, do the things according to which we classify beings exist in themselves or are they merely constructions of the mind? In his solution he found a way to harmonize the **realist** theory associated with **Plato**, that universals exist as separate "**Ideas**" or "Forms" (abstract entities), with the theory of immanent forms (existing in the mind) found in Aristotle. Universals, according to Albert, are of three types: those that exist prior to the individual things that exemplify them, whose existence is independent of thought; those that exist in individual things, whose existence is outside the mind; and those that exist in the mind as abstract concepts.

Saint Thomas Aquinas

An Italian Catholic philosopher, and perhaps the most significant medieval thinker in the scholastic tradition, Saint Thomas Aquinas synthesized the immensely persuasive philosophy of Aristotle, which had become central to medieval European thought, with Christian teaching. His work, at a time when the first universities were developing across Europe, called into question a way of thinking that had been accepted for centuries.

Born to an aristocratic family in the kingdom of Naples, southern Italy, the young Thomas Aquinas was educated at the Benedictine monastery of Monte Cassino. He attended the University of Naples, where he came under the influence of the Dominicans, a new order committed to study and preaching. Aquinas decided to join them, much to his family's dismay. They went to great lengths to dissuade him, by keeping him prisoner, even tempting him from chastity by offering a prostitute, but Aquinas resisted. Eventually his family gave way and Aquinas joined the order aged 17. Soon he was sent to Paris to study under **Albert the Great** (Albertus Magnus), a Dominican

friar who became known for his application of **Artistotle's** philosophy to Christian theology.

Despite his student nickname "Dumb Ox", which perhaps reflected his large stature and slow manner, Aquinas became respected for his rigorous application of reason, his precise language, and engaging lectures.

His philosophy applied the methods of Artistotle to Christian thinking. At the time, Christian thought was torn between the Augustinians (after **Saint Augustine**) and the Averroists (after **Averroës**). The Averroists argued that Aristotle's work justified

Essential philosophy

Aquinas recognized the persuasiveness of Aristotle's logic and realized the necessity of showing that Aristotle's system was compatible, more or less, with Christian theology. The unfinished *Summa Theologica* (1265-73), an immense work of some 60 volumes, contains the fullest statement of Aquinas' philosophy. It applies Aristotelian **metaphysics**, **moral philosophy**, and **philosophy of mind** to a Christian vision of the world. In particular, he makes a proof for the existence and nature of God.

Knowledge

Aquinas distinguished between truths arrived at through reason and truths of revelation. Matters such as God's existence or God's omni-potence, he held, should be accepted on the basis of divine revelation alone, but in some circumstances it was desirable to apply reason to arrive at genuine knowledge of such things. According to Aquinas' position, known as moderate **realism**, the intellect achieves knowledge of the world through the senses; **sense experience** of a particular object is necessary to formulate both a mental image of the object and a **universal** concept that applies to it and all similar objects. Knowledge of the object then comes through abstraction by the intellect.

Argument for the existence of God

Aquinas presented five proofs of God's existence based on logical argument, the Five Ways (*quinque viae*), each of which starts with a divine act – an effect – and argues back to its cause. The second proof,

perhaps the most famous, is the Argument of Efficient Causation. The first premise of this argument – nothing is a cause of itself – Aquinas presents as an **empirical** fact accepted by all. Causes are causes of other things: their effects. He demonstrates this through an example of a stone moving, which is caused by a stick pushing it, which in turn moves because there is a hand holding the stick and moving it, and so on. However, he argues, an infinite regression of causes is not possible, so there must have been a first uncaused cause. This first cause is God. The final step in the argument – that the first cause is God – most commentators agree requires a leap of faith, and is not proved by the premises alone.

The nature of God

Aquinas was concerned to show how we can understand terms used in the Bible to describe God, such as "good" and "just", when, as he believed was the case, we do not have insight into God's nature. His solution was that we can come by an imperfect knowledge of the nature of God by analogy and by negation. By negating the properties of material things for which we do have knowledge, we might learn, for example, that God is not changing and not finite. By making analogies with properties that we already know, for example human goodness, we must recognize that God has these perfections in the fullest way possible. Beyond these methods of analogy and negation, knowledge of the divine nature of God is possible only through revelation. In other words, there are certain revelatory truths that are not accessible by reason alone.

their claims, against the teachings of the Catholic Church, that the soul is not immortal, and the universe was not begun by a single, divine creative act but exists externally. In order to reconcile such ideas with Christian faith, they adopted a notion of "double truth": that something could be true in rational thinking but false in religious belief. Aquinas utterly opposed the separation of faith and truth, as much as he opposed the Augustinians who made truth a matter of faith. He held that the truths of faith are in harmony with the truths of reason – both are the gifts of God – thus defending Aristotle's work against those who saw it as inspiring the heretical commentaries of the Averroists.

Aquinas spent much of his life moving between places of learning in Italy and France. His writing output was vast, in one estimate eight million words, many in the form of commentaries upon the Gospels and upon Aristotelian treatises. His best known writings include two *Summations* (*Summae*) of theology. The first, *On the Truth of the Catholic Faith against the Gentiles* (*Summa Contra Gentiles*, 1259–64), may have been aimed at converting Muslims to the Catholic faith. The second, *The Summation of Theology* (*Summa Theologica*, 1265–73), though incomplete shows a systematic application of philosophical principles to theology.

His prolific writing stopped abruptly following a religious experience during Mass. He is reported to have said: "*All that I have written seems to me like straw compared to what has now been revealed to me.*" He died four months later, struck on the head by a tree branch on his way to a church council.

Detail of *The Triumph of Saint Thomas Aquinas over Averroes* by Gozzoli Benozzo, 1471.

Legacy, truth, consequence

■ Thomas Aquinas is remembered for finding a way to reconcile Aristotelian thought with Christianity and for his influence on other **scholastic** philosophers. His work is now recognized as a great intellectual achievement.

■ His influence on Christianity was so immense that his writings became the official doctrine of the Roman Catholic Church in 1879.

■ For centuries Aquinas was ignored by thinkers outside the Catholic Church and the philosophy of religion, but increasingly his vast output is studied by philosophers in the wider intellectual community for his insights into human nature, government, **logic**, **ethics**, metaphysics, **epistemology**, and the philosophy of mind.

■ He is the father of the **Thomistic** school of philosophy and theology, a movement that took Aquinas' ideas and developed them in many directions. Followers had to defend themselves against other movements, especially from the teachings of **John Duns Scotus** and **William of Ockham**. Neo-Thomism today continues the tradition, and Thomistic principles have also been applied to modern life by non-Catholics.

Key dates

1225	Born in Roccasecca, Italy.
c.1242	Joins the Dominican Order.
1245	Begins his studies in Paris under Albert the Great (Albertus Magnus), accompanying him to Cologne in Germany.
1252	Returns to Paris and becomes a professor of theology.
c.1259	Fulfils a role as professor and advisor at the papal court in Italy.
1259–64	Completes *On the Truth of the Catholic Faith against the Gentiles* (*Summa Contra Gentiles*).
1265–73	Works on his (unfinished) masterpiece, *The Summation of Theology* (*Summa Theologica*).
1269	Returns to Paris to combat a movement known as Latin Averroism.
1274	Dies on his way to the Council of Lyons, where he was to be a papal consultant.
1323	He is made a saint.

Three things are necessary for the salvation of man: to know what he ought to believe; to know what he ought to desire; and to know what he ought to do.

Two Precepts of Charity (1273)

John Duns Scotus

A theologian–philosopher, and a Franciscan friar, John Duns Scotus was the founder of a school of scholasticism known as Scotism, in which he extended and modified the teachings of Saint Augustine in the light of Aristotle's writings. One of the most influential logicians of the High Middle Ages, he earned the epithet "the Subtle Doctor" for his penetrating mind and subtle and critical philosophy.

Very little of John Duns Scotus' life is definitely known. It is thought that he was born probably in Scotland, though some claim him for Ireland. He joined the Franciscan Order and was a professor for several years at Oxford. We also know that he went to Paris around 1304, where he was presented for a doctor's degree. He stayed there for just a short time, going on to Cologne in 1308, as a professor at the university. He died there, relatively young, and was buried in the Church of the Minorites. There is a tradition that Duns Scotus may have been buried alive: it is said that sometimes he could be so caught up in contemplation that he would become completely insensible, to the extent that on one occasion, while in Cologne, he was declared dead and buried.

The pervading atmosphere for Duns Scotus' work was a combination of traditions emanating from **Aristotle**, **Saint Augustine**, **Saint Anselm of Canterbury**, Roger Bacon (c.1214–c.1294), and **Saint Thomas Aquinas**. Duns Scotus' writings are complex and address concerns in **logic**, **metaphysics**, theology, **epistemology**, and **ethics**. There are several philosophical

treatises, including his commentaries and questions on various works of Aristotle. His *Opus Oxoniense* was composed while at Oxford and is a commentary on the *Book of Sentences* of Peter Lombard (c.1100–60), essentially a philosophical approach to theological subjects. The *Opus Parisiense* collects his lecture notes composed while in Paris. The *Quaestiones Quodlibetales* was a dissertation for his doctor's degree.

Encyclopedic in scope, much of Duns Scotus' writing is in the form of interpretations and explanations of live theological issues of the day; his method was to discuss disputed questions from several angles and apply logic to refute the arguments of his opponents. Unlike Thomas Aquinas, he did not present a summary of his thought and his doctrine was not consistently applied through his work. Often obscure, and sometimes unfinished, his writings, which are still being disentangled from spurious works, have been misinterpreted. Nevertheless, it is still possible to find in his teachings a developed system of thought and ideas which have been influential into the modern period.

Essential philosophy

Duns Scotus was convinced that meticulous investigation and dissection of his predecessors' works would lead him to the truth. A follower of Saint Augustine, particularly in his **Platonism**, he was a moderate **realist** about the nature of **universals** (general descriptive terms), but he nevertheless abandoned certain Augustinian theses, in the light of Aristotelian thought, to arrive at a new form of **scholasticism**. Known as **Scotism**, this school of thought was often opposed to the **Thomism** of the followers of Saint Thomas Aquinas.

Haecceity as a principle of individuation
As a realist, Duns Scotus faced the question of how to tell individual things apart when they exemplify the same universal qualities, for example, how to explain what makes one red apple distinct from another red apple, when they both exemplify redness. In the realist tradition, redness would be an entity existing in individual things and outside the mind – not merely a concept of the mind, as a **nominalist** such as **William of Ockham** would come to believe.

Denying the Aristotelian-Thomist view that individual things are distinguished by their matter, he held that objects are identified by their qualities and characteristics (for example, the redness of an apple), and ultimately distinguished by the specific combination of qualities that are the form of a thing (thus borrowing from Aristotle the distinction between something's form and its substance). This combination of qualities is what he called the "*haecceitas*" or "thisness". For example, the quality of "intelligence" exists in both Aristotle and Plato, but in Aristotle it is made individual by Aristotle's *haecceitas* and in Plato by Plato's *haecceitas*.

Univocal predication
Duns Scotus taught that terms such as "humane" or "wise" can be applied univocally (with the same meaning) to both God and creatures. This was a departure from Aquinas, who insisted that a word as applied to God has an *analogous* meaning to the same word applied to human beings, not the *same* meaning. An argument

Legacy, truth, consequence

■ Duns Scotus' teachings marked a critical point in the history of scholasticism and its rival schools. The opponents of Thomas Aquinas and Thomism found a champion in Duns Scotus; while Franciscan teachers followed Duns Scotus, the Dominicans ranged themselves behind Saint Thomas. The controversy that raged between these two groups ultimately hindered the development of scholasticism to the extent that it was unable to grow and adapt to the burgeoning scientific movement at the beginning of the modern era (see pages 76–7).

■ Duns Scotus' work on individuation and the conception of logical possibility was taken up and developed by **Gottfried Leibniz**. Other philosophers influenced by him include **René Descartes**, **Martin Heidegger**, and **Charles Peirce**. His ideas still influence logical and linguistic debates at the heart of modern-day **philosophy of language**.

■ After his writings and followers (known as Dunses) were ridiculed in the sixteenth century, he became immortalized in the English language for giving his name to the term "dunce", meaning "a stupid person".

The liturgical celebration of the Conception of Mary and the doctrine of her Immaculate Conception were the object of much debate. John Duns Scotus defended the doctrine.

Key dates

c.1266	Born in Scotland or Ireland.
1291	Ordained to the priesthood.
c.1294–1304	Teaches at Oxford and writes commentaries on Aristotle's works, various disputations (*Collationes*), and treatises primarily in theology, *De Primo Principio* and *Quaestiones Quodlibetales*. While at Oxford he writes his commentary on Peter Lombard's *Book of Sentences*, the *Opus Oxoniense*.
c.1304	Sent to the University of Paris. His lecture notes are collected in his *Opus Parisiense*. He formulates his celebrated theological thesis on the Immaculate Conception of the Blessed Virgin.
1308	Moves to Cologne to teach at the Franciscan Scholasticate.
1308	Dies in Cologne.
1993	He is beatified by Pope John Paul II.

Thus, absolutely speaking, the primary efficient cause can exist in its own right; hence it exists by itself.

Opus Oxoniense (c.1300)

Duns Scotus uses against analogous **predication** is that if all our concepts come from creatures, then the concepts applied to God must come from creatures too, i.e. they are the very same concepts and not concepts that are merely *like* those that come from creatures (as in analogous predication). There are no other concepts to use, so if we can't use the same concepts from creatures, then we can't apply any concepts at all to God, which means we wouldn't be able to talk about him, which is false.

Proof of the existence of God

For Duns Scotus, proofs of God's existence must ultimately be *a posteriori* (knowable on the basis of experience of sensible things). Developing Saint Anselm's **ontological argument** (see pages 56–7), which he saw as a "probable persuasion", he held that God's existence is possible (can be thought without contradiction) but knowledge of that possible existence must be demonstrated from experience. Experience tells us that many things are possible,

all of which must be related to an Uncaused Being (the "primary efficient cause"). This, he argues, is because the objects of our experience must be produced (or caused) by something else. But there can't be an infinite regression of causes. Hence we are led to admit the existence of an Uncaused Being, outside the chain of succession and change, and justifying all the other objects of our experience. Since this Being is uncaused and unchanging, it is infinite perfection. Therefore, an infinite Being (God) is possible and, because the concept of the infinite involves no contradiction based on our experience, it actually exists.

Philosophy and theology

Where Aquinas taught that the omnipotence of God and the immortality of the human soul are demonstrable by reason, Duns Scotus insisted on the inferiority of philosophy, maintaining that human reason alone cannot prove such truths, thus placing theology and supernatural truth above all philosophical knowledge.

William of Ockham

A Franciscan friar, Ockham was also an influential scholastic philosopher and logician of the High Middle Ages. His controversial stance in various theological and political debates led to his excommunication by the Catholic Church and he spent much of his career in hiding. He is probably best remembered for "Ockham's razor", a methodological procedure, or principle of economy, one expression of which is: it is vain to do with more what can be done with less.

Little is known of Ockham's early life but he was born probably in the village of Ockham in Surrey, near London in England. He joined the distinguished educational establishment of the Franciscan Order in London, then proceeded with theological training at Oxford University, but returned to London before obtaining his master's degree. This earnt him the nickname "Venerable Inceptor" (Inceptor being one who has has not fully completed his degree). He acquired his other nickname, "More than Subtle Doctor", because he was thought to have surpassed the "Subtle Doctor", **John Duns Scotus**.

Ockham was a devoted follower of **Aristotle**, and wrote several commentaries on his works. Another influence was the French Franciscan philosopher Peter John Olivi (1248–98). Sometime before 1327 Ockham wrote his most important philosophical works, including his commentaries on Aristotle's **natural philosophy** and *Summa Logicae* (*Sum of Logic*), in which he presented his logical approach to **metaphysics**.

Ockham's academic career in England ended in 1324 when his theological views came under suspicion. He was summoned to the papal court in Avignon, charged with heresy. For four years he remained under a type of house arrest, during which time he defended apostolic poverty, the view held by the Franciscans that Jesus and his apostles owned no property of their own, and, like the Franciscans, survived by begging and from the gifts of others. This clashed with the beliefs of Pope John XXII, and Ockham, convinced that the papacy was corrupt, decided to flee by night with other sympathizers also on trial. He sought refuge in Italy under the protection of Louis of Bavaria, and then, with the same band of "outlaws", went on to Munich in Germany. He was excommunicated by the pope along with his colleagues in hiding. Ockham remained in Munich for the rest of his life, writing fervently against the papacy in several political treatises, and dying there, perhaps from the plague that was ravaging Europe at the time.

Essential philosophy

Ockham was convinced about the power of **logic** in the advancement of knowledge, particulary in theological matters. He used rigorous logic to show that many Christian beliefs – for example, that the human soul is immortal – cannot be proved by reason alone, only by divine revelation.

Summa Logicae

Ockham's logical writings are presented most fully in his *Summa Logicae*, which contains his extensive development of **syllogistic** logic – defined by Aristotle as discourse in which certain things being posited, something else necessarily follows; for example, if we have two statements of the form "All S are P" and "Q is an S", then it necessarily follows that "Q is P".

"Ockham's razor"

This principle of simplicity was not invented by Ockham – there are examples of its application in Aristotle and **Saint Thomas Aquinas**, among others – but Ockam used it with great effect. It states that the simpler theory is more likely to be true, and in Ockham's thinking this is because adding more hypotheses to your explanation increases the risk of it being false, as each hypothesis comes with its own risk of falsity. Another popular formulation of the principle is: entities are not to be multiplied without necessity.

Nominalism

In metaphysics Ockham developed a theory that **universals**, such as "blueness", "old", "humanity", exist only as concepts invented in our minds in order to help us understand how different things can be united by a common feature or form. In this he was responding to the challenge first posed by **Heraclitus**, to explain how things are the same despite their differences. Heraclitus concluded that nothing stays the same – you can never step into the same river twice – so all of reality must be in flux. But his conclusion made science impossible – we can never really know anything if nothing ever remains the same. This **scepticism** was avoided by **Plato** by positing abstract universal essences of things ("**Ideas**"), the invisible structures of material objects that explain their shared characteristics, such as the shared characteristic of being old, or young. However, Ockham rejected Plato's theory (known as **metaphysical realism**) because he thought it rested on a contradiction – that a universal essence is both

For logic is the most useful tool of all the arts. Without it no science can be fully known. It is not worn out by repeated use, after the manner of material tools, but rather admits of continual growth through the diligent exercise of any other science.

Prefatory Letter, *Summa Logicae* (c.1320s)

The Papal Palace, Avignon, where Ockham was summoned and charged with heresy.

Legacy, truth, consequence

- Ockham helped to reform **scholasticism** towards simplification. The principle of parsimony in Ockham's Razor, associated with Ockham, has made an important contribution to theory building both in science and philosophy to this day.
- His teachings marked a break with previous **medieval philosophy**, in particular the work of Thomas Aquinas.
- He came to believe that logic can be studied outside the province of metaphysics, a position that proved important in the development of scientific inquiry.
- In logic, Ockham formed a basis for what would later be termed "De Morgan's Laws" – after Augustus de Morgan (1806–71). Ockham's work towards a system of logic using three truth values (the standard being two truth values for each **proposition**: true or false) would be developed further by modern logicians, for example, Jan Lukasiewicz (1878–1956).

For nothing ought to be posited without a reason given, unless it is self-evident (literally, known through itself) or known by experience or proved by the authority of Sacred Scripture.

Ordinatio (1317–18)

Key dates

c.1287	Born, probably in the village of Ockham in the south of England.
c.1296	Educated at London Greyfriars, house of the Franciscan Order.
c.1309	Begins his theological training at Oxford University but returns to London Greyfriars before gaining his full qualification.
1317–18	Writes a commentary on the Sentences of Peter Lombard: *Ordinatio*.
By 1324	Writes an *Exposition of Aristotle's Physics* (incomplete) and *Questions on Aristotle's Books of the Physics*.
1324	Called to defend his views in front of a papal commission in Avignon, France. Becomes irretrievably entangled in a political–theological debate.
By 1327	Writes *Summa Logicae*, a lengthy treatment of logic and semantics.
1328	Flees to Italy and is excommunicated by the pope.
1329	Moves to Munich under protection of Louis of Bavaria.
1340–1	Writes *Eight Questions on the Power of the Pope*.
1347	Dies in Munich.

one thing and many things at the same time – and therefore cannot be true. Ockham's **nominalist**/conceptualist alternative was that universals are concepts caused in our minds when we perceive similar attributes of things in the world. Thus, there are only individual objects in the world; universals are not real things that exist in abstract form – as Plato's theory implied, and which Ockham condemned as *"the worst error of philosophy"*.

Direct realism

Like Aristotle, Ockham believed that knowledge is acquired through **perceptions** of the world, by observing the characteristics of objects – the theory known as **empiricism** (which contrasts with **rationalism**, where knowledge is gained through reason). On Ockham's version of empiricism, if you see the sea, for example, its blue color causes you to know that it is blue. Direct realism, as this theory came to be known, leads to scepticism because it doesn't explain the difference between perceiving something in reality and perceiving something through a dream or an hallucination that is not really there in the world. Many later philosophers rejected direct realism for this reason.

Niccolò Machiavelli

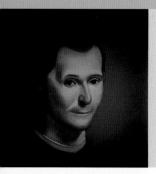

Niccolò Machiavelli was a Florentine diplomat and political philosopher. Although his name has become synonymous with political expediency, cunning, and the acquisition of power at all costs, this pejorative sense of "Machiavellian" does the philosopher many injustices. Machiavelli was a pragmatist and a patriot who yearned for Italian political stability.

Machiavelli was born in Florence, the second son of Bernardo di Niccolò Machiavelli, a lawyer, and of Bartolommea di Stefano Nelli. After a humanist education, he entered governmental service in Florence as a clerk and ambassador in 1498, soon after the city had expelled the ruling Medici family and restored itself as a republic.

Between 1499 and 1512, Machiavelli undertook a number of diplomatic missions on behalf of the Florentine republic to the court of Louis XII in France, Ferdinand II of Aragón, and the Papacy in Rome. He also bore witness, from 1502 to 1503, to the effective – if often brutal – state-building methods of Cesare Borgia, or Duke Valentino.

During the Renaissance, Italy was a scene of intense political conflict involving the dominant city-states of Florence, Milan, Venice, and Naples, plus the Papacy, France, Spain, and the Holy Roman Empire. Each city attempted to protect itself by playing the larger powers off against each other. Machiavelli's direct experience of this political turmoil during his diplomatic career was central to the formation of his **political philosophy**.

When, in 1512, the Medici family regained control of Florence, Machiavelli was banished, imprisoned, and tortured on suspicion of conspiring against the Medici. After his release in 1513, he withdrew from public life to virtual exile on his estate near Florence, where he devoted his last years to studying the ancients and to writing.

Machiavelli died in 1527, in the same year that Rome was sacked by Charles V, and the Medici rule of Florence was once more interrupted. It was not until five years after Machiavelli's death, however, that the bulk of his writing was to be published, including *The Prince* and *Discourses on Livy* – works that would ensure his contribution to the development of political philosophy.

> *No enterprise is more likely to succeed than one concealed from the enemy until it is ripe for execution.*
>
> The Art of War (1521)

Essential philosophy

Machiavelli's approach to political philosophy is an **empirical** one, based on his own observations of governance in Renaissance Italy and on his interpretations of the ancient Greek and Roman systems of government. Unlike the **humanists**, he does not seek to idealize the perfect state. Instead, he takes a pragmatic approach to the achievement of clear political objectives: national independence, security, and a well-ordered constitution.

The Prince

Machiavelli's most famous work, *The Prince* (*Il Principe*, 1513; pub. 1532), was not a work of detached scholarship, but a passionate treatise addressed to Lorenzo de Medici in an attempt to regain access to the political process from which the author found himself exiled. In that respect, it failed: Machiavelli was doomed to remain on the outside of political life until his death in 1527. But posthumous publication of *The Prince* in 1532 marked a turning point in political thinking.

The Prince clearly sets out a vision of monarchical **absolutism** as a program for effective government. Machiavelli's thesis is that the stability of the state is paramount, that law and order must be imposed, and that it is the duty of a prince to bring whatever mix of force, audacity, prudence, virtue, or apparent virtue is necessary to maintain the order and stability of his state. An effective prince must "*be a fox to recognize traps, and a lion to frighten wolves*", matching his ferocity or cruelty to the needs of the greater good:

> "*We may call cruelty well applied (if indeed we may call that well which in itself is evil) when it is committed once from necessity for self-protection, and afterwards not persisted in, but converted as far as possible to the public good.*" (*The Prince*)

The Prince has been interpreted in many ways: as sincere advice, as a plea for political office, as a detached analysis of Italian politics, as evidence of early Italian nationalism, and as political satire on Medici rule. The fact that Machiavelli saw fit to analyze political expediency in so ruthless and honest a fashion – or, in the words of **Francis Bacon**, that he wrote "*what men do, and not what they ought to do*" – marks out *The Prince* as a thoroughly "modern" text.

The work must also be seen as written against the backdrop of a Renaissance Italy riven by political intrigue, blackmail, and

Legacy, truth, consequence

- Machiavelli's apparent abandonment of morality in *The Prince* in favor of political expediency led to the work being placed on the *Index of Prohibited Books* by the Catholic Church in 1559.
- Other Renaissance **humanists**, such as Desiderius Erasmus (1466–1536) and **Francis Bacon**, also condemned the seeming immorality of *The Prince*.
- By the 1570s the term "Machiavellian" had been appropriated into the English language to mean "practicing duplicity in statecraft or in general conduct; astute, cunning, intriguing" (*Oxford English Dictionary*).

- Elements of Machiavelli's ideas on statecraft, kingship, and politics, as well as the popular misconception of him as an unscrupulous power-monger, can clearly be seen in the works of Shakespeare and other dramatists of the English Renaissance (see, for example, *Richard III*, *Othello* (the character Iago), *The Jew of Malta*).
- **Jean-Jacques Rousseau** defended Machiavelli as "*a proper man and a good citizen … veiling his love of liberty in the midst of his country's oppression*". Rousseau believed that the *Discourses* (and the *History of Florence*) were more representative of Machiavelli's true philosophy, maintaining "*that this profound political thinker has so far been studied only by superficial or corrupt readers*" (*The Social Contract*).

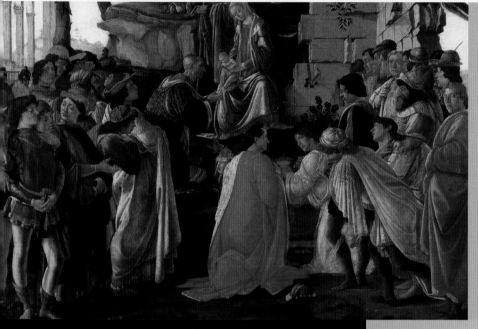

The Medici family pictured in Sandro Botticelli's *Adoration of the Magi*.

> **This, then, gives rise to the question whether it is better to be loved rather than feared, or feared rather than loved. It might perhaps be answered that we should wish to be both; but since love and fear can hardly exist together… it is far safer to be feared than loved.**
>
> *The Prince (1532)*

violence, and constantly at the mercy of invading foreign powers. In its conclusion Machiavelli issued an impassioned call for Italian unity, and an end to foreign intervention.

Discourses on Livy

Less widely read but more indicative of Machiavelli's politics is his *Discourses On The First Ten Books Of Livy* (1512–17; pub. 1531). In this work Machiavelli expounded a general theory of politics and government that stressed the importance of an uncorrupted political culture and a vigorous political morality:

> "*In a well-ordered republic it should never be necessary to resort to extra-constitutional measures.*"
>
> (*Discourses on Livy*, Book I)

Vaster in conception than *The Prince*, the *Discourses on Livy* clearly reveal Machiavelli's republican principles:

> "*the governments of the people are better than those of princes.*"

These principles are also reflected in his *History of Florence* (1520–5; pub. 1532), a historical and literary masterpiece that is entirely modern in concept.

Key dates

1469	Born in Florence, Italy.
1498	Made Secretary of "The Ten", a Florentine board which had management of foreign affairs.
1502–03	Sent on diplomatic mission to Cesare Borgia, the Duke Valentino.
1503–9	Responsible for the Florentine militia.
1507	Sent on diplomatic mission to Emperor Maximillian.
1509	Florence's citizen forces defeat Pisa under Machiavelli's direction.
1510	Sent on diplomatic mission to France, which consolidated the alliance of Florence and France.
1512	Restoration of the Medici rule in Florence.
1513	Imprisoned, tortured, and released; writes *The Prince*.
1513–27	Retires to an estate near Florence, where his key works are written.
1521	Publication of *The Art of War*.
1527	Dies in Florence.
1531	Posthumous publication of *Discourses on Livy*.
1532	Posthumous publication of *The Prince* and *History of Florence*.

Francis Bacon

Bacon was the first major figure in the change from the medieval scholastic intellectual environment to that of modern science. Poet, historian, essayist, scientist, lawyer, philosopher, and statesman, he was typical of a Renaissance humanist ideal, but his substantive achievement sees him widely acknowledged as the father of modern scientific method, and as inaugurator of the philosophical tradition of British empiricism.

Bacon was born into a family used to political influence. His father, Sir Nicholas Bacon, was Lord Keeper of the seal under Queen Elizabeth I; his mother was the daughter of Sir Anthony Coke, a leading **humanist**; and his uncle was Lord Burghley – Elizabeth's chief minister. The values of intellectual pursuit and public service were imbued from an early age and his philosophy can be said to be a merging of these two strands.

At college Bacon recognized the shortcomings of the prevailing intellectual orthodoxy: a broadly **Aristotelian rationalism** filtered through a tradition of **scholastic** commentary. By the sixteenth century, tired and bankrupt, it was producing nothing new. Established precedent, together with the manipulation of **axioms** (specifically following **Aristotle**'s logical principles) made for a climate that seemed to reduce intellectual ambition and the search for truth to the **logic**-chopping of individuals confined to university circles. The contrast with technological advance was significant: Bacon quotes with admiration the transforming inventions of printing, gunpowder, and the compass :"*Men have been kept back as by a kind of enchantment from progress in the sciences by reverence for*

antiquity, by the authority of men accounted great in philosophy", so that "*philosophy and the intellectual sciences … stand like statues, worshipped and celebrated but not moved and advanced*". Bacon was an intellectual optimist and believed science to be at the center of advance towards real and complete knowledge of the world, and the purpose of which was absolutely to improve the life of mankind in real practical ways.

Throughout his life Bacon's scientific and philosophical work ran alongside his life in politics. Having traveled early on to France as secretary to the English ambassador, he went also to Italy and Spain, acquainting himself with developments abroad and the work of his contemporaries Galileo Galilei and Johannes Kepler. Back in England he maintained these contacts by regular correspondence. It's astonishing how much he produced (the Oxford edition of his works runs to 13 volumes) given his level of activity in parliament, as lawyer and politician. Bacon's determination to succeed in politics seems less a selfish ambition than as an example of the moral requirement to act and effect in the public domain of lived human experience. That was where meaning lay and it was the ultimate source of significance in all his thought.

Essential philosophy

Bacon's entire philosophical system was summed up in his major work the *Instauratio Magna* of 1620. This "great restoration" of human knowledge lay incomplete at his death. He believed he was turning on its head Aristotle's science of **deductive reasoning** proceeding from **axioms**. In Aristotle, **syllogistic** argument takes the place of experiment even in investigating the natural world. For Bacon, science should end in the establishment of general axioms rather than begin from them; and it was to proceed **inductively**, from experience.

Idols

However, our analysis of the evidence of experience needs checking because of "*important and profound… fallacies in the mind of man*". Human faculties are subject to four "idols" or prejudices, which can prevent objective judgement:
1. Idols of the Tribe (i.e. mankind): it's not just that we make mistakes in interpreting what our senses seem to be telling us; it's also that "*the*

mind of man is far from the nature of a clear and equal glass … it is rather … full of superstition and imposture". We must "*consider the false appearances that are imposed upon us by the general nature of the mind*".
2. Idols of the Cave: those private prejudices we have as individuals due to our upbringing, education, personality. We have to learn to question these.
3. Idols of the Marketplace: in the public domain, where we meet, communicate, and deal with one another. Bacon is thinking about language, not just our own misinterpretations of each other and lack of clarity, but the philosophically suggestive fact that we have words for things that are not necessarily to be considered "things". We need evidence beyond words before we can assert the existence of things named by words.
4. Idols of the Theater: these are errors of traditional philosophy which he calls merely rhetorical or play-acting – asserted, not rigorously tested or experimented upon.

■ Bacon accomplished a radical shift in the governing intellectual climate. His project of establishing a sure footing for approaching questions of scientific fact by observing relevant instances and clarifying them by experiment and measurement has been seen as the initial step towards modern scientific values and the **Enlightenment**. He helped found the increasingly central preoccupation of modern **Western philosophy** with **epistemology**, and the philosophical tradition of **empiricism**. A procedure for finding an answer was for him essential. For succeeding philosophers like **Thomas Hobbes** and **John Locke**, this aim became a model for investigating questions of **metaphysics**, morality, religion, and politics.

■ Bacon was not so much concerned with knowledge as intellectual certainty, but rather its practical value in life. His experimental optimism didn't disguise his sense that scientific method could not produce positive logical certainly: experiments confirming a hypothesis do not prove it; however, negatively, an experiment can disprove a hypothesis with certainty, which can be more useful. One could say that Bacon was initiating a move that resonates in the work of Locke and **David Hume**, of allowing a place for probability over certainty. In the twentieth century **Karl Popper**'s work in the philosophy of science gave a central place to falsifiability and similarly put this principle of science at the center of the humanist enterprise.

■ The justification of scientific investigation and its aim (knowledge) Bacon saw in moral (societal) terms: a kind of utopia that he elaborated in his last work, *New Atlantis*. In this, the academy he called the House of Solomon was consciously drawn on by the founders of the Royal Society of London in the late seventeenth century, and it inspired Denis Diderot (1713–84), editor of the French *Encyclopédie*. In the twentieth century **John Dewey** saw in Bacon a precursor of his own **pragmatist** philosophy of science.

■ Bacon's belief that we could know about the natural world and that it was a moral requirement to do so, because thereby we could control its processes to benefit mankind, dominated Europe for generations: the Enlightenment ethic of benign scientific progress. To some thinkers from **Karl Marx** onwards (and especially in our own time **Martin Heidegger**), Bacon's romance of technology has been seen as a disastrous process leading to man's alienation from the natural world he seeks to exploit and dominate.

Frontispiece of *Instauratio Magna*, 1620. The ship is sailing into the open sea of knowledge, beyond the limits of classical scholarship.

Knowledge is power.

Meditationes Sacrae (1597)

New scientific method

The way forward must use the tool of experimentation. Inductive methods are not to be simply the adding together of instances. Rather, natural phenomena must be analysed from their complex to their simple parts or properties. Against Aristotle, Bacon takes a **pre-Socratic materialist** and **atomist** view: "*the natural motion of the atom, which is indeed the original and unique force that constitutes and fashions all things out of matter*". To investigate these properties, experimental evidence must establish lists of instances of their presence, absence, and increases and decreases in objects (his Tables of Presence, Absence, and Degrees or Comparisons). From these exhaustively carried out "natural histories", **hypotheses** can be formed and these can inform further experimental testing until general axioms are established.

Key dates

1561	Born in London.
1573	Attends Trinity College Cambridge.
1577	Begins his political career working for the English ambassador in Paris.
1581	Becomes a member of parliament – and remains so for 37 years.
1584	Writes "A Letter of Advice to Queen Elizabeth", among other things arguing for measures against Catholics.
1592	Becomes advisor to the Earl of Essex.
1597	Publishes first edition of *Essays*. He distances himself from Essex as the Earl loses favor.
1603	On accession of James I, Bacon's political fortunes begin to rise. He works for the new king and is knighted.
1605	Publishes *The Advancement of Learning*.
1618	Becomes Lord Chancellor and created a Baron.
1620	Publishes the *Instauratio Magna*, including the *Novum Organum*.
1621	Becomes Viscount St Albans, but largely for political reasons is impeached for corruption.
1621-6	Deprived of his offices and seat in parliament, he retires and spends his last years focusing on philosophical, scientific, and literary works.
1626	Dies of pneumonia – supposedly after experimenting with ice to ascertain its food-preserving qualities.
1627	*The New Atlantis* is published posthumously.

Thomas Hobbes

Hobbes is most famous for his counterintuitive conclusion that in society we must sacrifice individual freedoms in order to guarantee the wellbeing of the whole community. Although his idea of a "social contract" has seen him accepted as the father of modern political philosophy, actually more significant was his grounding of politics on a thoroughgoing materialist and mechanistic metaphysics.

Born in comparative poverty to a country vicar who died young, Hobbes' classical education was maintained by a wealthier uncle. After graduating from Oxford he became tutor to the Cavendish family. Moving in influential circles he met **Francis Bacon**, William Harvey, Galileo Galilei, and **René Descartes**.

The intellectual climate of the time had been influenced very strongly by the Protestant revolution against centralized authority; and the publication for the first time in the 1560s of the texts of Greek **scepticism** made central to philosophical thinking the question of knowledge: how possible is it? How certain can it be? It is difficult not to see this, and the intense ideological ferment of the years leading up to the civil war in England, as instrumental in motivating Hobbes' concerns and approach. He was impressed by successes in many fields of the sciences: astronomy, medicine (Harvey's discovery of the circulation of the blood), and mathematics, and was profoundly affected by the advances made

in physics in the work of Galileo on momentum and bodies in motion, and particularly by his study of Euclid's geometry. These showed conclusions reached with certainty. They seemed to promise stability beyond dispute, beyond the civil wars of philosophy or politics – the kind of self-defeating strife which was the epitome of chaos and anarchy, for Hobbes the ultimate evil.

Because of his pro-monarchist views he had to leave the country, joining Prince Charles in exile as his tutor. However, already considered a probable atheist, his defense of a monarchy as crucially dependent on the will of the people undermined the notion of the Divine Right of Kings and further antagonized the royal party in exile: he had to return to England.

Hobbes experienced little stability himself and, though left undisturbed through the Interregnum and the restoration of the monarchy in 1660 under Charles II, he lived in fear of persecution and was frequently the victim of opposing opinion.

Essential philosophy

Hobbes produced, over a long life, several versions of his system, often translating from his own Latin or English original. But it was *Leviathan* in 1651 that made him famous throughout Europe and in which he sums up and enlarges upon his previous thoughts on the whole of philosophy. At a time when thinkers did not yet distinguish within the field of "science" between philosophy and physics, it dealt with "bodies natural" (the physics of the natural world), the "dispositions and manners of men" (**moral philosophy**) and the "civil duties of subjects" (**political philosophy**).

Materialism and empiricism
Rather than proceeding simply on the basis of Bacon's **empiricist** methodology (producing a system as an **hypothesis** to explain the facts of experience), Hobbes begins by examining the experience of perceiving facts itself. The world can be known. It is known through the senses first and it is known as physical bodies in motion. In other words, **atomistic materialism**: reality is to be understood in terms of the mechanics of physical objects – from the planets to the inner workings of the mind. Philosophy's task is to produce a "geometry" of the laws of motion of bodies which

gives an account of the natural world. "*The gate of natural philosophy universal … is the knowledge of the nature of motion.*" Hobbes' empiricism, that knowledge begins in **sense perception**, and sense perception is ultimately to be seen as matter in motion, is a harbinger of modern science. He goes on to pioneer a materialist psychology (theory of mind): not only sensations but all mental activities (thinking, emotions, dreaming, imagination) are corporeal motions of the brain and certainly not separately existing entities.

State of nature
Emotions of individuals are to be analysed in terms of the mechanistic reactions of bodies to physical stimuli, either of attraction to what is desired or repulsion from what is to be avoided. Everything comes down to this – the natural world of the individual – and conflict necessarily ensues between the desires and fears of

> *The universe is corporeal; all that is real is material, and what is not material is not real.*
>
> Leviathan (1651)

- In furthering Francis Bacon's project of establishing a science of the natural world, Hobbes tried to give a "logic" to human affairs: his recommendations were not merely pragmatic, they were meant to be essential and necessary.

- In his own time Hobbes was controversial for his radical **metaphysics** and his ambiguously religious materialism. He has been influential on the whole succeeding history of political philosophy. The social contract in particular has been a source of fruitful opposition and development in **John Locke**, **Baruch Spinoza**, **Jean-Jacques Rousseau**, and even **Karl Marx**. It has contributed to **constructivist** ideas of morality and truth (that their reality is purely a useful construction).

- Hobbes' writing introduces a vocabulary and ethos that resonates through empiricism to **logical atomism** and later: philosophy's task as developing and assessing scientific endeavors with a view to revealing the ultimate building blocks of the natural world. His idea of the natural state as being necessarily one of conflict may have contributed to Charles Darwin's purposive modification in the "survival of the fittest", and Hobbes has a place in any discussion of scepticism, materialism, and **free will** and **determinism**. He has been fundamental to the development of the nineteenth-century ethical doctrine of **utilitarianism** in basing his moral recommendations on the rational working out of a metaphysical system (rather than the word of God).

- More recently it has been his extreme conservative authoritarian politics that have proved controversial. In both his politics and his metaphysics there are subtle ambiguities that still provoke debate, as does his controversial view of mankind as essentially machines in motion.

> *The passions that incline men to peace are: fear of death; desire of such things as are necessary to commodious living; and a hope by their industry to obtain them.*
> Leviathan (1651)

1588	Born in Malmesbury, England.
1608	Graduates from Magdalene College, Oxford. Begins a career as a tutor, chiefly within the Cavendish family (future Earls of Devonshire), during which time he travels on the continent and meets scientists and philosophers, such as Galileo Galilei and René Descartes.
1640	Publishes *The Elements of Law* – a defense of the king's position as Supreme Governor. Fearing parliamentarian reprisals he flees to France.
1642	Publishes *De Cive* (*On the Citizen*), introducing his political and moral philosophy.
1642–51	Civil War in England.
1651	Returns to England and publishes his magnum opus *Leviathan*.
1655	Publishes *De Corpore* (*On Bodies*), his materialist metaphysics.
1657	Publishes *De Homine* (*On Mankind*), his moral philosophy.
1679	Dies in Derbyshire, England.
1682	*Behemoth, or The Long Parliament* is published posthumously containing Hobbes' account of the civil wars, the experience of which motivates so many of his concerns.

competing individuals. Hobbes famously summed up life in its natural state as "*solitary, poor, nasty, brutish and short*" (*Leviathan*, 1651).

Social contract

In contrast to this natural state an artificial one, a "**Leviathan**", has been created: a social contract constructed to form a society in which all individuals assent to give up their natural rights and obey a sovereign authority for the sake of safety, protection, and freedom from the terrible and inevitable consequences of the natural life.

Absolutism

This central authority could be of various forms: a monarchy, an oligarchy, a **democratic** assembly, or a totalitarian party. Hobbes strongly favored a monarchy but the key point was that the authority itself was to have absolute power. There should be no separation of civil, military, judicial, or ecclesiastical power, because that might lead to internal conflict. However, the ruler's authority was to depend ultimately on the will of the ruled, and not on any outside authority, for example God. The contract had, by definition, to be upheld by both sides: obedience on the one, protection on the other.

Detail of the frontispiece from *Leviathan* (1651), showing the state as a giant made up of individuals.

René Descartes

The most important Western philosopher since Plato and Aristotle, and a key figure in the intellectual revolution of the seventeenth century, Descartes laid the scientific and philosophical foundations for the modern age. He is famous for prizing the certainty of reason above the fallible deliverances of the senses, and seeking to build our knowledge of the world on the foundation of our indubitable existence.

As a young boy Descartes was sent to the college La Flèche in Anjou in western France, where he was instructed in the **scholastic** philosophy that his own work would eventually supersede. Much of Descartes' early work would now be classed as scientific or mathematical rather than philosophical, though at the time no such clear distinction between science and **natural philosophy** was recognized. His *Le Monde*, written in the early 1630s, was a treatise on cosmology and physics; an attempt to explain the behavior of the physical world in terms of simple mechanisms rather than the opaque scholastic notions of "real

qualities" and "substantial forms". Descartes sought to explain the physical behavior of the universe in terms of uniform matter, hypothesized to be of the same type throughout the universe, on earth and in the heavens. In fear he withdrew the book in 1633 before its widespread publication, having heard about Rome's condemnation of Galileo Galilei (1564–1642) for claiming that the earth goes round the sun at the center of the universe.

In 1637 Descartes anonymously published three treatises on geometry, optics, and meteorology. Along with these he published his *Discourse on the Method of Rightly Conducting Reason and Reaching*

Essential philosophy

The method of doubt

Descartes' primary objective in his *Meditations on First Philosophy* (1641) was to place his knowledge of the world on some firm and unshakeable foundations. To do this he adopted a method of doubt, subjecting all of his previously held beliefs to scrutiny. In this way he aimed to cast out all of those beliefs that could possibly be in error and be left with those of whose certainty he could be assured. As a consequence he claimed that beliefs based on **sense experiences** all carry with them the possibility of error – as when a straight stick appears bent in the water or a curved object like the surface of the earth looks flat – and as such are doubtful.

> "*The senses deceive from time to time, and it is prudent never to trust wholly those who have deceived us even once.*"
>
> (First Meditation)

But Descartes recognized that, in most ordinary cases, possible doubts about the deliverances of sense experience can be alleviated. For example, I can check up on whether my experience is misleading me through further sensory experiences so as to guard against the possibility of one-off mistakes, as when I reach into the water and find the stick that looks bent to be straight. In a passage that has come to be known as the "dreaming argument", Descartes raises a more powerful form of doubt about our everyday beliefs. He asks us to consider our most vivid dreams, those that are indistinguishable to us from waking life so long as we are having them. During such dreams

there are no apparent marks that serve to identify the experience as a dream from the sufferer's point of view. Hence, it is conceivable that my belief that I am sitting here reading a book could be based on a misleading but inscrutable dream experience. As far as I can tell, I might be having a vivid dream such as this, rendering my belief false.

But the doubting does not end there. Even if deliverances of the senses could be doubted on the **hypothesis** they might constitute a dream world, we might think we could still rely on the existence of the external objects that make up a world beyond my dreaming. Descartes asks us to subject our beliefs to an even more pervasive form of doubt. He asks us to consider the possibility of a "*malicious demon of the utmost power and cunning*" that chooses to mislead us in the most fundamental ways. In such a scenario, the existence of external objects could be a delusion conjured up by the demon for his own sport. Moreover, the malicious demon might mislead us even in our mathematical and logical reasoning.

The *cogito*

Though Descartes subjected our ordinary beliefs to these three waves of doubt, he found that there was at least one belief that he could not coherently doubt and which provided him with the bedrock of certainty. This was his belief in his own existence:

> "*Let the demon deceive me as much as he may... I am, I exist is certain, so long as it is put forward by me or conceived in my mind.*"
>
> (Second Meditation)

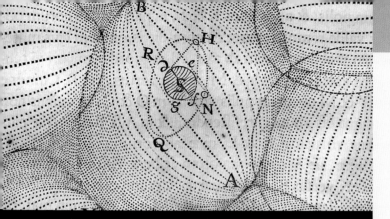

This image from Descartes' *Principles of Philosophy* (1644) desribes his mechanistic view of the universe, consisting of huge whirlpools ("vortices") of cosmic matter.

■ Descartes' **epistemological** project of finding a foundation for our knowledge of the world is still an influential one, and his forms of doubt provide the basis for contemporary accounts of **scepticism**.

■ The problems that Descartes raised about the mind and the body have been grouped together as the **"mind-body problem"** and continue to exercise philosophers today. The relationship between the objective world as described by the physical sciences and the inner world of the mind of which each of us is directly aware still raises deep puzzles (see the entry on **Gilbert Ryle** for a contrary view to Descartes'.)

... despite being cultivated for many centuries by the best minds, [philosophy] contained no point which was not disputed and hence doubtful.

Discourse on the Method (1637)

Key dates

Truth in the Sciences, which outlines his approach to philosophical questions as well as some scientific theses. The book engages with several of the central philosophical themes that Descartes would give a fuller treatment in his masterpiece *Meditations on First Philosophy*, published in 1641. Descartes' last work, *The Passions of the Soul*, was written shortly before his visit to Sweden in the winter of 1649–50. He was to teach a Swedish princess. But when forced to break his long-kept habit of sleeping to midday, he developed pneumonia on the cold Swedish mornings, and died before reaching his fifty-fourth birthday.

My putting forward or conceiving the **proposition** that I exist assumes or requires the existence of the "I" that is the subject of the proposition. This argument is often known as the *cogito*, taken from the Latin phrase "*cogito ergo sum*" ("I think, therefore I am"). As long as we are thinking, Descartes claimed, we cannot but be certain of our existence. It is from this certain foundation that he hoped to build up our knowledge of the rest of the world. His means of establishing our knowledge of the world on this basis was to use the powers of thinking mentioned in the *cogito* to prove the existence of God. Given the existence of a perfect God who is the source of all truth, Descartes then hoped to secure all our worldly knowledge. Though humans can make mistakes and believe things that are not true, Descartes thought that the benevolence of God establishes the overall reliability of the human mind. However, contemporaries of Descartes were anxious to point out that if we need to establish God's existence to ensure the reliability of our intellect then we cannot rely on that intellect in proving God's existence. This is known as the "Cartesian circle".

Cartesian dualism

Descartes believed that the mind, or thinking substance ("*res cogitans*"), is wholly distinct from the world of matter and physical substance. For Descartes, the matter, on which the mechanisms of the physical world operate, is extended, divisible, and spatially located. The mind is unextended, indivisible, and not spatially located. Descartes also held that each individual knows the existence of his own mind and its content better than we know the external world of matter. In contrasting mechanism and mind, Descartes raised legitimate questions about how the freedom of human thought and expression could be the result of mechanisms. He also raised an influential argument in favor of the conceivability of our existing independently of our body. He concluded that the mind, or soul, is "*entirely distinct from the body, and would not fail to exist even if the body failed to exist.*" (*Discourse on the Method*, 1637). But if we suppose that the mind is made up from a distinct sort of substance to the body, as Descartes did, many think it becomes impossible to give a coherent account of their intimate connection.

Baruch Spinoza

Baruch Spinoza was one of the great rationalists of seventeenth-century Western philosophy. Rationalism played a significant role in the development of Renaissance thought, and writers in this tradition set out to try to work out a system of knowledge that was derived by pure reason, logic, and contemplation rather than by observing facts as was the practice of the empiricists. Spinoza's writings made significant contributions in many areas of philosophy, in particular in ethics.

Together with **René Descartes** and **Gottfried Leibniz**, Spinoza was one of a triumvirate of **rationalists** in Continental Europe. Each of these three writers concluded that he could build his system on the basis of the certainty of God. However, their philosophical methods undermined the medieval dependence on the priesthood as the source of authority, by emphasizing the role of the individual in seeking knowledge, laying the groundwork for the eighteenth-century **Enlightenment**.

The order and connection of ideas is the same as the order and connection of things.

Ethics (1677)

Spinoza came from a Portuguese Jewish family, who lived in exile in Holland. He had a rabbinical education but was expelled from the Amsterdam synagogue for his defence of heretical opinions. Studying privately, he explored medieval Jewish thought, the philosophy of Descartes, and new scientific ideas. He made a living as a lens-grinder, and his death in 1677 may have been caused by this labor.

Spinoza's early philosophical works became known around Europe, and he was offered an academic post at Heidelberg in 1673, but preferred to retain his independence. His first published work, *The Principles of Descartes' Philosophy* (1663), included most of the basic tenets of his philosophical system, although his monumental, five-volume *Ethica Ordine Geometrico Demonstrata* (*Ethics*), published posthumously in 1677, was a more detailed account. During his lifetime he also published *Tractatus Theologico-Politicus* (*A Theologico-Political Treatise*, 1670), in which he attacked anthropomorphic conceptions of God, proposed historical and critical methods for biblical interpretation, and defended religious toleration.

Essential philosophy

In his philosophical writing, Spinoza took **Cartesian rationalism** as a starting point, and explored his conviction that the universe was a unitary whole. Like Descartes, he used mathematical reasoning and **logic** as his building blocks, and *Ethics* is laid out in the style of a geometrical set of definitions and self-evident **axioms**. There is also some influence in his writing from medieval **scholasticism** and Jewish tradition.

Spinoza describes the universe as a single, coherent whole in which the rigid laws of logical necessity hold sway. He talks of the single substance that makes up the universe as "God or Nature", which for him are alternative names for an identical reality. In his view, all things are determined by God or Nature to exist and to cause effects. The complicated chain of causes and effects is something that we can only partially understand. His view of **logical necessity** and cause and effect leads him to a thoroughgoing **determinism**. As ever, determinism leads him to have to confront the problem of **free will** – humans feel that they choose their own actions, so the idea that our every move is simply an effect of logical causation conflicts with our **perceptions** of the world.

Spinoza attempts to resolve this problem by pointing to our limited comprehension of **causality**. We believe we have free will because we are aware of our appetites but can't fully understand the reasons we have them. Our genuine freedom consists in our capacity to know that our actions are determined. If we form more adequate ideas about what we do and about our emotions, then we become active participants rather than passive actors – we become freer and more like God when we accept that our actions are mere effects of God or Nature. This is an ingenious piece of thinking, and one that prefigures the later work of **Arthur Schopenhauer** and **Friedrich Nietzsche** who wrote about rationality as merely an interpretation of will. However, for many it remains a unsatisfactory explanation of free will. Spinoza accepts that his **ethical** conclusions are difficult, but suggests that our only path to goodness comes from understanding our place in the structure of the universe and accepting it.

The unitary universe

Spinoza's entire system rests on his initial "proof" that the universe is a single substance. His justification for this conclusion depends

Legacy, truth, consequence

- In the period immediately following Spinoza's death, he was seen as a dangerous, anti-religious thinker. Even though God was at the center of his system, many thought that Spinozism would lead on to **pantheism**, or to atheistic **materialism**.

- By identifying God and nature, Spinoza did encourage those who were looking for a less authoritarian basis for religion – his popularity through the Enlightenment was partly based on this identification of spirit and nature.

- In the long run, Spinoza's reputation is a more complex one. He is a subtle, fascinating thinker, and philosophers as varied as **Friedrich Nietzsche, Ludwig Wittgenstein**, and Gilles Deleuze (1925–95) have praised his work.

- Whatever Spinoza's virtues, the project of rationalism can't be seen as a complete success. Each of the great rationalists claimed their system to have been deduced unfailingly from first principles – yet each reached very different conclusions, just as the **pre-Socratics** had when they debated the nature of reality. The differences even came down to basics such as whether the universe consists of atoms, Leibniz's "monads", or Spinoza's indivisible substance. The fact that rationalism produced such different results merely emphasized the limits of pure reason in resolving the classic problems of philosophy.

> *God, or substance, consisting of infinite attributes, of which each expresses eternal and infinite essentiality, necessarily exists.*
>
> Ethics (1677)

Key dates

1632	Born in Amsterdam in the Netherlands.
1656	Excommunicated from the synagogue; devotes his life to philosophy.
1663	*The Principles of Descartes' Philosophy* is published.
1670	*Tractatus Theologico-Politicus* (*A Theologico-Political Treatise*) is published anonymously due to its controversial content.
1676	Spinoza meets with Leibniz in the Hague.
1677	*Ethica Ordine Geometrico Demonstrata* (*Ethics*) is published posthumously by friends.

Inside the Portuguese synagogue in Amsterdam, Emanuel de Witte, c.1680. Spinoza was expelled from the synagogue for his heretical opinions.

on a detailed set of axioms. He assumes that substance cannot be dependent on anything else for its existence and that no two substances can share the same nature, or have a causal relation with each other. As a result he concludes that substance cannot be caused, that it must be infinite, and that there must therefore be only one substance. He essentially accepts an **ontological argument** for the existence of God, which is the argument that God's essence includes his inevitable existence and the possession of infinite attributes. So Spinoza's conclusion of a single unitary substance becomes an extreme form of **monism** in which every mind, body, thought, and action are simply aspects of God.

The two attributes of the divine substance that are known to us are "thought and extension"; that is to say we can only perceive ideas and things. Spinoza devotes some time to exploring the possibility of human knowledge, concluding that genuine knowledge is possible. He proposes practical, rational methods by which humans can attain the best knowledge of which they are capable. His **dualism** is similar to Descartes', in that he views ideas and things as separate realms, although since both are expressions of the same infinite substance they inevitably relate to each other in perfect correlation. The problem of knowledge for Spinoza revolves around our inability to be certain that the ideas in our minds have a correlation to the material facts to which we believe they relate. God's mind and body are of course in perfect correlation, but imperfect humans must struggle through rationality to approach an understanding of the universe.

Opinion, reason, intuition

Spinoza distinguishes three kinds of knowledge. Opinion is unreliable, being sensory or language based. Reason is the operation of rationality, which can lead to indubitable knowledge only if it is based on adequate building blocks. Whereas intuition allows us to perceive the true and indubitable facts from which reason must proceed. So to discover knowledge we must ignore misleading sensory testimony and conventional learning. Then we must reason back to understand the eternal nature of God or Nature. Once we have this knowledge, our capacity for good or free actions depends on our understanding and accepting the divine nature of the universe.

John Locke

John Locke, from a modest rural background, rose through academic achievement to take part in the significant political developments of his age. He was the first great political liberal, defender of religious toleration and the rights of man, and theorist of revolution. His greatest work aimed to put all future intellectual endeavor on a sure footing by establishing the nature of thought itself.

Locke's life and work echo his predecessors, **Francis Bacon** and **Thomas Hobbes**. Running through their efforts is a preoccupation with contemporary politics and an intellectual concern with the problem of knowledge. The underlying theme can be summed up in the idea of "authority". Truth and our knowledge of it came to be seen as not found through a tradition of revealed or respected authorities, but in the analysis of experience through the exercise of our own mental faculties. Locke's aim of investigating the mind was fundamentally to authorize its procedures and establish its remit for all thinking.

He found fault at Oxford with the traditional intellectual environment. **René Descartes**' work and the new impetus it had given to philosophy on the Continent proved more fruitful. Like Bacon and Hobbes he found inspiration in the world of science. He followed the experimental advances of his friends Robert Boyle and Robert Hooke, and knew Isaac Newton whose

mathematics and mechanics he regarded with awe. This group of scientists, with its commitment to experiment, later became the famous Royal Society of London – standard bearer of truth in the physical sciences.

Friendship with the Earl of Shaftesbury ensured a succession of government appointments for Locke – during periods the Earl was not out of favor. Locke became an acknowledged expert on matters of finance and trade. However, his association with opposition politics necessitated his fleeing abroad. In France he experienced the religious toleration inaugurated by the Edict of Nantes (from 1598) and saw its revocation in 1685 result in the return of persecution. At the Glorious Revolution of 1688, which overturned the English king, James II, Locke returned with the new regime of William and Mary, under whose auspices his cause of a liberal constitutional monarchy was to triumph. All this must have encouraged the working out of his own political ideas.

Essential philosophy

Locke's major concern was the human mind and the mental capacities that enable us to know what we do.

Ideas and the "*tabula rasa*"
Locke introduces (via Descartes) the term "idea" which "*stands for whatsoever is the object of the understanding, when a man thinks*": ideas are what happens when we think.

Where do we get them? Against **Cartesian** and Christian "innate ideas" or properties of the mind (e.g. the logical and moral senses), Locke argues that the mind is empty, a "white paper" or *tabula rasa*, that gradually is written on through experience. Ideas are either "of sensation" (the simple product of the external world's stimulation of our senses) or "of reflection" (the complex product of the operation of our minds on these simple sense ideas), generating concepts like those of mathematics, morals, and religion. These are the twin sources of all our ideas. The world revealed by these **sense-data** is similarly one of complexes (objects) made up out of simples (atoms). Locke distinguishes, for objects, between their "primary qualities"(properties which they have independently of us, like shape, size, solidity) and their

"secondary qualities" (which they have in terms of our perceiving them, like color, taste, and smell). Sensory interaction with the world is necessary for, and results in, ideas and knowledge. All mental activity is derived from the senses and we cannot have any knowledge apart from our ideas, i.e. that is not derived from experience. These distinctions lead to a definition of the limits of our knowledge. Truth is seen as concerning **propositions** about the world. The limits to our knowledge will show us which propositions are determinable (as true or false).

Political philosophy
In his *Two Treatises of Government* (1690), Locke attacks the Divine Right of Kings – the predominant theory of government before the upheavals of the seventeenth century – replacing it with theories of natural rights and the **social contract**. For Hobbes, an equality of ability and a desire to attain one's ends was "the natural state" among humans before civilization. The laws of nature are merely a description of the way things are (a physics or natural history). But for Locke they are a prescription for the way things ought to be. Out of this "state of nature", or "natural

- Independent, commonsensical, liberal: Locke established the characteristics of a particularly British tradition through George Berkeley, David Hume, Jeremy Bentham, John Stuart Mill, up to Bertrand Russell and G. E. Moore.
- He was the first substantial theorist of epistemology: the core issue behind **Western philosophy** up to the twentieth century. In his concept of the organizing aspect of the mind, Locke made a vital contribution to the theme being worked out from Bacon to Immanuel Kant: the mind's conditioning of our experience.
- Locke's theory of value and property was of considerable influence on Karl Marx's social theory.
- His account of the self gave a central role to education in the emergence of the individual. Locke regarded it as part of the responsibility of government to legislate for an improving environment for its subjects. This has been important within social science, and also influenced psychiatry and Freud's ideas of childhood development.
- Locke aimed to establish limits to the understanding to determine what could and what could not be known. This move was very influential and can be seen in the twentieth century in **logical positivism**'s notion of limits to the meaningfulness of language and the **verificationist** claim within the **philosophy of language** that propositions which cannot be verified by the senses or logic are meaningless. **Ludwig Wittgenstein's** *Tractatus* and his seeking a limit to what can be thought/said (see pages 150–1) seem part of the same development.

William of Orange landing at Torbay in 1688. On the success of the Glorious Revolution, John Locke returned to England.

If by this enquiry into the nature of the Understanding I can discover the powers thereof; ... I suppose it may be of use to prevail with the busy mind of man to be more cautious in meddling with things exceeding its comprehension.

An Essay Concerning Human Understanding (1690)

law", Locke develops the concept of "natural rights". In his more optimistic view, man's natural state of equality need not lead to a conflict that only **authoritarianism** (by social contract) can control. It is a state of affairs that government (by social contract) defines itself as having to maintain: in which all men are equal in their right to "*life, health, liberty, and possessions*". In Locke's view the social contract isn't a contract between men (to institute government) but between government and those governed. Nor do the governed give up freedoms to the sovereign power (as in Hobbes). Rather, the social contract is set up to defend those liberties against that power. Men's rights limit the authority of the state, which for Hobbes was to have no limits. This makes explicit the right, and indeed obligation, of the governed to revolution when a government acts against these natural rights.

Locke argued in favor of religious toleration and in this area his political ideas follow from his **epistemology**, being based on acknowledging the limits of knowledge. There should be toleration of opposing beliefs where there is no possibility of something being known as true or false, which especially applies to matters of religion.

Key dates

1632	Born in Somerset, rural southwest England.
1652	Enters Christ Church College, Oxford.
1658–63	Lectures in classics, **rhetoric**, and **moral philosophy**.
1666	Meets the Earl of Shaftesbury, who becomes his employer and patron. Moves with his household to London.
1667	Publishes *An Essay Concerning Toleration* on his religious views. Shaftesbury secures him various government appointments.
1669–75	Becomes secretary to the Lords Proprietors of Carolina and the Council of Trade. On Shaftesbury's fall from favor he travels to France, later returning to Oxford.
1684	Flees to Holland with Shaftesbury to escape prosecution for alleged involvement in a plot to assassinate the king.
1687	Becomes advisor to William of Orange.
1688	On success of the Glorious Revolution, he returns to England.
1689	Issues first *Letter Concerning Toleration*; two more follow.
1690	*An Essay Concerning Human Understanding* and *Two Treatises of Government* are published.
1693	Publishes *Some Thoughts Concerning Education*.
1696–1700	Becomes a member of the reconstituted Council of Trade.
1704	Dies at the home of family friends in Essex, where he had been living in retirement.

Gottfried Leibniz

Gottfried Wilhelm Leibniz was a German rationalist philosopher, logician, mathematician, and polymath. He argued that the world is composed of single units (monads), each of which is self-contained but acts in harmony with every other, as ordained by God, and so this world is the best of all possible worlds. Leibniz also made the important distinction between necessary and contingent truths and devised a method of calculus independently of Isaac Newton.

Leibniz was born in Leipzig, in Saxony (now Germany), at the end of the Thirty Years' War. He entered Leipzig University aged 15, took a degree in law, then in 1666 refused the offer of a professorship from Altdorf University at Nürnberg, preferring to embark on a political and diplomatic career.

From then on he earned his living by combining the roles of councillor, diplomat, librarian, and historian, first for the elector of Mainz (from 1666 to 1673), and then the electors of Hanover (from 1676 to 1716). In his spare time he worked prodigiously on questions of philosophy, mathematics, logic, geology, and physics.

Leibniz's employment took him to the principal courts of Europe, from Paris to Saint Petersburg, where he met and struck up prolific correspondence with the most eminent figures of the day. In his youth he had been attracted by the works of **René Descartes**; he conversed with **Baruch Spinoza**; he also wrote a criticism of **John Locke**'s *Essay on Human Understanding*,

chapter by chapter, which he refused then to publish following Locke's death.

In 1700 Leibniz founded the German Academy of Sciences in Berlin with the support of the electress Sophia Charlotte (who in 1701 became the first queen of Prussia). In 1710 he wrote *The Theodicy* for Sophia Charlotte, in which he set down his ideas on divine justice and established his "principle of sufficient reason" (see below).

Although *The Theodicy* was the only complete book on philosophy that Leibniz published in his lifetime, he did publish considerable philosophical work in the leading, learned European journals of the time, for example: "Meditations on Knowledge, Truth, and Ideas" (1684), "Brief Demonstration of a Notable Error of Descartes" (1686), "Whether the Essence of Body Consists in Extension" (1691), "New System of Nature" (1695), and "On Nature Itself" (1698).

Essential philosophy

Leibniz never published his philosophy in its complete form; much of it had to wait at least 150 years to be abstracted from vast numbers of manuscripts. Even so, from what he did publish his contemporaries could appreciate Leibniz's philosophy as a closely-knit system of speculative **metaphysics**. Its neatness and attractiveness led **Immanuel Kant** to say that Leibniz had built "*a kind of enchanted world*". Subsequent philosophers have generally found Leibniz's system as a whole too strange to be taken seriously, but some of his individual ideas have been extremely influential.

Mind and matter

Leibniz, like Spinoza, tried to overcome the **duality** of mind and matter that Locke had taken over from Descartes. His method, which sharply contrasted with that of Spinoza, involved adopting a new doctrine of substance that was closely allied to his dynamic theory of motion. This "New System" (1695), concerning the relationship of substances and the pre-established harmony between the soul and the body, asserted that God does not need to bring about man's action by means of his thoughts, nor to wind

some sort of watch in order to reconcile the two; rather, the Supreme Watchmaker has so exactly matched body and soul that they give meaning to each other from the beginning.

Principle of sufficient reason

In *The Theodicy* (1710), Leibniz showed his commitment to the principle of sufficient reason, i.e. the thesis that for every state of affairs that obtains there must be a sufficient reason why it obtains. This commitment contains his solution to the difficulty of reconciling the evil in this world with the conception of God as an omnipotent, morally perfect creator. For when applied to God's choice of a possible world to create, the principle of sufficient reason implies that God must have a sufficient reason for creating just this world; but, given God's moral perfection, this reason must have to do with the value of the world selected. Hence, the world selected must be the best of all possible worlds.

It was this thesis which the French **Enlightenment** writer **Voltaire** lampooned so savagely in *Candide* (1759). But Voltaire was unjust in treating Leibniz as a shallow optimist: Leibniz did not believe

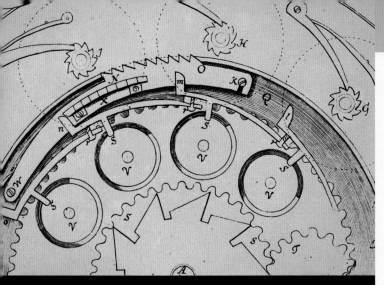

Details of the mechanisms of the Leibniz calculating machine.

Two things are identical if one can be substituted for the other without affecting the truth.

"Table of Definitions" (1704)

The House of Hanover, in whose service he remained from 1676 until his death, allowed him considerable leeway in pursuing his many interests in addition to his courtly duties. However, when Georg Ludwig, elector of Hanover, became George I of England in 1714, Leibniz was forbidden from following him to London, much to the philosopher's disappointment. Leibniz died in Hanover two years later in relative neglect.

this world is obviously perfect, but only that because a good God exists this must be the best world possible, however evil it may seem.

Monadology

Leibniz published *Monadology* in 1714. It is a logical synthesis, in the form of 90 **aphorisms**, of his life's contemplation of metaphysics. A monad (from Greek *monas*, "unit") is an elementary individual substance that reflects the order of the world and from which material properties are derived. If the physical world is made up of atoms, the metaphysical is made up from monads.

In Leibniz's system of metaphysics, monads are basic substances that constitute the universe but lack spatial extension and hence are immaterial. Each monad is a unique, indestructible, dynamic, soul-like entity whose properties are a function of its perceptions and appetites. Monads have no true **causal** relation with other monads, but all are perfectly synchronized with each other by God in a pre-established harmony. The objects of the material world are simply appearances of collections of monads.

Legacy, truth, consequence

- Leibniz made important contributions to philosophical theology.
- The leading principles of his philosophy became the orthodoxy of the German universities during the greater part of the eighteenth century.
- Leibniz's principle of the "identity of indiscernibles", where two things are held to be identical if and only if they share the same properties, is frequently invoked in modern logic and philosophy.
- Leibniz's methods and concerns often anticipate the **analytic** and linguistic philosophy of the twentieth century.
- Philosophically, Leibniz exerted a direct influence on Christian Wolff (1679–1754), Immanuel Kant, **Bertrand Russell**, and **Martin Heidegger**.
- Leibniz also made major contributions to mathematics, physics, and technology, and anticipated notions that surfaced much later in biology, medicine, geology, probability theory, psychology, linguistics, and information science.

Key dates

1646	Born in Leipzig in Saxony (now Germany).
1666	Awarded doctorate of law by Altdorf University. Enters service of Johann Philipp von Schönborn, elector of Mainz, and his minister, Baron von Boyneburg.
1673	Death of elector of Mainz in February; Leibniz makes his first visit to London, demonstrating his calculating machine to the Royal Society of London.
1675–98	Appointed courtier to John Frederick, Duke of Brunswick–Lüneburg, then to his brother, Ernst August, later elector of Hanover.
1687–90	Travels extensively in Germany, Austria, and Italy, researching history of the House of Brunswick.
1698–1716	Courtier to elector Georg Ludwig of Hanover.
1700	Founds Academy of Science in Berlin with support of Sophia Charlotte of Hanover, later queen of Prussia.
1710	Publishes *The Theodicy* (dedicated to Sophia Charlotte).
1713	Appointed Imperial court councillor by Charles VI, Holy Roman Emperor, at the Habsburg court in Vienna.
1714	Publishes *Monadology*. Elector Georg Ludwig of Hanover becomes George I of England.
1716	Dies in relative neglect in Hanover, Germany.

George Berkeley

In his own time not taken seriously by the philosophical community, Bishop Berkeley (as he became known) pioneered a development of empiricism called "subjective idealism", but was above all driven by a supra-philosophical concern to defend Christianity from the threat of a materialist philosophy he felt was dominating the age. His work has a paradoxical power and has come to be admired more for being thought-provoking than unassailable.

Berkeley's work is the product of a highly Christian sensibility's reaction to the stage at which he found himself in the philosophical tradition. At Dublin University he read **John Locke**, **René Descartes**, and Malebranche (1638–1715), in effect contemporary philosophy. The problems he identified with Locke's (and **empiricism's**) **materialism** were specifically philosophical problems, but the whole force driving – and perhaps driving too blindly – his philosophy as well as his life was his commitment to Christianity.

As an ordained minister of the (Irish) Anglican Church he lectured in biblical languages and theology, and gained a reputation for devoting himself to pastoral work. While in London he joined in establishing the famous Foundling Hospital: a home and school for abandoned children. In Ireland he was an early instigator of ecumenism between the denominations. He was engaged much of his life with the idea that materialism and hostility or indifference to religion were going to dominate the European tradition, a future era of hope lay with the New World.

His major practical project was to set up a college to provide and teach missionaries and which he envisioned including not only white Americans but also native Americans.

Berkeley seems always to have been something of a freethinker. He tells us in a diary of his ideas that he was "*distrustful at eight years old*". There is something maverick about his achievement, seen in his work and in his life. Much loved by all who came in contact with him, there is a kind of eccentricity that, comparing him with Laurence Sterne (1713–68) or his friend Jonathan Swift (1667–1745), one can almost think of as specifically Irish. He often used the word "amuse" for what philosophical thinking does. Fortunes were left him by strange women, he crossed the Atlantic on a scheme many thought ridiculous, took up a derivative of coal tar as a medicinal wonder, advocated "a tax on dirt", and always had an almost willful refusal to take anything for granted, but God. He himself said he was "*one who maintained the most extravagant opinion that ever entered into the mind of man*".

Essential philosophy

Empiricist tradition

Berkeley was an empiricist but his empiricism was a side-show to the major debate in his work: between materialism and immaterialism, the view, later called subjective **idealism**, that there are no material objects, only minds and ideas in those minds. His radical take on it shows how such a wide-ranging concept can include different and overlapping views under its banner. Modern empiricism – which began essentially with **epistemological** concerns – developed **ontologically** in Berkeley, reflecting his basic religious concern. He was worried about God's status within philosophy. Locke had maintained that we can have no knowledge beyond our ideas, which arise from experience (of the material external world). But it meant, as Locke accepted, that in **perception** we do not have direct access to physical objects, rather we are directly aware of the ideas objects "cause" in our minds and that "represent" the objects themselves.

Berkeley's approach is to accept the language developed by empiricism (ideas, sensations, reflections, simple and complex) and the basis in experience. But he makes an ontological move by asking

what the existential status is of objects in the world, or external reality. He rejects **Thomas Hobbes'** strong materialism (everything including God and the mind is ultimately material): "*Matter once allow'd I defy any man to prove God is not matter*". He also rejects Locke's less strong materialism-combined-with-immaterialism (ideas, which we can know, represent a world behind them which we cannot really know). Locke didn't try to prove the existence of a world behind the ideas and admitted it was a mystery how causation between the physical and mental takes place, how matter causes impressions and ideas. On Berkeley's view, the mind/body or material/immaterial **dualism** leads to **scepticism** because of its "*supposing a difference between things and ideas*", and atheism because of the impoverished sense in which God might relate to any external world. Once a distinction is made between our perception of material things and the things themselves "*then are we involved all in scepticism*".

Subjective idealism

Berkeley's response to this dualism is not, as in Hobbes, a complete materialism but rather a complete immaterialism in which,

Legacy, truth, consequence

- Berkeley was a kind of iconic eccentric, but eccentricity can highlight the absurdity of the world and it's assertions can surprise us into thinking. Ridiculed in his own time, Berkeley's work nevertheless forms a link between John Locke and the later **David Hume**, whose (sceptical) epistemology was influenced by Berkeley's anti-materialist ontology. Through Hume, Berkeley was important for **Immanuel Kant** and, later on, **Arthur Schopenhauer**'s idea of the world "*as will (or mind) and representation*".

- Contrary to what he would have wished, he gave an impetus to **phenomenalism** or **absolute idealism**, whereby God, for example, becomes a construct of our imaginations.

- Berkeley's work is still of interest because its intriguingly counterintuitive position is less assailable than commonsense might hope. And questioning common sense is one of the ways philosophy can defend it.

Both the University of California and the city of Berkeley were named after Bishop Berkeley in 1868 on the suggestion of one of the university's trustee, Frederick Billings, inspired by Berkeley's *Verses on the Prospect of Planting Arts and Learning in America*.

The furniture of the Earth ... all those bodies which compose the mighty frame of the world have not any substance without a mind.

A Treatise Concerning the Principles of Human Knowledge (1710)

furthermore, God's role can be central. He accepts that we know there are perceiving minds and objects of perception or ideas, but goes further to maintain that these are *all* there are.

His main point is what might be called a logical one: using **Ockham's razor** he insists there is no need to posit anything more than perception. For him perception is not intentional, essentially not "of" anything. From the fact that we perceive we can grant only the existence of perceptions; we don't need to infer anything beyond them.

If objects are what we perceive by sense, and perceptions are ideas, and ideas cannot exist unperceived: then objects cannot exist unperceived, for example when we are not in the room with them. He concluded: it must be God who grounds the perception in these and all other cases. In Berkeley's famous phrase "*esse est percipi*", to exist is to be perceived, ultimately by God.

Complete immaterialism (there is no world other than our perceptions) seems to commonsense more sceptical of the world's reality than the dualist view he opposes on anti-sceptical grounds. He defends the commonsense of his claims but his defense tends to be just a spirited re-assertion of his position, with the statement that it seems perfectly commonsensical to him.

He can and does claim, however, that by his immaterialism various problems for materialist dualism (whether matter can think, how it produces mental phenomena, the existence of an external world and other minds) "*are entirely banished from philosophy*".

No philosopher is studied because his work is unassailable. Criticisms of Berkeley have basically been of the logical status of his major theses. Firstly, that even if it is the case that something must "be" if it is perceived, it doesn't follow that something "cannot be" if it is not perceived. Secondly, that there is a difference, which he doesn't recognize, between something's perceptibility and its actually being perceived. One might say that something "cannot be" without being perceptible, but it doesn't follow that something "cannot be" without being perceived.

Berkeley might have proved the necessity of mind to account for the world, but not it's sufficiency – that mind alone is sufficient to account for the reality of the world.

Joseph Butler

Joseph Butler was a moral philosopher and an English cleric. His philosophy is an attempt to ground ethics on a proper understanding of human nature, and as such continues the tradition of Aristotle, Thomas Hobbes, and the Third Earl of Shaftesbury. Butler's refutation of ethical egoism – the view that people ought to do what is in their own self-interest – is a classic of moral thought. He carefully distinguishes self-love, benevolence, and the impact of conscience.

Born in England into a Presbyterian family in 1692, Butler was sent to the dissenting academy of Samuel Jones in Gloucester, destined for the ministry of the Presbyterian Church, the non-conformist church permitted in England from 1647. There he was grounded in the study of the ancient languages, logic, mathematics, geography, and biblical studies, and through Jones' lectures on logic he was introduced to **John Locke's** *Essay Concerning Human Understanding* (1690).

While at Jones' academy, Butler befriended Thomas Secker, future archbishop of Canterbury, and also struck up an unlikely correspondence with conformist philosopher Samuel Clarke (1675–1729), concerning matters of divine omnipresence and divine necessity. Clarke was so impressed by the young Butler's letters that he published them in 1716, thus cementing a relationship that was to serve Butler well in his future career.

In 1714 Butler decided to conform to the Church of England. A year later, he entered Oriel College, Oxford. Despite his misgivings over the intellectual caliber of his Oxford education, Butler nevertheless established at Oriel a great friendship with Edward Talbot, second son of William Talbot, bishop of Salisbury and, later, of Durham. The Talbots were to prove significant patrons of Butler's ecclesiastical career in the years to come.

Graduating in 1718, Butler was ordained as a Church of England minister by Bishop Talbot in the same year. For the next eight years he was preacher at the Rolls Chapel in London, where his sermons, addressing the practical side of Christian living, won him fame. He published some of these "Sermons on Human Nature" as *Fifteen Sermons Preached at the Rolls Chapel* in 1726.

Around this time, William Talbot, by then bishop of Durham, appointed Butler as parish priest at Stanhope, in County Durham. It was here that he wrote his most famous work, *The Analogy of Religion, Natural and Revealed, to the Constitution and Course of Nature*, which was published in 1736. In the same year he was made head chaplain to Caroline, wife of King George II, but after the Queen's death a year later he went to Bristol as bishop in 1738.

In 1740 he added Dean of St Paul's to his titles, the income from which enabled him to further his pastoral duties at Bristol, which was the country's poorest bishopric. He became bishop of Durham in 1750, but died only two years later.

Essential philosophy

Fifteen Sermons Preached at the Rolls Chapel

Butler's *Fifteen Sermons* (1726) is widely accepted as one of the most significant examples of eighteenth-century **ethical** writing. He uses a searching analysis of human nature as the foundation of an ethical theory which propounds that virtue consists in following nature, while vice is deviation from nature. One of Butler's targets is the psychological egoism of writers such as **Thomas Hobbes** – which asserts that people can only act in their own interest. Yet he is not an uncritical follower of the **moral sense theory**, or sentimentalism (the view that morality is based on moral sentiments or emotions) associated with Shaftesbury (1671–1713); rather he is seeking out a middle path between a moral sense approach to ethics and a **rationalist** one.

In his analysis Butler puts forward an essentially hierarchical view of human nature in which the various motivational principles in the human personality are ranked and need to be integrated properly if virtuous action is to ensue. Thus conscience, implanted by God, is the most important principle, which "*pronounces determinately some actions to be in themselves just, right, good; others to be in themselves evil, wrong, unjust*" (*Fifteen Sermons*).

The relationship between conscience and self-love is crucial in Butler's attempt to provide an account of moral behavior that avoids the extremes of psychological egoism on the one hand and a highly abstract **metaphysical** system on the other. Butler the preacher is concerned to help his congregation lead virtuous lives by stripping away the moral and intellectual confusion that may hinder them. His theological presuppositions – the existence of an ordered universe created by God, and the existence of a future life – enable him to argue that "*Duty and interest are perfectly coincident*".

Legacy, truth, consequence

- Butler's work impressed **David Hume** and Christian theologian John Wesley (1703-91). Hume commented: "*[Butler was one of those] who have begun to put the science of man on a new footing, and have engaged the attention, and excited the curiosity of the public.*"
- By the late eighteenth century Butler was widely read in Scottish universities; and from the early nineteenth century he was influential at Oxford, Cambridge, and many American colleges, perhaps because of the strong Scottish influence in America.
- Among the many thinkers subsequently influenced by Butler's arguments in favor of traditional theology was Cardinal John Henry Newman (1801–90), who attributed his own conversion to the Roman Church to his study of Butler – an attribution which may have counted against Butler's influence in Anglican circles.
- Aspects of Butler's theological **apologism** are reflected in the writings of twentieth-century Christian apologists such as C. S. Lewis and John Warwick Montgomery.

Key dates

1692   Born in Wantage, Oxfordshire, in England, into a Presbyterian family.

1711   Attends dissenting academy of Samuel Jones.

1713–14   Theological correspondence with Samuel Clarke is later to be published anonymously by Clarke.

1714   Conforms to Church of England.

1715–18   Undergraduate at Oriel College, Oxford.

1718   Graduates from Oxford; ordained Church of England minister.

1718–26   Preaches at Rolls Chapel, London.

1725–36   Parish priest at Stanhope, County Durham.

1726   Publishes *Fifteen Sermons Preached at the Rolls Chapel*.

1736   Publishes *The Analogy of Religion*; appointed chaplain to Queen Caroline.

1737   Death of Queen Caroline.

1738–50   Holds office of bishop of Bristol.

1740   Appointed dean of St Paul's Cathedral.

1750–2   Bishop of Durham.

1752   Dies in Bath, Somerset, southwest England.

> *Conscience and self-love, if we understand our true happiness, always lead us the same way. Duty and interest are perfectly coincident; for the most part in this world, but entirely and in every instance if we take in the future and the whole; this being implied in the notion of a good and perfect administration of things.*
>
> Fifteen Sermons (1726)

Durham Cathedral; Butler became Bishop of Durham in 1750.

The Analogy of Religion

Butler's principal contribution to theological debate is *The Analogy of Religion, Natural and Revealed, to the Constitution and Course of Nature*, published in 1736. Here Butler grapples with contemporary arguments that challenged the Christian faith, dealing methodically with their errors and inconsistencies. In particular he deals with the challenge of **Deism** – the outlook asserting the supremacy of reason over revelation in explaining religious faith.

In *The Analogy*, Butler counters the Deists by arguing both that the investigation of nature can show us more than Deist reasoning allows – the existence of a future life, for example, or that this life is a time of moral trial. Butler draws a parallel between the difficulties apparent in Christian revelation and the difficulties apparent in the account of natural religion offered by the Deists, and he criticizes his opponents for setting standards of proof for revelation that are not satisfied either by the Deistic beliefs that they proclaim or by a range of commonsense beliefs that they do not question.

In religion, as in ordinary life, what people need for reasonable belief is not certainty but enough probability to warrant action. Butler's arguments about the need to rely on probabilities ("*probability is the very guide of life*"), and the necessity of deciding in practice between alternatives that cannot be proved beyond doubt, have a universal resonance reaching far beyond his particular argument with the Deists.

Butler's *Of the Nature of Virtue*, which he appended to the *The Analogy*, presented a refutation of **hedonism** and of the notion that self-interest is the ultimate principle of good conduct.

Voltaire

Voltaire (pseudonym of François-Marie Arouet) was a philosopher and man of letters, a major playwright and novelist, and a brilliant scientific and philosophical popularizer. He is remembered as a courageous polemicist who indefatigably fought for civil rights, the right to a fair trial, and freedom of religion, and as one who denounced the hypocrisies and injustices of France's *ancien régime* and the Catholic Church.

Voltaire was born François-Marie Arouet, into a wealthy Parisian family, and educated at the Jesuit school of Louis-le-Grand. Despite his father's determination that he pursue a career in the law, Voltaire evaded such a fate in favor of a literary life. (It was probably partly in rebellion against his father that he adopted the pen name Voltaire.)

His early satirical writings led to exile in Holland (1713), imprisonment in the Bastille during which time he wrote *Oedipe*, his acclaimed first tragedy (1717), and exile in England (1726–9). Indeed, much of Voltaire's life can be seen in terms of exile and opposition.

Voltaire's period of English exile imbued him with an admiration for both the **liberalism** of England's institutions, and the English intrepidity in the discussion of religious and philosophical questions. He was convinced that it was because of their personal liberty that the English were in the forefront of scientific thought. On his return to France he wrote the *Philosophical Letters on the English Nation* (published 1734), whose respect for the liberal spirit of England forced him to retire to the country to avoid arrest.

For the next 15 years he took refuge in the château of his mistress, Mme du Châtelet, at Cirey in Champagne. Together they amassed a vast library, undertook Newtonian experiments, and pursued historical, theological, and philosophical investigations.

After Mme du Châtelet's death in 1749, Voltaire spent a period in Berlin at the request of Frederick the Great of Prussia. In 1755, however, following a dispute with Frederick, Voltaire retired once more to the country, settling in a château at Ferney, near Geneva. Here he published *Essays on the Manners and Spirit of Nations* (1756); his satirical masterpiece, *Candide* (1759); his *Philosophical Dictionary* (1764); histories of Peter the Great, India, and Louis XV; and his *Treatise on Toleration* (1763).

In 1778 Voltaire returned to Paris for the premiere of *Irène*, his last play. It was a triumph, and he was hailed in Paris as the greatest figure of the **Enlightenment** and his generation's most courageous spokesman for freedom and tolerance. He died in Paris soon afterwards.

Essential philosophy

Voltaire and England

Philosophically Voltaire absorbed the combination of science, **empiricism**, and religious awe characteristic of Isaac Newton (1643–1727) and **John Locke**, both of whom he came to admire during his period of English exile. His subsequent *Philosophical Letters on the English Nation* (1734) attacked the abuses committed by France's *ancien régime*, and held up England as a model of tolerance and liberty. The work was publicly burnt in Paris.

Candide

Voltaire's 1759 novella *Candide* is perhaps the work for which he is best remembered. It was an unashamedly satirical swipe at the **metaphysical** optimism of **Gottfried Leibniz**, whose principle of sufficient reason posited that this was "*the best of all possible worlds*".

In *Candide*, Voltaire satirizes Leibniz as young Candide's tutor Dr Pangloss, a character of unremitting optimism, who even when he has been infected with syphilis cannot agree with his tutee that such an act springs from the devil:

"*Not at all,*" replied this great man [Dr Pangloss], "*it was a thing unavoidable, a necessary ingredient in the best of worlds; for if Columbus*

had not in an island of America caught this disease, which contaminates the source of life… we should have neither chocolate nor cochineal."

(*Candide*)

Pangloss' naïve belief in "the best of worlds", where the arbitrary misery and brutality of the world mask a greater divine good, is held by Voltaire to be ridiculous, and offensive to his **rational scepticism**.

Voltaire and religion

Voltaire is often misrepresented as an atheist, the chief source for this misconception being his most famous epigram: "*If God did not exist, it would be necessary to invent Him.*" Interestingly, the poem to which this forms the opening line (*Epistle to the author of the book, The Three Impostors*) continues: "*But all nature cries aloud that He does exist.*"

In fact, like many other key figures during the European Enlightenment, Voltaire considered himself a **Deist**. He did not believe that absolute faith, based upon any particular or singular religious text or tradition of revelation, was needed to believe in God: "*Dogma leads to fanaticism and strife; morality everywhere inspires harmony.*" Voltaire's religious criticisms were not directed at the

[Men] use thought only to justify their injustices, and speech only to conceal their thoughts.

Dialogues (1763)

Legacy, truth, consequence

■ Voltaire's writings were hugely influential on the American Revolution of 1776 and the French Revolution of 1789.

■ Many themes of his writing would become key tenets of the social reform agenda of the late-eighteenth and early-nineteenth centuries. These included:
- the establishment of religious tolerance;
- the growth of material prosperity;
- respect for the rights of man;
- the abolition of torture and worthless punishments;
- the right to a fair trial.

■ Voltaire was one of the most prolific letter writers who ever lived – the extant 12,000 letters he wrote to over 700 correspondents are an invaluable historical source.

■ Voltaire's library, much of which he amassed with Mme du Châtelet, comprised more than 6,000 books. It was bought by Catherine the Great on the philosopher's death and is now housed in the National Library of Russia in Saint Petersburg.

Superstition sets the whole world in flames; philosophy quenches them.

Philosophical Dictionary (1764)

concept of religion itself, but were always focused on the actions of organized Christian religion, whose baleful effects were all too visible in the world of his time.

Causes célèbres

In the last 20 years of his life, while Voltaire enjoyed his role of philanthropic country gentleman at Ferney, he turned to positive social action and championed various victims of religious intolerance – most notably Jean Calas, Jean-François de la Barre, and Pierre-Paul Sirven, all of whom suffered horribly at the hands of Catholic zealots.

In his campaigns to right these and other abuses, Voltaire employed one of his most famous phrases: "*écrasez l'infâme!*" or "*crush the infamy!*" The "infamy" in question was not the monarchy itself, as future revolutionaries might claim, but the corrupt and bigoted aspects of the aristocracy and Catholic Church, and the superstitious intolerance that had been encouraged within the French people.

Voltaire remains a supreme example of the philosopher as a politically engaged, socially reforming liberal **humanist**.

The Arrest of Voltaire, a nineteenth-century engraving. Voltaire was imprisoned for 11 months in the Bastille in 1717, during which time he wrote *Oedipe*, his first tragedy.

Key dates

1694	Born in Paris, France.
1713	Exiled in Holland.
1717	Imprisoned in the Bastille. Writes *Oedipe*.
1726–9	Exiled in England. Meets with key literary and political figures of the day. Attracted to the philosophy and science of Locke and Newton.
1734	Publishes *Philosophical Letters on the English Nation*. Forced to flee Paris.
1735	Takes up residence with Mme du Châtelet, at Cirey in Champagne, France.
1749	Death of Mme du Châtelet.
1750	Accepts invitation of Frederick the Great of Prussia to visit Berlin.
1755	Forced to leave Berlin after disagreement with Frederick.
1756	Publishes *Essays on the Manners and Spirit of Nations*.
1758	Settles in voluntary exile at Ferney, near Geneva.
1759	Publishes *Candide*.
1762	Campaigns to clear the name of Jean Calas, a Toulouse Huguenot wrongly accused and put to death on the wheel by the Catholic authorities.
1764	Publishes *Philosophical Dictionary*.
1765	Jean Calas found not guilty. Begins campaign to help Pierre-Paul Sirven, a Protestant wrongly accused of murder.
1766	Intervenes to clear the name of Jean-François de la Barre, a Protestant nobleman beheaded and burned for blasphemy.
1771	Sirven family exonerated. Sirven writes to Voltaire: "*By enlightening people you have succeeded in making them human*".
1778	Dies in Paris and is buried in Champagne, although in 1791 his remains are interred in the Panthéon in Paris.

David Hume

No philosopher of the British empiricist tradition has had a greater influence on his successors or reputation among philosophers today. In Hume, empiricism, following on from implications in the work of Bishop Berkeley and John Locke, becomes open to a thoroughgoing scepticism, testing the basis of our commonsense notions of ourselves and the world.

Hume was an almost Socratean figure. Deeply loved and admired by his friends and colleagues for his kindliness, equanimity, unpretentiousness and wit. **Adam Smith** called him *"approaching as nearly to the idea of a perfectly wise and virtuous man as perhaps the nature of human frailty will permit"*. He met illness and death with the cheerful acceptance of his Greek predecessor, **Socrates**, which astounded those contemporaries who knew him as an infamous atheist and who received his views with a mixture of vitriol and incomprehension.

Encountering opposition from his family to his studying philosophy, without financial support and in considerable hardship, Hume pursued his passionate interest in the subject privately. Working out his ideas early on, there seems to have come a point when he realized the full **sceptical** force of what he wanted to say, inducing a kind of mental breakdown. Only having

overcome this was he able to proceed – working out, refining, and propagating his basic view for the rest of his life.

In many ways he was an outsider: from academic orthodoxy (never achieving a university position) and in terms of a philosophical stance, which regarded human society as its subject yet dismantled the very commonsense notions that tend to hold it together. Rather than the traditional science of how we know (**epistemology**), Hume's preoccupation was with the feelings, emotions, and beliefs that form the profoundest part of our lives: a view of human nature as primarily one of "sentiment" and passions. He seems to have had less grand schematic hopes for philosophy than his predecessors, marking a turn away from their high claims to the solutions of problems and towards a more doubting acceptance of reason's significance, almost in some sense a **mystical** view. These traits make him a precursor of the **Romantic** spirit rather than a child of the **Enlightenment**.

Essential philosophy

Hume's animating idea was the project of extending the seventeenth-century notion of a science of the natural world to man. In his major work *A Treatise of Human Nature* he seeks to maintain the observational and experimental method of the "new science" to give a Baconian (after **Francis Bacon**) "natural history" of mankind. His method is to establish some basic principles in terms of which a coherent account of human nature can be given, in the same way as Isaac Newton (1643–1727) – Hume's hero – accounted for the underlying principles governing the motions of everything in the universe. Not just within the realm of knowledge and understanding (the epistemology that had been so central to the concerns of his predecessors) but, rather, for man's feelings, emotions, and beliefs, both moral and religious. It was an holistic approach considering the whole life of mankind: an anthropology.

Impressions and ideas

An important characteristic of seventeenth- and eighteenth-century philosophy was to analyze and divide the phenomena under discussion into distinct categories. Within the phenomenon of **perception** (all mental activity), Hume distinguishes between "impressions" and "ideas". Different in degree rather than kind,

impressions (i.e. sensations) are stronger than ideas, which are a kind of copy, as in the difference between the memory of pain and the original sensation of it. Simplicity and complexity apply to both: simple ideas being based on a corresponding simple impression, and complex ideas not necessarily being based on simple impressions, as when in imagination we form new ideas like that of a unicorn from simpler elements of impressions like "horse" and "horn". This particular complex idea does not correspond to reality and thus we may be **sceptical** towards the existence of the thing (a unicorn) that is supposedly represented by the complex idea.

Matters of fact and relations of ideas

Within the field of epistemology another important distinction for Hume is between "matters of fact", which are propositions about the world assessed as true or false in the arena of experience; and "relations of ideas", which are found to be true or false by "the mere operation of thought", i.e. logically as in geometry and mathematics. Hume wants to look at every question in terms of where it fits within these distinctions. Relations of ideas produce logically certain results. But for matters not based on such **logical necessity**, Hume asks *"what is the nature of that evidence which assures*

Legacy, truth, consequence

■ Hume's characteristic rejection of metaphysics (his **empiricist** refusal to accept any ideas other than those of logic or immediate and concrete experience) made him a mentor to philosophers in the twentieth century, who turned their analytical eye against the excesses of the previous century's **idealism**. He wanted to abandon theoretical explanations of the supposed ultimate nature of reality, "*hypotheses which can never be made intelligible*". The idea that mistaken philosophical positions might have as their source conceptual incoherence rather than mere falsity is a precursor of the preoccupation in the twentieth century with the idea that philosophical problems may result from a failure to make our use of language sufficiently clear.

■ Hume takes a further step along the road of "knowledge" becoming more and more narrowly defined, and his view that a term, to be meaningful, must be based on sense impression or logic prefigures the **logical positivists**. For Hume, we can discern certain principles at work in human nature but their ultimate causes – as with gravity for Newton – are "*totally shut up from human curiosity and enquiry*". He defends a kind of humility, a reticence, even a sense of mystery in the face of the limited nature of strict knowledge, a sentiment which finds later expression in **Ludwig's Wittgenstein's** "*whereof we cannot speak thereof we should remain silent*". Similarly his "habit and custom" stands in a relation to Wittgenstein's "language game" and "form of life".

> *Reason is, and ought only to be, the slave of the passions, and can never pretend to any other office than to serve and obey them.*
>
> Treatise of Human Nature (1739)

David Hume's tomb is located, as he wished, on the eastern slope of Calton Hill overlooking Edinburgh. He wrote his own epitath: "Born 1711, Died [----]. Leaving it to posterity to add the rest".

… *any matter of fact?*" Matters of present and past fact are legitimately answered by our senses, but what of factual beliefs about the future, i.e. all our expectations based on the idea of a securely knowable external world? For example, that the sun will rise tomorrow. They are "*founded on the relation of cause and effect*". But how can we infer *necessarily* from cause to effect?

Causal connection

A **necessary connection** between events in the world, such as the sun rising every morning, is unknown either as a sensation (*a posteriori*) or a **logical necessity** (*a priori*). The idea of a necessary connection arises because of the repetition of various successions of impressions of sensation, as a result of which a mental habit forms. This "custom and habit" effect is a principle of human nature. Although basic to all our beliefs about the external world, it cannot be called reasonable in a strict sense; we must just accept it **empirically**. Nor can we really "know" anything that results from it. Hume similarly dismantles our notions of the self as anything more than a series of discrete sense impressions we tend to associate **inductively** but without justifying a claim to knowledge of any such thing. He makes a similar assessment of our

supposed knowledge of **other minds** and even the external world more generally, regarding these beliefs or opinions as a species of the emotions, "*which no reasoning or process of the thought and understanding is able either to produce or prevent*". And he groups moral and religious **propositions** with beliefs as "natural instincts", matters of "sentiment", feeling, or emotion as opposed to reason.

Does this make Hume a **sceptic** in the sense of recommending that we give up all such beliefs and judgements? He seems rather to be saying that it is just humanly impossible to refuse to hold such beliefs or to act on them. In this sense he is both downgrading traditional philosophy (basically **metaphysics**) and demanding more rigor and attention to our beliefs.

Jean-Jacques Rousseau

Jean-Jacques Rousseau was a French writer and philosopher who emerged from the French Enlightenment, yet whose most significant work was essentially counter-Enlightenment. He was profoundly influential on European romanticism and on the French Revolution, as well as on the philosophers Immanuel Kant and Karl Marx.

Rousseau was born in Geneva (now in Switzerland) and raised during his early years by his father, his mother having died shortly after giving birth. At the age of 16 he ran away to Savoy, eventually settling in Annecy, in the Rhône-Alpes region of eastern France, where he enjoyed the patronage of the wealthy baroness Madame de Warens.

In 1742 Rousseau arrived in Paris. By now a talented musician, he initially found work teaching and composing. His opera *Devin du Village* (1745) was highly successful, and performed before Louis XVI, but a growing friendship with the Parisian intelligentsia of the *Philosophes*, including Étienne Bonnot de Condillac (1715–80) and Denis Diderot (1713–84), propelled him towards philosophy rather than the potentially easy life of a court composer.

It was Diderot who encouraged Rousseau to enter the Academy of Dijon's essay contest of 1750. Rousseau's *Discourse on the Sciences and the Arts*, in which he condemned the arts and sciences as morally corruptible, won him first prize and brought both controversy and fame. His second discourse, *On the Origin of Inequality Among Men* (1753), stirred more controversy. Its

increasingly **Romantic**, anti-**Enlightenment** stance caused the *Philosophes* to break their connections with him.

Following this estrangement, Rousseau enjoyed the patronage of the Duc de Luxembourg, during which time he produced some of his most important works: *Julie, or the New Heloise* (1761), one of the best-selling novels of the century; *The Social Contract* (1762), his definitive work on **political philosophy**; and *Emile* (1762), a semi-fictitious work which expounded his views on education.

Both *The Social Contract* and *Emile* were condemned by the authorities, forcing Rousseau to flee, first to Switzerland and then, in 1766, to England at the invitation of philosopher **David Hume**. A year later, however, following a paranoid quarrel with Hume, Rousseau returned to France incognito.

In 1770 Rousseau was allowed to return to Paris. In his last years he copied music for a living and also wrote his autobiographical *Confessions*, as well as *Rousseau: Judge of Jean-Jacques* and the *Reveries of the Solitary Walker*. He died in 1778. His *Confessions* and later political writings were all published posthumously.

Essential philosophy

For Rousseau, human nature and society are fundamentally divided: he believed that man was good when in the "state of nature", but is corrupted by society. (Interestingly, "the noble savage", a phrase often attributed to Rousseau, was never used by him.) Rousseau's favoring of natural innocence, emotion, spontaneity, and solitude over reason, intellect, culture, and society mark him out as truly Romantic in sensibility, and profoundly anti-Enlightenment.

The *Discourses*

Rousseau's *Discourse on the Sciences and the Arts* (1750), which established themes he was to develop in much of his subsequent political philosophy, argued that the arts and sciences were merely the seductive characteristics of a modern society in which mankind had lost his natural liberty and entered a moral decline. Rousseau equated virtue with innocence which, once lost, could never be regained.

In his *Discourse on the Origin of Inequality* (1753) Rousseau argued that society's negative influence centers on its transformation of *amour de soi*, a positive self-love, into *amour-propre*,

or pride: the former represents the human desire for self-preservation; the latter is artificial, and derives from society, which urges humans to compare themselves to each other. This, and in particular the institution of private property, was the prime source of moral corruption.

The Social Contract

Rousseau's greatest and most influential work of philosophy was *The Social Contract* (1762). The earlier *Discourses* had established a problem. If society inherently corrupts humankind's natural goodness, and a return to solitary living is impossible, how can man continue to live in society? Rousseau's answer lay in the notion of the "*volonté générale*" or "general will" – he saw civil society as a single organic unity with a single will to which its citizens were contracted. Most significantly, freedom of the citizen is changed by this act of contract. Before contracting, man's freedom lies in pursuing his individual interests; afterwards, freedom consists in obeying the general will.

Legacy, truth, consequence

- Rousseau is one of the chief philosophical influences on the European **Romanticism** movement.
- His philosophy helped to shape that of **Immanuel Kant** and **Karl Marx**. Because Rousseau was one of the first modern writers to attack seriously the institution of private property, he is considered a forebear of **communism**.
- *The Social Contract* became the bible of the French Revolution but, as **Bertrand Russell** wrote, "*as is the case of bibles, it was not carefully read and was still less understood by many of its disciples*" (Russell, *A History of Western Philosophy*, 1945).
- "*Man is born free; and everywhere he is in chains*" (the opening words of *The Social Contract*) has been a rallying-cry for revolutionaries and reformers ever since.
- Many of Rousseau's ideas on education, as propounded in *Emile* and derided at the time, can be seen in the modern educational culture of child-centered, experiential learning.
- **Voltaire** on Rousseau: "*This arch-madman, who might have been something, if he would only have been guided by his brethren of the Encyclopedia.*"
- Rousseau on Voltaire: "*That trumpet of impiety, that fine genius, and that low soul.*"

Il retourne chez ses Egaux.

1755 edition of Rousseau's *Discourse on the Origin of Inequality*.

In effect, Rousseau argues for a version of sovereignty of the whole citizen body over itself, expressing its legislative intent through the general will, which theoretically applies to all equally because it comes from all alike. The general will tends to promote liberty and equality, in Rousseau's view, for it both arises from and promotes a spirit of fraternity. To his critics, however, the resulting state can be regarded as totalitarian: since freedom consists in obedience to the general will, those who do not obey must be "forced to be free".

Yet Rousseau insisted that the object of political right must be liberty and equality, and it is to these ends that his philosophy was directed.

Key dates

1712	Born in Geneva (in Switzerland). His mother dies weeks after giving birth.
1722	His father, a failed watchmaker, is forced to flee Geneva. Rousseau is sent to live with his aunt and uncle.
1728	Runs away to Savoy. Settles in Annecy, France, with baroness Mme de Warens.
1742	Arrives in Paris. Meets Therese Levasseur, an illiterate linen-maid, with whom he has five children - surrenders all to Paris orphanage.
1743–4	Acts briefly as secretary to French Embassy in Venice.
1745	His opera *Devin du Village* is performed before Louis XVI at Versailles.
1745–50	Contributes to Diderot's *Encyclopedie*.
1750	*Discourse on the Sciences and the Arts* wins first prize in Academy of Dijon contest.
1753	*Discourse on the Origin of Inequality* is published.
1758	Marries Therese Levasseur.
1761	Publishes *Julie, or the New Heloise*, which becomes a best-selling novel.
1762	Publishes *The Social Contract* and *Emile*. Both are banned in Paris and Geneva and Rousseau is driven into exile. His mental health deteriorates.
1766	Flees to England at invitation of David Hume.
1767	Returns to France under a false name after quarreling with Hume.
1770	Allowed to return to Paris on condition that he publishes no more works.
1778	Dies of apoplexy in Ermenonville, France.
1780s	Posthumous publication of: *Confessions* Vol. I (1782); *Rousseau: Judge of Jean-Jacques* (1782); *Reveries of the Solitary Walker* (1782); and *Confessions* Vol. II (1789).

Man is naturally good, and only by institutions is he made bad.

Discourse on the Origin of Inequality (1753)

Emile

Emile (1762) is part fiction, part didacticism. Rousseau propounds a new system of education through the story of how a boy, Emile, grows and is helped by his tutor (Rousseau) to become educated by nature. Emile has to feel himself free in developing his activities. The educator may never impose his will upon the pupil by precepts; rather, he should act as a facilitator, preparing the fittest external conditions for the free unfolding of the activities of his pupil.

In Rousseau's view, education should concentrate on the senses and bodily health at the expense of the intellect. Emile is discouraged from books, learning only those notions that will be necessary to his practical life as a carpenter. Rousseau keeps him safe from the corrupting influences of culture and the sciences, and encourages him to enjoy "*the sleep of reason*". *Émile* was promptly banned.

Adam Smith

Adam Smith was a pioneering political economist and moral philosopher. A key figure of the Scottish Enlightenment, he is known primarily as the author of *The Wealth of Nations* (1776), which argued that rational self-interest and the competition of a free market can lead to economic well-being and prosperity. Smith's work laid the foundations for the modern academic discipline of economics and provided one of the best-known rationales for free trade and capitalism.

Smith was born in Kirkcaldy, Scotland, and raised by his widowed mother. He won scholarships, first to Glasgow University and then to Balliol College, Oxford, after which he returned to Scotland in 1748 to lecture in Edinburgh under the patronage of the Lord Kames. During these years he first became acquainted with the philosopher **David Hume**, who became a close friend, and other figures of the Scottish **Enlightenment**.

In 1751 Smith was appointed professor of logic at Glasgow University, transferring a year later to the chair of moral philosophy. He lectured on natural theology, **ethics**, jurisprudence, and economics.

In 1759, at the age of 36, Smith published *The Theory of Moral Sentiments*, a groundbreaking work on **moral philosophy** which incorporated some of his Glasgow lectures. His abilities caught the eye of the Duke of Buccleuch, who between 1764 and 1766 engaged him as tutor to his son on the Grand Tour of Europe. During his travels Smith met other eminent thinkers such as **Voltaire**, **Jean-Jacques Rousseau**, and Benjamin Franklin.

On his return to Britain, he concentrated on the writing of his greatest work, *An Inquiry into the Nature and Causes of the Wealth of Nations*. This was finally published ten years later, in 1776, the same year that Smith moved to London.

The Wealth of Nations was the first major work of political economy, and it was almost immediately successful, securing Smith's financial future. His appointment as commissioner of customs for Scotland in 1778 took him back to Edinburgh, where he made his home with his aged mother in Panmure House, which still stands in Edinburgh's Canongate. Here he regularly entertained such Enlightenment figures as the physicist Joseph Black, James Hutton the geologist, and his old friend the philosopher David Hume.

Smith died in 1790 after a painful illness. He had left instructions to his executors to destroy all but his most notable papers. His *Essays on Philosophical Subjects* were duly published posthumously in 1795.

Essential philosophy

The Theory of Moral Sentiments

This work, which established Smith's reputation in his day, was based on Hume's doctrines. Smith argued that the essence of moral sentiments was sympathy – but a specialized, conscience-stricken sympathy, like that of an impartial and well-informed spectator. *The Theory of Moral Sentiments* established a new **liberalism**, in which social organization is seen as the outcome of human action but not necessarily of human design.

The Wealth of Nations

An Inquiry into the Nature and Causes of the Wealth of Nations examined in detail the consequences of economic freedom, such as **division of labor**, the function of markets, and the international implications of a **laissez-faire economy** (although that term was not used by Smith and did not cross the English Channel until the nineteenth century).

The basic doctrine of *The Wealth of Nations* was that labor is the only source of a nation's wealth. Smith advocated division of labor in the productive process, stressed the importance of individual enterprise, and argued the benefits of **free trade**. The true wealth of a nation, he held, lay not in gold but in the achievement of an abundance of the necessities of life; and he warned against unnecessary intervention by the state in this process.

> *It is not from the benevolence of the butcher, the brewer or the baker, that we expect our dinner, but from their regard to their own self interest. We address ourselves, not to their humanity but to their self-love, and never talk to them of our own necessities but of their advantages.*
>
> The Wealth of Nations (1776)

- The science of political economy, and indeed of economics as a whole, can be traced directly back to the publication of Smith's *Wealth of Nations* in 1776.
- *The Wealth of Nations* also provided one of the best-known intellectual rationales for free trade, the laissez-faire mode of government, and **capitalism**.
- Smith greatly influenced the writings of later economists, most notably Thomas Malthus (1766–1834), David Ricardo (1772–1823), and **Karl Marx**.
- Smith's political influence was also great, his advocates including William Pitt the Younger (1759–1806), Charles Fox (1749–1806), and Napoléon Bonaparte (1769–1821).
- Smith stipulated four maxims of taxation that are still held true today: proportionality, transparency, convenience, and efficiency.

> **How selfish soever man may be supposed, there are evidently some principles in his nature, which interest him in the fortunes of others, and render their happiness necessary to him, though he derives nothing from it, except the pleasure of seeing it.**
>
> The Theory of Moral Sentiments (1759)

Detail of a page of *The Wealth of Nations* showing the prices of wheat.

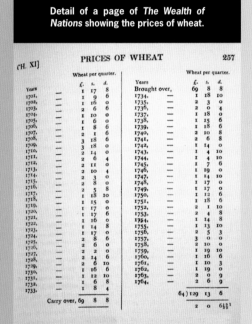

Free trade

When *The Wealth of Nations* appeared in 1776 there was a strong sentiment for free trade in Britain and in America, which had just declared its independence and was ready for a new system to alleviate economic hardship. This helps to explain the immediate success of the book both in Britain and abroad – it underwent five publications in Britain alone before Smith's death in 1790.

For centuries before 1776 it was taken for granted that it was the task of the government to regulate trade in what it thought was the best interests of the community. Smith challenged this system of regulation (known as mercantilism), whose main feature was a structure of tariffs on commodities.

The ideas of free trade expressed in *The Wealth of Nations* were enthusiastically taken up in Britain by William Pitt the Younger, who became prime minister in 1783. Pitt's reforms of trade tariffs were halted, however, by the French Wars (1792–1815) and it was not until the 1820s that momentum could be built once more to make Britain a free-trade nation.

The "invisible hand"

One of the main points of *The Wealth of Nations* is that the free market, while appearing chaotic and unrestrained, is actually guided to produce the right amount and variety of goods by a so-called "invisible hand":

> "By preferring the support of domestic to that of foreign industry, he intends only his own security; and by directing that industry in such a manner as its produce may be of the greatest value, he intends only his own gain, and he is in this, as in many other cases, led by an invisible hand to promote an end which was no part of his intention."
>
> (The Wealth of Nations, IV)

The image of the invisible hand was previously employed by Smith in his *Theory of Moral Sentiments*, and is a metaphor which has become synonymous with Smith and later advocates of free trade. Understandably, it has many detractors, who see the metaphor as central to the weaknesses of free market economics. As Nobel Prize-winning economist Joseph E. Stiglitz has written: "*the reason that the invisible hand seems invisible is that it is often not there*" (*Making Globalization Work*, 2006).

Immanuel Kant

Kant was one of the most influential European thinkers of the eighteenth century. In fact his essay "Answering the Question: What is Enlightenment?" can be seen as the work that defined the Enlightenment. Here he used the Latin phrase "*Sapere Aude*" ("Have the courage to use your reason") to extol the virtues of autonomous thinking, free of the influence of state or religious authority. The main body of his work was an erudite attempt to reconcile the two great philosophical movements that preceded him, rationalism and empiricism.

Kant is generally seen as a rather pedantic, precise type of man, something of an academic cliché. His life certainly wasn't one of adventure and remarkable events. He was the fourth of eleven children born to a Königsberg family in 1724. He never traveled far from the town, which was the capital of Prussia at the time. From an early religious education he moved to becoming a student at the city's university at the precocious age of sixteen. There he worked as a tutor, then as a lecturer, a role in which he covered many subjects, including philosophy, before attaining the position of professor of logic and metaphysics. Several of his early works were about scientific topics, including some rather accurate and progressive astronomical speculations on the origins of the universe and the Milky Way in particular.

Despite his writings in philosophy in his thirties and forties, and being the author of popular works such as *Observations On the Feeling of the Beautiful and the Sublime* (1764), Kant credited **David Hume**'s writing with waking him from a "dogmatic slumber". After reading Hume, in about 1770, he realized that in his early work he had failed to fully understand the way that our intellects and senses interact.

He didn't publish again for eleven years, although he did continue teaching. This period is known as his silent decade and marks the interval during which he developed his mature philosophy. Kant was a gregarious man, but for this time he became relatively withdrawn and focused firmly on his work. Later in life he became known for living a very regulated life in which he was woken at the same hour every day and went through identical routines – it was famously said that locals could set their clocks by the timing of his walks.

Essential philosophy

In 1781 Kant revealed the first fruits of his silent decade when he published the *Critique of Pure Reason*, one of the most remarkable philosophical works ever published. It was a difficult book, like the two further *Critiques* (of *Practical Reason* and *Judgement*) that followed it in his oeuvre, but it gradually gained a reputation among those of his peers who were able to follow its 800 pages of dense, dry argument. The three Critiques provide Kant's solutions to problems in **metaphysics**, **ethics**, and **aesthetics**.

Knowledge

In the *Critique of Pure Reason*, Kant was concerned to provide a foundation for metaphysics, understood as philosophical knowledge that transcends the bounds of experience (such as knowledge of whether free will exists, that there is a God, etc). In so doing, he aimed to solve the interminable war between the **rationalists** (such as **Gottfried Leibniz**) and the **empiricists** (such as **David Hume**), and to set limits and principles for the proper application of human reason.

The metaphysical knowledge that Kant sought to prove as possible was, he claimed, both *a priori* and **synthetic**, i.e. concerned with both **necessary truths** (derived from **propositions** that must

be true, as opposed to *a posteriori* knowledge based on empirical evidence about the world) and with synthetic truths (informative propositions that claim more information than can be derived merely from an analysis of the concepts contained in the proposition). An example of a synthetic *a priori* judgement would be "The three angles of a triangle add up to 180 degrees". The mathematical truths about a triangle are truths about the independent nature of reality and cannot be deduced simply from the proposition.

His innovation, often called his "Copernican revolution in philosophy" (to compare it with Copernicus' challenge to the accepted view of the universe), involved reversing the idea of how knowledge is acquired by the mind. Kant overturned the view that the mind is a passive recorder of experience conforming to a realm of objects in the world, a blank slate or *tabula rasa* waiting to be written upon, as the empiricists claimed; instead, the mind is active, playing a part in shaping the world of experience and constituting the objects of knowledge. The mind imposes categories, such as cause and effect, and ideas of space and time, upon the incoming sense-data of experience to help us interpret the world and generate knowledge. This led to Kant's claim that human

Enlightenment is man's leaving his self-caused immaturity. Immaturity is the incapacity to use one's intelligence without the guidance of another.

"What is Enlightenment?" (1784)

Legacy, truth, consequence

■ The subtlety and range of Kant's ideas make him a key influence on all Western philosophy in the last two centuries, particularly in his reconciliation of **rationalism** and **empiricism**.

■ He was a major influence on the Romantic and German **idealist** philosophers of the nineteenth century, and can be seen as the starting point for most of the philosophy that followed him.

■ His answer to how the mind acquires knowledge from experience greatly influenced the twentieth-century **phenomenologists** and **gestalt** psychologists.

Key dates

1724	Born in Königsberg in East Prussia (now Kalingrad, in an enclave of Russia, on the Baltic coast).
1740	Attends university.
1749–70	Various works are published, starting with *Thoughts on the True Estimation of Living Forces*.
1770	Made professor of logic and metaphysics.
1770–81	The "silent decade".
1781	*Critique of Pure Reason* (on metaphysics) is published.
1783	*Prolegomena to any Future Metaphysics that will be able to present itself as a Science* is published.
1784	His essay "Answering the Question: What is Enlightenment?" defines the **Enlightenment**.
1788	*Critique of Practical Reason* (on ethics) is published.
1790	*Critique of Judgement* (on aesthetics) is published.
1795	*Toward Perpetual Peace: a Philosophical Project* is published.
1804	Dies in Königsberg.

Kant's work helped to define the ideas of the Enlightenment. The signatories of the American Declaration of Independence were motivated by the same principles.

Human reason has this peculiar fate that in one species of its knowledge it is burdened by questions which, as prescribed by the very nature of reason itself, it is not able to ignore, but which, as transcending all its powers, it is also not able to answer."

Critique of Pure Reason (1781)

knowledge is limited to appearances or the **phenomenal realm** (the world of objects as they are perceived/experienced); whereas the things-in-themselves, the objects in the world belonging to the **noumenal realm**, are thinkable but not actually knowable. His project, known as **transcendental** idealism, explains how we can have *knowledge* of how things appear to us, but we can only *think* about things-in-themselves (the *noumena*). It explains how knowledge of the empirical world, including synthetic *a priori* knowledge, is possible, but rules out speculative metaphysics concerned with transcendental questions. Speculative metaphysics leads to contradictions because it attempts to attain knowledge of the *noumena* while using the categories that apply to the world as we experience it.

But although Kant rejects traditional metaphysics, he leaves room for the truths of morality. The idea of **free will** throws up contradictions between the causal **determinism** of nature and the free will required by morality only when it is considered as a thing-in-itself. Once this assumption is rejected, it at least remains *conceivable* that human beings, considered as things-in-themselves (*noumena*) are free (although we can never know with certainty that free will isn't subject to the forces of determinism). For Kant this is sufficient for morality and gives meaning to life.

The categorical imperative

Kant also considered ethics in relation to synthetic *a priori* judgements. He concluded that our morality is based on a single "categorical imperative" – that you should "*act only according to that maxim whereby you can at the same time will that it should become a universal law.*" Effectively, Jesus' "golden rule" ("do unto others as you would have them do unto you"), Kant's imperative is *categorical* because truly rational beings cannot fail to recognize it as rationally binding them irrespective of their particular circumstances and ends. Thus, for example, rational beings will desire that the moral imperative "do not murder" should become a universal law.

Moses Mendelssohn

A philosopher of the German Enlightenment, Moses Mendelssohn was also the "father" of the Jewish Enlightenment. A writer, critic, and translator, he argued convincingly for Jewish civil rights and for Jewish assimilation into German society. As well as writing about Judaism, his philosophy covered a range of topics from metaphysics to aesthetics.

Born in a fairly poor German–Jewish family, Mendelssohn studied traditional Jewish law, but taught himself secular subjects such as Latin, German, and philosophy. In the mid-1750s he began to publish noteworthy philosophical articles, sometimes with his friend the playwright Gotthold Lessing. Mendelssohn was the model for the eponymous Jewish hero in Lessing's 1779 play *Nathan the Wise*.

In 1763 he was given the formal status of "Protected Jew", which meant that he could live permanently in Berlin. At that time, in most European countries, Jews were not allowed to vote or play a part in civic life. As a result Jewish communities had not changed for centuries: they were insular, traditional, Yiddish-speaking, and isolated. Always an observant Orthodox Jew, Mendelssohn argued for equal rights and emancipation. He also worked to persuade Jews to learn European languages and modern scientific subjects, and to play a part in the wider community.

In 1769 he was challenged by the pastor Johann Lavater to debate arguments for Christianity, but he avoided this by pleading for tolerance and religious acceptance. However, when Lessing was accused of pantheism or atheism after his death, Mendelssohn jumped into the argument to defend his dead friend.

Essential philosophy

Reason

Mendelssohn believed that the existence of God and other religious truths could be discovered through reason. He accepted the reality of revelation and miracles, but argued that they were not the only basis for religious belief. He opposed empty superstition and religious threats such as excommunication.

In 1767 he discussed the immortality of the soul, through rational arguments, in a famous treatise *Phädon*, loosely modeled on Plato's *Phaedo* (fourth century BCE). This earned him the title the "German Socrates" or the "Jewish Socrates".

Tolerance

In many of his writings he pleaded for religious tolerance, and argued that the state has no right to interfere in the religious beliefs of people, whatever they happen to be. He took a pragmatic position that there may be several truths, and different individuals may need different religions.

Legacy, truth, consequence

■ His general philosophy helped shape the unique path of the German **Enlightenment** towards **mysticism** instead of **empiricism**.

■ Mendelssohn showed that it was possible to be an observant Jew and yet follow **rationalist** principles of the European Enlightenment. He helped bring about the cultural renaissance called the Jewish Enlightenment.

■ His arguments in favor of religious toleration helped further the cause of Jewish emancipation in Europe.

■ While some Jews welcomed the Enlightenment, others felt that his ideas simply led to cultural assimilation and an eventual loss of Jewish identity. His own grandchildren, including the composers Felix and Fanny Mendelssohn, converted to Christianity.

Key dates

1729	Born in Dessau (now in modern Germany).
1743	Studies with well-known Jewish scholars in Berlin.
1754	Begins lifelong friendship with playwright Gotthold Ephraim Lessing.
1755	Begins publishing philosophical works.
1763	Wins prestigious Berlin Academy literary competition.
1767	His treatise *Phädon* is published, making him famous in Europe as the "German Socrates".
1780–3	Translates the *Torah* (the first five books of the Old Testament) and other parts of the Jewish Bible into German.
1786	Dies in Berlin, Kingdom of Prussia (Germany).

My religion recognizes no obligation to resolve doubt other than through rational means; and it commands no mere faith in eternal truths.

Collected Writings (ed. 1971)

Edmund Burke

Edmund Burke was an Irish politician and philosopher. His political career came during a fascinating period of British history. He combined being an advocate of American independence with being an opponent of the French Revolution, which followed soon after. His philosophical work ranged from early musings on anarchism to writing on aesthetic theory.

Burke was raised in Dublin, and moved to London to pursue a legal career. Two of his most interesting philosophical works were written early in his life. *A Vindication of Natural Society* was an early exposition of anarchism, although Burke would later disown it as a satire. *A Philosophical Enquiry into the Origin of Our Ideas of the Sublime and Beautiful* was a study of aesthetic theory, which was an influence on writers as disparate as Denis Diderot (1713–84) and **Immanuel Kant**.

His life in politics revolved around problems specific to the period, for instance the role of representative **democracy**, and the restrictions on the power of the monarch. His attitude to the British Empire was an important one. Burke argued against the abuse of the colonies, and his views became influential. In the case of the American War, he was a strong proponent of peace and allowing the former colony its freedom. However, he saw the French Revolution in very different terms, believing it represented an unreasonable attack on authority and tradition of every sort. While the long-term implications of Burke's views can be questioned, his doubt in the value of the French Revolution was perhaps vindicated by the Reign of Terror that ensued under the leadership of Maximilien Robespierre.

Essential philosophy

A Philosophical Enquiry into the Origin of Our Ideas of the Sublime and Beautiful

Burke's investigation begins with the triggers for our emotions and passions. He divides the "passions" of humans into those of "self-preservation" (which turn chiefly on pain and pleasure and arouse in us a sense of "delight") and of "society" (which are founded on sexual love or love of mankind and the animate world in general). Love is a positive pleasure *"and its object is beauty; which is a name I shall apply to all such qualities in things as induce in us a sense of affection and tenderness…"* Thus, whatever arouses "delight" is sublime; whatever excites "love" is beautiful. In his "Essay on Taste", included in the second edition of the treatise (1759), he responds to **David Hume**'s 1757 *Dissertation on Taste*. Hume is sceptical that it is possible to determine a standard of taste, whereas Burke is convinced that laws of taste are scientifically verifiable. However, commentators are mostly agreed that Burke ignored the subjective element involved in apprehending beauty: that it is our personal "ideas" of objects that we call beautiful, and these ideas depend on personal interests, emotions, etc.

Legacy, truth, consequence

■ Burke is best remembered as a founding father of modern Anglo-American conservatism.

■ He has been an enduring influence on classical liberals such as **Karl Popper** and Friedrich Hayek (1899–1992).

■ One of the most interesting comments on his thinking comes from Winston Churchill who was defending him against a charge of inconsistency in his attitudes to the American and French Revolutions. He said that Burke's *"soul revolted against tyranny, whether it appeared in the aspect of a domineering monarch … or whether mouthing the watchwords of a non-existent liberty, it towered up against him in the dictation of a brutal mob and wicked sect"*.

Key dates

1729	Born in Dublin, Ireland.
1756	*A Vindication of Natural Society* is published.
1757	*A Philosophical Enquiry into the Origin of Our Ideas of the Sublime and Beautiful* is published.
1765	Enters the British Parliament.
1775	His influential speech: *Conciliation with America*.
1788	Burke argues against abuse of colonies in trial of Warren Hastings, Governor-General of India.
1790	*Reflections on the Revolution in France* is published.
1797	Dies in Beaconsfield, England.

Good order is the foundation of all things.

Reflections on the Revolution in France (1790)

Reflections on the Revolution in France

In this treatise Burke attacked **social contract** theory and argued for the idea that society is best run with respect for established values such as traditional religion.

1737–1809

Thomas Paine

Thomas Paine was a political philosopher, a republican, revolutionary, and consummate pamphleteer. A brilliant polemicist with an independent critical mind, Paine played a key role in arguing the case for revolution in both America and France. His opinion-forming rhetoric was also crucial in sustaining support for the American Revolutionary War once it began. Profoundly influential on later nineteenth-century radicals, his unorthodox thinking, especially on religion, left him with few friends in his own time.

Thomas Paine was born in Thetford, in the south-east of England, in 1737, the son of a Quaker father. His early career was not successful: he failed at his father's trade of corset-making, was dismissed twice as a customs officer, and failed as a shopkeeper. His first wife died in childbirth and his second marriage ended in separation.

In September 1774, jobless and debt-ridden, Paine met the statesman and scientist Benjamin Franklin in London. He took Franklin's advice, along with letters of introduction, and emigrated to the American colonies.

Paine arrived in Philadelphia on November 30, 1774 and soon began a new career as a journalist, contributing articles to the *Pennsylvania Magazine* on a range of topics.

In January 1776 he published a short pamphlet, *Common Sense*, which advocated American independence. It was read everywhere, from the coffee house to the pulpit, and had a huge impact on public opinion. Having established his reputation as a revolutionary propagandist committed to the cause of American

independence, he followed up *Common Sense* with a series of stirring articles and a pamphlet series called *The American Crisis* (1776–83).

After a brief visit to Paris in 1781 to secure funding for the war, Paine returned to Europe in 1787. He supported the moderate wing of the French revolutionaries, and produced his most famous work, *The Rights of Man* (1791–2), in response to **Edmund Burke**'s anti-revolutionary *Reflections on the Revolution in France* (1790).

From 1792 Paine sat in the French National Assembly, but fell foul of the Jacobins, the increasingly radical political club of the French Revolution, and narrowly escaped the guillotine in 1794. His *Age of Reason* (1795–6), a **Deist** manifesto that declared nature the only form of divine revelation and bitterly attacked the Church, made him even more enemies than before.

After wearing out his welcome in Paris, Paine finally returned to America in October 1802. His last years were marked by poverty, poor health, and alcoholism. He died a virtual outcast in New York in 1809.

Essential philosophy

Paine's first American pamphlet, *Common Sense* (1776), became the most widely distributed pamphlet of the American War of Independence. It made independence seem both desirable and attainable to the wavering colonists.

He wrote in accessible prose, couching his beliefs as the promptings of common sense, and insisting that the issues between Britain and America were of universal importance:

"*The cause of America is in a great measure the cause of all mankind ... 'Tis not the concern of a day, a year, or an age; posterity are virtually involved in the contest, and will be more or less affected, even to the end of time, by the proceedings now.*"

(*Common Sense*)

For Paine, America would remain the providentially chosen asylum for liberty while Europe crumbled into despotism. "*Society*", he announces in the opening paragraphs, "*in every state is a blessing, but government, even in its best state, is but a necessary evil*". This "necessary evil" best serves the end of protecting the freedom and security of

its people by taking a representative and republican form. Government by kings runs contrary to the natural equality of man:

"*'Tis a form of government which the word of God bears testimony against, and blood will attend it.*"

The American Crisis (1776–83) was a series of letters and pamphlets designed to muster the American people to the cause of independence and to set straight the record of military affairs. The opening of the first letter is as resounding a piece of political rhetoric as any political pamphlet published:

"*These are the times that try men's souls. The summer soldier and the sun-shine patriot will, in this crisis, shrink from the service of his country: but he that stands it now, deserves the thanks of man and woman. Tyranny, like hell, is not easily conquered: yet we have this consolation with us, that the harder the conflict, the more glorious the triumph. What we obtain too cheap, we esteem too lightly; it is dearness only that gives everything its value.*"

(*The American Crisis*)

Legacy, truth, consequence

■ Paine's writings greatly influenced his contemporaries, especially the American revolutionaries.

■ He inspired both philosophical and working-class radicals in the United Kingdom, and he is often claimed as an intellectual ancestor by United States liberals, libertarians, anarchists, freethinkers, progressives, and radicals.

■ Both Abraham Lincoln and Thomas Edison admired Paine's works. Lincoln is reported to have written a defense of Paine's Deism in 1835, and Edison regarded him *"as one of the greatest of all Americans. Never have we had a sounder intelligence in this republic"*.

■ *The Age of Reason* gave many working-class readers the resources to rethink their religious standpoint.

■ Paine was one of the earliest exponents of both a progressive income tax and the abolition of slavery.

Key dates

1737	Born at Thetford, Norfolk, England.
1774	Encouraged by Benjamin Franklin to emigrate to America. Arrives in Philadelphia on November 30.
1776	Publishes *Common Sense*, which quickly becomes a best-seller.
1776–83	Publishes *The American Crisis* both as a series of letters in *Pennsylvania Magazine* and as widely distributed pamphlets.
1781	Visits France to negotiate funding for the American War.
1787	Returns to Europe.
1791–2	Publishes *The Rights of Man*. Accused of seditious libel by the British, and put on trial in absentia.
1795–6	Publishes *The Age of Reason*, his Deist tract.
1797	Publishes *Agrarian Justice*.
1802	Returns to America. Warmly welcomed by President Thomas Jefferson, but his outspoken unorthodoxy soon alienates him.
1809	Dies an outcast and pauper. Only six attend his funeral.

> *Such is the irresistible nature of truth that all it asks, and all it wants, is the liberty of appearing.*
>
> The Rights of Man (1791–2)

A 1792 caricature of Thomas Paine, surrounded by injustices, holding a scroll labeled "rights of man".

> *The cause of America is in a great measure the cause of all mankind.*
>
> Common Sense (1776)

George Washington reputedly ordered the pamphlet to be read aloud to troops to boost morale on the eve of battle.

The Rights of Man

In 1791 Paine produced Part I of *The Rights of Man*, subtitled *Being an Answer to Mr Burke's Attack on the French Revolution*. When Burke responded, Paine replied with Part II (1792). What began as a defense of the French Revolution became an examination of discontent in European society – the evils of arbitrary government, poverty, illiteracy, unemployment, and war. *The Rights of Man* not only championed republicanism over monarchy; it outlined a plan for popular education, relief of the poor, pensions for aged people, and public works for the unemployed, all to be financed by the levying of a progressive income tax.

The Age of Reason

Like **Voltaire**, Paine's Deist beliefs, coupled with a gifted polemical ability to express them, earned him a lasting reputation as an atheist. In fact *The Age of Reason* (1795–6) was written with the express design of combating atheism, and it begins with a frank statement of Paine's faith: *"I believe in one God, and no more; and I hope for happiness beyond this life"*.

However, Paine's trenchant and uncompromising attack on organized "revealed" religion, the compilation of inconsistencies he found in the Bible, and his own advocacy of Deism, resulted in his work being denounced as epitomizing atheism and infidelity. (As late as 1888, Theodore Roosevelt described Paine as *"a filthy little atheist"*.)

Jeremy Bentham

Bentham was an English philosopher, political reformer, and theoretical jurist. He was the "father" of utilitarianism, which evaluates actions based upon their consequences, in particular the overall happiness created for everyone affected by their actions. His theories on the penal system, poor law, voting rights, and legal reform were hugely influential in the nineteenth century.

Jeremy Bentham was born in the city of London in 1748, and educated at Westminster School. A child prodigy, he was sent to Queen's College, Oxford, aged 12. After graduating he studied law and was called to the Bar in 1769. However, much to the disappointment of his father, an attorney, he did not practice law, preferring instead to study how the law might be reformed.

His first publication, *A Fragment on Government* (1776), was an unsparing criticism of William Blackstone, jurist and professor of English law. In the 1770s Bentham also wrote his *Introduction to the Principles of Morals and Legislation*. Although not published until 1789, this remained the main theoretical work to be printed in his lifetime.

Bentham's interests in penal reform, crime, and punishment grew throughout the 1770s, spurred by evidence of a failing system: squalid prison hulks on the River Thames, and the evident failure of capital punishment to act as a deterrent. His pamphlet *A View of the Hard Labour Bill* (1778) has been credited with influencing the seminal Penitentiary Act of 1779.

In 1781 Bentham began a fruitful friendship with William Petty, Earl of Shelburne (who became Marquess of Lansdowne in 1784). Lansdowne's patronage would be invaluable, as would the connections he brought to Bentham.

In 1785 Bentham journeyed to visit his brother Samuel in Russia. While there he was inspired by Samuel's scheme for an "inspection house" – a circular building with a central observation post – and developed the design as a Panopticon (a prison allowing the guards to observe the prisoners without the prisoners being able to tell they are being watched). After returning to England he tried in vain for over 20 years, with Lansdowne's help, to persuade the government to adopt the Panopticon as a solution to England's penal failings.

In the early 1790s, as France slipped into Maximilien Robespierre's Reign of Terror, Bentham's enthusiasm for the French Revolution declined. He made a scathing analysis of the French Declaration of the Rights of Man in his polemical *Anarchical Fallacies* (1791–5; published 1816), in which he famously ridiculed the notion of "natural rights" as a "perversion of language" and "nonsense on stilts".

Britain's long and painful participation in the Napoleonic Wars, however, rekindled Bentham's radical **liberalism**. He worked closely with his disciples, the "philosophical radicals", in the early decades of the nineteenth century to further the reform agenda. He also co-founded the *Westminster Review* in 1823 to act as a radical counterpoint to the conservative journals of the time.

Bentham died in 1832, shortly after the Great Reform Act had passed through parliament. The Act introduced wide-ranging reforms to the electoral system of the United Kingdom, including improved voting rights for adult males.

Essential philosophy

Influenced by the *Philosophes* of the **Enlightenment** (such as Cesare, Marquis of Beccaria (1738–94), Claude Adrien Helvétius (1715–71), Denis Diderot (1713–84), Jean le Rond d'Alembert (1717–83), and **Voltaire**) and also by **John Locke** and **David Hume**, Bentham's work combined an **empiricist** approach with a **rationalism** that emphasized conceptual clarity and **deductive** argument.

A Fragment on Government

Bentham's *Fragment on Government* (1776) was a small part of his enormous *Comment* on the jurist William Blackstone's *Commentaries*, which to Bentham constituted outmoded statements of conservative legal theory and resistance to legal reform.

Bentham disagreed with Blackstone's defense of judge-made law, his theological formulation of the doctrine of mixed government, and other legal matters. While Bentham was content to point out the confusions in Blackstone's thought without developing his own ideas at any length, his *Fragment* nevertheless contains, in embryonic form, the central themes of his future work, including the principle of utility as the foundation of his system.

Utilitarianism and reform

Bentham's *Introduction to the Principles of Morals and Legislation* (1789) explicitly defines "utility" as:

> "*that property in any object, whereby it tends to produce benefit, advantage, pleasure, good, or happiness … or to prevent the happening of mischief, pain, evil, or unhappiness*".

The rightness of actions depends on their utility; and utility is measured by the consequences which the actions tend to produce.

Legacy, truth, consequence

- Bentham's ideas were carried on by followers such as **John Stuart Mill**, legal philosopher John Austin (1790–1859), and other **consequentialists** (who held that the consequences of a particular action form the basis for a valid moral judgement concerning that action).

- Bentham's influence was strong in the first half of the nineteenth century, and contributed much to the reform of the penal code and of the Poor Law, as well as to electoral reform.

- **Utilitarianism** was revised and expanded by Bentham's student, John Stuart Mill. In Mill's hands, "Benthamism" became a major element in the liberal conception of state policy objectives. Mill called Bentham one of the "seminal minds" of the eighteenth century, "*the great questioner of things established*".

- Modern utilitarianism remains an important theme in contemporary moral and political philosophy (see **Peter Singer**, pages 194–95).
- His theories on crime, punishment, and penal reform were influential on **structuralist** philosopher **Michel Foucault**.
- Bentham helped to found University College London, where his embalmed body still keeps watch in the South cloister.
- The bulk of Bentham's hugely prolific writings (he left manuscripts amounting to some 5,000,000 words) would not see the light of day until many years after his death. Since 1968, the *Bentham Project* at University College London has been preparing a definitive edition of his collected work. So far, 25 volumes have appeared; there may be as many still to come before the project is completed.

Key dates

1748	Born in London, England, to a wealthy Tory family.
1760	Sent to Queen's College, Oxford.
1763	Gains Oxford degree.
1769	Called to the Bar but does not practice.
1776	Publishes *A Fragment on Government*.
1785–7	Visits his brother Samuel Bentham in the Crimea; returns with a design for a prison: the Panopticon.
1787	*Panopticon* and *Defence of Usury* are published.
1789	Publishes *Introduction to the Principles of Morals and Legislation*.
1792	Made honorary Citizen of France.
1793	*Emancipate your Colonies* is published.
1811	*Punishments and Rewards* is published.
1816	*Anarchical Fallacies* is published.
1817	*Parliamentary Reform Catechism* is published.
1823	Founds the journal *Westminster Review*.
1832	Dies in London.

As Bentham requested in his will, his body was preserved and stored in a wooden cabinet, called his "Auto-icon".

... want is not supply; hunger is not bread…. Natural rights is simple nonsense: natural and imprescriptible rights, rhetorical nonsense – nonsense upon stilts.

Anarchical Fallacies (1816)

Of all these varying terms describing the consequences, the most important for Bentham are pleasure and pain:

"*Nature has placed mankind under the governance of two sovereign masters, pain and pleasure.*"

For Bentham, these are clear, easily understandable terms that can give precise sense to all others: the principle of utility must be interpreted in terms of the maximization of pleasure and the minimization of pain, since that is the only universally comprehensible measure of value.

Upon this principle of utility ("*the greatest happiness of the greatest number*"), Bentham wished to build a perfect system of law and government. If the aim of such a system were to bring happiness ("*the fabric of felicity*") to the people, the means must be through reason and law. In Bentham's draft codes of law, each was attached to a "*commentary of reasons on this law*". The commentary demonstrated its value and also, Bentham hoped, improved its effect.

Bentham and democracy

Bentham's *Parliamentary Reform Catechism* (1809; pub. 1817) showed that he was converted to **democracy** by 1809. In the catechism he demanded equal electoral districts, annual parliaments, household franchise, and reform of electoral procedures. These were necessary on the grounds of utility, for England was being governed by a minority in the interests of a minority, and only the "*democratical, which is the universal interest*" could secure the greatest happiness.

Mary Wollstonecraft

A true pioneer, Mary Wollstonecraft was a writer who argued eloquently for the education, independence, and rights of women. At the time she was condemned by society, not so much for her radical views, but for her unconventional lifestyle, since she dared to live with a man without marrying him. Today, she is considered to be a feminist heroine for her courage and her writings.

Mary was the oldest girl in a family of seven children. Her father was a handkerchief weaver, but he dragged the family around Britain with him as he attempted – and failed – to make a better living from farming. In his desperation he even stole the small legacy that was due to Mary, leaving her without any means of support. In those days there were very few respectable jobs or opportunities for women, but in 1777 Mary managed to find work as a lady's companion, a position which kept her poor and unhappy.

In 1784 she began to display the revolutionary attitudes that set her against society of the time. Her sister Eliza was deeply depressed by an unhappy marriage, and Mary went against all the cultural norms by persuading her to abandon her husband and child. To help support Eliza and herself, together with her closest friend, she set up a school in a progressive community in east London, but the school failed, and in 1786 Mary became a governess. She hated the experience, and in that period grew to despise the aristocratic women who followed social expectation by behaving as if they were weak and passive, needing the guidance of men, yet were cunning and manipulative behind the scenes.

In 1787 she began to explore her ideas in print, in a pamphlet *Thoughts on the Education of Daughters*. This was a fortunate development, since she was sacked that year but was given a lifeline by her publisher, who offered her an editorial job in London on a new radical magazine. Mary began to move in intellectual circles, and wrote two significant works, *A Vindication of the Rights of Men* and *A Vindication of the Rights of Woman*, in response to recently published books that infuriated her: one by **Edmund Burke** argued against the radical changes in society brought about by the 1789 revolution in France; the second, by **Jean-Jacques Rousseau**, stated that the only purpose of a woman's education was to enable her to help a man.

Her second book made her famous in Britain and on the continent. While many reactionaries laughed off her ideas on the education and abilities of women, radicals embraced her.

To recover from an unhappy love affair, Wollstonecraft joined other British supporters of the French Revolution in France. There she fell in love with an American, Gilbert Imlay, and had a child, Fanny, with him, and, although they did not marry she began to call herself Mrs Imlay. Her timing was bad: the Terror had begun and France and Britain were about to go to war, making life dangerous for British citizens on the Continent. Even worse, Imlay left her and her baby alone in France.

Essential philosophy

Equality and reason

As a philosopher of the European **Enlightenment**, Wollstonecraft saw rationality or reason as the key to human society, but, unlike male philosophers, she applied this to women as well as to men. She pointed out that women are not naturally inferior to men, either rationally or intellectually, and if they appear so it was because of lack of education or because women were playing the passive role expected of them.

At the time wealthy women lived empty lives dedicated to gaining male admiration, usually by overemphasizing "sensibility" – focusing on areas such as fashion that relied only upon sensing and feeling. Wollstonecraft argued that this emphasis further reduced women's reason, making them less effective wives, mothers, educators, and members of society.

Education and independence

She argued that women could only improve their lives and show that they were intellectual equals of men through proper education, which would not only supply rational ideas but would also offer the possibility of independence. She proposed a detailed educational plan putting girls' education on the same footing as that of boys', and suggested co-educational schools where boys and girls would be educated together. She was well ahead of her times, for many male thinkers just laughed at this idea.

Sexuality

Wollstonecraft was also ahead of her times in writing about the right of women to express their sexuality. She explored this particularly in her two novels, *Mary: A Fiction* (1788) and *Maria: or,*

> *How many women thus waste life away the prey of discontent, who might have practised as physicians, regulated a farm, managed a shop, and stood erect, supported by their own industry, instead of hanging their heads surcharged with the dew of sensibility, that consumes the beauty to which it at first gave lustre.*
>
> A Vindication of the Rights of Woman (1792)

Key dates

1759	Born in Spitalfields, east London, England.
1787	Publishes her first pamphlet on women's education.
1790	Publishes *A Vindication of the Rights of Men*.
1792	Publishes *A Vindication of the Rights of Woman*.
1793	Lives in France with Gilbert Imlay.
1794	Her first daughter Fanny is born, illegitimately.
1797	Marries William Godwin.
1797	Dies in London of complications after childbirth.

The Tennis Court Oath, on June 20, 1789, sparked the French Revolution. Wollstonecraft left for Paris and its stimulating intellectual atmosphere in December 1792.

Always subject to depression, and well aware of her emotional needs, Wollstonecraft followed Imlay to Britain, but tried to commit suicide with an overdose of laudanum (a tincture of opium) when he refused to return to her. Desperate to win him back, she undertook a business trip to Scandinavia for him, traveling with only her baby and one maid. Some of her letters to Imlay, containing philosophical musings and inspirational travel writing, were published in 1796 as *Letters Written During a Short Residence in Sweden, Norway, and Denmark*. Back in London Imlay rejected her once more, and she attempted suicide by jumping into the river Thames, only to be dragged out by a passerby.

Wollstonecraft turned back to literary endeavors, and slowly formed a passionate relationship with the philosopher William Godwin (1756–1836). When she became pregnant again, they married in order to remove the stigma of illegitimacy from the child, and only then did it come out that she had never married Imlay. Society was scandalized, even some of the couple's friends. Mary's and William's life together was happy but short: she died after giving birth to her second child, who, as Mary Wollstonecraft Shelley, would find lasting fame as the author of the novel *Frankenstein*.

> *Till women are more rationally educated, the progress in human virtue and improvement in knowledge must receive continual checks.*
>
> A Vindication of the Rights of Woman (1792)

The Wrongs of Woman (published posthumously in 1798). In both of these the married heroines only find love and fulfilment in extra-marital relationships, whether sexual or platonic.

Legacy, truth, consequence

■ At first Wollstonecraft's arguments were supported by many women. But her reputation was completely ruined when it became widely known that she had had an affair before she was married. From then on, she and all her works became tainted in the eyes of polite society, and apart from one or two suffragettes, her philosophy was ignored for more than a hundred years.

■ Modern feminists see her as a pioneer who put forward compelling arguments that women have the same abilities of reason and intelligence as men, and should have the same rights. She is also admired as a courageous woman who was willing to ignore social prejudices in order to live according to her own views.

■ *A Vindication of the Rights of Woman* is now a feminist classic.

■ Wollstonecraft also celebrated feelings and sensitivity to nature, especially in her *Letters Written in Sweden, Norway, and Denmark*. This had an influence on the later **Romantic** movement.

Georg Wilhelm Friedrich Hegel

G. W. F. Hegel was a hugely influential philosopher in his lifetime and beyond. Along with J. G. Fichte and F. W. J. Schelling he was a creator of German idealism. His work constitutes a weighty philosophical system in which he attempts to unify many of philosophy's traditional dualities through the use of "dialectic", a type of logical and critical thinking.

Hegel was born in Stuttgart in southern Germany in 1770. He attended a Protestant seminary at the age of 18, where he met the poet Friedrich Hölderlin and the philosopher Friedrich Willhelm Joseph Schelling (1775–1854), both of whom were influential in the development of his thought. After working as a tutor and lecturer he became a professor at Jena, in central Germany, although financial problems that followed the Battle of Jena (Prussia was defeated by Napoléon I of France and Jena was occupied by the French army) meant that he had to go and work as a newspaper editor and headmaster. In 1816 his academic career restarted, first in Heidelberg, and then Berlin, where he became professor of philosophy in 1818. His fame spread throughout this period and his lectures were attended by students and academics from across Europe. He became rector of the University of Berlin in 1830, but died following a cholera epidemic in the city in 1831.

Essential philosophy

Hegel's philosophy was rooted in the ideas of his predecessor J. G. Fichte (1762–1814), who propounded a theory of **absolute idealism**. Fichte and other German idealists were responding to **Immanuel Kant**'s **metaphysical** system, which showed how we can only have knowledge of the "phenomena" presented to the mind (our ideas), and not any real knowledge of the **"noumenal" realm** (the real world of things-in-themselves lying behind the appearances).

The idealism of **Bishop Berkeley** had aimed to show that **absolute knowledge** is subject to our faith in God, but the German idealists took a more **humanist** approach, claiming we can attain real knowledge through philosophy that focuses more on the thinker than the thought. Fichte, in order to avoid **scepticism** about the external world, claimed that objects only exist as the objects of consciousness, and not as things-in-themselves belonging to a world outside our consciousness. Hegel, searching for another way to attain absolute knowledge, used the idea of historical progress: the gradual evolution of the history of thought is how we reach absolute truth, a conceptual notion in Hegel's philosophy, rather than an **empirically**-based notion about how things are in the world. Thus he talks about ideas or concepts, rather than **propositions**, being capable of truth and falsity. Ultimately, the unfolding process towards absolute truth leads to an absolute universal mind or spirit.

He also emphasized the importance of the "other" in the development of self-consciousness. Expanding on this idea in his dialectic of master and slave, he shows that the "self" (the "master") generally appropriates the "other" (the "slave"); the slave makes himself the corporeal body of the master's will.

Hegel is not an easy philosopher to read or understand. His response to Kant's limits of "pure reason" was to try to develop a new form of thinking: "speculative reason". He aimed thus to overcome the limitations of common sense and traditional philosophy in mapping the relation between thought and reality. "Speculative reason" is mainly remembered for the specific idea of "**dialectic**".

Dialectic

For Hegel, society and philosophy were fraught with contradictions and tensions, such as those between mind and nature, subject and object, self and other, freedom and authority, or knowledge and faith. As **Socrates** had done in his dialogues, Hegel tried to bring out the hidden contradictions in ideas (concepts). His main philosophical project was to interpret these contradictions and tensions as part of a comprehensive, evolving, rational unity that he called "the absolute idea" or "absolute knowledge".

This unity evolves through contradiction and negation, which Hegel referred to as dialectic. His ideas have often been popularly explained as taking a "thesis" and "antithesis" and combining these to produce a "synthesis". In fact he rarely used this terminology, and the actual process of his dialectic was more complex than this simplified summary suggests. Modern interpreters of Hegel focus on the "dialec-tical moment", when things or thoughts are transformed into their opposites or have their inner contradictions revealed. This is preliminary to the "speculative moment", which ascertains the unity of these opposites or contradictions. This process doesn't lead to the stable unity of "synthesis" but to a further unstable state of "recognition". So for Hegel, reason is endlessly speculative. Synthesis is never reached because a "remainder" or anomaly always remains, but in the process our ideas are continually refined, leading ever closer to "absolute knowledge".

Legacy, truth, consequence

- Hegel's attempt at building an impregnable system of philosophy has been given many interpretations. In his lifetime, Hegelian philosophy was highly regarded. To later critics, such as **Friedrich Nietzsche** and **Arthur Schopenhauer**, he was a pompous thinker, using deliberate obfuscation and sleight of hand to support his structure.
- **Karl Marx** and **Friedrich Engels** adopted Hegel's dialectical method, but inverted it to suit their pure **materialism**, rather than accepting Hegel's idealism.
- To some degree Hegel fell out of favor, before being rediscovered in the twentieth century. Writers such as **Jacques Derrida** and the psychologist Jacques Lacan (1901–81) did not accept the absolute Hegelian system, but found inspiration in his ideas of self, the "other", and difference.

> **What is rational is actual and what is actual is rational. On this conviction the plain man like the philosopher takes his stand …**
>
> *Elements of the Philosophy of Right* (1821)

Identity in difference

At the heart of Hegel's **epistemology** is the idea of "identity in difference". He describes the mind as externalizing itself in various forms and objects that are outside it ("the other"). When the mind recognizes itself in these different forms and objects, a unity is reached of mind and other.

As he considers different areas of knowledge, such as consciousness, philosophy, art, nature, history, and society, he views them each undergoing dialectical development until a rational unity is achieved. The same logical order and development underlies all of reality, and is identical with the structure of rational thought. However, the dialectical process is not fully conscious at all times. Only through philosophical meditation and higher stages of history can the dialectical process come to an understanding of itself. Thus our conceptions of "self" and "other" join in a unified, continually developing whole. Hegel claims this creates a path to genuine knowledge, because the living process of the brain, the entire process of thinking, is the subject of our study, and the real world is only the external form of "the idea".

The end of history

Hegel's conception of historical progress has often been seen as progression towards greater perfection. The one time he clearly used the "thesis/antithesis/synthesis" terminology (which he attributed to Kant) was in discussing the French Revolution (1789–99). In this context he sees the attempt to claim freedom via revolution as the thesis, but one so radical that it provokes the antithesis of the Reign of Terror. Arising out of this is the possibility of a synthesis – the constitutional state where citizens have their liberty without needing to make a radical claim for it.

Key dates

1770	Born in Stuttgart, in southern Germany.
1801	Secures a position as an unsalaried lecturer at Jena University after submitting his dissertation. The same year his first book, *The Difference between Fichte's and Schelling's Systems of Philosophy*, is published.
1805	Promoted to extraordinary professor but is still unsalaried.
1807	His long awaited book, *Phenomenology of Mind* (first volume), is published – an introduction to Hegel's system.
1812	*Science of Logic* is published (first volume; second and third volumes are published in 1813 and 1816 respectively)
1816	Becomes a professor in Heidelberg. *Encyclopedia of the Philosophical Sciences* is published.
1818	Accepts the chair of philosophy at the University of Berlin.
1821	*Elements of the Philosophy of Right* is published.
1830	Becomes rector of the University of Berlin.
1831	Dies following a cholera epidemic in Berlin.

A depiction of Hegel teaching. Hegel's lectures were attended by students and academics from across Europe.

Some have seen this as describing a progress towards an "end of history". Both **Marxists** and neo-conservatives have adopted a dialectical approach to history which suggests that their preferred endpoint is an inevitable result of the tides of history. In fact, Hegel didn't see the dialectical progression as resulting in a stable endpoint. However, he did describe it as an inexorable movement towards higher forms of civilization and intellectual achievement, in which each country's genius would contribute to the development of the "world spirit" (an idea that was seized upon by revolutionary thinkers). And it is fair to suggest that Hegel had a rather complacent view both of his own importance as the high point of all previous philosophical thought and of the near-perfection of the Prussian state of his lifetime.

Arthur Schopenhauer

Schopenhauer is an anomalous, and often misrepresented figure in the history of Western philosophy. He has been called a pessimist, an ascetic, an anti-Semite, or a misogynist, and all of these labels have some foundation. But there is more to his thought, and he repays careful study. His philosophy, which takes Immanuel Kant as its starting point, can be seen as a bridge to the aesthetic and psychological aspects of twentieth-century philosophy.

Schopenhauer's life story is a strange one. Born in 1788 in the city of Danzig, his father died when he was seventeen, possibly from suicide. His mother, though friends with writers such as Johann Goethe, never got along well with her son. The young Schopenhauer studied philosophy in Berlin, especially **Plato** and **Kant**, and became a fervent opponent of the philosophy of **G. W. F. Hegel**, which he regarded as pompous, self-serving and intentionally mystifying. When he became a university lecturer he purposefully scheduled his first lecture at the same time as the far more famous Hegel. Only a handful of students attended Schopenhauer's lecture and he never taught again. After becoming embroiled in a bizarre lawsuit with a woman who had been noisy outside his apartment, he finally settled in Frankfurt, where he lived alone, except for his pet poodles. Such details make him appear a tragicomic figure, but along the way he produced some fascinating philosophical work.

> *This actual world of what is knowable, in which we are and which is in us, remains both the material and the limit of our consideration.*
>
> The World As Will And Representation (1819)

Essential philosophy

"Will" and "representation"
Schopenhauer's key work, *The World As Will And Representation*, was published in 1819. Regarding himself a follower of Kant, he was deeply critical of other contemporaries such as Johann Fichte (1762–1814) and Friedrich Schelling (1775–1854). He opposed Hegel for personal and theoretical reasons. Hegel's politics were meaningless and "respectable" in Schopenhauer's view, by which he meant that Hegel was an establishment figure who wanted acclaim more than he wanted the truth. In theoretical terms, Schopenhauer returned to Kant's division of the world into **noumena** and **phenomena** (see pages 100–1). Like Kant, he defined *phenomena* as ideas (or "representations"). But while Kant had referred to *noumena* as "things-in-themselves", Schopenhauer took a different view, referring to them as "will". For him, representations or ideas were simply the way we experience the world's basic drive, which is "will".

David Hume had argued that we do not directly experience objects in the world that are external to us. Schopenhauer took issue with this idea, asserting that we can have direct knowledge of our own body, and that this allows us to conceive of objects in the real world. We experience drives and desires in our own bodies, and we interpret these as representations. It is crucial to understanding Schopenhauer to realize that he is thus asserting that we do not fully understand these drives and desires. We simply find ways of translating them into ideas. This is one of the respects in which Schopenhauer prefigured **psychoanalysis**.

The "river of will"
Schopenhauer sees us as individuals swept along on a "river of will", acting and thinking, and then trying to comprehend our own actions and thoughts. This causes suffering for the individual. There are only two ways we can deal with the condition of life. One is through denial of the "will", ascetic living, which is only appropriate for some people. For others, the best way to deal with the "will" is through a kind of universal compassion for the human condition, by understanding that this suffering is experienced by everyone else too.

From here, Schopenhauer developed a theory of **aesthetics**. He saw tragedy as the highest art form. If the human condition is defined by suffering, tragedy is the art that attempts to come to terms with and comprehend that suffering. This conception of tragic art has been an extremely influential one, and was the

■ Schopenhauer is a writer of great significance in the birth of modern **psychology** and the development of aesthetics. He was influential on thinkers as varied as Nietzsche, **Ludwig Wittgenstein** and Sigmund Freud (1856–1939).

■ He was an important predecessor of two of the most significant strands of thought over the twentieth century. The Freudian notions of libido and of unconscious forces shaping our thoughts are essentially a restatement of Schopenhauer's thinking about the "will". Charles Darwin's conception of natural selection (though not connected historically or intellectually) is another echo of Schopenhauer, as it sees our reproductive behavior as rooted in forces that are for the good of the species rather than arising from individual needs.

■ For the modern reader Schopenhauer's weaknesses can be offputting. Politically he had some fairly indefensible views, seeing women as inferior, and talking of Jews and other races in derogatory terms. He also talked positively of eugenics. Of course such prejudices were widespread at the time in his society. In other respects he was more progressive, opposing the taboos on suicide and homosexuality and speaking out against the treatment of African slaves.

■ Schopenhauer was ahead of his time in his attitude to Eastern religion. As he saw the "will" as the cause of suffering, he was interested in **Buddhist** thought and in the Upanishads (part of the Hindu scriptures), both of which advocate asceticism as a way of escaping the tyranny of the "will". It was rare for a Western philosopher of this period to consider these religions, although it would become more common in the twentieth century.

■ Nietzsche admired Schopenhauer but saw his emphasis on asceticism as a passive, feeble response to the "will". For Nietzsche denial of the "will to power" was a weakness that led to what he regarded as Schopenhauer's corrosive pessimism, and in others to *ressentiment* and the "slave mentality" of Christianity. Nietzsche's response would be to call for his readers to seek self-affirmation. One doesn't have to agree with Nietzsche's analysis to see Schopenhauer's pessimism as depressing.

starting point for **Friedrich Nietzsche**'s early work *The Birth of Tragedy* (1872), although Nietzsche went on to reject some of his predecessor's ideas, especially his pessimism.

Schopenhauer had a high regard for the aesthetic value of music, which he described as a direct interpretation of "will". In the aesthetic contemplation of tragedy and music, he found a third way (following self-denial and compassionate sympathy) of achieving temporary respite from the suffering that the "will" causes us.

From aesthetics to psychology

Schopenhauer's ideas about the will were also at the root of his writing on **psychology**. He wrote extensively about love, a subject which has often been skated round or ignored by major philosophers. His real love life was a rocky one, but perhaps this gave him a keen insight into the passions and sufferings of lovers. Love has often been described in terms of beauty, companionship, or family. Schopenhauer took a rather more violent approach, acknowledging the passion and irrationality of love. He described love in terms of his fundamental idea of the "will", the driving force that carries us along in spite of our incomprehension.

1788	Born in Danzig (now Gdansk, in Poland).
1811–12	Attends the University of Berlin.
1814	Starts work on *The World As Will And Representation* (published 1819).
1820	Briefly becomes a lecturer.
1831	Flees a cholera epidemic in Berlin (in which Hegel died).
1833	Settles in Frankfurt.
1836	*On The Will in Nature* is published.
1839	*On the Freedom of the Will* is published.
1840	*On the Basis of Morality* is published.
1860	Dies of heart failure.

The composer reveals the innermost nature of the world, and expresses the profoundest wisdom in a language that his reasoning faculty does not understand . . .

The World As Will And Representation (1819)

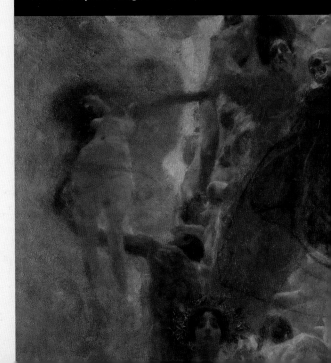

Composition draft of *Medicine*, a painting by the symbolist artist Gustav Klimt, now destroyed. The Symbolists shared Schopenhauer's theory of aesthetics and tended to look to art as a contemplative refuge from the world of strife and "will".

Auguste Comte

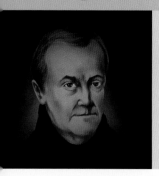

Auguste Comte, philosopher and father of French positivism, did much to further the development of the social sciences, and is generally credited with having coined the term "sociology". As a vigorous proponent of a scientific approach to human phenomena, Comte acted as a harbinger of modern social and behavioral science. However, the mysticism of his later years somewhat damaged his philosophical reputation.

Isidore Auguste Marie François Xavier Comte was born in 1798 in Montpellier, southwest France. He attended Montpellier University before studying in Paris at the École Polytechnique, which was noted for its republican, progressive ideals.

Soon after the École's temporary closure in 1816, Comte took up residence in Paris, eking out a living through occasional tutoring and journalism. During this time he read widely and began to construct his own system of **positivist** thought, while also forming an influential friendship with Henri de Saint-Simon (1760–1825), social reformer and one of the founders of socialism, though he broke with Saint-Simon in 1824.

In 1826 Comte began a series of lectures on his "*system of positive philosophy*" for a private audience, which he developed into a successful lecture series in 1828–9, despite suffering a severe nervous breakdown. He devoted the following twelve years to completing his *Course of Positive Philosophy* (published in six volumes, 1830–42).

Between 1832 and 1842 Comte taught at the École Polytechnique. However, he lost his post following a quarrel with the school's directors, and for the rest of his life was financially dependent on his French disciples as well as admirers such as the English philosopher **John Stuart Mill**.

Comte married Caroline Massin in 1825, but they were unhappy and separated in 1842. From 1844 he became profoundly involved with Clotilde de Vaux, in an intense platonic relationship, but de Vaux died in 1846 of tuberculosis. Comte idealized their love to a quasi-religious status, and in his later writings saw himself as founder and prophet of a new "religion of humanity", in which scientists and industrialists would replace priests.

The years following Clotilde de Vaux's death were devoted to composing his last works: *The System of Positive Polity* (1851–4), in which he completed his blueprint of sociology and his idealized positivist society; *The Catechism of Positive Religion* (1852); and *Subjective Synthesis* (1856).

Comte lived to see his writings widely analyzed throughout Europe. He was influential in England, where his work was translated and disseminated. The number of French devotees also increased, and a large correspondence developed with positivist societies throughout the world. Comte died of cancer in 1857.

Essential philosophy

Comte sought a system of philosophy that could form a basis for political organization in tune with modern industrial society. His dual achievement was in establishing such a system, "positivism", and allying it to the newly defined discipline of sociology.

His gift was in synthesizing the most diverse intellectual streams: he derived his conception of positivism from **David Hume** and **Immanuel Kant**; he used the Catholic Church as a model for a disciplined, hierarchical framework for social organization; from **Enlightenment** philosophers he adopted the notion of historical progress; and from Saint-Simon he came to appreciate the need for a basic and unifying social science, for which he coined the word "sociology".

Comte shared Saint-Simon's faith in the capacity of modern science and scientific methods to improve society. Furthermore, he believed that the ultimate aim of sociology's innovation and systematization should be the control of social planning. Comte also believed a new, secularized spiritual order was needed to supersede the outmoded supernaturalism of Christian theology: his "religion of humanity", outlined in *The Catechism of Positive Religion*, 1852.

Positivism and sociology

Comte saw positivism as a theory based on the idea that theology and **metaphysics** are earlier, imperfect modes of knowledge and that positive knowledge comes from natural phenomena and their properties and relations as verified by the **empirical** sciences. According to his "law of the three stages" (defined in the first volume of his *Course of Positive Philosophy*, 1830), society has passed through three distinct phases in its quest for the truth: the theological, the metaphysical, and the positive.

During the theological stage, the world and human destiny were explained in terms of gods and spirits; in the metaphysical stage (from the **Renaissance** to the Enlightenment), explanations were in terms

Legacy, truth, consequence

■ Comte laid the foundations for the discipline of sociology. His belief in the importance of the scientific study of human society remains an article of faith among contemporary sociologists.

■ Social scientists such as Émile Durkheim (1858–1917), Herbert Spencer (1820–1903), and Sir Edward Burnett Tylor (1832–1917) were all influenced by Comte.

■ Comte was also highly admired by John Stuart Mill. Mill said of Comte's *Course of Positive Philosophy*: "*This book is, I think, one of the most profound books ever written on the philosophy of the sciences*" (Letter to John Nichol, Dec 21, 1837).

■ Comte's secular "religion of humanity" attracted adherents both in France and internationally, most notably in Brazil. In 1881 Miguel Lemos (1854–1917) and Raimundo Teixeira Mendes (1855–1927) organized the "Positivist Church of Brazil".

■ The motto *Ordem e Progresso* ("Order and Progress") in the flag of Brazil is inspired by Comte's motto of positivism: "*Love for the system, and order for the base; progress for the goal*" (*The System of Positive Polity*, 1851–4).

Key dates

1798	Born in Montpellier, France.
1814	Enters École Polytechnique, Paris.
1816	Leaves École Polytechnique following its temporary closure.
1817	Meets Henri de Saint-Simon in Paris.
1824	Breaks with Saint-Simon.
1825	Marries Caroline Massin.
1826	Begins lecturing on his "system of positive philosophy". Suffers nervous breakdown.
1828–9	Continues lecturing successfully.
1830–42	Publishes *Course of Positive Philosophy* in six volumes.
1832–42	Teaches at Ecole Polytechnique, Paris.
1842	Separates from Caroline Massin.
1844	Meets Clotilde de Vaux; begins unrequited love affair.
1846	Death of Clotilde de Vaux.
1851–4	Publishes *The System of Positive Polity*.
1857	Dies in Paris and is buried at the Cimetière du Père Lachaise.

> ### [Man] was a theologian in his childhood, a metaphysician in his youth, and a natural philosopher in his manhood.
>
> *Course of Positive Philosophy*, Vol. 1 (1830–42)

Ordem e Progresso, the motto in the flag of Brazil, inspired by Comte's writings on positivism.

of essences, final causes, and other abstractions; and in the modern, positive stage, society has become aware of the limitations of human knowledge – absolute explanations are therefore better abandoned in favor of laws based on the observable relations between phenomena.

Although Comte did not originate the concept of sociology or its area of study, he greatly extended and elaborated the field and systematized its content. His development of sociology grew out of his perception that scientific, or "positive", methodology should be extended to the study of politics and society as a way of bringing order to the post-revolutionary, industrialized world of the nineteenth century. To adopt the positive method meant avoiding metaphysical speculations by tying scientific laws to concrete facts; once established, all ideas would be scientific, homogenous, and unified. Then by extending such science to society, in sociology, attention could be focused on humanity, and agreement reached on essential intellectual and moral principles. Thus sociology, through positivism, would bring a new consensus, forming the basis for a stable, industrial social order.

Comte divided sociology into two branches: social statics, or the study of the forces that hold society together; and social dynamics, or the study of the causes of social change. Both stressed the interconnectedness of human beings as a way of countering the egoism of the modern age.

In addition to delineating the two divisions of sociology, Comte outlined the three key methods of this new science: observation, experimentation, and comparison. Sociologists should observe ordinary events, customs, languages, and other social phenomena; like biologists, they should study pathological cases as a means of experimentation; and they should compare human societies against animal ones, as well as different, and consecutive, states of human society. Comte's methodologies were revolutionary, and many aspects are still relevant to current theory.

John Stuart Mill

J. S. Mill is recognized as the major English-speaking philosopher of the nineteenth century. He presided over the progressive opinion of an era that saw the demise of the intellectual idea of Christianity; political argument over liberal social and economic reform; massive growth of industrialization with the commodification of the working population that Karl Marx criticized; and the British Empire's growing responsibilities as governor of a significant part of the globe.

John Stuart Mill's life was fundamentally influenced by, and came to influence, the British **empiricist** tradition. Raised as the product of **utilitarian** ideals, under the strict auspices of his father specifically to become the genius of utilitarianism and carry forward its radical social program, Mill learnt Greek at three, Latin at eight, and had studied extensively in logic, mathematics, history, science, and economic theory by the time he was fourteen. This human engineering was based on **Jeremy Bentham**'s idea of psychological development, stemming from **John Locke**'s account of the mind as a blank slate on which experience (education in the widest sense) writes our character.

The relentless intensity of this process brought Mill to a "mental crisis" in which, feeling almost manufactured, he came to regard his education as lacking room for feelings, emotions, and cultural life. Poetry and a growing love of nature rescued him. The insight he gained from the experience influenced his whole life: which can be seen as a refining and developing of the utilitarian idea, along subtler lines responding to a richer and more deeply human, and social, understanding of "experience". It colored his ideas of education, the role of environmental influence, and governmental or legislative intervention. Continuing his father's radical political (utilitarian) involvements, J. S. Mill's liberal, even **socialist**, concerns drove his actions and his view of the import and purpose of philosophy itself.

Mill's works run to more than 30 volumes, all written while busy in other fields: a highly successful career in the East India Company, an MP, and editor of the (radical) *Westminster Review*. He was also involved in agitation for many specific reforms, exemplifying the ideals of social change he dedicated his life to, including his early arrest for distributing birth control literature, having seen in London unwanted babies abandoned to die. He himself credited his wife's influence as decisive emotionally and intellectually, and she was certainly vital to his promotion of women's suffrage.

Mill's moral philosophy marks a fundamental shift from the detached pronouncements of reason to a concern with the expediency of human affairs, practical needs, and the happiness of human kind.

Essential philosophy

Usually thought of in terms of **ethics** and **politics**, Mill also wrote on traditional **metaphysical** subjects like **epistemology**. The unifying principle was the **empiricism** of his predecessors, which he carried further. He was always committed to the idea that the best method of explaining the world was that of the natural sciences: everything questioned is seen as part of the **causal** order of the natural world and examined by their methods.

Logic and induction

In his *System of Logic*, following the position reached by **David Hume**, Mill argues that it is not only **propositions** about the world (involving causation, the external world, and **other minds**) that are **inductive**, i.e. *a posteriori* and never more than probable. So also are the truths of mathematics. Our ideas of number, for example, are abstractions from our experience of 1, 2, 3 ... objects in the world. For Mill the laws of mathematics are inductive generalizations.

To answer **Bishop Berkeley**'s problem of accounting for unperceived entities, Mill's epistemology introduces the idea that physical objects are "permanent possibilities of **perception**". He also makes clear his major theme (not openly admitted in Hume) of defending the status of **inductive reasoning**. **Deductive logic** (**analytic**, *a priori*) adds nothing to our knowledge. Inductive reasoning (**synthetic**, *a posteriori*) is the only form of "ampliative" **inference**, i.e. contributing new information. The ultimate uncertainty of such inference shouldn't lead to **scepticism** about its use, but rather to a new assessment of rational justification in support of inductive reasoning. In order to live we cannot avoid making all sorts of inductions (that the sun will rise tomorrow, and so on), so it is strictly unreasonable, he says, to propose that we abandon the process. We ought to utilize it. Mill defends as rational the fallible knowledge of induction.

Ethics

The utilitarianism Mill inherited from Bentham had sought to give a sound basis to the answering of moral questions that Hume's empiricism had made a matter of opinion or "sentiment",

Legacy, truth, consequence

■ Hugely influential on the opinions of his own times, Mill's popular significance lies in expressing the progressive soul of the nineteenth century. In many practical fields – the voting system and proportional representation, workers' rights, education, economics, women's suffrage – Mill's work is a liberal starting point. His attempt to show that justice can be described in utilitarian terms is still important for those opposing, for example, **John Rawls'** contemporary theory of justice.

■ In logic his work was opposed by **Gottlob Frege's** and **Bertrand Russel's** innovations in the early twentieth century, but there has been some movement against this attack in the work of, for example, **W. V. O. Quine**. His discussion of deductive knowledge in terms of its analytic, non-ampliative nature leads on to the notion of **Ludwig Wittgenstein** (and **logical positivism**) that all **necessary truth** is tautological. In metaphysics his assertion of the mental nature of our experience of the world was the first statement of **phenomenalism**.

■ Mill was also an early environmentalist, who argued for population control as an antidote to the growing destruction of nature for man's use, and for the abandonment of the aim of unquestioned economic growth. All in all, he gave the standard account of **empiricist liberalism** – humane, progressive – written in prose that was celebrated in his own time as its perfect expression, and still stands the test today.

> *Whatever crushes individuality is despotism, whether it professes to be enforcing the will of God or the injunctions of men.*
>
> On Liberty (1859)

Key dates

1806	Born in London, England.
1818	Aged twelve, his notes on his father's economy lessons become the basis for a book: *Elements of Political Economy*.
1823–58	Works for the East India company, achieving the highest position of examiner.
1826	Experiences a mental breakdown.
1830	Meets Harriet Taylor and begins lifelong relationship, only being able to marry – after her husband dies – in 1851.
1843	Publishes first major work, *A System of Logic Ratiocinative and Inductive*.
1848	Publishes *Principles of Political Economy*.
1859	Publishes *On Liberty*.
1863	Publishes *Utilitarianism*.
1865	Elected MP and continues to work for many radical causes.
1869	Publishes *Subjection of Women*.
1873	Dies in France and is buried next to his wife. His last works *Autobiography* and *Three Essays on Religion* are posthumously published.

East India House, London, headquarters of the British East India company where Mill worked from 1823 to 1858.

unjustified as "knowledge". Bentham had done this by putting forward the famous maxim that actions are good or bad according to whether their consequences tend to produce the greatest happiness or unhappiness in the greatest number of people. Mill's innovation was to mitigate this soulless view, in which happiness is simply quantifiable and "**egoistic**", with a stress on qualitative aspects of pleasure (and therefore the good) that was central to an "altruistic" utilitarianism: man as cultural animal, not just a selfish mechanistic unit. Mill's ethics express, in contrast to Bentham's blythe self-confidence, the subtle and difficult reality of ethical questions.

Politics

The association of philosophy with the advancement of the moral and practical welfare of mankind had been present in empiricism since **Francis Bacon** and can be seen in all Mill's work. Mill gives the best nineteenth-century account of liberal interventionism and reformist aims in politics. He defends individual freedom in compliance with restrictions against harming others, even in cases of what we might consider self-harm (e.g. suicide). More than Bentham he takes into account the difference between the individual's happiness and the common happiness. He is particularly worried about the "tyranny of the majority"; for Mill there should be no prohibitions of individual behavior (for the good of the community or the individual himself) except where it would lead to the harm of others.

He similarly defends free speech: because we cannot guarantee any opinion is not true, in prohibiting it we may lose some genuine insight. It is a **necessary condition** of intellectual and social progress, and all "personal development" – a moral aim for Mill.

Religion

On matters of religion Mill was an atheist from boyhood, but postponed the full publication of his opinions until late in his career so as to prejudice as little as possible the reception of the rest of his work.

Alexander Herzen

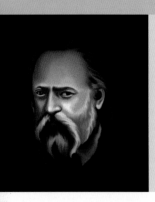

Alexander Herzen is one of the most intriguing and humane thinkers of the Russian nineteenth century. He has been described as the father of Russian socialism, although he was in many respects opposed to the kind of radicalism that eventually turned into Marxism, and can also be claimed as a founding father of liberalism. He was a campaigning journalist and publisher, and his widely read newspaper, *The Bell*, played an important part in campaigning for the emancipation of the serfs, which was achieved in 1861.

Herzen was born in Moscow in 1812. As a young man in the early 1830s he witnessed the oppressive regime under the Tsar, and the increasingly vocal opposition of a small group of radicals. He himself was inspired to become a radical by the failure of the Decembrist uprising. While followers of the revolutionary Mikhail Bakunin (1814–76) looked towards **G. W. F. Hegel**'s idea of the progress of the "world spirit" (see page 111), Herzen led a group who saw the French Revolution and utopian **socialism** as their inspiration. He was arrested in 1834, for having attended a festival at which the Tsar had been publicly criticized.

The next 13 years were spent in banishment or exile, before he finally managed to leave Russia, taking a considerable inherited fortune with him. For the remainder of his life he was a resident in various European cities, including London and Geneva. He fervently supported the wave of 1848 revolutions across Europe, but became frustrated with the European socialist movements after their failures. In 1852 Herzen moved to London, where, from 1857, he published frequent editions of *The Bell* along with

another review, *The Polar Star*. He still believed in a socialist future for Russia, but he was also in favor of individual rights. His strongest campaigns in Russia, where *The Bell* was widely distributed, were for liberty – the emancipation of the serfs, free speech, and individual rights within the law.

Herzen's reputation gradually waned in the 1860s. The increasing liberties accorded by the Russian state meant that his initial aims had been achieved, while the continuing inhumanities of the Tsarist regime reduced hopes of further progress through campaigning alone. When Herzen defended the Polish insurrection in 1863, he lost many liberal admirers in Russia (because they had supported the Tsar's harsh treatment of the Poles). After moving to Geneva to try and keep *The Bell* in business (which he ultimately failed to do), he finally moved to Paris, where he died in 1870. His autobiography *My Past and Thoughts*, which dealt frankly with the personal tragedies he had experienced as well as his detailed political thoughts, became widely read, and would keep his reputation alive.

Essential philosophy

In his most popular period, Herzen often fell between two opposing camps. The failure of the 1848 revolutions had created a gloomy atmosphere in European radicalism, in which the pessimism of **Arthur Schopenhauer** gained a following, as it seemed to catch the mood of the times. Herzen was a self-proclaimed socialist, but Russian radicals often felt he was too ready to accept a gradualist approach, rather than to call for the violent overthrow of the Tsar. Meanwhile the liberals, who advocated a more gradualist approach themselves were at odds with him over his view of history. The Hegelian idea of historical progress had been adopted by both camps – for the radicals, a violent revolution was required to move Russia into a new phase of history, while the liberals trusted that gradual increases in liberty could steadily lead to a better condition of society.

Herzen, in spite of being a Hegelian in his youth, rejected historical inevitability. He insisted that history was contingent, and that change is achieved by individual action rather than historical inevitability, and

that to describe current suffering as justifiable in achieving the final revolution was immoral. His belief in the rights of the individual was too strong for him to accept that individual freedom should be subjugated to the greater progress of man. However, he did advocate the ongoing struggle to reform society, believing that only through individual action would a better society be achieved.

For this reason Herzen despised the politics of **Karl Marx**, who lived in London at the same time as he did. In particular, he didn't accept Marx's abstract, **materialist** idea of human progress. Herzen would always argue for the individual over the collective, and for actual, verifiable fact over theoretical, untested ideals. Having seen the malaise that affected the attempted revolutions in 1848 he knew how **idealism** could degenerate into **despotism**. He would have been unsurprised by the failure of post-revolutionary Russia, and dismayed to see his beloved Russia succumb to what he perceived as Marx's mechanical theory rather than to a more humane **socialism**.

Legacy, truth, consequence

■ After a period of being somewhat out of fashion, Herzen became more popular in Russia through the 1880s. Leo Tolstoy was quoted as saying that he had never met anyone "*with so rare a combination of scintillating brilliance and depth*".

■ Vladimir Lenin was another admirer. He rejected the supposedly "bourgeois" interpretation of Herzen, claiming him as a proto-revolutionary who had opposed the liberal forces and their passive approach to reform. This wasn't the first time that Marxist–Leninists chose to rewrite history in their own image, nor would it be the last.

■ One of the problems with Herzen as a political hero is that he was a prolific writer who could side with radicals or liberals of his time on varying issues, and thus can be claimed by different traditions. Lenin's admiration for him demonstrates this point. But what shines through in the end are the qualities that Berlin admired in him – his passionate belief that individuals could build a better society, and his unending battles for individual freedom.

■ He is also one of the most likeable intellectual figures of his time. His autobiography and letters reveal an honest, self-doubting man, who contemplated the possibility that his life had been a failure. He expressed the angst and uncertainty of his times, and can be placed alongside Ivan Turgenev and Fyodor Dostoevsky as a chronicler of the mood of the era.

> If all our progress takes place only through the government, we will give the world an unprecedented example of an autocracy armed with all the achievement of freedom ...
>
> *The Bell* (c.1860)

A riot scene in Paris in 1848. Herzen supported the wave of revolutions across Europe, but became frustrated with the socialist movements after their failures.

Liberty and progress

Herzen was a passionate opponent of the harsh regimes of European monarchies, but he also understood how easily radicalism could slip into excesses and disregard of individual liberty. It was this that made him a hero to **Isaiah Berlin**, who would become one of his strongest proponents in the twentieth century. In Berlin's well-known book, *Russian Thinkers*, he praised Herzen's humanity in his defence of individual freedom. Berlin lauded Herzen for suggesting that individuals should always be as free as possible to make their own choices, and that state intervention should be as minimal as possible. This fitted in well with Berlin's own ideas on negative and positive freedom (see pages 174–5).

Berlin also admired Herzen's views on historical progress. He reiterated Herzen's message that "*the end of life is life itself*", meaning that any historical age should be viewed as its own end, rather than as a pawn to be sacrificed to an abstract future goal.

Key dates

1812	Born in Moscow, Russia.
1834	Arrested and banished to Vyatka, now Kirov in northeastern Russia.
1842	His first work is published, *Dilettantism in Science*.
1847	Leaves Russia for the last time.
1852	Moves to London.
1857–67	Publishes his newspaper, *The Bell*.
1861	Emancipation of the serfs.
1864	Moves to Geneva.
1870	Dies in Paris, France.

> *Russia is in darkness and in chains but her spirit is not captive.*
>
> *The Bell* (1861)

Søren Kierkegaard

Kierkegaard is a fascinating figure in the history of philosophy. Like Arthur Schopenhauer and Friedrich Nietzsche, he can be seen as a bridge between traditional thinkers and the twentieth-century philosophical tradition. As well as a philosopher, he has been described as a poet, a theologian, a humorist, and one of the first existentialists.

Søren Kierkegaard was born into a prosperous Copenhagen family in 1813. In early life he was exposed to the religious teaching of his father, who took a rather severe view of Christianity, cursing God for his misfortunes, and focusing on the suffering of Christ. In 1830 Kierkegaard began studying at the city's university. He started keeping his well-known journal in 1834 in an attempt to come to an understanding of his own life. Living a strange double existence, he created a public image of a witty, convivial man, while privately suffering from depression and immersing himself in serious, introspective philosophical thought. He was well known in Copenhagen, becoming involved in controversies and feuds with journalists at one of the city's newspapers. In 1840 he became engaged to Regine Olsen, but then broke off the engagement to focus on his philosophical calling; he never quite got over Regine, and she remained a strong influence in his life and work. His major

works were produced over the subsequent decade, before his early death from a spinal condition in 1855.

Kierkegaard's writing often deals with problems of religion and faith in the Christian Church. He reacted against what he regarded as the pomposity and vacuousness of both the Danish church of his time, and the prevailing **Hegelian philosophy**, which dominated European academia. By contrast his focus was on the difficult choices and problems facing the individual who struggled with problems of faith and truth. He often wrote under pseudonyms, taking different viewpoints of a variety of characters, and concealing his message with understatement and irony. This leaves the reader the awkward task of interpreting when it is Kierkegaard directly speaking and when he is simply presenting a point of view – Kierkegaard himself said that "*the task must be made difficult, for only the difficult inspires the noble-hearted*".

Essential philosophy

It isn't easy to sum up Kierkegaard's thinking, as it is so quixotic and multi-faceted. He reacted strongly against **G. W. F. Hegel**'s system-building, believing that it was impossible to create a complete, impregnable system of thought. Two of his best-known ideas are the "leap of faith" and "subjectivity". He used subjectivity to mean the differences between the varied individual connections that are made to the same truths about the world. With the leap of faith, he was looking at the way in which an individual comes to believe in God, or to fall in love. They simultaneously hold faith and doubt in their minds, but choose to make the leap of faith – which may not be a rational decision. In fact it is something that goes beyond rationality, into the realm of faith. The doubt is an essential element, without which the faith would not have the same value. These ideas were at the heart of Kierkegaard's fascination with the self, and the way that we use self-examination to relate to the world. In *Fear and Trembling* (1843) he wrote about the way that the biblical figure Abraham was forced into an impossible, incomprehensible decision when he chose to obey God's order to kill his son. Kierkegaard concludes that Abraham's choice only makes sense seen as a decision made on the basis of faith.

Kierkegaard rejected Hegelian **dialectic** (see pages 110–11) pointing out that the "synthesis" could only contain ideas that had already been present in the thesis and antithesis. But he was fascinated by **Immanuel Kant**'s suggestion that we sometimes choose to embrace the unknowable as a way to avoid the intolerable possibility that life is meaningless (see pages 100–1). He felt that Hegel's attempt to solve the problems of philosophy through dialectic was an empty promise, and that we only reach resolution of these problems through the leap of faith.

From aesthetics to religion

Kierkegaard despised the way that people crave for recognition in society and the church. This was one reason why he chose to write so often under a pseudonym. At times his writing feels closer to the Russian novelist Fyodor Dostoevsky, a near-contemporary, than to traditional philosophers. Faced with Kant's concept of the "borders of reason", the point at which our rational thought can take us no further with certainty, he digressed into a meditation on the idea of human freedom. Rejecting Hegel's "world spirit" (see page 111) as a meaningless notion, he argued that the crowd of humanity is

Legacy, truth, consequence

■ Kierkegaard's subjectivity can be seen as a kind of **relativism** in which it might even be better to hold a passionate, but false or immoral belief than to have a milder belief in truth and goodness. This was something that would be echoed in twentieth-century thinkers, including some of the **existentialists**. However, his special appeal lies in the intensity of his writing and the vigor of his thought.

■ He also influenced some intriguing philosophers who adapted or expanded on his rather playful approach to writing. Jacques Derrida, the **deconstructionists**, and even the **situationists** would use humor, irony, and understatement to try to capture the opacity of meaning.

■ Just as Friedrich Nietzsche would use confrontational, **paradoxical** techniques to demolish the Hegelian idea of truth as a monumental system, later thinkers influenced by Kierkegaard would use the act of writing, a particular style or indirect approach, in treating the difficult issues of truth and meaning.

■ His influence can also be seen in **Marxists** such as Herbert Marcuse (1898–1979), and theological thinkers such as Karl Barth (1886–1968). In the end, rather than Kierkegaard's Christian message, it was his focus on individual subjectivity and the problems of writing about truth from a subjective point of view that became his strongest legacy.

Life must be lived forwards, but understood backwards.

Kierkegaard's Journal (1843)

Søren Kierkegaard in the coffee-house, 1843.

often hopelessly wrong, and that only a defiantly individual action can be the responsible reaction.

But this leaves us more or less alone in the cosmos, which is a deeply unsettling concept. He was one of the first writers to use the concept of "angst" (a deep-seated form of anxiety) to describe the fear an individual feels when they realize this – there is a dizzying moment of freedom and responsibility which a human must deal with in their life.

In *Either-Or* (1843) Kierkegaard wrote about different ways of living. The **aesthetic** life is one where we live for the present, and have beauty as our goal. The **ethical** life is one where we try to live in accordance with the truths of morality. For Kierkegaard, neither of these spheres is complete and suffcent. Neither can be fully rational or grounded and so they fail to satisfy our wills.

He thus proposed the religious life as an alternative, but accepted that this wasn't a fully rational choice either. He clearly distinguished **objective truth** and **subjective truth**. The search for objective truth is a scientific undertaking, where we try to make sure our internal beliefs match the external world. For Kierkegaard this is insufficient. We must search for subjective truth, where the relationship between the subject and the world is an innate part of the system. The religious life involves believing in objective contradictions, such as Jesus' dual role as God and man. The leap of faith is a leap towards subjective truth. We need passion as well as reason. To believe in God in order to conform to society is worthless. But to make a passionate leap into this belief leads us towards fulfilment as human beings. How we believe is almost as important as what we believe for Kierkegaard.

Karl Marx

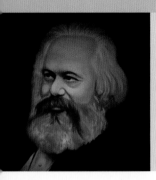

Few people have had such an impact on the world as the nineteenth-century German philosopher, historian, social scientist, and revolutionary, Karl Marx. His ideas formed the philosophical foundation for communism, and by the late twentieth century nearly half the world lived in countries whose regimes were supposedly based on Marxism. Even though many communist countries have now altered their political and social systems, his philosophy remains influential.

Karl Heinrich Marx was born into a middle-class German–Jewish family. His father, a lawyer, converted to Christianity when racial discrimination threatened his job, but Karl was an ardent atheist, later proclaiming that "*Religion is the opium of the people*".

Marx first studied law at the University of Bonn, but after several student pranks and a duel (possibly the only time the revolutionary actually used a weapon himself), his father sent him to the more serious academic environment of the University of Berlin. There Marx switched to philosophy and became a **Young Hegelian**, agreeing with the group's radical ideas inspired by **G. W. F. Hegel**. He later repudiated the group.

Marx became a journalist, and in October 1842 was editing the influential liberal newspaper *Rheinische Zeitung* in Cologne, where he first met **Friedrich Engels**. When the government closed the paper down in 1843, Marx emigrated to France, where he met Engels again. The two became lifelong friends and collaborators.

Expelled from France in 1845 for revolutionary writings, Marx and Engels went to Brussels. They joined **communist** groups, began to develop Marxist economic theories, and wrote *The Communist Manifesto* in 1848. That same year revolutions broke out, first in France, then across Europe, and Marx and Engels rushed to France to support the revolution, then to their homeland of Prussia. There they soon were in trouble with the authorities again, and when the revolution was crushed, they fled to London, England, where, despite requests from Prussia for their extradition, they were allowed to stay.

There, in what he called the "*long, sleepless night of exile*", Marx lived sometimes in extreme poverty, even though he and his family were partly supported by Engels, who went back to work for his father's firm to raise enough money. Marx himself earnt a modest income writing articles (which Engels often had to finish).

By now Marx was convinced that economics was the foundation of all human society, but he was distracted from his studies by the political organizations of early communism. In 1864 he wrote the inaugural address for the "First International", the first International Working Men's Association, and he encouraged it for its ten years of existence, helping with congresses and preventing an anarchist take-over attempted by the Russian Mikhail Bakunin (1814–76). In 1872 the association's council was transferred to New York, US, and the International began to decline.

In collaboration with Engels, Marx wrote a great many papers and books, as well as letters to fellow communists around the world. But his most important work, *Das Kapital* or *Capital*, was only completed by Engels after his death. In his address at Marx's memorial service, Engels said presciently, "*Marx was before all else a revolutionist … His name will endure through the ages, and so also will his work.*"

Essential philosophy

The Communist Manifesto

This document outlined the essential principles of class struggle and predicted the nature of a communist revolution and society. It was the work of both Marx and Engels. Engels wrote an accessibly-written first draft (see Friedrich Engels, pages 124–5, for more about *The Manifesto*).

Dialectical materialism and Historical materialism

Hegel (1770–1831) had first proposed the dialectic: change occurs because of the contradiction between opposites; a thesis is opposed by an antithesis, and from the best ideas of both comes a synthesis, after which the process starts again (see pages 110–11). Marx argued that the background to this process was not God or human consciousness, but was material: the economic conditions surrounding the individual and society. Therefore, human history is best assessed through its economic stages.

Applying his theory of history, Marx concluded that the existing economic arrangements would be overthrown when they could no longer fully exploit the existing means of production. From this he predicted the collapse of the current economy (industrial **capitalism**) and its replacement by communism. He thought that the inherent flaws in capitalism, such as its inequality and its cycle of boom and bust (he also predicted falling rates of profit), would lead to its own downfall and that the urban workers, or

Legacy, truth, consequence

- Marx's view that all aspects of human society – art, politics, religion, morality – are rooted in the economic structure was revolutionary. The strength of his ideas is shown by the fact that Marx is still a figure who inspires extreme reactions. He is often revered or hated. Marxism is followed slavishly by some people, and viciously attacked by others. His ideas are now part of our cultural heritage.

- The communist revolutions in Russia, China, Cuba, and other countries all looked to Marxism for their ideological foundation. He himself did not expect working-class revolutions in those countries – he anticipated a proletarian uprising in advanced, industrialized nations. However, Vladimir Lenin, Leon Trotsky, Joseph Stalin, Mao Zedung, Fidel Castro, Che Guevara … all the revolutionaries who transformed the twentieth-century world were inspired by Marx.

- In some cases communist revolutionaries developed their own form of Marxism. Marxist–Leninism became the basis of the Soviet Union, adopting Lenin's ideas that professional revolutionaries would have to lead the proletariat, and that the resulting communist state could ruthlessly impose its ideals. In China, Mao Zedong argued that revolution could be led by rural peasants, not industrial workers, and proved his point when he led a peasant army to victory in the civil war.

- Although the East European communist countries have changed their systems of government, Marxism still suggests valuable ways to view society, particularly through economic factors or as class conflict. As a result there are ongoing Marxist analyses (offering a critique from the point of view of political and social function) of literally everything – from the structure of society to popular blockbusters such as J. R. R. Tolkien's *The Lord of the Rings*.

> *It is not the consciousness of men that determines their existence, but, on the contrary, their social existence determines their consciousness.*
>
> A Contribution to the Critique of Political Economy (1857–8)

Key dates

1818	Born in Trier, Prussia (now Germany).
1835	Goes to university, in Bonn, then the following year in Berlin.
1842	Edits liberal newspaper *Rheinische Zeitung* until it is closed down.
1843	Goes to Paris, France. Joins up with Friedrich Engels.
1845	Expelled from France; goes to Brussels, in Belgium, with Engels. Becomes a communist.
1848	Publishes *The Communist Manifesto* with Engels. Goes to France then Germany to support revolutions.
1849	Chased out of Germany; seeks refuge in London, England, with Engels.
1859	Publishes *Critique of Political Economy*, which includes a summary of historical materialism.
1864	Elected to the general council of the International Working Men's Association in London, the "First International".
1867	Publishes volume I of *Das Kapital* (*Capital*) analyzing capitalist processes of production. Finishes volumes II and III of *Das Kapital* during the 1860s, but continues to refine them for the rest of his life. Engels publishes them posthumously.
1871	Writes pamphlet *The Civil War in France* in support of the defeated Paris Commune.
1883	Devastated by his wife's death in 1881, dies in London after a long period of ill-health and depression.

Karl Marx, here shown arrested in Brussels, was more than once in trouble with European authorities.

proletariat, would from historical necessity overthrow the existing system. Marxism therefore includes the idea that human society – its economic, political, and social life – is always in a state of change, with conflict and challenge forever creating a new synthesis and status quo, which in turn is challenged by new institutions. However, in Marx's ideal classless society there would be no more conflict since everyone would benefit justly from their own labor, and government would "wither away".

Class struggle

Marx saw the struggle between classes as rising from the system of material production. Class was defined by the ownership or lack of ownership of the means of production, but his proposed ideal communist state would do away with private ownership.

Das Kapital

In *Das Kapital* or *Capital*, Marx elaborated his idea that the whole of human society and history is centered around economics, particularly the means of production of goods and the distribution of goods. He offered an explanation of how capitalism developed and how it could be transformed, and pointed out that everyone in a capitalist society has their freedom circumscribed by the economic system.

Friedrich Engels

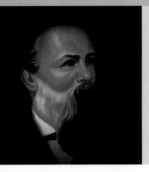

As the supporter and collaborator of Karl Marx, the German socialist and philosopher Friedrich Engels helped provide the theoretical basis of communism. Although usually overshadowed by Marx, his ideas underpinned the social and political revolutions in Russia and China and smaller countries around the globe that transformed the twentieth-century world.

From a family of wealthy German industrialists, Engels was exposed to the conditions of the working class when he was a young man, helping out in a family-owned factory in Manchester, England. Ironically, his father sent him there in the hope the work would rid him of the **Young Hegelians**' radical ideas (named after **G. W. F. Hegel**). Instead, Engels was appalled by the poverty, filth, and exploitation in the heavily industrialized city, and began to campaign for improvements. His articles soon brought him into contact with **Karl Marx**, who was then editing a radical journal in Paris, and the two men – who had not impressed each other when they first met – became lifelong collaborators in their plans to change society.

From early on in their partnership, the better-off, practical Engels supported Marx financially, giving the more scholarly philosopher the time to study and expound his theories. While Marx could easily wrestle with complex, abstract philosophical points, Engels had a straightforward writing style that helped the two of them reach a wide audience. He wrote the first draft of the paper that was to become *The Communist Manifesto*, keeping it in a style that would be accessible to a mass audience. Published in 1848, this was their basic summary of the struggle for social revolution, and outlined the **communist** society that would

follow the **proletariat**'s, or urban workers', overthrow of the property-owning class or **bourgeoisie**.

Engels helped define the aims of the International Communist League's Central Committee as "*the overthrow of the bourgeoisie, the domination of the proletariat, the abolition of the old bourgeois society based on class antagonisms, and the establishment of a new society without classes and without private property*".

In 1848 a wave of revolutions and social protests spread across Europe. The two philosophers rushed to France to support the cause, then returned to Prussia, where they started a radical magazine. Engels joined the armed uprising against the government, and had to flee for his life when Prussia crushed the revolt. They sought refuge in London, England, where they were allowed to stay even though Prussia asked for their deportation. To support Marx and his family, Engels returned to work for his father, but the two revolutionaries continued to correspond regularly before Engels settled back in London.

Engels disapproved of marriage, since he considered it to be an unnatural institution treating women unfairly, but he lived for 20 years with Mary Burns, whom he had met in Manchester. After she died in 1862 he lived with her sister, Lizzy.

Essential philosophy

The Communist Manifesto

This booklet was not originally intended to publicize communism, but rather to explain the ideology to other communists. The **socialists** and utopian idealists who were beginning to adopt the label "communist" wanted a clear outline of communist principles, so Engels and Marx were commissioned by London's Communist League (mainly comprising German exiles) to provide one.

The result was the most famous and hotly debated political document of all time.

The Communist Manifesto's view of history was that it should not be understood just as a list of rulers or great people and battles, but that the story of human development was the story of the struggle between social classes: "*The history of all hitherto existing society is the history of class struggles*". It defined the progression of historical societies

from slave to feudal to the modern bourgeois society consisting of bourgeois and proletarian classes, in which the bourgeois have stripped everything down to exploitative, market value terms.

The Manifesto was a blueprint for action, laying out the ten steps that would have to be taken to transform society, beginning with the abolition of private ownership of land and ending with free education for all children. Engels and Marx predicted that once the proletariat had seized political power, there would be a brief transitional period of "dictatorship" while the mechanisms of class, private means of production, and state control were disposed of, before the state itself would wither away, leaving an ideal communist society.

Having addressed the needs of the working class, they ended *The Manifesto* with an appeal for action – "*Working Men of All Countries, Unite!*"

Engels also contributed to the theories of historical materialism and economics that Marx pioneered (see Karl Marx, pages 122–23).

Legacy, truth, consequence

- Engels wrote in an elegant and lucid style, leaving an important body of work on socialist and communist theory. Many articles and papers that appeared under Marx's name were in fact written by Engels.
- His financial support enabled Marx to work on communist economic theory in *Das Kapital* and other writings.
- Engels has usually been overshadowed by Marx, particularly since the philosophical basis of communism is often simply called Marxism. But, the two of them discussed and developed **socialist** theory together, hardly ever disagreed, and it was Engels who persuaded the international communist movement to accept and adopt their ideas.

Detail of the only remaining manuscript page of *The Communist Manifesto*.

> Let the ruling classes tremble at a Communistic revolution. The proletarians have nothing to lose but their chains. They have a world to win.
>
> The Communist Manifesto (1848)

The Condition of the Working Class in England

In this classic social science book, Engels combined his own observations and critical analysis with contemporary reports and social statistics to show how poverty, disease, and the death-rate had risen among urban workers since the Industrial Revolution. While in Manchester he had pounded the streets to discover the details of working-class life at first hand, so he was able to eloquently describe the overcrowding, the dangerous work, the long hours, poor pay, the filth, squalor, and hopelessness in an industrial city.

His book was an educational document, an appeal to the working class to politicize as a way to improve life.

Feminism

Engels was an early **feminist**, arguing that the concept behind monogamous marriage was to enable the man to control the woman, and that the whole institution led to the inequality of women. He put this in communist terms: when human societies introduced capitalism and the idea of private property, women became just another property to be owned, and her "means of production" of children had to be strictly controlled so that a man could be sure that only his own children inherited his property. Before that historical stage, Engels argued, women inherited property and social status for themselves, and many societies acknowledged matrilineal rather than patrilineal descent. He compared marriage to the struggle for control of the bourgeoisie over workers, writing: "*The first class oppression that appears in history coincides with the antagonism between men and women in monogamous marriage …*"

In his proposed future communist society, there would be no such economic constraints determining private relationships.

Charles Peirce

Charles Sanders Peirce has a strong claim to being the "father" of pragmatism. This was a theory developed in the United States that focused on the practical, observable outcome of beliefs, explaining meaning and truth in terms of the effects that believing in an idea would have in practice.

Born in Cambridge, Massachusetts, in the United States, Peirce was an extremely promising student. His father, a well-known professor of astronomy and mathematics, introduced him to many of the country's most prominent thinkers and gave him an education suitable for a child genius, while refusing to administer any kind of discipline. It is said that Peirce read his older brother's copy of *Elements of Logic* by Richard Whately (1787–1863) at the age of 12, beginning a lifelong interest in **logic**.

Peirce studied philosophy and chemistry at Harvard, and was a member of the "Metaphysical Club" – together with **William James** and Oliver Wendell Holmes (who would later become the well-known jurist) – where he proposed some of his early ideas. His academic career started within the field of science. He studied gravitation with the US Coast and Geodetic Survey,

before going on to teach logic and philosophy at Johns Hopkins University.

In 1876 Peirce left his first wife Melusina for Juliette Froissy Pourtalès, a French gypsy who would become his second wife. The resulting scandal led to his academic career ending prematurely in 1884, and in 1887 he retired to a house he built at Milford, Pennsylvania. He lived there for much of the rest of his life, in poverty and illness, doing odd-jobs and surviving for the most part on the charity of family and friends, in particular his great friend William James.

Despite Peirce's complicated private life, and his reputation being at one stage eclipsed by those of other pragmatists such as William James and **John Dewey**, his contribution to the development of **pragmatism** is now recognized as highly significant.

Essential philosophy

Peirce's approach to philosophy grew from his background in science and logic. His early thinking derived from **Immanuel Kant**, but he grew frustrated by **syllogistic** reasoning and instead started to study the way that language and belief operate. His early, decisive contribution to pragmatism came in two essays: *The Fixation of Belief* (1877) and *How to Make Our Ideas Clear* (1878). In these essays, he considered the philosophical method from a new angle. He asked how human beings work towards a true opinion and described doubt as an "irritation" that drove us to search for beliefs which would lead us to successful habits of action.

Taking this line of thought further, in the second essay he claimed that even our concepts and categories are derived in this way. If an idea or concept leads to successful actions, it will be useful to us. So concepts and categories are justified pragmatically – true beliefs are more useful to us, because they lead us to make better decisions.

Abduction

He put this in logical terms by taking the traditional methods of **deduction** and **induction**, and adding the idea of "abduction", a scientific process by which we observe facts and come up with **hypotheses** that might explain them. **David Hume** had, centuries before, proved that induction could not be relied upon, and

abduction is equally fallible. But this didn't worry Peirce, as he felt he had found a way to evaluate the usefulness of ideas which didn't assume that our logic must be unchallengeable. In fact, Peirce went further, attacking the kind of Hegelian **rationalism** (see **G. W. F. Hegel**, pages 110–11) that took deduction as the one pure method of reason. For Peirce, techniques such as abduction and induction were as likely to be tools for the discovery of real truth as deduction.

This led him back towards a distinctive new take on Kantian **metaphysics**. He presumed that our sensations did point towards objects in the real world, and that our categories and concepts were an attempt by the interpreting subject to grope towards the truth, by whatever means were most likely to lead him to true beliefs. Adding to this he asserted that the way that we judge a belief to be true is that "*if acted on it should . . . carry us to the point we aim at and not astray*".

Pragmatism and meaning

Possibly the most interesting aspect of Peirce's philosophy was the way that he applied pragmatism to meaning itself. Because he viewed the entire notion of clear and distinct ideas as being dependent on the practical consequences of belief in those ideas, he was led to consider the social basis of meaning. Humans as a

Legacy, truth, consequence

■ In spite of his turbulent life, Peirce made a decisive contribution to the method of pragmatism, with its faith in experimental reasoning, and its identification of the meaning of concepts with reference to their consequences in action. Pragmatists such as Jane Addams (1860–1935), George Herbert Mead (1863–1931), John Dewey, and William James developed these ideas in their own ways.

■ Peirce himself went on to claim that where judgements could not be evaluated according to future consequences, they could be regarded as meaningless. While other pragmatists attempted to find solutions to metaphysical and **ethical** problems, Peirce's legacy was a markedly anti-metaphysical one.

■ In this respect there is an obvious connection between Peirce and **logical positivism**, which would be developed in the decades after his death. However, while both shared a **verificationist** outlook (meaning that they judged a statement's truth and meaning on the basis of its verifiability), there was little direct influence between the pragmatists and the logical positivists, and the latter were generally more keen to eliminate metaphysics from the arena of philosophy.

■ Peirce's contributions to **logical analysis** have perhaps had the most enduring influence. Philosophers as varied as **Richard Rorty**, Hilary Putnam (*b.* 1926), and **W. V. O. Quine** have created work that derives from elements of Peirce's thinking.

... the machinery of the mind can only transform knowledge, but never originate it, unless it be fed with facts of observation.

How To Make Our Ideas Clear (1878)

group are clearly subject to irrationality, self-deception, and error. However, they also tend to converge on the same conception of the world, at least to a degree, because our pragmatic relation to reality requires us to try to find true beliefs, and at least some of those beliefs will overlap. Meaning and truth are thus partly socially defined, at least in so far as beliefs grow out of a collective scientific, experimental approach to our world.

Peirce the logician

Some of Peirce's later work has been influential on logicians. It is hard to summarize complex logical concepts here, but he completed important work on subjects as varied as infinitesimals in the number system, Bayesian logic, and probability. His achievements in this area are perhaps best understood as a testament to his enduring genius, even if they are not easily digested.

As he grew older, Peirce became disenchanted by the fact that other pragmatists (including William James, who did give Peirce due credit in his own writing) had become better known than him. Many of his later projects stalled either because he failed to complete them or because he couldn't find a publisher. In 1905 he wrote *What Pragmatism Is*, in an attempt to claim his share of the credit for pragmatism, for which he perversely chose a different name, "pragmaticism".

Peirce's House in Milford, Pennsylvania, where he retired in 1887, recorded in a Historic American Buildings Survey in 1888 (top) and in 1914, the year of his death (bottom).

William James

William James was a multi-talented thinker, whose work ranged across the fields of religion, physiology, psychology, and philosophy. Together with Charles Peirce, he was one of the founders of pragmatism, the theory developed in the United States that focused on the practical, observable outcome of beliefs, explaining meaning and truth in terms of the effects that believing in an idea would have in practice. He was also a well-known academic who frequently commented on public affairs.

William James grew up in an intellectual environment. His father was an eccentric theologian, his sister kept a literary diary, while his brother Henry was the well-known novelist. William graduated in medicine from Harvard, where he was a member of the "Metaphysical Club", along with **Charles Peirce**, and through his life he interacted with such luminaries as philosophers **John Dewey**, George Santayana (1863–1952), **Henri Bergson**, Ernst Mach (1838–1916), his godfather Ralph Waldo Emerson (1803–82), philosopher and psychologist **Sigmund Freud**, and writers Mark Twain (1835–1910), H. G. Wells (1866–1946), and Gertrude Stein (1874–1946). He had a successful academic career, spent entirely at Harvard, but was prone to depression and melancholy. In spite of this, he managed to produce a remarkable body of work on disparate subjects.

James' early writing spanned science and philosophy. Like Peirce he took an essentially scientific attitude to problems of consciousness and truth. He also made some interesting observations on the tendency of philosophers to produce work that suits their own temperaments rather than being pure reflections of truth. He carried this sense of subjectivity into his observations on belief, particularly religious belief. In this connection he vacillated between asserting on the one hand that a study of human nature could lead us to a more scientific understanding of religious experience, and on the other hand that religion was something that science could not penetrate, a matter that the human subject could only approach on an individual basis.

James made some of his most important philosophical contributions in the last decade of his life. In a burst of writing between 1904 and 1905 (collected in *Essays in Radical Empiricism* in 1912) he set out the **metaphysical** view most commonly known as neutral **monism**, according to which there is one fundamental "stuff" that is neither material nor mental. In *A Pluralistic Universe* (1909) he made a case against the **intellectualism** of philosophers such as **G. W. F. Hegel**, defending instead a **mystical** and anti-pragmatic view that concepts distort rather than reveal reality. Preferring the anti-intellectualism of Henri Bergson, he argued that the "*concrete pulses of experience appear pent in by no such definite limits as our conceptual substitutes are confined by. They run into one another continuously and seem to interpenetrate*". In his influential *Pragmatism* (1907) he presented systematically a set of views about truth, knowledge, reality, religion, and philosophy that had permeated his writings from the late 1870s onwards.

Essential philosophy

James and psychology

In 1890 James published the monumental *Principles of Psychology*. This work did a great deal to establish the foundations of psychology as a serious science in which our introspective study could lead us to an understanding of how the mind works. He analyzed the individual mind in terms of a "stream of consciousness", arguing that we could study this through a combination of self-analysis and comparative study, and that the individual did exercise **free will**.

Pragmatism and empiricism

James developed Peirce's ideas on pragmatic method into a more complete system. In *Pragmatism* (1907), he defined truth as being whatever is "*expedient in our way of thinking*", and accepted that the only way to define truth and meaning was through a pragmatic examination of the consequences of acting as though a statement was true or meaningful. In *Essays in Radical Empiricism* (1912) he developed his basic **empiricism** into neutral **monism**. This is a theory that **Bertrand Russell** would also examine. James made it into a form of **phenomenalism**, which is the theory that our sensations give us no evidence of the existence of anything beyond themselves. While **idealists** take this as the starting point for rejecting the external world, James avoided such metaphysical questions, drawing only the pragmatic conclusion that the reality we know and talk about is the reality of sensation and experience and not an external world beyond it.

Belief and religion

In *The Will To Believe* (1897) James considered the idea that it is the consequences of believing that are most important. He saw belief as an individual choice, and argued that we can rationally choose to believe in some **propositions**, even though we know they lie beyond the realm of certain truth. So where the **logical positivists** would later use

Legacy, truth, consequence

- By finding ways to justify religion and ethics within a pragmatic theory, James took a more humane approach to the basically scientific definition of truth which pragmatism had outlined.

- Pragmatism was an influence on numerous philosophers in the twentieth century, although the logical positivists and logicians such as Bertrand Russell would take a more rigorous approach to theories of truth.

- James outlined an interesting theory of emotion – known as the James–Lange theory as Carl Lange (1834–1900) independently outlined a similar theory. He claimed that we don't feel fear as a separate emotion. If we see a bear and run, our experience of fear is really an experience of the physiological consequences of flight – the increased heartbeat, adrenaline surge, and so on. This is a debatable theory, but it does have an interesting relation to **Ludwig Wittgenstein**'s later work on private language and the social development of shared ideas about internal emotions.

- James' work on psychology helped to lay the foundations of a fledgling science. His concept of the stream of consciousness would be hugely influential in literary as well as psychological circles. Even the later **existentialists** would adopt a phenomenalist approach that treated the stream of consciousness as the primary human experience.

> **Truth happens to an idea. It becomes true, is made true by events. Its verity is in fact an event, a process: the process namely of its verifying itself, its veri-fication.**
>
> Essays in Radical Empiricism (1912)

An extract from James' *Principles of Psychology*, 1890.

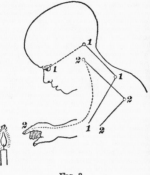

time, and, by virtue of a reflex tendency common in babies of a certain age, extends his hand to grasp it, so that his fingers get burned. So far we have two reflex currents in play : first, from the eye to the extension movement, along the line 1—1—1—1 of Fig. 3; and second, from the finger to the movement of drawing back the hand, along the line 2—2—2—2. If this were the baby's whole nervous system, and if the reflexes were once for all organic,

FIG. 3.

a **verificationism** similar to that of James to reject the possibility of metaphysics, he preferred to analyze the way that we choose to believe in metaphysical statements, in spite of the impossibility of certainty.

This line of thinking fed into his writing on religion, in particular in *The Varieties of Religious Experience* (1902). To some degree, James' viewpoint allowed him to treat religion as a rational choice. On the one hand the individual subject might choose to believe in God in the spirit of "Pascal's Wager" (after Blaise Pascal, 1623–62), believing that the consequences of being wrong are worse for the person who chooses atheism than for the person who chooses belief. But on the other hand there is a more subtle application of James' thinking. Since truth for him is about the personal consequences and coherence of belief as much as it is about the congruence with an external reality, it is possible to judge the expedience (and thus truth)

of a belief in God by judging its consequences in our life. If the belief in God leads to better outcomes then we can judge it to be a useful or even true belief.

Emotion and choice

James started from a pragmatic view that the only way to judge truth is according to whether a belief leads us to better actions. But rather than rejecting categories of knowledge on this basis, he made a noble effort to understand how people do actually reach metaphysical and **ethical** beliefs such as religious ones. As well as describing the way we acquire beliefs as a complex process in which we judge new beliefs according to their coherence with our existing beliefs, he also considered the possibility that we need some "over-beliefs" which we use as heuristic guides for our acquisition of further beliefs.

Friedrich Nietzsche

A moralist and culture-critic, Nietzsche challenged the very core of Western moral values and Christianity. Controversial and unconventional, he proved deeply influential in artistic and avant-garde twentieth-century Continental Europe, particularly after the misappropriation of his theories by the Nazis and Fascists had receded. He is often referred to as one of the first "existentialist" philosophers.

Born in Germany, to a Protestant pastor father, Nietzsche was a deeply religious child. He proved to be a brilliant student at university. The cultural and literary movement known as **Weimar classicism** had an impact on him, and his interests turned to philosophy, in particular, to **Arthur Schopenhauer**, whose atheistic and turbulent vision of the world, and passion for music, appealed to the young Nietzsche.

Nietzsche was a strange individual: a passionate loner, and a frequent traveler in search of climates that would aid his faltering health. Perhaps remembered most for his sustained attack on Western moral culture of the last 2,000 years, he criticized the "Apollonian" forces of logical order and stiff sobriety, which he saw as emanating from the classical Greeks. He hoped for a cultural rebirth of the instinctual, amoral "Dionysian" energy within **pre-Socratic** Greek culture, which he regarded as infinitely more creative and healthy. In his first book, *The Birth of Tragedy* (1872), he advocated the resurrection and fuller release of the Dionysian artistic spirit. In effect this adulated the German artists of the time, especially Richard Wagner, whose operas he greatly admired and considered to be the true successors to Greek tragedy, though later he was openly to criticize him.

His mental breakdown in 1889 was triggered when he witnessed a horse being whipped by a coachman in Turin. He never recovered his sanity. His sister Elisabeth, having returned from Paraguay after attempting to set up an Aryan, anti-Semitic German colony there with her husband, assumed responsibility for Nietzsche's welfare and the promotion of his work. It was through her solicitations with Adolf Hitler and Benito Mussolini that the Nazis and Italian Fascists came to selectively assemble quotations from Nietzsche's work and use them to justify their doctrines, which most scholars today regard as a perversion of Nietzsche's philosophy.

Essential philosophy

Perspectivism

Written early in his career, the unpublished essay "On Truth and Lies in a Non-Moral Sense" is considered by some commentators to be the key to Nietzsche's thought. In it, he rejects the idea of universal constants: "truth", he claims, is nothing more than the invention of fixed conventions for practical purposes. The *Genealogy of Morals* (1887) includes a clear expression of his idea of "perspectivism": that there is no absolute, "God's eye" standpoint from which one can survey everything that is, and therefore it is important to draw upon many different perspectives when analysing something.

"God is dead"

Nietzsche was convinced that no religion was really true, and, like the French *philosophes* who preceded the 1789 Revolution, he objected to the submission to the will of God. He thought that Christianity fosters weakness in men, and by devaluing aspects of life that are naturally attractive to humans it dampens vitality and creativity. Likewise, most moral systems he held are contrary rather than conducive to the enhancement of life and need to be re-evaluated. In particular, the dominant "slave" morality, as typified in Christianity, is based on a "herd-animal" instinct ideally suited to mediocre and weak types. In modern times it has eclipsed the "master" morality peculiar to the aristocracy. Life has become dominated by the all-too-human needs and weaknesses associated with less favored human types and is rarely lived to the full. It is only through art that we are afforded a rare glimpse of the type of life that could be lived. Both Christianity and our present moral systems have run their course and should be replaced.

"Supermen" and the "will to power"

In *Beyond Good and Evil* (1886) Nietzsche challenged accepted views of what is "good" and what is "evil". He strongly resisted the **democratic** urges of the times, seeing them as producing a dominion of "inferior" men. His conviction that the moral basis underpinning Western civilization was fundamentally flawed led him to search for a new alternative for humanity to avoid the advent of **nihilism**. His concept of "the will to

> ## That which is done out of love is always beyond good and evil.
>
> *Beyond Good and Evil*, Aphorism 153 (1886)

Legacy, truth, consequence

- Nietzsche was influential in **Continental philosophy** and the emerging movements of **existentialism** and **postmodernism**. He particularly influenced **Derrida**, **Foucault**, **Heidegger**, and **Sartre**.
- The Nazis and Fascists during the 1930s and 1940s were able to latch onto elements of Nietzsche's work. They saw it as promoting a "desire for and of power"; some Nazis even upheld a biological interpretation, giving it a meaning relating to **Social Darwinism**. Heidegger criticized this misreading, arguing that Nietzsche's concept was closer to an inner force of nature, a fundamental instinct or drive.
- His other great influence has been among literary and artistic circles. His "God is dead" declaration, perspectivism, and emphasis upon the "will to power" provided inspiration in the 1960s–80s to consider the foundations of our basic assumptions in life.
- His sister Elisabeth's edited and altered collection of Nietzsche's writings, published after his death as *The Will to Power*, did much to harm his reputation in the twentieth century, despite concerted efforts by academics to set the record straight.

> *I know my fate. One day my name will be associated with the memory of something tremendous — a crisis without equal on earth, the most profound collision of conscience, a decision that was conjured up against everything that had been believed, demanded, hallowed so far. I am no man, I am dynamite.*
>
> Ecce Homo (1888)

power" is the urge within an individual to take charge of his own life, and is something to be pursued and affirmed. The strong have learnt to channel the will to power into a creative force and are more complete as human beings. His ideal is to create a society where this type of "strong" being is the norm. Often translated as "superman", the sense is more an "overman", or someone who stands over and above humans as they exist at present: a different type of man representing the highest passion and creativity possible, who lives at a level of experience beyond our standards of good and evil. In order to bring this superman into existence it is necessary to destroy the way man currently thinks, his ideas of good and evil. Ultimately, this is an internal battle: the values of good and evil are within ourselves.

Doctrine of eternal recurrence

In *The Gay Science* (1882) Nietzsche set forth the idea that one is, or might be, fated to relive forever every moment of one's life. This was intended to turn our attention away from all worlds, heavenly or otherwise, towards the one in which we currently live, since eternal recurrence precludes the possibility of any final escape from the present world.

Lou Andreas Salomé, Russian-born psychoanalyst and author, Paul Rée, author and compulsive gambler, with Nietzsche *(right)* in 1882; all three were close friends and traveled together, but Salomé and Nietzsche fell out after Salomé believed that he was desperately in love with her.

Gottlob Frege

A mathematician, logician, and philosopher, Frege is the founder of modern mathematical logic. His contribution to, and influence on, contemporary Western philosophy of language, logic, and mathematics is arguably peerless.

Friedrich Ludwig Gottlob Frege was born in 1848 in Wismar, part of the Grand Duchy of Mecklenburg-Schwerin, in Germany. His parents ran a girls' high school and his father had written books on grammar and logical reasoning. Frege gained a doctorate from the University of Gottingen with a thesis on geometry. He then taught at the University of Jena from 1874 until he retired in 1918.

Frege's early work was mathematical, focusing on geometry in particular, before he became interested in more fundamental issues in **logic**. His life was solitary and peaceful, with few noteworthy events. In 1879 he wrote his *Begriffsschrift* (*Concept Script*), a pamphlet of less than 100 pages. This set out a new logical symbolism which made logical structure perspicuous and brought out logical properties that ordinary language masked. Frege attempted to show how arithmetic could be derived from logic using these ideas. In pursuing this agenda he hit upon new questions and techniques that would animate philosophy for over

a century to come. The ideas of the *Begriffsschrift* were formulated in less formal terms in the *Foundations of Arithmetic*, in 1884, and in *The Basic Laws of Arithmetic*, 1893, the latter published at Frege's own expense.

Sadly, Frege's work received very little attention in his lifetime. But he had a huge, if indirect, impact on **analytic philosophy** through his influence on **Bertrand Russell** and **Ludwig Wittgenstein** (whom he had advised to work with Russell). **Rudolf Carnap** was one of his students and his work owes Frege a great debt. Outside analytic philosophy, Frege also had an important influence on **Edmund Husserl**, whom he managed to convince that logic was not psychological.

In the last years of his life, Frege attempted a full length exposition of his philosophy of logic. He only managed to complete a series of articles on the relationship between logic and the mind called *Logische Untersuchungen* (*Logical Investigations*).

Essential philosophy

Predicate calculus

Frege's *Begriffsschrift* contains the first systematic exposition of the "propositional calculus". This is the system of logic that deals with the **inferences** which depend on logical connectives such as "not", "and", "or", and "if … then …" that apply to whole sentences. The propositional calculus treats the truth or falsehood of sentences which contain logical connectives as a function of the truth or falsehood of the component sentences that are linked by the connectives. So, for example, sentences of the form "A and B", where A and B can be replaced by any two sentences, are true just when both the sentence A is true and the sentence B is true. But Frege's most revolutionary contributions to logic were his invention of the "predicate calculus" and "quantification theory". A **predicate** calculus is a system in which one can represent valid **inferences** among predications rather than only among combinations of sentences. A statement of predication involves ascribing a property to something, as in the sentence "Tomatoes are red", where redness is predicated of tomatoes. The ideas that Frege developed to do this are still central to the **philosophy of language**.

Quantification theory allowed Frege to deal with inferences that depend for their validity on expressions of quantity within

sentences, such as "all", "some", "any", "every", and "none". Frege's invention of a method for describing quantified variables, such as "For all x …", meant that he could disambiguate sentences like "Every boy loves some girl", which has two possible logical construals: according to one, there is some girl, say Daisy, that every boy loves; but according to another, for every boy there is some girl or other, whether it's Daisy or Mary or Jane or any of the other girls, that he loves. Frege's new logic made such logical structure absolutely clear through its use of quantified variables and the ordered relations between them.

Logicism

Logicism is the view that arithmetic is a branch of logic. Frege wanted to determine whether mathematical proofs could be based upon logical laws or whether they relied upon other non-logical facts. He thought that arithmetic was a branch of logic because it could be stated without appealing to any non-logical notions or laws whatsoever, and in *Die Grundlagen der Arithmetik* (1884) he set out to establish this view. Frege's logicist views on mathematics were sharply at odds with those of **Immanuel Kant** and **John Stuart Mill**. Kant had claimed that mathematics was **synthetic** and known through

Legacy, truth, consequence

- Frege's invention of modern logic facilitated not only the development of the philosophy of language and mathematics but also provided resources for the invention of computers and contemporary linguistic theory. His predicate calculus was referred to in Bertrand Russell's *Principia Mathematica*, **Kurt Godel's** "incompleteness theorem", and the theory of truth of Alfred Tarski (1901–83).
- Frege wrote some founding documents in the philosophy of language, including *Begriff und Gegenstand* (*Concept and Object*). *Sinn und Bedeutung* (*On Sense and Reference*) is perhaps his most widely discussed contribution to the theory of meaning.
- Frege's predicate calculus provided a logic that could handle inferences between quantified sentences. He developed other areas of logic but more recently philosophers have used the tools Frege made available to explore **modal logic** (the logic of possibility and necessity) and tensed logic (the logic of temporal statements).

It is natural, now, to think of there being connected with a sign (name, combination of words, letter), besides that to which the sign refers, which may be called the reference of the sign, also what I should like to call the sense of the sign, wherein the mode of presentation is contained.

On Sense and Reference (1892)

An example of Frege's notation system of mathematical logic, in his work *Begriffsschrift* (1879).

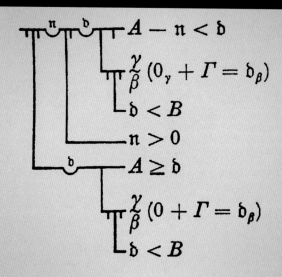

Key dates

1848	Born in Wismar, Mecklenburg-Schwerin, northern Germany.
1873	Receives a doctorate in mathematics from the University of Gottingen.
1879	Publication of pamphlet setting out his *Begriffsschrift* (*Concept Script*). In the same year he takes up a professorship at the University of Jena, Thuringia, in Germany.
1884	Publishes *Die Grundlagen der Arithmetik* (*The Foundations of Arithmetic*).
1892	Writes founding texts in the philosophy of language: *On Sense and Reference* and *Concept and Object*.
1893	Publishes *Die Grundgesetze der Arithmetik* (*Basic Laws of Arithmetic*).
1925	Dies in Bad Kleinen in northern Germany.

a priori intuition, while Mill had maintained that the truths of mathematics were **empirical** generalizations known through their confirmation by experience. Frege held that arithmetic was **analytic**: it could be defined in purely logical terms and proved from logical principles. This would provide arithmetic with a certainty that intuitions and empirical theories seemed to lack. However, **Bertrand Russell** showed that Frege's attempt to derive arithmetic from logic relied on an inconsistent and **paradoxical** assumption (see page 142).

Sense and reference

Frege became interested in identity statements like the statement "George Orwell is Eric Blair". The statement tells us that George Orwell, the writer of *Animal Farm*, is identical to, is one and the same as, the man Eric Blair. The statement is true because "Eric Blair" was George Orwell's real name. Frege noticed a certain puzzle about these sorts of statements that has come to be known as "Frege's puzzle". Suppose, as J. S. Mill thought, that a name like "George Orwell" or "Eric Blair" has as its meaning the object that it refers to. Given that "George Orwell" and "Eric Blair" refer to the same person, they should have the same meaning. But then "George Orwell is Eric Blair" should have the same significance as

"George Orwell is George Orwell". Yet everyone can recognize the truth of "George Orwell is George Orwell", while not everyone knows the truth of "George Orwell is Eric Blair". Knowledge of the latter statement is only had by those that do some historical investigation, while the former statement can be known just by inspecting the statement itself. So the two statements must differ in their significance. But if the only difference is that one contains "Eric Blair" where the other contains "George Orwell", and these names have the same meaning because they refer to the same thing, then how can the statements differ in their significance? Frege claimed that names have a *sense* as well as a *reference*. The nature of sense is still a live topic of inquiry but Frege's view was that the sense of a name is a way of presenting its referent. So, although "George Orwell" and "Eric Blair" refer to the same person, they present that referent in different ways; they can be used to think different thoughts and say things with a different sense. Frege also held that sense is something non-psychological – abstract and objective – that we grasp in thinking and speaking. Russell disputed Frege's notion of sense in his paper "On Denoting" (1905). It has been a central issue in the philosophy of language ever since.

Edmund Husserl

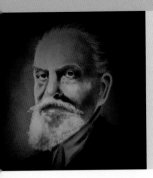

Edmund Husserl is recognized as the main founder of the German movement of phenomenology. His thinking was influential on areas as varied as linguistics, sociology, and psychology, but at its heart, phenomenology was based on a deep logical analysis of the problems of consciousness.

Edmund Gustav Albrecht Husserl was born in 1859 to a Jewish family living in Moravia, part of the Austrian Empire at the time, and now in the Czech Republic. He went to Vienna in 1881, where he studied mathematics and logic, but he became interested in the lectures on philosophy and psychology that Franz Clemens Brentano (1838–1917) was giving and decided to change course from mathematics to philosophy.

His first major work *Philosophie der Arithmetik*, published in 1891, was a study of the philosophical and logical roots of arithmetic. His early work focused on the use of philosophy and psychology to create a sound foundation for mathematics – whereas his contemporaries **Gottlob Frege** and **Bertrand Russell** were seeking to ground mathematics in logic.

Later on, in 1933, the now-retired Husserl became a victim of anti-Semitic Nazi legislation, including a ban from the library at Freiburg, where he had been an academic since 1916. His former pupil **Martin Heidegger** (whose work Husserl saw as an aberration from his own theories) was now rector of the university and a member of the Nazi party. The Nazi period overshadowed Husserl's last years to some degree, but he continued to work and write up until his death in 1938.

Husserl's work was clearly influenced by his mentor, Brentano, who had taught an earlier form of **phenomenology**. Brentano had suggested that the main characteristic of mental states is **intentionality** – that is to say that the mental state represents something beyond itself. For Husserl, phenomenology was "*the reflective study of the essence of consciousness as experienced from the first-person point of view.*" By "bracketing" our natural beliefs, he wanted to use the phenomenological method to study pure "phenomena" (a term that was used by **Immanuel Kant** to refer to the contents of consciousness, or "*things as they appear to us*", rather than "*things as they really are*"). Husserl thus aimed to focus on the essential nature of our experience, and on the **transcendental** self, which would be both the object of study, and the active agent in this process.

Essential philosophy

Phenomenology starts from a **logical analysis** of the distinction between meaning and object. Logical philosophers of this period paid close attention to the problems of **reference** and **naming**. Names can operate in a few different ways. Proper names such as "Edmund Husserl" have no meaning but refer to a specific object (although of course there may be more than one man of that name). In other cases, such as "the morning star" and "the evening star" we may find that two names, which have different meanings, nonetheless refer to the same object (the star known as "the morning star" and "the evening star" being one and the same object). One of the challenges for anyone trying to build a system of knowledge that rests on logic is to understand the ways in which names might refer to objects in the real world.

The attack on psychologism

Husserl came to reject psychologistic theories of mathematical logic, that is to say theories that attempted to describe mathematics in terms of purely psychological relations. For Husserl, logic is a formal theory that studies the way that *a priori* (self-evident) statements relate to each other, whereas mathematics studies the possible forms of being. Each is related to the other, and each studies formal categories rather than the relationship between these formal categories and the sensible objects they may refer to.

In *Logical Investigations* (1901/2) Husserl uses this rejection of psychologism as the basis for marking out a separate area of study for logic, philosophy, and phenomenology, independently from the **empirical** sciences – a field that can be completely independent of empirical science. This is where the "bracketing" of consciousness comes into the equation. Since mental states and the relationships between them can be studied independently of the external objects to which they may or may not refer, phenomenology aims to separate out the contents of experience and study them alone.

This isn't a denial of the external world, as in the extreme **idealism** of **Bishop Berkeley**. Instead it is an attempt to attain knowledge of our essential experience by bracketing all

> *In truth, of course, I am a transcendental ego, but I am not conscious of this; being in a particular attitude, the natural attitude.*
>
> *Cartesian Meditations* (1931)

The burning of the German Reichstag in February 1933 – at the time explained as a communist terrorist plot – helped the rise to power of Hitler's Nazi party, a period that would overshadow Husserl's last years.

Legacy, truth, consequence

- Husserl influenced a variety of philosophers who adapted his ideas on phenomenology, including Merleau-Ponty and Heidegger. He is also associated with the **existentialists,** who saw him as a significant predecessor and focused on the details of his disagreements with Heidegger.
- His logical analyses were especially influential, and writers who were interested in mathematical logic, including **Kurt Gödel** and **Rudolf Carnap**, expressed appreciation for details of his work.
- Meanwhile figures as varied as **Jacques Derrida** and Wilfrid Sellars (1912–1989) also developed elements of the philosophy of Husserl.
- Problems of bracketing and the whole question of meaning, naming, and reference would absorb **analytic philosophy** in the twentieth century. The logical problems identified by Husserl continued to be a preoccupation of Western philosophers at least up until the famous work, *Naming and Necessity* (1980), by Saul Kripke (*b.* 1940).

Key dates

assumptions about that external world and the inessential, **subjective** aspects of the objects that are referred to by **intentional** thought. Husserl used the word *epoché* for this process.

He thus aimed to exclude any **hypothesis** that relied on the existence of external objects. His method of phenomenological reduction simply removed them from the field of study, leaving us with the pure transcendental ego, as opposed to the concrete, empirical ego. In later work Husserl would adapt his philosophy from the early **realist** phenomenology to transcendental phenomenology. Later phenomenologists, including Heidegger and **Maurice Merleau-Ponty**, would cast doubt on this step, arguing that the ego always exists in the empirical world.

Does bracketing work?

Much of the conversation about phenomenology has revolved around the question of what "bracketing" actually consists of and achieves. Phenomenologists have debated issues of exactly what one is left with after the bracket is applied. Others have questioned whether bracketing is the big step forwards in philosophy that Husserl treated it as, or whether it is really just a subtle restatement of the **Cartesian method** of beginning from those thoughts and mental states which one cannot doubt. Some have criticized the whole process of phenomenology as being simply a new kind of **foundationalism** (the idea that there is a level of indubitable beliefs or mental states from which we can derive certain knowledge), of which classical empiricism and **rationalism** were both examples.

Opponents of foundationalism include **Friedrich Nietzsche** and **Michel Foucault**, who both appealed to genealogical models of knowledge. Others have appealed to Otto Neurath's (1882–1945) well-known comparison of human knowledge to a boat being built at sea – one can never strip it down to its bare foundations, but one can nonetheless improve and repair aspects of it while staying afloat.

Henri Bergson

Henri Bergson attracted both a cult status and strong criticism in the years between the World Wars. Along with William James and several modernist writers, he attempted to give a novel account of our inner and psychological life. In particular, he tried to integrate new research in biology with a theory of consciousness that would challenge the mechanistic and rationalistic interpretations of evolutionary theory which seemed to miss the very essence of life and creativity involved in evolution. He was awarded the Nobel Prize for Literature in 1927.

Born in Paris to a Jewish–Polish father and an English–Irish mother, Henri Bergson spent part of his childhood in London, and then settled with his family in France. His talent first emerged in mathematics, but he chose to study humanities at the École Normale Supérieure in Paris; his math teacher famously said, "*You could have been a mathematician; you will be a mere philosopher.*"

He taught at several schools before becoming a professor at the Collège de France, where he was appointed chair of philosophy. Leading the typically quiet life of an academic, it was the publication of his remarkable works that brought Bergson into the limelight. Their new perspectives on life and powerful expression captured the imagination of both scholars and the wider public. His philosophy was so compelling that **William James** felt impelled to introduce it to the Anglo-American public. Although Bergson, unlike James, was far from being a **pragmatist**, there are ideas common to both their philosophies, for example, in their notion of consciousness as a stream of thought and their rejec-tion of the "intellectualist method". For James, Bergson's influence "*was what had led me personally to renounce the intellectualist method and the current notion that logic is an adequate measure of what can or cannot be … reality, life, experience, concreteness, immediacy … exceeds our logic, overflows, and surrounds it.*" (William James, *A Pluralistic Universe*, 1909).

Creative Evolution (1907) is the work that made Bergson world-famous in his own lifetime. Its original contribution to the philosophical assessment of the theory of evolution was a milestone, taking a completely new direction in thought. In it he applied his theory of time to the study of living things.

He traveled to Oxford University and Birmingham in England, and to several American cities, lecturing to large audiences on subjects later published as *The Perception of Change*, *Life and Consciousness* (which became the first essay in his collection *Mind-Energy*, 1919), *Spirituality and Liberty*, and *The Method of Philosophy*.

In 1927, while living with his wife and daughter in Paris, he was awarded the Nobel Prize for Literature for *Creative Evolution* but was unable to attend the ceremony in person due to crippling arthritis. His illness forced him to retire from public life but he still managed to publish another major book in 1932, *The Two Sources of Morality and Religion*, which inevitably fuelled new debates and misunderstandings about his philosophy.

Before his death in 1941, Bergson attracted the public eye once more in his stand against the Vichy government of occupied France when he renounced all his previous awards rather than accept an exemption from their anti-Semitic laws.

Essential philosophy

Bergson's philosophy is one of mobility, novelty, freedom, and creativity. Known as a "process philosophy", it explores matters such as consciousness, time, identity, **perception**, change, **free will**, memory, and the limits of reason.

Consciousness and free will

In *Time and Free Will: An Essay on the Immediate Data of Consciousness* (1889) Bergson develops his theory of consciousness and time. The essay is a response to **Immanuel Kant**'s claim that free will is at least conceivable, but we cannot know with certainty whether free will exists because it belongs to a realm beyond the realm of our experiences (the **phenomenal** realm – see pages 100–1). On Bergson's model, consciousness involves a method of intuitive

introspection, and this deep level of consciousness is the seat of free will and creativity. At this level of consciousness free will is possible because the human experience of psychological time or "duration" is not perceived as a succession of individual conscious states, spatially extended, with one segment of "duration" succeeding and causing another, but as a continuous flow and diverse in character. Therefore, **determinism** (the theory that all human actions are predetermined) does not apply, and free will is able to move freely (freedom is mobility).

"Intuition" and rejection of the "intellectualist method"

In *Introduction to Metaphysics* (1903) Bergson further develops the method of intuitive introspection and explains why psychological

Legacy, truth, consequence

- Bergson's influence in France has been considerable among such thinkers as **Maurice Merleau-Ponty** and **Jean-Paul Sartre**. He has also had an impact in Britain and the United States, in the work of William James, George Santayana (1863–1952), and Alfred North Whitehead (1861–1947).

- His rejection of rationalist systems led many philosophers in the analytical **Western tradition** to criticize his approach. **Bertrand Russell**, in *The Monist* in 1912, claimed that classifying Bergson was impossible because his philosophy cuts across all divisions, whether **empiricist**, **realist**, or **idealist**.

- Bergson's conception of "duration" was a major influence on such modernist writers as Virginia Woolf, James Joyce, and Thomas Mann in the development of the "stream of consciousness" novel.

- The influence of Bergson's philosophy faded in the 1920s, but in 1966 Gilles Deleuze's *Bergsonism* marked the beginning of a renaissance of interest in Bergson's work. The insights Bergson develops in his essays and lectures contained in *Mind-Energy* remain highly pertinent to contemporary work in the **philosophy of mind**.

- The Roman Catholic Church banned Bergson's writings in 1914.

In *Laughter: An Essay on the Meaning of the Comic* (1900), Bergson develops a theory of how laughter can be provoked and describes the process of laughter used by comics and clowns.

Key dates

1859	Born in Paris, France.
1877–81	Studies at the École Normale Supérieure, then becomes a philosophy teacher.
1889	Publishes his first major work, *Time and Free Will: an Essay on the Immediate Data of Consciousness*.
1896	Publishes his book, *Matter and Memory*.
1900	Becomes a professor at the Collège de France and the same year publishes *Laughter: an Essay on the Meaning of the Comic*, a theory of how laughter can be provoked.
1903	Publishes *Introduction to Metaphysics*.
1907	Publishes his key work, *Creative Evolution*.
1908	Meets William James in London.
1914	Elected to the Académie Française.
1919	Publishes *Mind-Energy*, a collection of essays concerned with **metaphysical** and **psychological** problems.
1921	Resigns his position at the College of France to dedicate himself to writing.
1921–6	President of the International Commission on Intellectual Cooperation – a body of the League of Nations and an ancestor of today's UNESCO. Participates in a debate with Albert Einstein, his reflections on which are published as *Duration and Simultaneity*.
1927	Awarded the Nobel Prize for Literature.
1932	Publishes his final major work, *The Two Sources of Morality and Religion*.
1934	Publishes a collection of essays, *The Creative Mind*.
1941	Dies in Paris.
1957	*The Philosophy of Poetry* is published posthumously.

... no two moments are identical in a conscious being.

The Creative Mind (1934)

time or "duration" does not lend itself to analysis through immobile concepts. Intelligence, he claims, has developed in the course of evolution as a tool for survival, thus the knowledge it gathers is relative knowledge (it is not disinterested); when we use the intellect to achieve comprehensive knowledge, we analyse things by breaking them down and then synthesize the many perspectives gained through analysis. But this synthesis, although providing us with general concepts, never gives us the essence of things because it never reaches the mobile and flowing realm of life. To attain **absolute knowledge** of the world, reality must be grasped by "intuition", an experience that involves the use of imagination and sympathy to get to the things themselves. Without "intuition" we may as well experience life though a series of photographs; with "intuition" we experience the reality of being there.

Élan vital (creative energy)

The final essential component of Bergson's philosophy, which he developed in *Creative Evolution* (1907), is a type of vital impulse that shapes all life. Through this concept Bergson challenged the mechanistic Darwinist theory (*On the Origin of Species*, 1859) that evolution happens through primarily small, random adaptations helpful for survival, a process known as natural selection. Bergson argued that the course of evolution is better understood through the immaterial force of *élan vital*, or the creative urge.

John Dewey

John Dewey, who worked across the fields of philosophy, psychology, and education, became influential in the United States and across the world. Recognized as an important voice in American pragmatism, he also played a key role in developing a strand of applied psychology known as functional psychology.

Dewey grew up in Vermont, US, and gained a doctorate at Johns Hopkins University, where he encountered the ideas of **Charles Peirce**. He went on to become a professor of philosophy at Michigan, Chicago, and Columbia universities, and to found the American Association of University Professors. While in Chicago he formulated his **empirically**-based theory of knowledge, and began to support the newly developing theory of **pragmatism**. Along with Peirce and **William James**, he would become one of the key proponents of pragmatism, although Dewey preferred to describe his philosophy as "instrumentalist". Also at Chicago, Dewey succeeded in developing an influential biologically-based functional **psychology** that treats a person's mental states from the perspective of their active adaptation to the environment. This

approach allows the scientist a tool for examining psychological phenomena that are not easily studied in a laboratory or experimental situation.

Dewey was a reformer in the area of education, and in Chicago he set up a progressive laboratory school where some of his experimental reforms in education were tried out. His political concerns went far beyond philosophy and he was involved in liberal political movements for social reform. During his years at Columbia he traveled widely, lecturing on philosophy and social and political theory, and acting as an educational consultant. At home in America he was an outspoken critic on education, domestic and international politics, and numerous social movements. He died in New York City in 1952.

Essential philosophy

Dewey started his philosophical life under the influence of **idealism**, but after being exposed to the pragmatism of Peirce and James he changed his approach and developed a version of philosophical naturalism. **Naturalism** includes any theory that states that objects, events, and even values can be explained through the study of scientific facts and causes, rather than through **metaphysical** means.

The fallibility of truth

Like James and Peirce, Dewey took the approach that truth was merely the best practice, the belief that would lead us to the most successful actions. This very scientific attitude to truth meant that **epistemology**, the study of knowledge, was for Dewey best understood as a kind of practical problem solving. The human subject tests **hypotheses** against his or her experience to try to find beliefs that satisfy the criteria of warranted assertability (that are reasonable for us to assert) – beliefs that pass this test are coherent guides to action, and thus "true".

In *Logic: The Theory of Inquiry* (1938) Dewey lays out six steps in the process of belief formation. We start with doubt when we are confronted with an indeterminate situation. We recognize this as a problem. We invent hypotheses as possible solutions. We reason about the meaning of each solution. Then we apply the results of this

thought to the facts as we perceive them, and observe the results of assuming different theories. Finally we come to a common-sense belief about the situation that we originally were in doubt about.

Dewey was more explicit than William James in acknowledging that this means that the pragmatist concept of truth is a **fallibilistic** one; in other words, the results of our search for knowledge are always open to further doubt – we don't achieve certain knowledge and what is true now may not be true in future or for another person.

Moral progress or relativism?

In the long run this has been a problem for pragmatism, as it exposes it to the charge of **relativism**. If truth can be different from different points of view, then why do we care about the search for truth at all? Of course, Dewey's attitude is not that truth doesn't matter, merely that we cannot know that our beliefs are true, at least in the sense that they can be measured against some eternal yardstick.

Dewey's fallibilistic theory of truth allowed for an investigation of moral truth. Just as James had tried to understand how we can believe moral statements, even though they are in a sense untestable, Dewey tried to analyze the way that moral beliefs develop. Drawing from his concerns with education, Dewey saw moral statements as confirmable hypotheses that develop in a social setting. In this

Legacy, truth, consequence

- Dewey's legacy is a mixed one. By the time of his death in 1952, pragmatism had largely come to be seen as a rather woolly theory that tried to evade real questions of metaphysics and ethics. **Analytic philosophy** had in some respects replaced and superseded the thinking of the pragmatists. However, Dewey's naturalism continued to reverberate in the philosophy of writers such as **W. V. O. Quine**.

- Dewey also suffered from a backlash against the progressive, liberal thought he represented. His experimental thinking on education came to be seen in a less generous light as progressive schooling continued to face problems in the real world.

- However, Dewey is still revered by many as a powerful advocate of social reform, and some of his writings have been revisited with a more sympathetic eye in recent years.

- Interest in the epistemological approach of pragmatism has revived recently. Writers as varied as Hilary Putnam (*b.* 1926), **Noam Chomsky**, and **Richard Rorty** have gone back to Dewey and reconsidered his analysis of the ways in which we acquire beliefs.

In 1937 John Dewey was the chairman of the "Commission of Inquiry into the Charges Made Against Leon Trotsky in the Moscow Trials". The findings were published in the book *Not Guilty*.

respect, his work closely aligned with the thinking of George Herbert Mead (1863–1931), who tried to apply pragmatic principles to the emerging field of sociology. Mead developed an idea of self-consciousness that was grounded in our interactions, making our understanding of moral statements an essentially social one. Both Dewey and Mead were concerned with how pragmatism could be used to improve society. By grounding moral statements in a scientific, pragmatist setting, they hoped to show how new hypotheses about social reform could be tested and developed in a rational way.

Ethics and aesthetics

Dewey believed that his observations allowed the project of **empiricism** to be extended to the fields of **ethics** and **aesthetics**. In *The Construction of Good* (1929) he asserted that moral and aesthetic judgements are best understood as scientifically testable. By subjecting them to an experimental approach, we observe the consequences of our actions and choices and make moral judgements based upon these observations. This prevents us from being too influenced by subjective **egoism** and encourages us to accept that our beliefs are subject to error.

Key dates

1859	Born in Burlington, Vermont, US.
1884	Receives doctorate from Johns Hopkins and begins to teach at the University of Michigan.
1887	First of Dewey's many books, *Psychology*, is published.
1894	Becomes a professor of philosophy at the University of Chicago.
1896	Publishes *The Reflex Arc Concept in Psychology*, the basis for his future work on psychology. Sets up the University of Chicago Laboratory Schools.
1899	Elected president of the American Psychological Association.
1899	His first major work on education, *The School and Society*, is published.
1903	*Studies in Logical Theory* is published and contains his essays written while at Chicago.
1905	Begins teaching at Columbia University, where he stays until his retirement.
1905	Becomes president of the American Philosophical Association.
1910	*How We Think* is published.
1916	His work on progressive education, *Democracy and Education*, is published.
1919	With a group of intellectuals, sets up a progressive free school, The New School for Social Research, New York City.
1919–28	Tours Japan, China, Turkey, and Russia, lecturing and studying educational methods.
1929	Retires from formal academia.
1929	*The Construction of Good* is published.
1934	His major work on aesthetics is published, *Art as Experience*.
1938	*Logic: The Theory of Inquiry* is published.
1952	Dies in New York City.

> **... more important is the fact that the human being acquires a habit of learning. He learns to learn.**
>
> *Democracy and Education* (1916)

Of course there are problems with this theory. Firstly, Dewey is confronted by all the issues that had made **utilitarianism** a flawed theory, as we struggle to understand how moral issues can always be measured in a practical way. Secondly, Dewey's theory seems to reflect his own personality, which is that of a socially-concerned liberal who can accept their own fallibility. His theory seems less persuasive when we apply it to a world in which many people desire certainty rather than scientific fallibility and act from a position of self-interest.

Reading Dewey on moral issues, one can end up wishing he was right but suspecting that pragmatism cannot deal with these issues in the way that he hoped it could. But his belief that society could be improved through experimental progress can also be admired nonetheless for its optimism and belief in the human spirit.

Nishida Kitaro

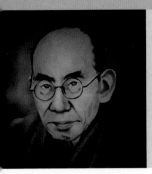

The foremost Japanese philosopher of the twentieth century, Nishida Kitaro was instrumental in introducing Western philosophy to Japan. The founder of what is called the "Kyoto School", he was the first person to explore Eastern spirituality such as Zen Buddhism through the lens of Western philosophical methods. He went beyond mere synthesis to create his own unique system of thought.

Nishida (his surname comes first according to Japanese custom) was born at a time of intense change in Japan. The Meiji Emperor, who inherited the throne in 1868, changed official policy by ending Japan's self-imposed period of isolation from the rest of the world, and introduced European or Western customs, education, and training. As a result Nishida was in the last generation whose early education followed the classical Japanese tradition, including the principles of Chinese **Confucianism**. However, he was also in the first generation to be encouraged to study European languages, philosophy, and technical subjects.

While at school in Kanazawa, Nishida made a lifelong friend in Suzuki Daisetz Teitaro (1870–1966), who, as D. T. Suzuki, was later to introduce **Zen Buddhism** to the Western world.

After graduating with a philosophy degree Nishida began to teach at junior colleges in Kanazawa and Yamaguchi, coming to specialize in **ethics**, **logic**, **psychology**, and German. In 1910 he began his association with the Imperial University in Kyoto, Japan's former capital and an important intellectual center. He became professor of philosophy there in 1914, building up a modern philosophy department and remaining in that post until he retired.

At the same time Nishida also became deeply involved in Zen Buddhism, which involves intense and disciplined meditation. It was the spiritual experiences that he gained through this practice that he tried to merge with **Western philosophical** ideas such as logic.

In 1905 he began to make his philosophical mark with essays that later formed part of his first book, *Zen No Kenkyu* (*An Inquiry into the Good*). With further publications and his work at the university, he became known as Japan's most eminent philosopher. As such, in the 1930s the government asked him to provide a theoretical justification for Japanese nationalism and expansionism. Nishida's ensuing exploration of culture and nationhood did not satisfy any politicians: aggressive expansionists thought he was too wishy-washy or abstract and vague, yet after World War II his philosophy was criticized for supporting the nationalist policies that had contributed to Japan's involvement in the war.

Essential philosophy

Although Nishida developed different insights over the course of his life, he maintained his same overall approach, which was to explore Eastern religions – particularly Zen Buddhism – with the rigor and logic of Western philosophical methods of inquiry. He felt that Western reasoning provided a rational foundation, but Zen supplied the ethics and the feeling or emotion. He was particularly influenced by the ideas on culture put forward by **Neo-Kantians**, and he wrote on a wide range of topics, including art and morality, from the perspective of a theory of consciousness and the will.

Experience

Nishida's starting point was to explore consciousness and experience, arguing that reality is nothing except experience or self-awareness (also defined as the phenomena of consciousness). In his 1911 book *An Inquiry into the Good* he defined "pure experience" as a state in which "*there is as yet neither subject nor object, and knowledge and its object are completely united. This is the purest form of experience*".

Thus his fundamental reality is a unity of the **subjective** and **objective**, where subject and object are the two relative sides of one reality and do not exist separately. He claimed that there is thus no separate objective reality at all – it depends entirely on subjective consciousness, and the self itself does not exist apart from the world that it sees. Conversely, all we know about the world is our experience of self.

From this fundamental reality everything else is manifested by a process of differentiation, separating into the subject that does the experiencing and the object that is experienced, into nature and spirit, intuition and thought, and so on.

In a later stage of his thinking Nishida proposed that experience is united with intuition in basic self-awareness, and he developed it further to say that the most fundamental form of self-awareness can be seen not as knowing but as "willing" or as an expression of "absolute **free will**". Throughout, however, he continued to believe that reality is a unity and that consciousness cannot be separated from it.

Legacy, truth, consequence

- Nishida succeeded in his aim of helping to introduce to Japan the full range of concepts explored by Western philosophers. He also succeeded in making philosophers around the world sit up and take notice of traditional and modern trends in Japanese thinking. The very labels of "West" and "East" are now considered by many to be too restrictive.

- Although he encouraged his students to branch off in independent directions, many of his colleagues and students were linked in the minds of others as the "Kyoto School", of which he was the pioneering founder. Most of the Kyoto School shared common interests in comparative philosophy, absolute nothingness, and an expression of Japanese thought through Western philosophical techniques.

- After World War II members of the Kyoto School were heavily criticized for their political ideas that supposedly contributed to Japanese nationalism and expansionism. In recent years, however, their unique philosophies have come to be reassessed.

Philosophy not only clarifies basic notions of reality, but must also elucidate the ideals of human life, the "ought" itself. Philosophy is not simply a worldview; it is a view of human life.

Art and Morality (1923)

Key dates

1870	Born near Kanazawa, Ishikawa Prefecture, Japan.
1891–4	Studies philosophy at Tokyo University.
1899	Becomes a professor in a junior college in Yamaguchi Prefecture.
1900s	Studies and practices Zen Buddhism.
1910	Begins to teach at Kyoto Imperial University; remains there for the rest of his teaching career.
1911	Publishes a key work, *An Inquiry into the Good*.
1914	Appointed professor of philosophy at Kyoto Imperial University.
1920s	Attracts top lecturers and students; creates the "Kyoto School".
1928	Retires from teaching; appointed emeritus professor.
1938	Lectures and writes on "The Problem of Japanese Culture" exploring nationalism.
1940	Awarded Japan's Cultural Medal of Honor.
1941	Invited to give a talk to the emperor and imperial court.
1945	Dies of an infection at Kamakura, in Kanagawa Prefecture.

The Philosopher's Walk in Kyoto, Japan, named after Nishida who used to walk the path to meditate.

Theory of place

In the mid-1920s Nishida developed one of his key ideas, the theory or logic of place or "*topos*", called "*basho*". He formulated a hierarchy of places containing different levels of differentiation, suggesting that his overall model can be seen as a series of inclusive circles, with the most comprehensive and concrete circle or place having no circumference and a center that is everywhere.

Nothingness

Several Asian religions, including some forms of Buddhism and Hinduism, contain the concept of "nothingness" or "emptiness", and Nishida applied this concept to the unitary source of all forms, which cannot itself be described as any one single thing, therefore is nothing ("*Mu*"). It is from *Mu* or nothingness that experience, self-consciousness, and free will come.

Nishida's most inclusive place, or ultimate *topos*, is that of the absolute nothingness. This place of nothingness, the "*Mu no basho ronri*", is effectively the state of pure experience that is part of Zen meditation, in which the division between self and the rest of the world disappears. He saw this as a way to avoid distinctions of oppositions such as subject and object, knower and object known.

Method

Nishida had a unique approach that was probably rooted in traditional Japanese art forms such as calligraphy as well as in his Zen practice: instead of presenting a linear chain of thought, he would address one idea in several different ways and from different approaches. His method has been described as spiraling around a topic, touching it in many places. He would also reverse concepts, treating abstract ideas as concrete notions, and vice versa.

International philosophy

Nishida argued that concepts such as "nothingness" might have originated within **Eastern thought** but they should not be only debated within the context of comparative religion. Instead, they should be considered part of the global philosophical movement.

Bertrand Russell

Russell was a great logician, mathematician, and philosopher, and campaigner for social reform. Along with Gottlob Frege and Ludwig Wittgenstein, he was a pioneer of analytic philosophy as it is practiced today. Russell was a prominent pacifist, resisting World War I on the grounds that it was immoral, and campaigning tirelessly for nuclear disarmament.

Born in 1872 in Monmouthshire, Wales, into an aristocratic and highly political family, Bertrand Russell was the third Earl Russell. His grandfather, the first Earl Russell, had twice served as prime minister. Russell's parents were radical for their times. His father consented to his wife's affair with the children's tutor and was an open atheist. Both his parents and his godfather, the philosopher **John Stuart Mill**, died while Russell was young, and the boy was put in the care of his grandmother who instilled in him a strong sense of social justice. He won a scholarship to Trinity College, Cambridge, in 1893, where he excelled at mathematics, gaining a fellowship in philosophy. Russell was first married in 1894 but had fallen out of love by 1901. Between this time and finally obtaining a

divorce in 1921 he had a number of affairs of which he made no secret, most famously with Lady Ottoline Morrell.

In 1911 Russell was visited by the young **Ludwig Wittgenstein** and came to consider him a genius. He hoped that his own work in **logic** would be continued by Wittgenstein, but their relationship deteriorated and Russell had no sympathy for Wittgenstein's later philosophy.

During World War I Russell was stripped of his job at Trinity College, and at one point jailed, because of his pacifism. With his new wife Dora Black he traveled to Russia and China. He had hoped to be impressed with Russia but was put off by his meetings with Vladimir Lenin, whom he thought very disappointing. In between

Essential philosophy

Logicism

Like his contemporary **Gottlob Frege**, Russell sought to ground the truths of mathematics in the laws of logic. This is the project of his famous book *Principia Mathematica* (1910–13), coauthored with Alfred North Whitehead (1861–1947). Like Frege's "logicism" (see pages 132–3), Russell drew upon the notion of classes or sets of objects to define the numbers. Thus Russell thought of the number one as the class of all one-membered classes, the number two as the class of all two-membered classes, and so on. He came to realize that there was a special **paradox** surrounding the assumption of classes.

Russell's paradox

Russell noticed a central paradox in the theory of classes. It was a paradox that undermined Frege's version of logicism. The paradox begins with the observation that most classes are not members of themselves. For instance, the class of all the red things is not a member of itself because it is not a red thing. But some classes are members of themselves. For instance, the class of all the things that are not men is a member of itself, not being itself a man. Now consider the class of all the classes that are not members of themselves. Is this class a member of itself? The reply might be: if it is a member of itself then it is not a member of itself, and if it is not a member of itself then it is a member of itself. But this is patent contradiction. One response would be to claim that such a class does not exist. But this conflicts with the

definition of a class as determined by a coherent condition, such as being red or not being a member of itself, together with the idea that we can have classes of classes. Russell's response was to construct a theory of types which limited the existing classes in a principled way so as to include all the classes needed by mathematics but exclude the class of all classes which are not members of themselves.

Philosophical logic

Russell invented the term "philosophical logic" to describe the analytical approach to philosophy he adopted. This involved working out the logical form of problematic **propositions** using a formal language he developed in *Principia*. Russell sought clarity in philosophy by breaking down troublesome propositions into their logical components and by going beyond the surface forms of ordinary language to reveal underlying logical forms. He was suspicious of the misleading forms taken by ordinary speech, saying that they "*enshrine the superstitions of cannibals*" (*Mind and Matter*, 1925) and disguise fundamental philosophical distinctions. For example, the word "is" in ordinary language obscures the differences between claims that something *is* in the sense that it exists, that one thing *is* identical to another ("George Orwell *is* Eric Blair"), and claims that one thing has a property ("The door *is* red"). All these differences can be brought out by analysis in philosophical logic. Russell saw this kind of logical analysis as the philosopher's primary tool. His theory of descriptions is often taken as a paradigm of philosophical logic and

MEN OF THE EMPIRE!
Rally Round the Flag
and
**Join the Army to-day.
Your Country needs you.**
ANOTHER HALF MILLION MEN REQUIRED AT ONCE.

During World War I, Russell engaged in pacifist activism against British participation in the war.

the wars, he was instrumental in organizing a number of meetings of prominent scientists and intellectuals devoted to world peace. He took a rather different view towards World War II, recognizing early on the danger that Hitler was to the freedom of Europe.

Russell tried to bring philosophical ideas to the general reader, and his *Problems of Philosophy* (1912) is still the best introduction to philosophical problems. In 1950 he won the Nobel Prize for Literature for his vast body of work, which defends complete freedom of thought and a belief that the exercise of human rationality, rather than God or political controls, is the answer to human problems.

> ## *... to my mind, a man without bias cannot write interesting history — if, indeed, such a man exists.*
>
> From Russell's autobiography (1967)

the analyses it can offer. The theory states that sentences such as "The present King of France is bald" should be analyzed as a description, the logical form of which is that there exists an x, x is the present King of France, and x is bald, and for all y, if y is the present king of France, then y is identical to x. One of several important consequences of Russell's logical analysis is that it allows us to make sense of such sentences without appealing to some non-existent object denoted by "the present king of France". The statement says of some existing individual that he is the present king of France but as no such individual exists the statement is false.

Logical atomism

Russell's **logical atomism** was the view that the world is composed of atomic parts (which are properties like patches of color) and the facts that the atomic parts compose. The logical atomist tries to account for our knowledge of entities like trees by building them up as logical constructions from things that can be immediately known and demonstrated, including the objects we immediately sense. This direct contact with things, Russell called knowledge by "acquaintance". He refused to rely on any entities that might be doubted saying:

> *I think on the whole the sort of method adopted by Descartes is right: that you should set out to doubt things and retain only what you cannot doubt because of its clearness and distinctness.*
>
> (*The Philosophy of Logical Atomism*, 1918)

Legacy, truth, consequence

■ Russell's work, along with Gottlob Frege's, was a powerful influence on **Ludwig Wittgenstein** in the writing of the *Tractatus* (1921). Russell was also instrumental in getting the *Tractatus* published.

■ His philosophical logic and theory of descriptions are often held up as paradigms of the method of analysis.

■ Russell's logical atomism directly, but also indirectly via Wittgenstein, shaped **Rudolf Carnap**'s project in his *Aufbau* (1928). One key difference is that Russell did not think of **sense-data** as mental objects.

■ The work of Russell has been a great influence on modern philosophy in the English-speaking world, in particular on **A. J. Ayer** and **W. V. O. Quine**, but also **Noam Chomsky** and **John Searle**.

■ Russell is also remembered as a great popularizer of philosophy, through his historical and introductory works on the subject, as well as his writings on social and political matters.

George Edward Moore

G. E. Moore was one of the most respected British philosophers of the early part of the twentieth century. A Cambridge professor, and a contemporary of Bertrand Russell and Ludwig Wittgenstein among others, he was one of the founders of the movement known as analytic philosophy. He was also the editor of the philosophy journal *Mind*.

George Edward Moore grew up in South London in a large family and had an excellent grounding in Greek and Latin at Dulwich College. From 1892 he studied classics at Cambridge University, where he became friends with **Bertrand Russell** and J. M. E. McTaggart (1866–1925). Under their influence he added philosophy to his studies. McTaggart and F. H. Bradley (1846–1924) were known as strong exponents of **absolute idealism**, which in the wake of **G. W. F. Hegel** was the dominant philosophy across Europe.

At Cambridge, Bradley put forward a rather stodgy version of idealist **metaphysics**, which emphasized the internal relations of truth and reality within a single "absolute". While Moore's early thinking was strongly influenced by absolute idealism, he would (along with Russell) become known for his later repudiation of this way of thinking.

As a young man, Moore joined the secretive Cambridge club, the Apostles, at a time when it counted among its members such famous names as Rupert Brooke (1887–1915), Lytton Strachey (1880–1932), and John Maynard Keynes (1883–1946). Moore's friendship with the literary, London-based Bloomsbury Set, combined with his role at Cambridge in a period when it was the pre-eminent center of **Anglo-American philosophy**, put him at the heart of the intellectual zeitgeist.

Essential philosophy

Moore's philosophy starts from the viewpoint that much philosophical controversy is superfluous. Rather than follow idealists and **sceptics** in questioning whether or not our common-sense beliefs can be shown to be uncertain or falsifiable, Moore started by assuming that our common-sense beliefs are correct, and that the role of philosophy is to analyze the nature and significance of those beliefs.

In his early works, *The Nature of Judgment* (1899) and *The Refutation of Idealism* (1903), he criticizes Bradley's concept of internal relations and carefully distinguishes between consciousness and the objects of consciousness. He goes on to reject the idealist slogan *esse est percipi* (to be is to be perceived), pointing out that the entire project of idealism relies on this idea, when it is clearly not a **necessary** (indubitable) truth. Against this background, Moore asserts his own version of **realism**. In the later work *A Defence of Common Sense* (1925), he states that we all know some basic truths about ourselves and the world around us. He rejects the doubts of idealists and sceptics, and asserts the primacy of common sense.

The role of propositions

From this point he needs to explain the nature of truth and reality. Moore's theory of truth relies on the idea of "**propositions**". Rather than define a proposition as the content of a thought, he sees it as an independent entity. For him, a proposition is what a declarative sentence conveys.

So if I say that the cat is on the mat, my sentence expresses the proposition that the cat is in a certain relation to the mat. If this proposition is in agreement with the fact (in other words the cat is indeed on the mat) then the proposition I have expressed is true. This is known as a "correspondence theory of truth" – the truth of a proposition depends on its relation to a fact. "Propositions" are a somewhat **metaphysical** concept and **analytic philosophers** have struggled to define exactly what they are. But Russell, **Ludwig Wittgenstein** (in his *Tractatus* period), and others relied on a similar theory as the foundation of their analysis of meaning and truth. Wittgenstein at one stage treated propositions as though they were a kind of picture – if we think about a fact, the thought is like a picture, and if the picture is an accurate representation of that fact, then it is true.

Moore thus assumes that a mental state creates a relation between the thinker and the object of thought. This is as much of an assumption as the idealist assumption that the state of being and **perception** are inextricably linked, but it does allow Moore to escape the **solipsism** that tends to result from idealism. After making his assumption, the role of **analytic philosophy**, in Moore's view, is to analyze and clarify the relationship between propositions and facts.

Legacy, truth, consequence

■ Moore had a significant influence on the project of analytic philosophy. His theories on truth were similar to his contemporaries Russell and **Gottlob Frege**, both of whom were also known as founders of this tradition. It is the form of philosophy that became dominant in the first half of the twentieth century, which seeks to study our use of ordinary language, and uncover concealed logical and philosophical assumptions in an attempt to achieve clarity in our thought.

■ Moore's own philosophy is sometimes frustrating in retrospect, in that his reliance on common sense can fail to convince. Later philosophers, such as Wittgenstein (with whom Moore had many conversations), **Gilbert Ryle**, and **Richard Rorty** – in entirely different ways – would bring greater clarity to some of the problems that Moore had identified.

■ Some would argue that Moore's influence is an unfortunate one, in that Anglo–American philosophy would, under the sway of analytic philosophy, turn away from what was perceived as the pretensions of Continental thinking. The result was a rather dry obsession with detailed analysis of problems of meaning and reference, rather than with the grander questions of life.

A proposition is composed not of words, nor yet of thoughts, but of concepts. Concepts are possible objects of thought; but that is no definition of them.

The Nature of Judgment (1899)

Trinity College Great Court, Cambridge University, where the Apostles, a secret society of which Moore was a member, was centered.

Moore's ethics

Moore's book *Principia Ethica* (1903) laid out the foundations of his **ethical** philosophy. His first instinct was to analyze the meaning and use of the idea of "goodness". He argued against attempts to reduce good to some other quality or list of qualities, asserting that this was a "naturalistic fallacy" (meaning that one couldn't equate "good" with a natural quality). He pointed out that there is always an "open question" left over when we try to define good in this way. If we say that something is good when it gives pleasure or when it makes the world a better place, we can always go on to wonder "but is that always good?"

For Moore, "good" is a simple, but non-natural quality. We can't reduce it down to meaning in terms of other qualities. But this doesn't mean that it is a pointless or meaningless term, since we know perfectly well what we mean when we use the term in everyday life. We intuit the concept of good, even if we can't elucidate what it means.

It perhaps says more about Moore as a man than as a philosopher that he went on to identify our experience of good as being most clear in our **aesthetic** appreciation of art and in our experience of human friendship. This kind of **ethical intuitionism** may not be a very satisfactory explanation of our moral judgements, or of why different people intuit different ideas of goodness, but for Moore it is the best we can do as common-sense philosophers.

Key dates

1873	Born, and grows up in South London, UK, where he is educated at Dulwich College.
1892	Begins studies at Trinity College, University of Cambridge.
1898	Wins a fellowship at Trinity and remains at Cambridge until 1904. Becomes involved in various philosophical societies.
1899	*The Nature of Judgment* is published.
1903	*The Refutation of Idealism* is published.
1903	*Principia Ethica* is published.
1911	Returns to Cambridge as lecturer in moral science.
1916	Marries Dorothy Ely, his former student, with whom he has two sons.
1918	Elected a fellow of the British Academy.
1921	Appointed editor of the journal *Mind*.
1925	*A Defence of Common Sense* is published.
1925	Appointed professor of mental philosophy and logic at Cambridge.
1939	*Proof of an External World* is published; retires as professor.
1944	Retires as editor of *Mind*.
1951	Awarded the British Order of Merit.
1958	Dies, and is interred in the burial ground of the Parish of the Ascension, Cambridge.

José Ortega y Gasset

The journalist and essayist José Ortega y Gasset aimed to bring about a cultural and literary renaissance in twentieth-century Spain. Promoting better education, introducing ideas from the rest of Europe, and writing prolifically, he succeeded in reinvigorating Spanish philosophical debate, and inspired developments in the arts, literature, and even science.

José Ortega y Gasset came from a well-off but liberal background and grew up in a literary atmosphere; his mother's family owned a newspaper, which his father, a journalist, helped run. Ortega was educated at a school and college run by Jesuits, later condemning them for a narrow, intolerant outlook. He also found the quality of education at the University of Madrid, where he studied philosophy, to be disappointing and mediocre, especially when compared to the advanced and disciplined approach to education and training that he found when he undertook further studies in Germany.

While in Germany, Ortega was influenced by **Neo-Kantian** ideas, although he eventually forged his own unique path. He was particularly keen to introduce new ideas in philosophy to the rather hide-bound Spanish intellectual world; the magazine he founded in 1923, *Revista de Occidente*, aimed to bring contemporary European culture to Spain.

Ortega was only 19 when he published his first article, setting the scene for his method of working. Instead of academic textbooks and papers, he wrote articles and essays that were published in newspapers and magazines for a general readership. His actual books were usually later compilations of a series of articles or lectures.

As well as journalism and teaching philosophy, Ortega was deeply involved in politics, opposing the 1923–30 dictatorship of Primo de Rivera and supporting the republican movement that led to the abdication of the monarchy in 1931. He was elected to the constituent assembly of the new Spanish republic, coming to lead a group of parliamentary intellectuals known as La Agrupación al Servicio de la República (The Group in the Service of the Republic). But disillusionment set in, and after just one year he left parliament. When the Spanish Civil War broke out in 1936 he felt unable to actively support either side, though he inclined towards the republic. He refused to stay and teach in Madrid under Franco's Nationalists, so went into voluntary exile until 1948.

Essential philosophy

Ortega was part of the so-called "Generation of '98", who grew up in the years after 1898 when Spain had finally lost the last vestiges of its empire and its historical glory. At a time of cultural depression and stagnation, the Generation of '98 aimed to reinvigorate society and culture, and restore to Spain a sense of pride and glory. Ortega believed that the way to do this was through education, and as a philosopher he thought he could inspire change through presenting philosophical ideas.

As a result his writings range over a huge variety of cultural and philosophical topics, from history and art criticism, to **metaphysics** and **epistemology**.

Circumstances

Ortega felt that the only reality was simply life itself, and he saw this as a dynamic interplay between the individual self and the circumstances it finds itself in. He summed this up in the phrase, which is central to his thinking: "*I am myself and my circumstances*", arguing that everyone is affected by their environment or situation, which means that each person has their own unique individual perspective on life and that there is no **absolute truth**.

One's circumstances can impose limits on freedom or choice, and Ortega was to some extent a fatalist, saying that freedom "*is being free inside of a given fate. Fate gives us an inexorable repertory of determinate possibilities, that is, it gives us different destinies. We accept fate and within it we choose one destiny*".

But, while some people will blindly accept their circumstances and their fate, Ortega said that an individual can create themselves by exerting reason and will, choosing to influence their circumstances through "tasks" or "projects of life". His thinking in this area led to Ortega being identified with the **existentialist** movement.

True to his own argument, Ortega said in later years that his thinking had continued to evolve because of changing circumstances.

Vital reason

Reason played many parts in Ortega's thought. It is fundamental to developing a "life project", and he also proposed a new term "vital

Legacy, truth, consequence

- Ortega was considered to be the most influential Spanish intellectual of his time. His dynamism and enthusiasm for his ideas and the causes he supported revolutionized philosophy in Spain, and he drew to the University of Madrid other modern thinkers who formed the loose group called "The School of Madrid".
- By writing in everyday language in popular newspapers and magazines, Ortega's influence extended well beyond purely philosophical or intellectual circles.
- Partly through his magazine *Revista de Occidente*, he succeeded in introducing contemporary Western culture to Spain.
- Some of Ortega's ideas, such as "life projects" and his argument that the only thing that is real is life, not the self or the mind, influenced existentialism.
- Several of his students worked to implement his ideas on education by reforming teaching methods in Spain and in some Latin American countries.

A Nationalist Air Force bombing raid during the Spanish Civil War. Ortega felt unable to support either side and went into voluntary exile in 1936.

reason" for the process of thinking through and living out philosophy. In this respect he is popularly thought to have turned **Descartes**' famous saying on its head – instead of "*I think, therefore I am*", Ortega said "*I live, therefore I think*". Finally, his "historical reason" was reason consciously founded in one's history or circumstances.

Elitism

In his 1929 book, *The Revolt of the Masses*, Ortega condemned twentieth-century society as dominated by mediocrity, full of masses of people who were content to be mediocre themselves, enjoying and even celebrating a popular culture that had no depth and a complete lack of vision. Despite his support for republicanism, Ortega was basically an elitist at heart, believing that these mediocre masses should be led by an elite minority of intellectually independent men and women who would be able to develop a more meaningful culture. This book became well known outside Spain, stirring up intense intellectual arguments around the world.

Key dates

1883	Born in Madrid, Spain.
1904	Gains a doctorate in philosophy from the Complutense University of Madrid.
1904–08	Studies in Germany.
1910	Appointed professor of metaphysics at the University of Madrid.
1914	Publishes his first important book, *Meditaciones del Quijote* (*Meditations on Quixote*).
1917	Begins to write essays for *El Sol* newspaper, many of which are later compiled into books.
1922	Writes *España Invertebrada* (*Invertebrate Spain*).
1923	Founds the literary and philosophical magazine *Revista de Occidente* (*Review of the West*), introducing ideas from other European countries.
1929	Publishes one of his best-known works, *La Rebelión de las Masas* (*The Revolt of the Masses*).
1931	Involved in social movement leading to collapse of monarchy. Elected to republican parliament.
1932	Disillusioned by politics, retires from parliament.
1936	On outbreak of Spanish Civil War goes into exile in Europe and South America.
1948	Returns to Madrid; founds the Institute of Humanities.
1955	Dies in Madrid.

I am I, and my circumstance. This expression, which appears in my first book and which, in the final volume, condenses my philosophical thought, does not only mean the doctrine which my work expounds and proposes, but also that my work is an effective instance of that same doctrine. My work is, in essence and presence, circumstantial.

Commentary on *Meditations on Quixote* (1932)

Education

Inspired by his own poor experiences at school and university, Ortega felt very strongly that a better education system was an optimistic, forward-looking way to solve "*the problem of Spain*". He argued that education should aim to shape a child's whole life with positive qualities, not just teach bare facts – "*Elementary teaching should be constantly governed by the final purpose of producing the greatest number of vitally perfect human beings*". And at the other end he felt that "*The university consists, first and foremost, of the education which the average person should receive; above all, the average individual must be made into a cultured person, able to meet the challenges of his times …*"

Sarvepalli Radhakrishnan

A politician as well as a philosopher, the Indian Hindu Sir Sarvepalli Radhakrishnan was concerned to show that Western philosophy could be compatible with Eastern religion. He helped kickstart a two-way flow of ideas, introducing traditional Indian religious philosophy to the West, and applying Western philosophical methods to Indian religions.

Sarvepalli Radhakrishnan was born a **Brahmin**, the highest caste in **Hinduism**, but his family was not well-off, and he relied on scholarships for his education. He spent several years at Christian missionary schools, where he first learnt about comparative religion. In 1904, the year he turned 16 and got married, he went on to the prestigious Madras Christian College, where he studied the classic Hindu texts. He was also introduced to European philosophy, eventually gaining a master's degree in the subject when he was only 20.

He began his teaching career at the same time as he started writing papers exploring and comparing Indian and Western religions. From his schooldays he knew how little most Europeans understood about the details of Asian religions, particularly their philosophical bases, so he was particularly keen to be published in European magazines. In 1911 he succeeded in reaching a large European audience when part of his master's thesis on "The Ethics of the Bhagavad Gita and Kant" was published in *The International Journal of Ethics*.

Many more papers followed, and as he refined his own interpretation of Hinduism and definition of experience, he found inspiration in the work of the Bengali poet and visionary Rabindranath Tagore. An Indian nationalist, in the early 1920s Radhakrishnan began to criticize European philosophy as dogmatic and sometimes irrational, and particularly for underpinning the despotism that he saw in much of the world, including British-run India. His many papers and books gained

him an increasing international reputation, and during a lecture tour in Oxford, England, he took the opportunity to make the case for independence, arguing: "*India is not a subject to be administered but a nation seeking its soul.*" The book based on those lectures, *An Idealist View of Life* (1932), is considered to be one of Radhakrishnan's most significant works. He obviously made an impact, since he was invited back to Oxford ten years later to take the newly created Spalding Chair of Eastern Religions and Ethics.

A renowned and committed teacher, Radhakrishnan saw education as a crucial element of the proposed independent India. In all his university posts he made efforts to strengthen the entire institution, and he was asked to chair the newly independent India's first University Education Commission in 1948.

Following independence in 1947, Radhakrishnan kept some academic roles but became increasingly involved in politics, as a member of the Indian Constituent Assembly and representing his country in the newly created United Nations Educational, Scientific, and Cultural Organization (UNESCO), and then as ambassador to the USSR. Apparently the **idealist** philosopher and the **communist** dictator Stalin got on very well together.

In 1952 Radhakrishnan was elected vice-president of India, serving two terms and becoming famous for calming down political tempers. After one term as president, during which he urged the world to restore a sense of unity and international fellowship, he retired.

Essential philosophy

Study of religion

Radhakrishnan wrote several commentaries on and analyses of Hindu texts such as the Bhagavad Gita and the Upanishads (part of the **Vedas**). He wrote to European academic standards, ensuring that his books were accepted in universities as a worthy subject of study, and thereby achieving his aim of introducing the rich traditions of Hindu philosophy to the West.

His own religious stance was a modern version ("Neo-Advaitin") of the Advaita Vedanta – a sub-school of the Vedanta school of Hindu philosophy incorporating a non-duality or **monistic** system of thought. But he tried to show that there is an underlying unity in the world's great religions, one that rose from his own tradition. He felt that the "authority" and "soul" of religion were personal intuitive experience and inner realization, which are

in fact the defining features of the Vedanta. Therefore, he claimed, it was not a religion, but religion itself. Other religions are only interpretations of the Vedanta. (See Traditional Indian Philosophy, pages 40–1, for more on Radhakrishnan's Vedanta beliefs.)

Through his studies of comparative religion and philosophy Radhakrishnan came to believe that there was a degree of self-deception in many Western philosophers, who did not acknowledge the religious origin of some of their tools and techniques, which he felt were rooted in different Christian dogmas.

Religious hierarchy

Radhakrishnan proposed a hierarchy of religious ideas. In his 1927 book *The Hindu View of Life* he wrote: "*The worshippers of the Absolute are the highest in rank; second to them are the worshippers*

Legacy, truth, consequence

- With his many books, academic papers, and lectures, Radhakrishnan succeeded in giving foreigners an introduction to Indian religions, and in showing the depth and complexity of Hindu philosophy.
- Philosophy in Europe tended to embrace only European intellectuals, thinkers from classical Greece and Rome, and perhaps one or two of the major Arab or Jewish scholars. Partly because of Radhakrishnan's influence, modern philosophy now acknowledges the contributions of Asian philosophers, even if their concerns have mainly been different from European thinkers.
- Radhakrishnan's distinction between a logical, dogmatic West and a mystic, spiritually-open East actually perpetuated old stereotypes, and is not seen nowadays to be a helpful definition of categories.

The art of discovery is confused with the logic of proof and an artificial simplification of the deeper movements of thought results. We forget that we invent by intuition though we prove by logic.

An Idealist View of Life (1932)

The Presidential Palace of India in New Delhi; Radhakrishnan was elected president in 1962 after serving as first vice-president from 1952.

Key dates

1888	Born in Tiruttani, Tamil Nadu, south India.
1909	Begins a teaching career at Presidency College, Madras, lecturing on **psychology** and European philosophy. Writes and publishes many philosophical papers.
1911	His master's thesis, "The Ethics of the Bhagavad Gita and Kant" is published.
1918–21	Becomes professor of philosophy at Mysore University.
1921	Takes the King George V Chair of Mental and Moral Science at the University of Calcutta.
1923	Publishes first volume of a major book, *Indian Philosophy*.
1926	Invited to Oxford, England, to give a lecture series, published the next year as *The Hindu View of Life*.
1927	Publishes second volume of *Indian Philosophy*.
1931	Receive a knighthood.
1931–6	Serves as vice-chancellor of Andhra University.
1932	Publishes his important work *An Idealist View of Life* (based on 1929 lectures).
1936–52	Appointed Spalding Professor of Eastern Religions and Ethics at Oxford University, England.
1939	Publishes *Eastern Religions and Western Thought*.
1947	Elected a member of India's first independent government.
1948–9	Elected chairman of executive board of UNESCO.
1949–52	Appointed Indian ambassador to the Soviet Union.
1952–62	Serves as first vice-president of India.
1954	Awarded India's new honor, the Bharat Ratna.
1953–62	Appointed chancellor of the University of Delhi.
1955	Publishes *East and West: Some Reflections*.
1962	Elected India's second president.
1962	His birthday, September 5, is declared Teachers' Day.
1967	Retires from politics.
1975	Dies in Mysore.

of the personal God; then come the worshippers of the incarnations like Rama, Krishna, Buddha; below them are those who worship ancestors, deities and sages, and the lowest of all are the worshippers of the petty forces and spirits."

Idealism

In his 1932 book *An Idealist View of Life*, Radhakrishnan outlined his ideas on the supremacy of experience (or subjective awareness) and intuitive thinking in reflecting what is real about the world. He saw this emphasis on idealism as an alternative to the rampant commercialism that he feared would exploit India and Indians.

Intuition

Radhakrishnan felt that intuition was integral in several ways, not least because it is the basis of all other experiences and is the origin of the creative energy that inspires progress. He defined it in many ways: sometimes as **mystical** and spiritual, such as revelation or spiritual idealism; sometimes as all-inclusive – self-sufficient, pure comprehension, complete.

He deplored the Western urge to reduce the intuitive to the logical, saying that although **logic** deals with known facts, intuition goes further by revealing the path to new facts. He also pointed out that intuitive experience is actually outside the realm of **logical analysis**.

Ludwig Wittgenstein

In his first major work, the *Tractatus Logico-Philosophicus*, Wittgenstein shaped the evolution of the philosophy of language, the philosophy of mind, the foundations of logic, and the philosophy of mathematics from the 1920s. He considered that it solved all the problems of philosophy, but his second masterpiece, *Philosophical Investigations*, then went on to criticize the *Tractatus* and the whole tradition that it rested upon.

Born in Vienna, Wittgenstein was the youngest of eight children, all of whom were baptized as Roman Catholics. He grew up in an artistic and intellectual environment and his devotion to music remained important throughout his life: his philosophical writings make frequent use of musical metaphors.

He studied at the Realschule in Linz, attending at the same time as Adolf Hitler, then, in 1906, began a course in mechanical engineering in Berlin, followed by a doctorate in engineering at the Victoria University of Manchester. His interest in the foundations of mathematics was sparked after reading **Bertrand Russell**'s *Principles of Mathematics* (1903) and **Gottlob Frege**'s *Grundgesetze der Arithmetic* (1883). In 1911 Wittgenstein joined Trinity College, Cambridge. He made a great impression on Russell and **G. E. Moore**, and started to work on the foundations of **logic** and mathematical logic. But in 1913 he retreated to the solitude of a remote village in Norway. There he was able to concentrate on his work and develop ideas that would eventually go into his *Tractatus Logico-Philosophicus*.

His secluded life was shattered at the outbreak of World War I. He volunteered for the Austro–Hungarian army, won several medals for bravery on the Russian front, and became a prisoner of war. An atheist during his stint at Cambridge, it is said that he discovered Leo Tolstoy's *The Gospel in Brief* and carried the book on the battlefield, recommending it to anyone in distress.

Wittgenstein published only one philosophical book in his lifetime, the *Tractatus Logico-Philosophicus* in 1921. His early work was influenced by **Arthur Schopenhauer**, and the ideas of **Immanuel Kant**, especially in relation to **transcendentality**. With the completion of the *Tractatus* Wittgenstein believed he had solved all the problems of philosophy. However, in 1929, he returned to Cambridge, where he was awarded a doctorate. He renounced or revised much of his earlier work, and his development of a new philosophical method culminated in his second magnum opus, the *Philosophical Investigations*, published posthumously.

Essential philosophy

Tractatus Logico-Philosophicus

Wittgenstein's early work was concerned with the relationship between language, thought, and reality. In particular he was concerned with the structure of language.

After Russell, he held that both the world and language consist of constituent or atomic parts, out of which larger facts are built. Following Frege, he held that the meaning of linguistic expressions is determined by facts about the world that exist independently of thought. The next step was Wittgenstein's own: he claimed that thought, expressed in the **propositions** of language, exactly mirrors the facts of the world by sharing the same "logical form". This claim that thought and language picture the structure of reality became known as the "picture theory" of meaning: sentences are pictures, or representations, of how the world is, or how the world could possibly be. Further, any thoughts or sentences that we cannot show to have a logical form in common with the order of the world, including contradictions and the so-called **necessary truths** of logic, such as tautologies, cannot be meaningfully discussed in philosophy. "*Whereof one cannot speak, thereof one must be silent.*" Those things to be passed over "in silence" may be important but they are not appropriate for philosophical analysis.

Some commentators have pointed out that the sentences of the *Tractatus* do not pass Wittgenstein's test of what is meaningful. This he admits when he writes in proposition 6.54: "*My propositions are elucidatory in this way: he who understands me finally recognizes them as senseless.*"

Philosophical Investigations

Wittgenstein's later work, the *Philosophical Investigations*, is an extremely rich source of ideas for contemporary philosophers. Unhappy with his earlier thesis, that meaning is essentially tied to the nature of reality, and that meaningful propositions stand in a "picturing" reality, he sought an

> **The limits of my language mean the limits of my world.**
>
> Tractatus Logico-Philosophicus (1921)

Legacy, truth, consequence

- Wittgenstein's work has been a major influence in **analytic philosophy**, **logical positivism**, and the "ordinary language" school of philosophy.

- He examined philosophical issues in ways that no one before had done. The logician Warren Goldfarb describes him as "*a philosopher whose major concern is to fight against **a priorism**, to demolish pictures of how things must be, to expose 'preconceived ideas to which reality must correspond'*" ("Wittgenstein on Understanding", *Midwest Studies in Philosophy*, XVII, 1992).

- Philosophers influenced by him include Bertrand Russell, **A. J. Ayer**, members of the **Vienna Circle**, Daniel Dennett (*b.* 1942), Saul Kripke (*b.* 1940), and **Gilbert Ryle**.

- His work has significantly influenced **psychology** and psychotherapy. Social therapy has also made use of Wittgenstein's language games as a tool for emotional growth.

In *Philosophical Investigations* (1953), Wittgenstein discusses the duck-rabbit picture: an example of something that can be seen in two different ways depending upon what we are most familiar with.

> *... my work consists of two parts: of the one which is here, and of everything I have not written. And precisely this second part is the important one ... All of that which many are babbling I have defined in my book by remaining silent about it.*
>
> Letter to Ludwig von Ficker, 1919 (translation by Ray Monk)

alternative description for the nature of language. This time he found that objects in the world are not literally the meanings of words (or names), but help us (along with other methods) to explain what words mean when we point to the objects in reality. In a clear break from the *Tractatus* and the idea of "meaning as representation", he found that the meaning of a word is essentially determined through its use in the language. Wittgenstein also realized that language is used for many different purposes – not only to describe or represent things, but also to joke, ask questions, give directions, play games, etc. Meaning is determined by all these applications and the specific context in each case. This idea that a particular context explains the meaning of an expression gave rise to Wittgenstein's famous notion of language use being a multiplicity of language-games: these are what give language its meaning. Wittgenstein's insistence that meaning cannot be seen in isolation from the behavior and activities of language users has had an enormous impact on modern philosophy.

This new understanding of language, he contended, would help to dissolve the problems of philosophy. Philosophers have applied **logical analysis** to seemingly intractable problems for centuries, but Wittgenstein explained that these are in fact "bewitchments" or confusions that arise when philosophers misuse language by forcing it into a metaphysical context. In its ordinary use in daily life, the problems do not arise. He advised philosophers to "*bring words back from their metaphysical to their everyday use*" and such problems will dissolve.

Key dates

1889   Born in Vienna, Austria. Begins studying mechanical engineering in Berlin (1906). Later enters Victoria University of Manchester to study for a doctorate in engineering.

1911   Visits Gottlob Frege and on his advice attends Trinity College, Cambridge, under the tutelage of Bertrand Russell.

1913   Retreats to a remote village in Norway; his writings and notebooks from this period become the source of much of the *Tractatus*.

1916   As a recruit of the Austro–Hungarian army in World War I he is sent to the Russian front. Wins medals for bravery.

1918   Finishes the *Tractatus* on leave in summer. Taken prisoner of war in the southern Tyrol in October.

1921   The *Tractatus Logico-Philosophicus* is published with an introduction by Russell (bi-lingual edn pub. 1922). Wittgenstein returns to Austria to work as a primary school teacher, a gardener at a monastery, and on the construction of his sister's new house.

1929   He returns to academic life at Cambridge after being drawn into philosophical discussions by the Vienna Circle.

1939   Appointed to the chair in philosophy at Cambridge. By this time his views on the foundations of mathematics have changed; he now believes there are no mathematical facts to be discovered.

1947   Resigns his position to concentrate on his writing.

1951   Dies from prostrate cancer. Notebooks, papers, and lectures published after his death include: *Philosophical Investigations* (1953), *The Blue and Brown Books* (1958), *On Certainty* (1969), *Remarks on the Foundations of Mathematics* (rev. edn 1978), *Remarks on the Philosophy of Psychology* (1980).

Martin Heidegger

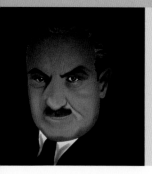

One of the most significant philosophers of the twentieth century, Heidegger epitomized the major dichotomy between Anglo–American and Continental philosophical culture. Recently there has been more stress on elements that connect the work of Heidegger and Wittgenstein, the major protagonists of each tradition. Heidegger's main concern is the question of the meaning of "Being": making this a real question for us and attempting a way of answering or at least responding to it.

Martin Heidegger once summarized the biography of **Aristotle** in a lecture by saying the philosopher *"was born, lived, and died"*. He would have liked the study of his contribution to similarly eschew biography and concentrate on thought. In fact this has been very much overshadowed by his involvement with Nazism – the nature and significance of which is still hotly contested. The fact that he accepted an official position (as university rector) under the Nazis has to be weighed against his reasons for doing so, his brief tenure of the post, his alluding in lectures during the war to Nazism as a movement indicative of philosophical decline, his help of various Jewish individuals, and indeed his two affairs with Jewish women. But it is still a matter too much of gossip and prejudice – where a dislike or liking of Heidegger's philosophical stance produces an account pro or anti his behavior. What can be said is that in the light of the frequent, legitimate impulse of philosophers from **Plato** to **Karl Popper** for their work to apply to the political life of their times, Heidegger initially misjudged the spirit of the Nazi movement. In a poetic **aphorism** he declared *"all who greatly think also greatly err"*.

Heidegger placed himself in a locality: southwest Germany, with Freiburg its intellectual center. Out of this area he rarely strayed. His hut on the mountainside overlooking the agrarian landscape of the Black Forest became an essential place to think and write. The forest that always surrounds is metaphorically manifest in much of his thought, the rich German vocabulary of woodland influencing particularly his later **philosophy of language** and meaning (his first post-war work *Holzwege* means "wood ways" or "ways through the wood").

His early education was Catholic and the **scholastic** expression of the **mystical** strongly leaves its mark on his psyche, even if he rejected Christianity or indeed any institutionalized religion.

Above all, his work is a constant developing dialogue with the **Western philosophical** tradition. From the **pre-Socratics**, Plato, and Aristotle to **Immanuel Kant**, **G. W. F. Hegel**, and **Friedrich Nietzsche**. **Eastern philosophy** influenced him too. The British **empiricist** tradition is notably absent from his commentaries/involvements, as is obvious (some would say) from the lack of its beneficial effect on his style and thinking.

Essential philosophy

Heidegger's whole project is a responding to the question *"What is the meaning of Being?"* Not this or that particular being, but the "Being" which all beings have. German has two words to express this "**ontological** difference"; English has to capitalize its primary sense. He speaks, like **Ludwig Wittgenstein**, of experiencing the question *"Why is there something and not rather nothing?"* Wondering of the world or any part of it not so much what it is, but that it is.

Wittgenstein defined this as "the mystical" – it may be where he wanted philosophy to stop, but this is where Heidegger begins. He wants to make central to the whole enterprise of our lives the realization of the meaning of the term "Being", what it is to be.

Being and Time
In his major work published in 1927, Heidegger sets out to explain this question and how much it has been forgotten by the tradition, and makes positive proposals for approaching it anew. He applies the methods of **phenomenology** to ontology. Where **Edmund**

Husserl had intended such methods to be applied to consciousness (i.e. **epistemological** questions), Heidegger applies them to the question of "Being", and he does this through an analysis of man because he is the only consciousness for whom his existence is an issue, for whom "Being" is a question. *Being and Time* supplies this subtle, complex, seemingly exhaustive analysis. He finds that we are not **Cartesian** "subjects", for whom the external world and **other minds** are problematic. Such **dualism** is a (**metaphysical**) construction. The world's existence separate from the mind is not in need of being **inferred**. It is given. The philosopher's task is instead one of describing our being-in-the-world.

Heidegger is not indulging in speculative metaphysics, he is describing human being as a way of approaching the "Being" of all beings. Among much else, he finds our sense of "being thrown" into existence, and most importantly the whole nature of our human being, is temporal, grounded in time particularly through the prospect of death. We experience "anxiety" at our contingency

Legacy, truth, consequence

■ Heidegger's complete works will run to 100 volumes. Much is still unpublished. His influence has already been widely felt in areas of theology, psychology, the arts, cultural theory, and beyond.

■ Overcoming metaphysics; a post-**idealist** and post-**positivist** sensibility; dissolving traditional questions of philosophy as delusions of the tradition; making language central; finding a place for the poetic in the theory of meaning; a concept of not saying but showing; a resistance to **scientism**; a view of philosophy as not a body of doctrines but an activity: all these traits connect Heidegger and Wittgenstein. For many philosophers now (such as **Richard Rorty**), their common ground offers the way forward.

The Black Forest, an essential place to think and write.

Finally, his encounter with modern technological society was decisive. In the 1940s and 1950s he anticipated the idea of the computer and its influence, speaking of a "language machine" essential to a world where communication and information are increasing exponentially but also in which man often feels himself unattached, not belonging, and alienated (see **Karl Marx**, pages 122–3).

> ## Every man is born as many men and dies a single one.
>
> *Being and Time (1927)*

and finitude – a mood Heidegger brings out in a complex and surprising way. The nearest he comes to an **ethics** for the individual is requiring that the human condition be faced. In the light of death, what meaning does my life have? Each person answers in his or her own way but to really ask the question is to live "authentically".

Language, poetry, technology

After *Being and Time*, particularly during the war years, Heidegger's thought undergoes a change. The so-called "*Kehre*" or "turn" is characterized by being less systematic, deliberately more obscure or oblique, with more emphasis on interpreting the history of philosophy. The development of the forgetfulness of "Being" is shown in the history of metaphysics; to "overcome metaphysics" is to remember "Being". A transforming centrality is given to the question of language, particularly poetic texts. It is poetry that shows the essence of language (rather than the **propositions** of **analytical philosophy**). We do not so much use language to speak our meaning: "*language speaks us*". "*Language is the house of the truth of Being*". Language is the place where "Being" shows itself. So man, in his caring for language, becomes "*the shepherd of Being*".

Technology in our time is a kind of metaphysics of the practical world, showing the extent of the forgetfulness of "Being", in which man has abandoned his poetic role, becoming instead the mere controller of language, world, and nature. Heidegger's later work has frequently elicited the response that it's not philosophy but poetry. For Heidegger that is philosophy's loss. The major sense we get from him is that a new approach to thinking is a requirement of our time. A new language and a new "poetic thinking", which he offers as a beginning (in the form of a return to the original) and a way forward.

Rudolf Carnap

Carnap was a German empiricist philosopher and logician, a part of the group of philosophers known as the Vienna Circle, and a principal advocate of logical positivism in America. He made important and technically rigorous contributions to logic and the philosophy of language, as well as making a lasting mark in epistemology and the philosophy of science.

Rudolf Carnap was born in Ronsdorf, Germany, in 1891. In 1910 he began to study physics at the University of Jena, where he made a careful study of **Immanuel Kant's** *Critique of Pure Reason* and was one of only a handful of students to attend **Gottlob Frege's** classes in mathematical logic. Carnap was much influenced by Frege, **Bertrand Russell**, and also **Ludwig Wittgenstein**, who later visited him in Vienna.

During World War I he served in the German army for three years, after which he was given permission to go to Berlin to continues his studies in physics (1917–18). He moved to the University of Freiburg, where he wrote a thesis on space and time. However, the physics department found Carnap's thesis far too philosophical to be published as a physics paper, and the philosophy department found it of little philosophical import. Carnap rewrote the whole thesis, bringing out more clearly its connections to Kant, and eventually had it published. His interest in philosophy was growing, and when neither he nor Freiburg University could afford a copy of Russell's three-volume *Principia Mathematica*, Carnap wrote a famous letter to Russell in 1921, who responded by copying out large swathes of his book in long-hand for Carnap's benefit.

Essential philosophy

The Logical Structure of the World (Carnap's Aufbau)

Carnap aimed to develop a rigorous form of **empiricism** in which all scientific discourse could be built out of immediate (**sense**) **experience** and logical constructions. The formal systems of Carnap's *Aufbau* categorized immediate experiences as qualities at space-time co-ordinates. These qualities (like redness or heat) were understood in terms of their resemblance to one another. In Carnap's system, scientific statements about the world were to be built up by logically compounding these immediate impressions of qualities so as to reconstruct our scientific knowledge on the rational basis afforded by sense experience and **logic**. The original aim was to extend the program beyond even the physical sciences to the social sciences.

But eventually Carnap became sceptical of the view that the language of physics is exhaustively translatable into the language of sense experience. And, in a series of highly influential papers, Quine argued that Carnap's project was not only Herculean, but doomed to failure in principle: individual scientific statements can never be reconstructed out of remembered similarities between immediate experiences and the application of logic because no individual statement really has a discrete set of experiences that are associated with it. According to Quine, only whole theories, not individual statements, have **empirical** significance. We can, on Quine's view, only hope to make sense of whole theories meeting the evidence of experience, but there is no hope of translating statements one by one into experiential terms. And as there is no hope for rationally reconstructing the statements of science, Quine

suggested that we should opt for empirical **psychology** over rational reconstruction, and study how we do in fact construct whole theories on the basis of sensory evidence. Carnap came to have a more pessimistic view about the project of the *Aufbau* and didn't publish the book in English until 1967.

Pseudoproblems in Philosophy

Carnap thought that many traditional philosophical statements were meaningless and the problems involving them were pseudo (false) problems. In particular, he considered that most metaphysical statements failed to express a meaning. Carnap's criteria for testing meaningfulness were a consequence of the **verification principle** he had adopted. According to Carnap, there are two sorts of meaningful statements: **analytic** statements, which, if true, are true in virtue of the meaning of their constituent terms, and **synthetic** statements, which, if true, are true in virtue of the facts of the world.

The verification principle, which **A. J. Ayer** also adopted, states that the meaning of a factual, synthetic statement is its method of verification. So a factual statement is meaningful if and only if it is in principle verifiable, i.e. has a method of verification. But where does this leave philosophical statements, such as those of metaphysics? Carnap thought that they suffered from a fundamental defect: they had no method of verification as there were no observations or other methods that could serve to verify them, and so he counted them as meaningless. The only alternative

Carnap was soon introduced to Moritz Schlick (1882–1936), who got him a job at the University of Vienna, and Schlick in turn introduced Carnap into the **Vienna Circle**, a group of philosophers sympathetic to his views. In November 1928 Carnap became part of the secretariat of the Vienna Circle, then known as the Ernst Mach Association (after the Austrian physicist Ernst Mach, 1838–1916, known for his stand against the misuse of **metaphysics** in science). In the same year, Carnap wrote two very important books. The title of the first, *Der Logische Aufbau der Welt* (sometimes known as "Carnap's *Aufbau*"), translates as *The Logical Structure of the World*, and the second as *Pseudoproblems in Philosophy*. In 1929 he wrote a famous pamphlet with Otto Neurath (1882–1945) and Hans Hahn (1879–1934), *The Scientific World Conception: the Vienna Circle*, which summarized the views of the group and acted as a manifesto to be presented to the wider philosophical world. The manifesto stated the central doctrines to which members of the Circle adhered, such as metaphysics being largely meaningless and there being no **synthetic *a priori*** knowledge.

The Vienna Circle disbanded in the early 1930s when Schlick died and Austria was beset by political troubles. It was at this time that Carnap developed his views on the language of science in *The Logical Syntax of Language* (1937), a book he discussed at great length with **W. V. O. Quine**. Quine became a lifelong friend and was instrumental in bringing Carnap to America in 1935. Carnap developed his philosophy at Harvard, Chicago, and the University of California. He died in 1970 in Santa Monica, California.

was to construe them as analytic, in which case they would be merely tautological, their truth ensured by the meaning of the words rather than any facts.

Apart from general concerns about the severity of the verification principle, it has faced some trenchant criticisms. Not only does the principle seem to fail to have meaning by its own measure, being neither verifiable nor analytic, it also seems that *any* statement can have verifiable consequences when conjoined in the right way with other verifiable statements.

The Logical Syntax of Language
Carnap wanted to give a rigorous account of the structure of any possible language, seeing this as a prerequisite to proper **logical analysis**. In the foreword to his *Logical Syntax of Language* he wrote:
"*Philosophy is to be replaced by the logic of science [and] the logic of science is nothing other than the logical syntax of the language of science.*"
Carnap advanced the principle of tolerance, according to which there is no such thing as a "true" or "correct" logic or language. One is free to adopt whatever form of language is useful for one's purposes.
"*It is not our business to set up prohibitions, but to arrive at conventions… In logic there are no morals. Everyone is at liberty to build up his own logic, i.e. his own language, as he wishes. All that is required of him is that, if he wishes to discuss it, he must state his methods clearly, and give syntactical rules instead of philosophical arguments.*"
(*The Logical Syntax of Language*, 1937)

Legacy, truth, consequence

- Carnap's work is the single biggest influence on W. V. O. Quine, though Quine was also to become Carnap's most powerful critic.
- While few now accept his starting point in **sense-data**, many agree with Carnap's view that **epistemology** is the project of rationally vindicating our knowledge. His position, in that respect, seems to have aged better than Quine's view that epistemology should be empirical psychology.
- Carnap's later work focusing on the semantics of natural and formal languages is set out in his book, *Meaning and Necessity* (1947), which laid foundations for the subsequent developments in **modal logic**.

It is not our business to set up prohibitions but to arrive at conventions.

The Logical Syntax of Language (1937)

Key dates

1891	Born in Ronsdorf (now a district of Wuppertal), in Germany.
1910	Attends University of Jena in central Germany to study physics.
1928	Joins the Vienna Circle and publishes *The Logical Structure of the World* ("Carnap's *Aufbau*") and *Pseudoproblems in Philosophy*.
1935	Moves to America.
1937	Publishes *The Logical Syntax of Language*.
1950	Publishes *The Logical Foundations of Probability Theory*.
1970	Dies in California, US.

Carnap became part of the Vienna Circle, a group of philosophers which held meetings in Viennese coffee houses.

Gilbert Ryle

Ryle was instrumental in calling into question the Cartesian conception of the mind as an essentially private realm and helping philosophers see how the mind might be integrated into the physical world. He is best known for exorcising Descartes' "ghost in the machine", drawing out the conceptual connections between the mind and behavior, and for his painstaking attention to the logical structure of ordinary language as a means of tackling philosophical problems.

Gilbert Ryle was born in Brighton, England, in 1900. He was among the ten children of a well-off and liberal family. Ryle attended Queen's College, Oxford, and there was attracted to philosophy, having undertaken to study classics. He was a keen rower while at Oxford, nearly winning a blue, an award earned for competing at the highest level of the sport. Graduating in 1924, he won a lectureship in philosophy at Christ Church, Oxford, and remained there until his retirement in 1968. During World War II, he was recruited to work in intelligence for the Welsh Guards, rising to the rank of major.

Ryle wrote on the history of philosophy, **philosophy of language**, and the nature of philosophical dilemmas, but perhaps his most important work was in the **philosophy of mind**. Having focused on questions concerning language and philosophical methodology in the 1920s and 30s, he applied himself to the central questions about the human mind. His 1949 book *The Concept of Mind* includes a sustained attack on **Cartesian dualism** and an argument in favor of an account of the mind that has been called **behaviorism**, though the label may not be apposite.

Ryle is also remembered fondly for his skill and patience as a teacher (many of his students, including **A. J. Ayer**, went on to contribute important work to philosophy). He was an engaging conversationalist in addition to being a distinctive and subtle writer. Having attended some of his famous meetings, he befriended **Ludwig Wittgenstein**, with whom he shared a suspicion of philosophical jargon and a dislike of affectation.

A bachelor throughout his life, Ryle lived with his twin sister Mary and spent his spare time walking, gardening, and smoking his pipe. He died in the autumn of 1976 after spending the day out walking on the moors.

Essential philosophy

The "Ghost in the Machine"
In *The Concept of Mind*, Ryle dubbed his target the "Official Theory", which he traced back to **René Descartes**. The "Official Theory" holds that a mechanistic explanation of the world (as was typically advanced in the science of Descartes' time) in terms of the mechanical operation of physical parts leaves no place in the physical world for our minds to which each person has direct and incorrigible access. Descartes was convinced that minds are not simply a more complicated form of mechanism, because their existence is more certain to us, and their contents are more transparent to us, than are the mechanisms of the physical world. He concluded that mind and body must be two completely different types of substance. The body is pure physical substance, such as plays a role in mechanism, while the mind is pure mental substance, such as constitutes our thinking and consciousness. This is Cartesisan dualism, the "two-world" view according to which the mind is a "Ghost in the Machine", an immaterial substance somehow intermingled with the physical stuff of the body. Ryle was instrumental in unravelling this picture. He drew out the important connections between conceptions of our mind and our behavior. This is why his view of the mind is sometimes called a form of behaviorism.

Behaviorism
Ryle argued that if our mental concepts, such as our concepts of belief and desire, really picked out a strange and immaterial substance, privately known to us but outside the physical world, then we would be unable to use those mental concepts in ways that we manifestly do. We use these concepts when we say that someone *wants* to catch the number 29 bus and *believes* it is on its way. We might make this assumption because we see them running very quickly after it, or checking the bus timetable, or because we hear them say

> *Such in outline is the Official Theory. I shall often speak of it, with deliberate abusiveness, as "the dogma of the Ghost in the Machine".*
>
> The Concept of Mind (1949)

Legacy, truth, consequence

- Cartesian dualism now has few advocates. The **substance dualism** that Ryle argued against is rarely defended though there are some who defend a **property dualism**.
- Behaviorist views of the mind, with which Ryle became associated, have gone out of fashion (see pages 182–3: **Noam Chomsky**) as mental vocabulary proved not to be translatable into statements about behavior. Contemporary **functionalist** views of the mind hold onto much of what was important about behaviorism, characterizing mental states in terms of their functional role, with environmental stimuli as inputs and observable behaviors as outputs.
- Ryle's notion of a "category mistake", whereby a philosopher attempts to classify an object or event according to the wrong sort of category, constantly crops up in philosophical debate. Ryle argued that mental and physical concepts belong to different logical categories and this view is still influential.

Key dates

1900	Born in Brighton, southern England.
1949	Ryle's most famous and widely read work, *The Concept of Mind*, is published.
1966	Ryle's book *Plato's Progress* receives scathing criticism from classicist Allan Bloom (1930–92) for trying to incorporate **Plato**'s ideas into a modern philosophical context.
1968	Retires from Christ Church, Oxford, where he has spent his whole academic life.
1976	After a day out walking, Ryle dies peacefully.

Christ Church College, Oxford, where Gilbert Ryle spent his whole academic life.

as much. So, just as we usually know what we believe and desire, we often know about other people's mental states. We acquire this knowledge of other people's minds on the basis of their behavior: what they say and do. But this would be impossible if our mental concepts applied to an immaterial substance that interacted with our physical bodies to generate a private stream of consciousness. So, Ryle suggested, the meaning of mental concepts must be intimately connected to the behaviors that minded creatures engage in, and what such creatures would do in certain circumstances.

A number of critics, including A. J. Ayer, have pointed out that Ryle's account of the mind in terms of behavior struggles to accommodate our inner life of imaginings, dreams, calculations, and the like, the "honest ghosts" that remain private to their possessors. And many now feel that a full account of our mental life requires us to understand the events and processes that underlie our behavior (see **Chomsky** on pages 182–3). Though Ryle himself was not committed to the behaviorist program of defining such mental phenomena as imagining and dreaming in behavioral terms, he recognized that *"the general trend of [my] book will undoubtedly and harmlessly be stigmatised as behaviorist"* (*The Concept of Mind*, 1949).

Against intellectualism

Ryle went on to combat an associated intellectualist conception of thinking and understanding. According to the intellectualist conception, what differentiates minded behavior that involves thought or understanding from mere movement of our body is a sequence of hidden mental events. These hidden mental events serve to rationalize the behavior. The clown-like behavior of a real clown is thereby distinguished from mere clumsiness by a series of hidden intentions to act in an outlandish and clumsy manner.

Ryle agreed that intelligent behavior involves *"thinking what we are doing"* but thought the intellectualist pushed this ordinary phrase too far. Ryle's problem with the intellectualist picture was that it leads to a regress, now known as "Ryle's regress". If we explain intelligent behavior in terms of the thought processes that go on behind it, then we need to know what makes these processes thoughtful or intelligent. We can't posit further intelligent processes on pain of starting a vicious regress. So Ryle thought that intelligent behavior can't be explained by assuming that there are hidden, rational operations going on in the mind.

Karl Popper

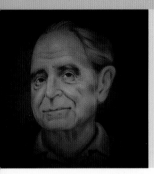

Sir Karl Popper was an Austrian philosopher who was best known for his theories in the philosophy of science, but who also wrote on social and political philosophy. He rejected the traditional account of how science advances through observation, induction, and proof. Instead he suggested that knowledge advances through a creative process of theorizing in which hypotheses are only rejected when they are falsified.

Karl Raimund Popper was born in 1902 in Vienna, in Austria-Hungary, into a middle-class, book-loving family. He was brought up a Lutheran and educated at the University of Vienna. It was here, while still a teenager, that he became interested in **Marxism**, following the 1917 Russian Revolution. However, he soon turned against the **historical determinism** of **Karl Marx** (the idea that history is traveling towards an inevitable end-state) and was a liberal thinker for the rest of his life, rejecting **autho-ritarianism** of all kinds.

Popper studied **psychology** and earned a modest living as a schoolteacher before publishing his first work, *The Logic of Scientific Discovery*, in 1934, in which he propounded his own view of scientific methodology and, in particular, his criticism of **logical positivism**. In 1937 the Nazi regime in Germany looked increasingly likely to move towards the unification of Austria with Greater Germany (the so-called Anschluss), so Popper emigrated, first to New Zealand, and then to England. The annexation of Austria was an important trigger for Popper to begin writing on social and political matters.

In England, Popper became a professor in logic and scientific method at the London School of Economics in 1949, and went on to have a distinguished academic career.

Essential philosophy

Popper's best-known theory was his account of the way that scientific method advances through falsificationism. He described his theory as the first non-justificational philosophy of criticism, although some might argue that the work of the **pragmatists**, including **Charles Peirce**, predated him in this respect. (When Popper read Peirce's work late in life, he declared that he wished he had read him when he was younger.)

However, Popper's approach was very distinctive. He pointed out that scientific theories are never confirmed – we can never have final proof that they are true. (This of course is an echo of the **fallibilism** of Peirce and **John Dewey**, who had concluded that the pursuit of certain scientific knowledge was an impossible one.) Instead, Popper argued, scientific theories stand until they are falsified by results. At which point they must be modified or replaced.

Critical rationalism

Popper referred to his theories as "critical rationalism", by which he deliberately meant to set himself in opposition to **empiricism**. For Popper the whole concept of scientific knowledge as a series of observed data leading to a conclusion was simplistic and misleading. He wanted to replace this with an idea of human knowledge as essentially conjectural. We creatively come up with explanations for our **perceptions**, and then those **hypotheses** are tested until they are falsified. Those that are not falsified remain but we can't be sure that they won't be falsified in future.

Since no theory can ever be finally verified, but they can be falsified, Popper went on to suggest that the test by which something should be considered a real science was that it was falsifiable. He used this observation as a basis for rejecting Marxism and psychoanalysis as pseudo-sciences, as their claims could never be falsified.

Popper and verificationism

In the 1930s the logical positivists saw Popper as a kindred spirit. They were working on the theory that a statement was only meaningful if it was verifiable, and this had an obvious relationship to Popper's thinking. However, Popper was far more interested in explaining how human knowledge advanced than in rejecting **metaphysics** and **ethics**. In the end his thinking took a rather different path from that of the logical positivists.

One potential problem with Popper's theory of falsificationism is how it explains scientific progress. For Popper, the progress of knowledge was akin to an evolutionary process. The theories that survive are the ones that are most fit for purpose and best help us to survive and prosper. Knowledge is an adaptive process of human rationality and, as we manage to find solutions to old problems that at least work, we move on towards ever more interesting problems. When a new theory is tested, we see how it fits into our overall belief system and reject the theory that is most expendable, or that has the least **inductive** evidence going for it.

Popper did a great deal to bring the **philosophy of science** into modern **analytic philosophy**. His theory of falsificationism has been attacked or superseded in a variety of ways. Probably the most influential work on the subject this century, *The Structure of Scientific Revolutions* (1962) by Thomas Kuhn (1922–96), argued that science advances through a process of observing anomalies in existing theories and then making a "paradigm shift" to a new theory. This was at odds with Popper's views, although he made some similar observations in his early work.

The Quine–Duhem thesis, named after the two philosophers who proposed it (**W. V. O. Quine** and Pierre Duhem, 1861–1916), also casts doubt on Popper's approach, simply by suggesting that hypotheses can never be falsified in isolation. As scientific theory is an interdependent set of theories, any anomalous observation could be taken to falsify a number of different hypotheses. The process by which falsification thus proceeds seems to be closer to Kuhn's conception, in which knowledge is adaptive as an organic whole.

Nonetheless, Popper's thinking was influential and was adapted or challenged by many successors, including two respected writers, Imre Lakatos (1922–74) and Paul Feyerabend (1924–94), both of whom studied under Popper.

One can see echoes of Popper's evolutionist approach to human knowledge in Richard Dawkins' theories about "memes" as the unit of evolution in ideas.

Popper also had a long friendship with Friedrich Hayek (1899–1992). It is probably true that each was an influence on the other, especially in their political thinking on the nature of liberal democracy.

The financial speculator and philantropist George Soros, a former student of Karl Popper, is the Chairman of the Open Society Institute, a foundation promoting democratic governance.

> *The open society is one in which men have learned to be to some extent critical of taboos, and to base decisions on the authority of their own intelligence.*
>
> The Open Society and Its Enemies (1945)

Key dates

1902	Born in Vienna in Austria-Hungary (now capital of modern Austria).
1918	Attends the University of Vienna.
1919	Briefly joins the Association of Socialist School Students.
1928	Attains a doctorate in philosophy.
1934	His first book, *Logik der Forschung* (*The Logic of Scientific Discovery*), is published.
1945	*The Open Society and Its Enemies* is published.
1946	Moves to England and becomes a reader at the London School of Economics.
1949	Becomes a professor in logic and scientific method at the London School of Economics.
1957	*The Poverty of Historicism* is published.
1959	*The Logic of Scientific Discovery* is published in English.
1963	*Conjectures and Refutations: The Growth of Scientific Knowledge* is published.
1965	Knighted by Queen Elizabeth II of England.
1969	Retires from his professorship but remains active as a writer and speaker until his death.
1976	*Unended Quest; An Intellectual Autobiography* is published.
1976	Elected a fellow of the Royal Society.
1994	*The Myth of the Framework: In Defence of Science and Rationality* is published.
1994	Dies in London. His ashes are taken to Lainz cemetery, Vienna, to be buried with those of his wife, Josefine Anna Henninger.

Popper also claimed to have solved the ancient problem of induction, which is the problem of how we know, for example, that the sun will rise tomorrow. Popper accepted that we cannot have certainty in induction, but he regarded a belief such as "The sun will rise tomorrow" as a "well-tested" theory, that has served us well in the past. Of course this doesn't really solve the problem, it merely explains why we feel justified in the belief that the sun will rise tomorrow.

Political philosophy

Popper became known as a strong advocate of liberal **democracy** and the "open society". He argued that an open society and the active involvement of citizens led to a process of advancing knowledge similar to the one he had described happening in the scientific sphere. He saw social planning and centralization as dangerous, as they would perpetually fail to adjust to their own failures, and asserted that the citizens of a country always needed to be able to criticize and change the political state in which they lived. He continued to reject the historical determinism of Marxists and others, regarding it essentially as an excuse for authoritarianism and abuse of the open society.

Sayyid Abul Ala Maududi

A Muslim journalist and political philosopher, Maududi formulated the theory of Islamism, the belief that a state must be run solely on Islamic principles. His philosophy inspired a renewal in Islamic thinking, but also gave rise to some Islamist separatist and fundamentalist movements that have moved away from political discussion towards terrorism.

Sayyid Maududi (also spelt Syed Mawdoodi) was born to a devout **Sunni Muslim** family whose ancestors had moved to India from Afghanistan in the fifteenth century. His father, a lawyer, could trace his ancestry back to the prophet Muhammad.

Maududi studied at a religious school, but had to leave when his father died. He began to work as a journalist, and continued to study Islam on his own, reaching his own independent and original conclusions. His career flourished and in 1925 he became editor of a Muslim newspaper in Delhi, which he forged into the most important publication for South Asian Muslims, and in 1933 he took over the monthly magazine *Tarjuman al-Qur'an* (*Interpreter of the Qur'an*). This became the main vehicle for his writings.

He first became interested in politics when he joined a group opposing British rule of India. At the same time, he was continuing to explore Islam and began to write about major political and cultural issues from an Islamic perspective rather than from political or economic viewpoints. In 1941 he founded a political party, Jamaat–e–Islami, to campaign for an Islamic state founded on Islamic law, and was its leader until 1972.

Maududi initially opposed the creation of Pakistan, a separate Muslim country, since he opposed secular nationalism and wanted to see the whole of India become Islamic. But after India's independence and the separation of Pakistan in 1947, he did migrate to Pakistan, where he argued against liberal policies and continued campaigning with his political party for a fully Islamic state. Unpopular with the military government, he was arrested in 1953 when he accused the Ahmadiyya sect of heresy, sparking off riots and attacks on them. He was sentenced to death, but after a popular outcry this was commuted to life imprisonment, and he was later freed.

Although he mainly wrote in Urdu, he was widely translated and became well known internationally. Plainly controversial, he has been criticized not only by secularists but also by other Muslim scholars for his interpretation of Islam.

Essential philosophy

The Qur'an
Maududi wrote more than 200 books and pamphlets, but his greatest work was his **exegesis**, *Tafhim al-Qur'an* (*The Meaning of the Qur'an*), which he produced over a period of 30 years. In this work he included introductions for each chapter of the Qur'an, giving relevant historical background, and explained the Qur'an's message and meaning in accessible, modern language. He also applied the Qur'an to social and individual problems, showing that it can be a guide to overcoming the difficulties of today's world. It is considered to be the foundation work for the revival of Muslim scholarship in the twentieth century.

Religion and ideology
Maududi wrote about the failure of Western ideals such as **capitalism** and **Marxism** to bring about world peace, security, and prosperity. He offered a third ideology, Islam, as a global political framework.

Instead of being just a personal choice, Maududi believed that religion pervades all human thought and activity, so should be the basis of the economic, legal, and political apparatus of the state, as well as regulating social and personal behavior. In particular, he interpreted the Qur'an to mean that only God can dispense law and judgement, and therefore government must strictly follow religious laws.

As a pious Muslim, he believed that Islam was the one true religion, and that it could transform the world starting with the individual. One believer inspires others, leading to a faith community, building up to a mass movement, resulting in a truly religious, Islamic society founded on the will of the people.

The Islamic state
In writings such as *Islamic State, Islamic Law and Constitution, How to Establish an Islamic State*, Maududi laid out his blueprint for the structure of his ideal country. One of his basic principles was that it would be the complete opposite of a secular **democracy** as seen in the West, since it would be Allah's sovereignty, expressed through the sovereignty of true religious people, that would be paramount, not a fluctuating popular vote.

His state would be single party, since the government's sole role would be to explore the applications of Islamic law as described in

Legacy, truth, consequence

- At a time when most of the Islamic world, from the Middle East to southeast Asia, was struggling with either colonialism or poverty, Maududi's writings galvanized a new wave of Islamic intellectual activity. He is probably the most widely read Muslim scholar and writer of modern times.

- Maududi was an important influence on Sayyid Qutb (1906–66) who founded the revolutionary **Islamist** group, the Muslim Brotherhood in Egypt, and his ideology is also thought to have inspired the terrorist group al-Qaeda and its leader Osama bin-Laden. His theory of an Islamic state was particularly popular in countries with a Muslim population who felt they had been exploited by Western colonialism, such as Egypt.

- His political party Jamaat-e-Islami has never achieved much success in elections, but in Pakistan it has had a significant political influence by pressurizing the government into passing strict blasphemy laws and other measures. For example, members of the Ahmadiyya sect are banned from public preaching in Pakistan as a result of campaigns by the Jamaat. Members of Maududi's party have also been involved in violent attacks on non-Muslims.

Key dates

That is why the Islamic state offers them [non-Muslims] protection, if they agree to live ... by paying Jizya*, but it cannot allow that they should remain supreme rulers in any place and establish wrong ways and establish them on others. As this state of things inevitably produce chaos and disorder, it is the duty of the true Muslims to exert their utmost to bring an end to their wicked rule and bring them under a righteous order.

The Meaning of the Qur'an (1972)

* Jizya: a tax paid by non-Muslims in an Islamic state so that they could enjoy the protection of the state.

the Qur'an and other main Muslim texts. He argued that this system is all-encompassing, ranging from international affairs to family relationships, and that any other political system is in fact "evil".

In his Islamic state, non-Muslims would be tolerated but would effectively be second-class citizens, prevented from having any political power since they would not understand the underlying **ethics** of the system. Any non-Muslim adults who did not provide military service would have to pay a special tax to pay for state protection. Women, who had to look after children, so could not devote their whole lives to religion, would be relegated to nothing but domestic roles.

Jihad

Because Islam embraces the whole world, Maududi believed that every country should become an Islamic state, and he argued that it was the duty of every Muslim to try to bring this about through **jihad**, literally "struggle". He was particularly scathing about previous Muslim leaders, both religious and political, who had not put into practice a full Islamic system.

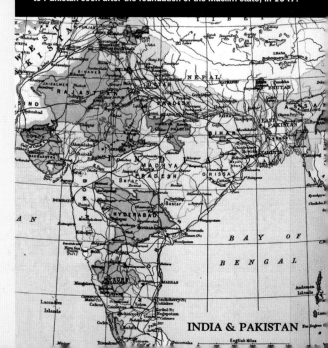

Proposed map of the partition of India from the British Indian Empire, leading to the creation of Pakistan. Maududi emigrated to Pakistan soon after the foundation of the Muslim state, in 1947.

INDIA & PAKISTAN

Jean-Paul Sartre

The French intellectual John-Paul Sartre was one of the best-known philosophers of the twentieth century, a key figure in the founding of existentialism, and a literary and philosophical icon in the decades following World War II. He was a successful novelist, playwright, critic, and biographer, expressing his ideas in all those forms, and he also became a well-known social activist.

Jean-Paul Sartre did not enjoy a particularly happy childhood. He had a strictly bourgeois upbringing, which Sartre was to intellectually rebel against, and he felt he was an ugly child, small, wall-eyed, and often ill. He had few childhood friends, and he often withdrew into his own world of books, both reading and writing.

However, Sartre later said that he would not have been the same man if his childhood had been different.

He chose to study philosophy, and won a place at the prestigious École Normale Supérieure in Paris, where fellow students included Jean Hippolyte (1907–68), **Maurice Merleau-Ponty**, Claude Lévi-Strauss (*b.* 1908), and Simone Weil (1909–43). Even as a student he gained a reputation for challenging the status quo, but Sartre actually failed to pass the postgraduate *agrégation* teaching qualification, perhaps because he put too many of his new ideas into it. It was while studying for the retake in 1929 that he met **Simone de Beauvoir**, who was to become his lifelong partner and lover. Sartre confined himself to standard philosophy in that year's *agrégation* exam, and took first place. De Beauvoir came second.

Sartre told her that they shared an "*essential* love", but they should "experience contingent love affairs", which, despite the conventions of the time, they did. They also shared a desire to explore the meaning of existence and the need for freedom, and to express their ideas through the medium of novels and plays as well as essays.

Sartre taught for a while before gaining a grant to go to Berlin, where he studied philosophers such as **Edmund Husserl** and **Martin Heidegger**. He was captured by the Germans in the early stages of World War II, but released from the prisoner-of-war camp because of ill-health. Rejoining de Beauvoir, he became involved with several Resistance magazines. After the war Sartre embraced left-wing causes: Algerian independence, Vietnam War protests, the student protests of 1968. With de Beauvoir he traveled widely, visiting **communist** China and Fidel Castro in Cuba, although he condemned the Soviet USSR for its invasion of Hungary in 1956.

In his last years he became partially blind, and recorded his discussions with de Beauvoir. She worked tirelessly to make sure that he kept his dignity – and his ability to work – until the end.

Essential philosophy

Sartre's philosophy encompassed concepts of individual freedom, atheism, consciousness, personal choice, a lack of restricting definitions, objectivity, and a central concern with the experience of being human. He came to describe the whole package as **existentialism**, but he called his book *Being and Nothingness: An Essay on* **Phenomenological Ontology**, or a look at the relationship between things and the human consciousness of them. In later years, he also developed a new direction, a synthesis of **Marxism** and existentialism.

Being and Nothingness

The title of his major work on existentialism, *Being and Nothingness* (1943), sums up Sartre's answer to the question "*What is human existence?*" He discussed two types of being: "for-itself" and "in-itself".

Being in-itself is everything that is not consciousness. It is the being of non-human objects that just exist solidly and concretely as they are, without any self-awareness, and also without any gaps in their being "*through which nothingness might slip in*".

Being for-itself is consciousness, the level of self-awareness that cannot be reduced to just a thing-in-itself, because it is always more than just one single thing. It is therefore no-thing, a nothingness, or a blank canvas, outside the given order of things.

Freedom

The nothingness of consciousness is full of possibilities of what it might be. And from this comes freedom. We are perfectly free to imagine what we might be in the future and it is through our choices that we express value and give meaning to our lives. The future is always changeable, or, as Sartre put it, we have the potential to always become.

Existence is already there; it is the prerequisite for personal choice, so what we actually choose is our essence. As Sartre said, "*Existence precedes and commands essence.*" An atheist, he argued that we have no essence before we individually come to exist because there is no creator to give an eternal essence.

■ Sartre is generally held to be the main figure in the foundation of existentialism, and was a leading light in the intellectual life of the Western world after World War II.

■ He produced some brilliant, contentious books and plays that influenced philosophers, writers, and even artists around the world.

■ Apart from his philosophy, he was famous for his unconventional, open love life, his rejection of the authority of the church, and his social and political activism. While he attracted and inspired the younger "Beat" generation, he won the disapproval of the Roman Catholic institution: in 1948 the Vatican banned all his books.

Everything is gratuitous, this garden, this city and myself. When you suddenly realize it, it makes you feel sick and everything begins to drift ... that's nausea.

Nausea (1938)

After World War II, Sartre embraced left-wing causes: he is seen here meeting Che Guevara in 1960.

Key dates

1905	Born in Paris, France.
1929	Meets Simone de Beauvoir, his lifelong companion.
1938	His first novel *La Nausée* (*Nausea*) is published to instant success.
1939	Drafted into the French army after the outbreak of World War II; captured by the Germans and released because of poor health in 1941.
1943	Publishes his major philosophical work, *L'Etre et le Néant* (*Being and Nothingness*), the basis of much of modern existentialism.
1944	Co-founds and edits the intellectual magazine *Les Temps Modernes* (named after Charlie Chaplin's film *Modern Times*).
1945	Refuses to accept the award of the Légion d'honneur.
1946	Publishes an introduction to his philosophy, *Existentialism and Humanism*, originally presented as a lecture.
1950s	Becomes more politically active.
1964	Turns down the Nobel Prize for Literature.
1971	Suffers a first heart attack.
1973	Suffers a second heart attack. His health deteriorates.
1980	Dies in Paris.

Although the for-itself is always free, choice-making is actually determined by the "facticity" or circumstances of one's life that cannot be changed.

Sartre added a third kind of being: for-others. He acknowledged that we express our humanity through relationships with other human beings, and if we do so while fully aware of our own freedom, we are living life to its full, realizing our actuality.

Nausea

In the novel *Nausea* the central character comes to realize that the things of the world cannot be categorized beyond the simple fact that they are just there. There is no explanation for the existence of things – they just are. Moreover, the world itself is totally indifferent to him; he is completely responsible for the meaning of his own existence and for his actions and the impact they might have. This knowledge brings about the sense of disorientation, anguish, or nausea of the title.

Some existentialists do say that because there is no meaning to existence it is absurd, but Sartre always argued that it is an optimistic concept, since it puts individuals in sole charge of their destiny.

Bad faith

Freedom brings responsibility, and in Sartre's terminology "bad faith" is the act of turning away from freedom and from making one's own meaning out of nothingness. Bad faith can take many forms, such as self-deception, falling into a stereotypical life style, or obeying convention or the expectations of others.

Kurt Gödel

Kurt Gödel was one of the twentieth century's greatest mathematical logicians and a bold, unorthodox philosopher of mathematics. For Gödel the boundary between mathematics and philosophy was an artificial one, and he became increasingly interested in crossing and blurring that boundary. He made some of the most important contributions to modern mathematical thinking, leading, among other things, to the development of computer science.

Kurt Gödel was born in 1906 in what was then the Austro-Hungarian city of Brünn (now Brno in the Czech Republic). After an uneventful childhood, albeit one marked by ill health, he entered Vienna University in 1924.

Although physics was Gödel's initial field of interest, his attention was soon drawn to both mathematics and philosophy. He attended philosophy lectures by Heinrich Gomperz (1873–1942), and learned his logic from **Rudolph Carnap**; in 1929 he graduated under Hans Hahn (1879–1934) with a doctorate in mathematics.

While at university, Gödel became acquainted with the **Vienna Circle** of **logical positivists**, which revolved around Moritz Schlick (1882–1936). Although Gödel's philosophy was to be diametrically opposed to logical positivism, this period was a fruitful and influential one for him.

In 1930 Gödel published his doctoral dissertation – his completeness proof for the first order functional calculus. The following year he published his groundbreaking theorems on the incompleteness of various **axiomatic** systems, which have become known as "Gödel's theorem" (see below). This changed the whole philosophical view of the basis of mathematics.

Between 1933 and 1938 Gödel was a non-salaried faculty member at the University of Vienna, during which time he made several appearances at Princeton University as a visiting lecturer. In 1935 he established the relative consistency of the axiom of choice, and in 1938 that of the generalized continuum hypothesis.

He married Adele Porkert in 1938, and in 1940, alarmed by the Nazi occupation of Vienna, he immigrated to the US with his wife. Joining the Institute of Advanced Study at Princeton, he became good friends with Albert Einstein, his daily walking companion. He was granted US citizenship in 1948.

From 1940 onwards, Gödel's interests turned more to philosophy, physics, and the philosophy of mathematics. He made a study of **Gottfried Leibniz's** work, and published a number of papers, including "On Russell's Mathematical Logic" (1944) and "What is Cantor's Continuum Hypothesis?" (1947). In 1949 he published "A Remark on the Relationship between Relativity Theory and Idealistic Philosophy", in which he demonstrated the existence of **paradoxical** solutions to the field equations of Einstein in general relativity.

Princeton appointed him to a professorship in 1953, a post he held until his retirement.

Essential philosophy

In an undelivered lecture from 1961, Gödel offered up a "schema" of philosophy which attempted to classify philosophical "world-views" (*Weltanschauung*) according to how near or far they stood from **metaphysics** or religion:

"*In this way we immediately obtain a division into two groups: scepticism, materialism and positivism stand on one side, spiritualism, idealism and theology on the other.*"

("The Modern Development of the Foundations of Mathematics in the light of Philosophy", 1961)

Gödel traced the general philosophical drift since the **Renaissance** "*from right to left*" in this schema, i.e. from **idealism** to **scepticism**. However, he elevated mathematics to a higher level, capable of rising above such a drift:

"*The conception of mathematics, by its nature an **a priori** science, always has, in and of itself, an inclination toward the right, and, for this reason, has long withstood the Zeitgeist that has ruled since the Renaissance ... Indeed, mathematics has*

evolved into ever higher abstractions, away from matter and to ever greater clarity in its foundations ... thus, away from scepticism."
(Ibid.)

The sceptical **empiricism** of **Bertrand Russell**, which lay behind Russell and Alfred Whitehead's *Principia Mathematica* (1910–13), was in line with the shift from right to left. Thus by undermining Russell's findings with his incompleteness theorems, Gödel effectively reshaped the orthodoxy of twentieth-century mathematics.

Incompleteness theorems

Gödel published his incompleteness theorems in 1931 as "On Formally Undecidable Propositions of *Principia Mathematica* and Related Systems". Despite their specifically mathematical application, they are also of huge philosophical importance.

Gödel's theorem, as these have become collectively known, states that for any consistent logical system able to express arithmetic there must exist sentences that are true in the standard

Legacy, truth, consequence

■ Gödel's techniques led directly to a new concept of effectively calculable function, which had a major influence on the development of computers and the study of computer science.

■ His procedure and results opened the way to a fully rigorous treatment of the notion of a computable function, and to our modern understanding of the power and limits of computation, and also the possibility or otherwise of programs that test for consistency and completeness.

■ The Kurt Gödel Society was founded in his honor in 1987. It is an international organization for the promotion of research in the areas of logic, philosophy, and the history of mathematics.

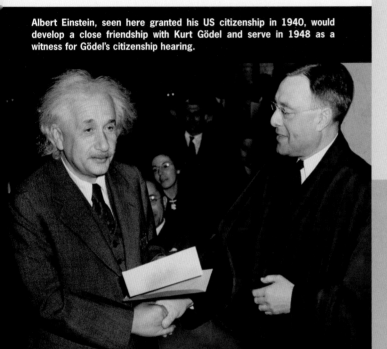

Albert Einstein, seen here granted his US citizenship in 1940, would develop a close friendship with Kurt Gödel and serve in 1948 as a witness for Gödel's citizenship hearing.

Mathematics has a form of perfection ... We may expect that the conceptual world is perfect, and, furthermore, that objective reality is beautiful, good, and perfect.

Gödel, quoted in H. Wang, *A Logical Lourney: From Gödel to Philosophy* (1996)

interpretation of that system, but which are not provable. Moreover, no such system – such as the vast structure of Whitehead and Russell's *Principia Mathematica* – can be powerful enough to prove its own consistency.

These results determined the limits of purely formal methods in mathematics. Additional philosophical significance attaches to the way Gödel proved his first result: by defining a formula *P* that, while unprovable, can be seen to be true given the way it is constructed. The implied moral is that truth in some way outruns provability, at least when the latter is considered formally. This accords with his **Platonist** world-view, and it counters the prevailing spirit of logical positivism in mathematical thinking at the time.

Gödel and rationalism

Gödel's **rationalism** has its roots in the Leibnizian thought that the world is perfect and beautiful, rational and ordered. Gödel extrapolates this belief from the perfection and beauty of mathematics:

"*Rationalism is connected with Platonism because it is directed to the conceptual aspect rather than toward the (real) world. Mathematics has a form of perfection.*"

(Gödel, quoted in H. Wang, *A Logical Lourney: From Gödel to Philosophy*, 1996)

Thus Gödel asserts that, given the conceptual world is perfect, it follows that **objective reality** is "*beautiful, good, and perfect*" – something Gödel admits is "*a Leibnizian thought*":

"*We should judge reality by the little which we truly know of it. Since that part which conceptually we know fully turns out to be so beautiful, the real world of which we know so little should also be beautiful.*"

(Ibid.)

Although the roots of Gödel's belief in rationalism were metaphysical, he had always held practical aspirations to develop exact methods in philosophy, to transform it into an exact science. In practice, this meant adopting a level of rigor in philosophical arguments approaching that which is found in mathematical proofs.

Nelson Goodman

Nelson Goodman was an intriguing and inventive American philosopher who produced a series of interesting theories and ideas on topics ranging from aesthetics and logic to problems of symbolism. He is best known for his "new riddle of induction" and for his work on counterfactuals (sentences of the form "If A, then B", where A is known to be false), and the meaning of symbols when used in art.

Nelson Goodman graduated from Harvard University in 1928. He had a lifelong interest in art – while studying for his doctorate in philosophy, he ran an art gallery in Boston, Massachusetts. After serving in the US army during World War II, he began teaching at the University of Pennsylvania in 1946. Among his students were Noam Chomsky and Hilary Putnam (*b.* 1926), both of whom would go on to become respected thinkers in their own right. He became a professor at Harvard in 1968. His later work, reflecting his interest in art, focused more on **aesthetic** theory than on the analytic, logical philosophy of his earlier career.

Essential philosophy

Goodman was a quixotic thinker who delighted in finding interesting new approaches to old problems. In his early work he struggled with some classic problems of **analytic philosophy**, in particular the **ontological** question of "what sorts of things exist". Since analytic philosophy needed to explain how a **proposition** (the idea expressed by a sentence) referred to facts in the world, it was an important task to work out problems of **naming** and **reference**. Mathematical **set theory** seemed likely to be of help in defining categories of objects and facts, so this was an area of particular interest to Goodman. He completed some complex work with **W. V. O. Quine**, centering on the difficulty of identifying **universals**. For instance, he addressed the idea that the universal "cat" derives from a collection of individual cats; logicians had been attempting to identify the universal "cat" with the set of all cats.

Goodman's nominalism

Goodman came to doubt that the logicians' task of identifying universals with sets of all individual instances was a feasible task. He argued that while individuals might exist, various objects that are labeled by the same term actually have nothing in common other than their name. This defined the theory of **nominalism**, which is a rejection of **realism**, in the sense in which the term was used in **medieval philosophy** – a realism which asserts that when we use universal terms, such as "cat", "blue", or "hard", we are referring to individual incidences of universal forms. **Plato** had introduced the concept of "Forms", or "**Ideas**", as representing the eternal universe, which we only perceive through our imperfect **perceptions**.

From the nominalist point of view, this connection between universals and forms is quite unnecessary. We can instead take a pragmatic point of view, seeing the names we use for things as simple manners of speaking that happen to work for us. The nominalist thus asserts there is no such thing as the universal "cat" or "blue" existing as an abstract entity.

Nominalism creates problems for those who want to ground analytic philosophy in mathematical rigor, and Quine later repudiated nominalism. But in Goodman's hands this was the start of a way of thinking about how we conceive of things in the world, which he would put to other interesting ends.

Induction and the color "grue"

Goodman is best known for his "new riddle of **induction**", a problem that continues to baffle and irritate new philosophy students to this day. The problem of induction was that no matter how many times we observe a pattern, such as the sun rising in the morning, this does not prove that the pattern will continue in the future. **David Hume** had argued that to believe something on inductive grounds is merely a habit of thought.

There had been some apparent progress on this problem in the form of Hempel's confirmation theory – formalized by Carl Hempel (1905–97) in *Studies in the Logic of Explanation* (1948). Hempel had started from a different logical conundrum. He had noted that the statement that "All ravens are black" is logically identical to the statement that "Everything that is not black is not a raven." He went on to observe that while seeing a black raven is a piece of evidence for proving that all ravens are black, seeing a green apple is also evidence for the same conclusion. This is because a non-black apple that is a non-raven is a piece of evidence towards the second statement, which is identical with the first. Hempel suggested that some inductive arguments are more reliable than others because they rely on "lawlike **hypotheses**". In other

Legacy, truth, consequence

- Goodman's new riddle of induction is a staple of undergraduate philosophy courses to this day and has provoked many anguished or amusing discussions on whether or not it actually makes sense.
- His early work on **logic** and nominalism has been influential – many have followed Quine in preferring to turn away from nominalism, but Goodman's work did a great deal to identify problems faced by set theory and universals.
- Goodman's writing on **counterfactuals** was also influential, and was one of the forerunners of David Lewis' (1941–2001) fascinating theory about possible worlds.
- Always an intriguing and challenging philosopher, some of his best writing came in his later works on aesthetic theory.

> *The meaning of the symbol is given by the system of meanings in which it exists.*
>
> Languages of Art: An Approach to a Theory of Symbols (1968)

Using emerald as an example, Goodman invented the term "grue", which applies to things that are green and that have been examined before the present time, but also that are blue and that are examined after the present time. "Grue" is now used as a linguistic concept for the translation of languages which do not have separate terms to distinguish blue and green.

words the kind of connection we make between data and an induction can be more or less reliable as a guide to future instances.

Goodman came up with a new counterexample to this. He invented the predicate "grue", which applies to things that are green and that have been examined before the present time, but also that are blue and that are examined after the present time. He pointed out that if every emerald I have seen in the past was green that gives me a reason to believe that emeralds I see in future will be green. However, every emerald I have seen has also been grue, which gives me an equally good reason to believe that the next one I see will be grue, that is to say, blue.

This seems like mere pedantry, and some would say that it is. But for Goodman, the point is that the universal **predicates** we use are arbitrary and there is no reason why we should use "green" rather than "grue", other than habit. So to attempt to solve the problem of induction by appealing to "lawlike behavior" is a more difficult task than it first appeared.

Irrealism and symbolism

In *Ways of Worldmaking* (1978) Goodman proposed an "**irrealist**" position. Philosophers have often been divided between **phenomenalists**, who see the contents of the mind as the primary reality, and **physicalists**, who see only physical objects as real. Goodman claimed that neither is true. But he went on to say that the two are just alternative versions, although not of the same world; he suggested that we actually "make alternative worlds" by conceptualizing the world in different ways. Again, he was emphasizing that the ways we symbolize the world can't be reduced to a simple **Platonic** system, but are a matter of choice and habit. For Goodman, there was no one "way that the world is", just a variety of versions that are defined by the symbolism we use to create those worlds.

He took this line of thinking into his writing on aesthetic theory. For him, artistic genres and forms were symbolic systems that didn't attempt to represent the world, but that relied on internal symbolic relations.

Maurice Merleau-Ponty

Merleau-Ponty is an intriguing and subtle French philosopher, who developed and refined the theory of phenomenology. Though is writing is dense, his project is clear: to find a new description of perception. His analysis of the difficulties of human existence has associated him with existentialists Jean-Paul Sartre and Simone de Beauvoir, although arguably his work found relevance in fields as diverse as cognitive science, medical ethics, psychology, and sociology.

Like many of his generation, Maurice Merleau-Ponty lost his father to World War I. His mother sent him to school in Paris and he went on to study philosophy at the École Normale Supérieure at the same time as **Jean-Paul Sartre**. Though he was later associated with the **existentialists**, he often argued against Sartre's theories, in particular his **Marxism**, and these differences contributed to the famous ending of their friendship.

After serving in the infantry during World War II, Merleau-Ponty returned to teaching in Chartres and Lyon. He then moved to Paris for professorial posts, first at the Sorbonne and finally at the Collège de France.

His first two books, *The Structure of Behavior* (1942) and *Phenomenology of Perception* (1945), were very influential and made his reputation. Also a political figure, he edited the political journal *Les Temps Modernes* from 1945 to 1952. When he argued with Sartre over the role of Marxism, it was Sartre who carried on as editor of this journal.

Merleau-Ponty died suddenly from a stroke at a relatively young age in 1961, leaving a body of unfinished writing.

Essential philosophy

Early in his career, Merleau-Ponty became interested in the ideas of the **gestalt** psychologists. They proposed a theory of the mind and brain that explained consciousness as a **holistic** process, in which the whole is different from the sum of its parts. They also argued that the atomic units of **perception** and learning (the **sense–data**) take the form of a structure which can't be reduced to the interaction of those units. Merleau-Ponty felt they had not carried through the philosophical implications of this idea; the concept of gestalt meant that we had to entirely revise our notions of how knowledge works and our **ontology** of *"what kinds of things exist"*. The notion of perception and the way it interacts with the world, especially through our corporeal (bodily) experience, was always at the heart of his thinking.

The body-subject

In *Phenomenology of Perception* (1945), Merleau-Ponty proposed the "body-subject" as an alternative building block to **René Descartes'** cogito (see pages 80–1). This marked his departure point from the **phenomenology** of **Edmund Husserl**, who had basically accepted that sense-data in the mind could be bracketed and the world left behind (see pages 134–5). For Merleau-Ponty, the "primacy of perception" meant that the body-subject always existed partially in the world. The phenomenon was thus not a pure mental state, but a result of the mind intertwining with the world via the body and perceptions.

Strongly influenced by **G. W. F. Hegel**, not least in his approach to **dualisms**, Merleau-Ponty argued that the divisions into subject and object, self and world didn't take account of the primacy of living experience of the existential body. He said *"the perceiving mind is an incarnated mind"*, so he refused to treat the body as external, preferring to treat it as being in continuity with the world.

This difficult concept means that as the body-subject and perception are in the world, when we reflect on the world we are in the state that we are considering. If the perceiving subject changes, so does the relation of the subject to the world. So consciousness is constantly in flux and cannot be studied separately from perception.

One of Merleau-Ponty's specific examples through which he developed his ideas about the body-subject was the case of someone who has lost a limb, but still feels as though it is there. He talks about how the experience of phantom limbs shows us that we structure the world through those aspects of the world that "speak" to the missing limb. So the doorknob or light-switch we try to reach towards has been experienced through the bodily perception of our hand, and until we restructure our perceptual scheme, we continue to experience it in the same way.

The structure of language

Like other contemporary French thinkers, Merleau-Ponty was fascinated by **structuralist** and linguistic theories of meaning. Writers such as the anthropologist Claude Lévi-Strauss (*b.* 1908) and the linguist Ferdinand de Saussure (1857–1913), who wrote about the importance of "difference" in language, were important influences on his thought. Saussure's writing fitted in with the ideas about **gestalt** propounded by Merleau-Ponty, who wanted to

■ Merleau-Ponty's views on the corporeal nature of perception were an obvious influence on his fellow existentialists, including Jean-Paul Sartre and **Simone de Beauvoir**, although his thinking was generally the most subtle of this group.

■ Through de Beauvoir, he has also had an interesting influence on the tradition of **feminist** philosophy. Writers as diverse as Rosalyn Diprose (of the University of New South Wales, Australia) and Bulgarian–French philosopher Julia Kristeva have talked of the way that the body is intertwined with the world, but have brought a feminist slant to this by contrasting the male and female experience.

■ **Jacques Derrida** followed Merleau-Ponty in refusing to accept a clear distinction between thought and language in his *Speech and Phenomena* (1967), and this idea would become central to the project of **deconstruction** in general.

■ Anti**cognitivists** in the **philosophy of science** picked up on Merleau-Ponty's use of gestalt ideas and applied this to question the limits of **artificial intelligence**. As a result there is a growing body of work in which cognitive scientists analyze the meaning of phenomenology.

1908	Born in Rochefort-sur-Mer, France.
1930	Graduates from the École Normale Supérieure, Paris.
1942	*The Structure of Behavior* is published.
1945	*Phenomenology of Perception* is published.
1945–52	Editor of the political, literary, and philosophical magazine, *Les Temps Modernes*.
1949	Appointed to the chair of child psychology at the Sorbonne, Paris.
1952	Aged 45, he is elected to the chair of philosophy at the Collège de France, Paris, and retains the position until his death.
1955	*Adventures of the Dialectic* is published.
1961	Dies of a stroke and is buried in Père Lachaise Cemetery, Paris.

> *We must not, therefore, wonder whether we really perceive a world, we must instead say: the world is what we perceive.*
>
> Phenomenology of Perception (1945)

In his essay "Cézanne's Doubt" (1945), Merleau-Ponty defines Cézanne's impressionistic theory of painting as analogous to his own concept of reflection.

emphasize that meaning could not be defined simply or by appeal to historical reflection, especially in the case of a "speaking language", but must reside partly in the structure of language and interplay between the subject and the world.

So where Husserl had separated "expression" and "indication" and many other writers had regarded language as the expression of a pre-existing thought, Merleau-Ponty regarded language and thought as being intertwined. He wrote about those moments when one searches for a forgotten word as indicative of the fact that thought itself is incomplete without the word. And he outlined a gestural theory of language – noting that when I speak, "*I reach back for the word, as my hand reaches toward a part of my body which is being pricked; the word has a certain location in my linguistic world and is a part of my equipment*"; the act of speech is the act of making a gesture within the structure of language.

Merleau-Ponty and Marxism

Like many of his contemporaries, Merleau-Ponty started as a Marxist. He had been inspired by the lectures of Alexander Kojève (1902–68), who gave an essentially **Hegelian** interpretation of Marxism, and who taught that we were progressing towards an "end of history" – though Kojève's conception of this endpoint was far more liberal in character that Marx's theory suggested.

Immanuel Kant had once written that we choose to view human history as though it is a progress towards a better state, because otherwise we would be forced to view it as a farce. This was essentially Merleau-Ponty's view for a long time – he felt that

to reject Marxism would be to reject all hope of meaning in history. He was never a strong apologist for the regime in the USSR, recognizing the evil of the purges and the show trials. However, it was the Korean War that finally made him revise his opinion: he felt that Soviet Marxism had clearly transformed itself into **imperialism**, and he castigated Sartre for not sharing this opinion. Later in life he came to a more **humanist** view of the value of parliamentary **democracy** as the alternative to totalitarian solutions.

Simone de Beauvoir

Although she called herself a writer rather than a philosopher, and she was often overshadowed by her lifelong partner, Jean-Paul Sartre, it is now accepted that Simone de Beauvoir's novels, articles, and feminist writings contain important philosophical ideas. She played a major part in France's unique twentieth-century intellectual world, and made significant contributions to existentialism and feminism.

Simone de Beauvoir came from a middle-class or bourgeois family that fell on hard times. As a result, the question of how to escape the dual restraints of a narrow moral code and poverty were to be of major concern to her. As a teenager she became an atheist and was determined to be a writer, choosing to study philosophy and literature at the Sorbonne University in Paris. In 1929, while studying for the *agrégation* (teaching qualification) in philosophy, she met fellow student **Jean-Paul Sartre**, who was to be her lifelong friend and lover. Only 21, she became the youngest person ever to gain the *agrégation*, taking second place to Sartre in the final examination. Some accounts say that the jury decided not to give her top place because she was a woman and because Sartre (who had failed first time round) was older at 24.

It was when she was a student that she was given an enduring nickname, Castor (in English: Beaver), partly a play on the English word's similarity to her name, but mainly because she worked as hard as and was as sociable as a beaver.

Obsessed with Sartre both sexually and intellectually, de Beauvoir agreed with his proposal that they should not marry, but have "contingent" relationships in addition to their own

"essential" pairing. For a woman at the time it was a courageous step to ignore convention to such an extent.

Supporting herself by teaching, she spent all her spare time debating with Sartre. In the 1930s there was no overall label for their discussions, which focused on the meaning of human existence, but included intellectual anarchy, **rationalist** atheism, **individualism**, a lack of politics, and freedom from bourgeois restrictions. The term "**existentialist**" was applied later on, but it wasn't until 1939 and World War II that her final philosophy was shaped, when she embraced political causes and put her energy and intellect into solidarity with others apart from just Sartre.

The war years were to prove productive. Her first published novel appeared and she wrote articles for the French Resistance magazines (both hers and Sartre's and one run by the writer Albert Camus), as well as preparing other important works, both novels and articles. As a result, in the early post-war period she found herself at the heart of France's intellectual life, and her lifestyle – of intense debates in Parisian cafés and jazz clubs – caught the imagination of young intellectuals around the world.

Essential philosophy

The Second Sex

In this most influential of all her works, published in 1949, de Beauvoir defined the world as one in which "male" was the norm, embodying power and status, while woman was "other", and had to contort to fit male expectations of femininity while forever being relegated to second class. She was the first philosopher to tackle the details of women's lives and to look at the cultural, economic, and psychological conditions that controlled women's freedom. *The Second Sex* outlined ways that women could challenge this status quo and achieve full independence and freedom, in particular by discarding the mystification surrounding ideals of the "eternal feminine". But, paradoxically, she often shaped her own personal life to fit around Sartre.

Existentialist ethics

The Ethics of Ambiguity, de Beauvoir's 1947 essay, was her most overtly existentialist work. In this she was responding to the

existentialist view that we have many alternative possibilities open to us, and a fear by some of the terror of a completely open future with no guiding light. She was concerned to show that an ethical theory is compatible with Sartre's view that there are no moral rules. Ethical worth, she argued, comes in how we face up to our freedom; we can face up to our freedom or try to escape it. Existentialism offers meaning to our lives through the life projects we adopt, through which we define ourselves. Ambiguity comes because meaning must be constantly won through such projects: sometimes it can be tempting to follow a course that avoids the responsibility of actively choosing freedom, and instead lets one just stagnate in a static identity. The virtues needed to face one's freedom resolutely are certain classical excellences such as courage, patience, and fidelity.

Above all, we have to accept responsibility for the impact our projects and choices have on other people's situations and conditions, within which they have to act to find their own

Simone de Beauvoir and Jean-Paul Sartre, pictured here in 1954: a lifelong, unique relationship.

One is not born a genius, one becomes a genius; and the feminine situation has up to the present rendered this becoming practically impossible ...

The Second Sex (1949)

Key dates

1908	Born in Paris, France.
1929	Meets Jean-Paul Sartre.
1943	Publishes her first novel *She Came to Stay*.
1944	Co-founds and edits the intellectual magazine *Les Temps Modernes* (named after Charlie Chaplin's film *Modern Times*).
1947	Publishes the essay *The Ethics of Ambiguity*, on existentialist ethics.
1949	Publishes her classic feminist work, *The Second Sex*.
1954	Wins the prestigious Prix Goncourt award for her novel *The Mandarins*.
1957	Begins social activism against colonialism in Algeria, and for women's liberation, abortion rights, and **socialism**.
1958	First part of her philosophical autobiography appears.
1980	Depressed after Sartre's death.
1986	Dies from pneumonia in Paris, France, and is buried next to Sartre.

In 1988 her letters to Sartre were published, revealing details of their affairs, including her lesbian relationships and their shared lovers. Even in so-called modern times, many people were shocked, but others realized that she had been writing her existence into her work for decades.

De Beauvoir became a **feminist** icon after the publication of *The Second Sex*, and soon was considered one of the leading intellectuals of the left. She became more socially active and as part of the campaign for the woman's right to choose an abortion, in 1971 she signed the "Manifesto of 343", admitting to having had an illegal abortion (although in fact she had not had one).

As devoted as ever, for ten years from 1970 she organized the care and comfort of an ailing Sartre, only returning to her work after he died.

freedom. De Beauvoir's **humanist** ethics stress this personal responsibility by arguing that evil lies in denying freedom to self and to others.

Metaphysics

De Beauvoir's novels *She Came to Stay* and *The Mandarins* also reflect her own life experiences, but through a **metaphysical** mirror that emphasized some things that are essential, or do not change, in human life and relationships. Both these books are semi-autobiographical (although names are changed) and show the multi-faceted ways in which we relate to our basic existence.

In her novels she further explored the ambiguity in the relationships of responsible individuals to each other, particularly when each has consciously chosen their own "project". Once more she concluded that our freedom is only meaningful if it expands the freedom of others as well as ourselves.

Other works

De Beauvoir's four-volume autobiography embraced fundamental philosophical ideas in its narrative. Her basic ideology of personal freedom but responsibility to others as an expression of existence shines through her story of her life.

Her many other writings include discussions on her visits to **capitalist** America and **communist** China, a denouncement of the torture by French forces of an Algerian girl accused of terrorism, her farewell to Sartre, and another groundbreaking look at the lives of "others", this time elderly people. In the latter, as in her discussions of death, she was concerned to show the reality of existence at all stages of life.

171

Willard Van Orman Quine

An American philosopher and logician of undoubted brilliance, Quine wrote on issues in metaphysics, epistemology, the philosophy of science, the philosophy of mathematics, and the philosophy of language. Though Quine is often classed as an analytic philosopher, he was in fact the most powerful critic of the view that philosophy reveals conceptual or linguistic truths through analysis, and he actually thought philosophy continuous with natural science.

Quine was born in Akron, Ohio, in 1908. His father was a manufacturer and entrepreneur and his mother was a schoolteacher. In 1930 he studied at Harvard under Alfred North Whitehead (1861– 1947), who had co-authored *Principia Mathematica*, a landmark in mathematical logic, with **Bertrand Russell**. Quine's doctorate thesis was on mathematical **logic** and **set theory**, in which he would prove important results. In 1932 he made a visit to the Polish logician Alfred Tarski (1901–83), which ensured Tarski's work on truth, now of great interest in the **philosophy of language**, became known to a philosophical audience. In the same year, he went to meet with the **logical positivists** in Vienna, forging a long friendship with **Rudolf**

Carnap, whose work exerted a great influence over him (though Quine's criticisms of Carnap's views are now recognized as devastating).

Quine's major works in philosophy began to appear after World War II with his 1953 book *From a Logical Point of View*, containing the classic papers "On What There Is" and "Two Dogmas of Empiricism". Though Quine often wrote on very technical issues, he is known for his good-humored turn of phrase and his powerful vision of philosophy as on all fours with natural science. He was fluent in many languages, a great traveler, amiable, and known to close friends as "Van". Having retired in 1978, Quine was actively associated with Harvard University until his death on Christmas Day 2000.

Essential philosophy

"Two Dogmas of Empiricism"

Quine argued that modern **empiricism** had been conditioned by two dogmas. The first is that there is a fundamental distinction between **analytic** and **synthetic** truths. Analytic truths are statements that are true purely "in virtue of" their meaning. Statements like "Bachelors are unmarried men" had been thought analytic because the meanings of "bachelors" and "unmarried men" seem to ensure its truth. Synthetic truths are statements that are true "in virtue of" meaning and non-linguistic fact, such as "Bananas are yellow", which is true because bananas are yellow and the sentence says as much. Logical positivists, such as **A. J. Ayer** and Rudolf Carnap, and, in their own terms, earlier empiricists such as **David Hume**, had made this distinction among true statements central to their philosophy. Quine argued that no one had ever drawn this distinction in clear terms that didn't suffer from circularity by assuming the very notion of "analytic" that they had sought to clarify. He described the distinction as a *metaphysical article of faith*".

The second dogma of empiricism Quine called "reductionism". This is the view that every meaningful statement can be translated into terms that refer only to immediate experience, or **sense-data**, and logical terms, such as "not", "and", "or", and "if…then". This view was held by **logical positivists** like Rudolf Carnap who attempted to ground all our knowledge of the world in our certainty of our immediate experiences and our knowledge of

logic. Quine thought that the project failed. He argued that statements taken in isolation do not have a set of sense experiences that would confirm or disconfirm them at all:

"Our statements about the external world face the tribunal of experience not individually but only as a corporate body."

("Two Dogmas", 1953)

In other words, an individual statement cannot be reduced to a set of sense experiences as sense experiences are not associated with any individual statement but only with the totality of statements, the "corporate body", that makes up our theory of the world. This view is known as **holism**.

Quine foresaw one of the results of rejecting the dogmas as a blurring of the line between philosophy, which many contemporaries thought to reveal truths of linguistic analysis, and natural science, the investigation of worldly facts through empirical observation. For, if all statements depend for their truth on worldly fact as well as on their linguistic meaning, they are all part of our empirical theory of the world. A further consequence is that any of our statements might be subject to revision given the disconfirmation of our theory by our experience of the world. Quine held that we could even hold the truths of **logic** and mathematics to be false given recalcitrant experience. But in practice, he argued, we would very rarely revise logic or mathematics if our theories fail since logical and mathematical statements are less sensitive to empirical

Legacy, truth, consequence

■ Prior to Quine, philosophers might have asked opponents whether what they said was analytic or synthetic. The implication was that if it was analytic then it was just a truth about the language, hence vacuous, and that if it was synthetic then it was really something for a scientist to decide. After Quine, philosophers became very wary of the terms and it was more likely for them to question whether an opponent's position might be *assuming* the analytic-synthetic distinction.

■ Quine convinced far fewer philosophers of his thesis of the Indeterminacy of Translation and his ensuing meaning **scepticism**. His description of the radical translator's evidence rested on a **behaviorist** conception of language (see Chomsky, pages 182–3, for opposition to behaviorism), which many now reject.

> As an empiricist I continue to think of the conceptual scheme of science as a tool, ultimately, for predicting future experience in the light of past experience.

"Two Dogmas of Empiricism" in *From a Logical Point of View* (1953)

To explain the thesis of the "indeterminacy of translation", Quine took the example of the word "gavagai" said by a native seeing a rabbit. The linguist can translate this as "a rabbit", but other translations are also possible: "food"; "let's go hunting"; "there will be a storm tonight"; or any other translation triggered by the context. Quine denied an absolute standard of right and wrong in translating one language into another: no unique meaning can be assigned to words and sentences.

evidence and serve to organize our theories. Quine thought of the totality of our statements, our theory of the world, as like a "*web of belief*" which "*meets the tribunal of experience*" with mathematics and logic at the center of the web and statements about immediate experience at the periphery.

Indeterminacy of translation

A view that Quine thought followed from his rejection of analytic truth, explored in his later work, is "meaning **scepticism**". If there are no statements that are true purely in virtue of meaning then, Quine wondered, how could there be true statements about the meaning of the sentences of languages? Quine developed this idea by considering the predicament of a "radical translator" who tries to translate the language of a completely unfamiliar community on the basis of the objectively available evidence. His conclusion is that there are always at least two ways of translating any language that are consistent with all the radical translator's evidence but incompatible with one another. Hence, there is no fact of the matter about correct translation. This is Quine's thesis of the "indeterminacy of translation", from which his meaning scepticism followed. For if there are always two inconsistent ways of translating any language compatible with all the objective evidence, then there is no objective fact about the correct translations of the sentences, and hence no objective fact about the correct statement of their meanings.

Isaiah Berlin

Sir Isaiah Berlin was a philosopher and writer who was well known for his defence of liberalism, his distate for extremism and authoritarianism, and for his work on the history of ideas. His 1958 essay "Two Concepts of Liberty" remains one of the most influential pieces of writing on the idea of freedom and has been a starting point for much subsequent discussion of the issue.

Isaiah Berlin was born in Riga in Latvia (then part of the Russian Empire), the only child of a Jewish timber merchant. He witnessed the Russian Revolution in Petrograd (Saint Petersburg) in 1917, before emigrating to London with his family in 1921, at the age of 12. At Oxford University he studied classics, philosophy, politics, and economics, before becoming a lecturer there, in 1932, and was the first Jewish person to be elected to a Prize Fellowship at All Souls College – a prestigious achievement.

During the 1930s, Berlin was involved in the philosophical establishment at Oxford, where his colleagues and friends included J. L. Austin (1911–60) and **A. J. Ayer**. After working for the British government's information services in the US and Russia during World War II, he returned to academic life, but chose to focus his attention more on the history of ideas than on pure philosophy. He continued to teach at Oxford and to travel between Britain and America.

His famous essay, "Two Concepts of Liberty", delivered as a lecture in 1958, became a key text in twentieth-century **political philosophy**. It set out the core concepts of **liberalism**, and, reflecting the turbulence of the Cold War and his rejection of **authoritarianism**, proposed a plurality of **moral values** as a goal for humanity.

Essential philosophy

The two strands of philosophy that Berlin first encountered were British **idealism** and the **logical positivism** of colleagues such as Ayer. He was also influenced by **Immanuel Kant**, in particular in his attempt to define the concepts and categories with which we try to organize our experience. However, for Berlin these were not fixed concepts – he saw our interaction with the world as being influenced by contingent historical circumstance, and this was one of the observations that led to his increasing interest in the history of ideas.

He opposed the logical positivist belief that philosophy should be modeled on natural science. Instead he classified philosophy as a human science, arguing that it had a different task and intention from science. He believed that philosophy attempts to answer questions for which we don't know the answer, indeed we aren't even sure what form an answer might take. It is thus a subversive discipline that focuses on the anomalies in our thinking, and pushes us towards new formulations.

While the positivists attempted to reject any question that couldn't be framed with scientific rigor, Berlin insisted that philosophy addressing these difficult questions had a socially useful role to play. He wrote that philosophy's aim was to "*to assist men to understand themselves and thus operate in the open, and not wildly, in the dark*".

The abandonment of certainty

In opposition to contemporary **analytic philosophy**, Berlin opposed the idea that philosophy should strive after certainty. He rejected what he called the "Ionian fallacy" or the "**Platonic** ideal" of **monism**, the idea that everything is reducible to or made out of the same kind of "stuff".

He identified this "fallacy" as the notion that all meaningful questions must have a single true answer, that there must be a dependable path to discovering true answers, and that true answers must form a compatible picture of the world. For Berlin, certainty was an impossible ideal, and there might be different true answers to the same meaningful questions.

Value pluralism

Berlin's rejection of the "Ionian fallacy" took on a new significance in his work on "**value pluralism**". Here, he resisted the idea that ethical values could be reduced to a single, compatible system (such as a system based on **utilitarianism**, or Kant's **categorical imperative**). He argued that there was a plurality of genuine values, and that they could often come into conflict with one another. Liberty and equality or truth and beauty might in many situations be incompatible. But he went even further, asserting that they could even be incommensurable, meaning that there was no reliable way to measure conflicting values against each other.

This did not mean that morality was a free-for-all. Berlin's thinking was always guided by **humanism** and liberalism. For him, moral collisions were unavoidable, but could be softened or solved through compromise. Philosophy might not be able to solve the problem of plural values but it could still cast light on the roots of moral conflicts and help us to avoid illusory solutions.

Legacy, truth, consequence

- **Libertarians** have used Berlin's advocacy of negative freedom to argue for a minimal state. Berlin himself didn't take this approach, as he took a more nuanced view that balanced the virtues of the liberal state and a focus on liberty.
- There has been much recent interest in the idea of value pluralism. Some argue that Berlin's pluralism is indistinguishable from **relativism**, although he would have rejected that accusation. Others claim that liberalism is reliant on universal value claims and is thus in contradiction with pluralism, something Berlin would also have rejected.
- In the end it is Berlin's conception of the two kinds of freedom that will be his most lasting legacy.

Berlin believed that throughout history the concept of "positive liberty" very often gave rise to the abuse of power and political totalitarianism, as in the Nazi or Marxist ideologies.

But to manipulate men, to propel them towards goals which you – the social reformer – see, but they may not, is to deny their human essence, to treat them as objects without wills of their own, and therefore to degrade them.

"Two Concepts of Liberty" (1958)

Berlin's political philosophy

In political philosophy, Berlin saw **Alexander Herzen** as a hero, and shared with him an aversion to the idea of inevitable historical progress. He rejected the idea of **determinism** in general, insisting on the importance of human **free will**. **Historical determinism** he saw as an excuse to treat men as pawns. Just as Herzen and Kant had warned against using men as means to an end, rather than ends-in-themselves, Berlin argued that the authoritarian mindset used historical determinism to justify the sacrifice of current people and virtues in the name of some future endpoint.

This thinking informed Berlin's "Two Concepts of Liberty", in which he contrasted negative and positive liberty. Negative liberty he associated with philosophers such as **Thomas Hobbes**, **Adam Smith**, and **John Locke**, defining it as "freedom from", meaning that a man has "negative liberty" if others do not impose upon him or interfere with him. By contrast "positive liberty", which he associated with **Jean-Jacques Rousseau**, **Karl Marx**, Johann Fichte (1762–1814), G. W. F. Hegel, and others, is about "freedom to": the ability to, and opportunity to fulfil one's potential.

In Rousseau's writing, he identified a shift from the idea of negative freedom as an individual, to positive freedom as a "citizen", at which point the individual's desires are subsumed into the idea of what a citizen "ought to desire". Fichte (a follower of Kant) had gone further, arguing that the individual only achieves freedom through overcoming their false, **empirical** self, and submerging themselves in the group (which for Fichte meant the *Volk*, or people). This is obviously a forerunner both of the Nazi ideology and the Marxist idea of "false consciousness", which rejects individual choices on the basis that they are not "authentic".

It's important to note that Berlin did accept that positive liberty could have value, and also that a narrow focus on negative liberty could lead to unfortunate consequences such as the exploitation that occurs under **laissez-faire economics**. His main aim was to point out the dangers of misinterpreting the idea of positive freedom, and to show how it could be abused by the authoritarian mindset.

Alfred Jules Ayer

The British empiricist Sir A. J. Ayer introduced logical positivism to the English-speaking world, stirring up controversy with provocative arguments such as that metaphysics, aesthetics, and other areas of traditional philosophy state no meaningful truths, and that moral statements are expressions of emotion.

Known familiarly as Freddie, Alfred Jules Ayer came from a financially comfortable background. He discovered philosophy at school in Eton, and in 1929 attended Oxford University to read philosophy and Greek. Already a committed atheist, he was labeled by a Jesuit priest as "dangerous" following a university debate on religion.

Ayer found his true philosophical home in 1933 when he went to Vienna to visit Moritz Schlick (1882–1936), then the acknowledged leader of the **Vienna Circle** of **logical positivists**. That year Ayer began writing *Language, Truth, and Logic*, which was published in 1936 to both acclaim and outrage.

In the 1930s Ayer also began his involvement in left-wing politics, actively supporting the Labour Party until 1981, when he joined the recently formed Social Democrats. He campaigned for many social issues such as gay rights and abortion rights, opposed racism, and supported **humanist** and secular organizations.

After serving in the Welsh Guards and with the British Intelligence Services during World War II, Ayer lectured at Oxford before moving to University College London, where, as professor of philosophy, he built the department up into a major intellectual center.

He also began his long relationship with the broadcast media, and became one of the BBC's (British Broadcasting Corporation) favorite intellectuals, happy to debate and argue about religion, philosophy, politics, or sport. He published several other books and many papers, but none had the impact of his first publication.

In the 1950s Ayer embarked on a series of worldwide lecture tours before moving back to the University of Oxford as Wykeham Professor of Logic.

As one of Britain's best-known atheists, he shocked himself and the world when he went through a near-death experience in 1988 after choking on a piece of food, but he hastened to state that he still did not believe in God.

He was a gregarious womanizer himself, but at a party in America in 1987 he tried to stop the boxer Mike Tyson from molesting the model Naomi Campbell. Tyson reportedly said, "*Do you know who the fuck I am? I'm the heavyweight champion of the world,*" upon which Ayer said, "*And I am the former Wykeham Professor of Logic. We are both pre-eminent in our field. I suggest that we talk about this like rational men.*"

Essential philosophy

Logical positivism

The logical positivism of the Vienna Circle (**Rudolph Carnap**, Moritz Schlick, and others) originated as a philoso-phical response to the new twentieth-century sciences. Their stance was that truth should be explored only through the empirical verifiability or logic of language.

Ayer was firmly in the camp of British **empiricism**, and like **John Locke**, **David Hume**, and **Bertrand Russell** he rejected the idea of **synthetic *a priori*** knowledge, claiming instead that all knowledge of the world outside the mind comes from the experiences of the senses. He enthusiastically embraced the Vienna Circle's approach as "logical empiricism", a way of giving philosophy the same certainty as science.

In *Language, Truth, and Logic* Ayer showed how this approach can be applied to questions of reality, knowledge, **perception**, and

meaning. He contrasted it with philosophical discussions of religion, **ethics**, and the meaning of life, which, he claimed, are imprecise, have no solutions, and are unverifiable. Philosophers, he said, should concentrate only on areas where critical analysis could be applied, such as the philosophy of science or language, and the theory of knowledge. They should not attempt to offer ethical guidelines.

Principle of verification

The keystone of Ayer's philosophy was his argument that for a statement to be empirically verifiable is not for it to be shown to be true by the experience of the senses, but for it to be possible for it to be confirmed or disconfirmed by sensory experience. Hence, false empirical statements can still be meaningful. He wrote: "*We say that a sentence is factually significant to any given person, if, and only if, he knows how to verify the proposition which it purports to express.*"

Legacy, truth, consequence

■ Written in a clear, elegant style, brimming with enthusiasm for the subject, Ayer's first book, *Language, Truth, and Logic*, was a shock to the philosophical world. Students loved it while many older philosophers immediately hated its iconoclastic ideas. Soon after it was published a group of Oxford students tried to discuss it at a seminar, only for their tutor to throw the book out of the window. Ayer had an immediate, major impact, stirring up a fruitful debate about the purpose and scope of philosophy.

■ *Language, Truth, and Logic* became a best-selling philosophy book, introducing new concepts to the general public. Although he later modified his stance slightly – his introduction in later editions openly admits to early flaws – Ayer remained faithful to the principles of logical positivism. Later on he did admit that sentences can have a meaning beyond their verifiability by sense-data.

■ Philosophers today have a mixed response to his work: either they embrace *Language, Truth, and Logic* as a classic text in the empirical and analytic tradition, or they reject it as obsolete.

Key dates

1910	Born in London, UK.
1929	Goes to Oxford University to study philosophy.
1933	Learns about logical positivism from the Vienna Circle.
1936	Only 26, publishes his masterpiece *Language, Truth, and Logic*.
1946	Appointed Grote Professor of Mental Philosophy at University College London.
1956	Publishes *The Problem of Knowledge*.
1959	Appointed Wykeham Professor of Logic at University of Oxford.
1965–70	Serves as president of the British Humanist Association.
1970	Awarded a knighthood.
1989	Dies of a collapsed lung.

Ascent of the Blessed (detail), Hieronymus Bosch, c.1490. A. J. Ayer described his near-death experience in a 1988 article entitled "What I saw when I was dead".

> *We say that a sentence is factually significant to any given person, if, and only if, he knows how to verify the proposition which it purports to express – that is, if he knows what observations would lead him, under certain conditions, to accept the proposition as being true, or reject it as being false.*
>
> Language, Truth, and Logic (1936)

The implication of the principle is that all meaning must ultimately be expressed in terms of **sense-data** or sense-contents.

The verification principle as a criterion of meaning makes it possible to distinguish between sense and nonsense in areas such as perception and knowledge. Statements to do with **metaphysics** and religion, such as "There is a God", are not verifiable, so according to this methodology they are factually meaningless and are classified as nonsense. In this way Ayer discarded many traditional philosophical ideas as not worth pursuing because **hypotheses** concerning them did not have any meaning.

Emotivist ethics

Ayer argued that moral statements such as "That action is evil" cannot be verified, so they do not have any cognitive content and are neither true nor false. They are simply expressions of emotion. When people discuss ethical issues, they are just showing their personal approval or disapproval of the issue, and are seeking to gain agreement for their emotional stance. Moral debate is simply a debate about which attitudes to hold. This view, known as emotivist ethics, was one of the most controversial points of his philosophy.

In his system, value judgements on artistic beauty are, like moral opinions, emotional attitudes, not facts.

Continental philosophy

Always happy to be combative, Ayer publicly ridiculed many of the new French philosophical ideas, describing them as "*preposterous*" and "*chiefly an exercise in misusing the verb 'to be'*".

John Rawls

1921–2002

John Rawls is one of the most influential twentieth-century writers on the subject of political philosophy. His theory of "justice as fairness", together with the idea that fairness can be defined in terms of how members of a society would choose to live if they were choosing from behind a "veil of ignorance", represents one of the most subtle attempts to underpin political ideology. He was a liberal thinker himself, but his ideas have been reinterpreted by thinkers of many hues.

John Borden Rawls was raised in Baltimore, Maryland, US, and attended Princeton University, which is where he first developed an interest in philosophy. It was here too that he was elected to the privileged and academic Ivy Club. He fought in the Pacific in World War II, losing his previous religious faith as a result of seeing the horrors of war at first hand. In the 1960s he would be a strong opponent of the Vietnam War, an event that would significantly influence his attempts to formalize the ideal relations between the individual and the state, and between state and state.

Rawls began his academic teaching career in 1950, and in 1952 was awarded a fellowship to study at Oxford University in the UK, where he was influenced by **Isaiah Berlin** and the legal philosopher H. L. A. Hart (1907–92). In 1964 he moved to Harvard University, where he taught for many years. His 1971 book *A Theory of Justice* was quickly recognized as a key work of **political philosophy**, although he continued to modify and extend his theories in his subsequent writings. In 1999 he received the National Humanities Medal from President Clinton in recognition of his contributions to thought on justice and **democracy**.

Essential philosophy

Rawls' main achievements came in his work to establish founding principles for a just, **liberal** society. He started by examining the idea of fairness and created a number of concepts in the process. These included "reflective equilibrium", a process of rationality which, rather than appealing to a set of fundamental beliefs, strives to find a coherent set of beliefs starting from the beliefs that are most important to us. He also talked about "public reason", by which he meant that public discourse about the state and political ideas should be based on simple ideas that everyone can acknowledge rather than on private inspiration or ideas that are too specific to a minority viewpoint.

However, his most important contribution came in his theory of "justice as fairness". Rawls was trying to address the basic political question of how to balance liberty and equality among individuals in a society. He assumed a well-ordered society with adequate resources, and then followed **Thomas Hobbes** in accepting that, because the liberties of individuals will clash with one another, there is a need for some form of **social contract**. However, the problem with social contract theory has always been that we are not given the choice of what social contract we accept – we simply live in a society that already has a certain balance of powers, rights, and responsibilities.

The veil of ignorance

Rawls attempted to solve this problem by asking a different question: what society would we choose to live in if the negotiations for the social contract were carried out by representatives who didn't know the specifics of our circumstances? (Some have depicted these decisions being made by imaginary versions of ourselves acting in a kind of limbo.) If they didn't know whether we would be from a rich or poor family, what our religion or race would be, if they didn't know if we were young or old or able-bodied or otherwise, what kind of society would they create?

This extraordinary and enlightening idea led Rawls to state two new principles of justice. He adapted these slightly over time to answer objections, but one version of them was as follows:

• **First principle:** Each person should have the same indefeasible claim to an adequate scheme of equal basic liberties, which is compatible with the same scheme of liberties for all.

• **Second principle:** Social and economic inequalities are to satisfy two conditions:

  (1) They are to be attached to offices and positions open to all under conditions of "fair equality of opportunity".

  (2) They are to be to the greatest benefit of the least-advantaged members of society (the "difference principle").

By starting from the "original position" of the veil of ignorance, Rawls was looking for principles that any individual could assent to regardless of their position in life. He thus aimed to remove the question of political legitimacy from problems of egotism and altruism, instead finding principles that could apply to any rational, reasonable person. His first principle creates a very simple statement

Legacy, truth, consequence

- Some have argued that Rawls' theories smuggle in assumptions. The difference principle is criticized by **Robert Nozick** and others for assuming that from behind the veil of ignorance we would automatically be risk-averse, rather than risk-taking.

- Rawls tried to adapt his thinking to different problems such as relations between states – some of his original followers were disappointed that his later writing in this area seemed more conservative than earlier works.

- Animal rights philosophers have doubted that there is a clear reason for excluding non-humans from the veil of ignorance. And as we face global warming and the end of oil, to what extent should the rights of future humans be included? (Rawls did consider this issue, but it is still a vexed one.)

- In spite of these questions, Rawls transformed political philosophy, bringing a whole new approach to the problem of how to justify systems of democracy and justice. Even those who disagree with him can respect the brilliance of his basic conceptions.

Key dates

The principles of justice are chosen behind a veil of ignorance.

A Theory of Justice (1971)

The aftermath of the Hiroshima bombing in 1945. Rawls lost his religious faith after witnessing the horrors of war.

of universal liberty. In his view, this justifies basic rights and liberties such as the liberty of conscience, freedom of association and of speech, liberty of the person, the right to vote, and the right to be treated equally by the law. Since unequal rights would be detrimental to those who got the lesser share of rights, none would assent to this situation from behind the veil of ignorance.

The difference principle

Rawls' second principle (in two parts) adds further detail to his theory. The first part aims to make sure that "*in all parts of society there are to be roughly the same prospects of culture and achievement for those similarly motivated and endowed*". One consequence of this for Rawls was that public elections should be funded by the state so that wealthy people were not given undue privilege (whereas it is reasonable that wise or respected people have an unequal chance in this sphere).

The second part states one of Rawls' most interesting and disputed ideas, the "difference principle". He confronts the conundrum that an unequal society can nevertheless be a decent, just one, and one in which all are better off than in one of enforced "equality". **Aristotle** had suggested that unequal societies resulted from "natural justice" and few philosophers in the intervening centuries had managed to address this issue satisfactorily.

Rawls suggests that behind the veil of ignorance we would accept an unequal outcome so long as all were better off under that outcome. In particular we would choose the outcome in which the worst-off gained the most advantage. Imagine we can choose between the following income arrangements: X(A=100, B=100, C=100), Y(A=200, B=300, C=1000), Z(A=300, B=400, C=600). Y and Z are better than X, because A, B, and C are all better off in these scenarios. But according to the difference principle, the most just outcome is Z, because all are better off and the least advantaged are better off than in Y, so we should prefer that possibility.

Michel Foucault

Michel Foucault was a French philosopher whose historical examinations of the human condition were aimed at changing the status quo of modern society. He was one of the twentieth century's most influential and controversial academics. Labeled both structuralist and poststructuralist, and resistant to both labels, Foucault spanned the disciplines of social sciences, history, literary theory, psychology, and politics.

Michel Foucault was born in Poitiers, France, into a stolidly bourgeois family – a background he would spend his life rebelling against. A brilliant, unpredictable student, he entered the École Normale Supérieure in Paris in 1946. Here he flirted with both **Marxism** and **existentialism**, soon turning decisively away from both.

Foucault graduated in 1952 with degrees in both philosophy and **psychology**, briefly teaching the latter at the University of Lille. Between 1955 and 1960 he worked as a cultural attaché in Sweden, Poland, and Germany. Returning to France, he took up a philosophy post at the University of Clermont-Ferrand, where he met Daniel Defert, who became his lifetime partner.

This was the period of Foucault's early works, or "archaeologies" as he termed them: *Madness and Civilization* (1961), on the birth of the asylum, offered an archaeology of how the exchange between madness and reason was silenced; *The Birth of the Clinic* (1963) was "an archaeology of the medical gaze"; and *The Order of Things* (1966) was "an archaeology of the human sciences". In 1970 he was elected to the Collège de France as Professor of the History of Systems of Thought.

Foucault's politicization increased after the 1968 student riots, as did his fascination with issues of power and knowledge ("*pouvoir-savoir*"). His interest in prisoners and delinquency fed into *Discipline and Punish* (1975), a study of how modern forms of punishment exercise more insidious control than in the pre-modern age, enabling society "*to punish less, perhaps; but certainly to punish better*". (There are echoes of **Jean-Jacques Rousseau** in Foucault's critique of the relationship between citizen and state.)

He further considered the interaction between knowledge and power in *The Will to Knowledge* (1976), the first volume of a projected six-volume *History of Sexuality*, conceived on the model of **Friedrich Nietzsche**'s *Genealogy of Morals*. However, only two other volumes were completed in his lifetime – *The Use of Pleasure* (1984) and *The Care of the Self* (1984).

As Foucault's reputation grew, he traveled widely, spending extended periods in Brazil, Japan, Italy, Canada, and the United States. He became particularly attached to the University of California at Berkeley, where he was a visiting lecturer for several years. Foucault died of an AIDS-related illness in Paris in 1984.

Essential philosophy

Foucault placed himself in the critical tradition of philosophical inquiry stemming from **Immanuel Kant**. He rejected both **Hegelianism** and Marxism but took both quite seriously. The writings of Nietzsche directed him to the history of the collusion between power and knowledge. He followed **Martin Heidegger** in rejecting existentialist **humanism** in favor of a new form of philosophical anti-humanism: as Foucault declared in *The Order of Things* (1966): "*Man is only a recent invention … [that] will disappear again as soon as our knowledge has discovered a new form*".

The Archaeologies

Foucault's analogy of the historian as archaeologist sprang from his desire to devise a properly specific history of subjects. By seeing the historian's collection of statements about subjects produced and presumed true at any given historical moment as the artifacts of some archaeological site or complex, he was able to reveal the inherently local and transient qualities of past conceptions of being human.

Madness and Civilization (1961) is an intellectual excavation of the radically different discursive formations that governed talk and thought about madness up to the nineteenth century. Standard histories saw the nineteenth century's "reforms" of medical treatment of madness as an enlightened liberation from the ignorance and brutality of preceding ages. But Foucault argued that the alleged scientific neutrality of modern medical treatments of insanity were in fact covers for controlling any challenges to the conventional bourgeois morality, and that what was presented as an objective scientific discovery (that madness is mental illness) was in fact the product of eminently questionable social and **ethical** commitments.

Foucault's next archaeology, *The Birth of the Clinic* (1963), can be read as both a standard history of science and a critique of modern clinical medicine. Its central motif is that of the "medical gaze", used to denote the often dehumanizing method by which medical professionals separate the body from the person. *The Order of Things* (*Les Mots et les Choses*, 1966) was controversial more for its

Legacy, truth, consequence

■ In the late 1960s Foucault was grouped with the new wave of **structuralist** thinkers such as Jacques Lacan (1901–81), Claude Lévi-Strauss (*b.*1908), and Roland Barthes (1915–80). He quickly tired of being labeled a structuralist, and was equally dismissive of the "**post-structuralist**" and "**postmodern**" labels that were later applied to him.

■ The terms "discourse", "genealogy", and "power-knowledge" have been embedded in the lexicon of contemporary social and cultural research.

■ Foucault's influence extends across many disciplines, including: literary and media studies, history, politics, sociology, psychiatry, cultural studies, organizational theory, social constructionism, and education.

■ Recent studies of colonialism, law, technology, gender, and race all owe much to Foucault.

■ The first volume of *The History of Sexuality* has become canonical for students of sexual and gender studies.

In this 1559 engraving, after a drawing by Pieter Bruegel, Justice stands blindfolded as people around her are being tortured. Foucault's *Discipline and Punish* is a genealogical study of prison and punishment.

It might be said that all knowledge is linked to the essential forms of cruelty.

Mental Illness and Psychology (1976)

philosophical attacks on **phenomenology** and Marxism than for its complex and nuanced analysis of the human sciences.

By the end of the 1960s, Foucault had come to acknowledge the shortcomings of his "archaeology of knowledge". Among other things, its consideration of both power and power-knowledge was at best partial, if not oblique. His inaugural lecture at the Collège de France, "The Discourse on Language" (1971), was a transitional text in which he subordinated "archaeology" to the "genealogical" form of discourse. The purpose of "genealogical" discourse was to show that a system of thought, uncovered through "archaeology", was the result of particular, contingent (not inevitable) historical events.

The Genealogies

Discipline and Punish: The Birth of the Prison (1975) is a genealogical study of prison and punishment. Foucault charts the rapid shift in the nineteenth century from "monarchical punishment" – brutal acts of public torture or execution designed to repress the populace – to

"disciplinary punishment", in which certain figures (prison officers, psychologists, parole officers) are given power over the prisoner. He used **Jeremy Bentham**'s Panopticon – a circular prison design in which a central, unseen guard observes all prisoners and all instances of "deviance" – as the epitome of power-knowledge (*pouvoir-savoir*).

Foucault emphasizes how this modern mode of discipline extends to the effective control of an entire society, with factories, hospitals, and schools modeled on the same paradigm. The modern world's systems of examination, observation, assessment, and surveillance are all vehicles of control or "normalization".

In *The Will to Knowledge* (1976), Volume I of his incomplete *History of Modern Sexuality*, Foucault delineates sexuality as a system of discourses that came into existence during the nineteenth century – created, he argued, by the desire to regulate sex, and to define and prohibit certain kinds of behavior. Sexuality, then, is a nexus of concepts and relationships brought into being through a complex process of naming the forbidden, in order to control and regulate it.

Noam Chomsky

A linguist, who revolutionized the science of language and mind, Chomsky famously claimed that our knowledge of language is innate. A prominent critic of corporate organization and the US political system, he is now equally renowned for his political activism and his writings on value and society. As well as being a scientist and philosopher of the first rank, Chomsky is also an important public figure.

Born Avram Noam Chomsky in 1928, in Philadelphia, Pennsylvania, to Jewish parents, Chomsky was the son of a Hebrew scholar. He grew up immersed in Hebrew culture and language.

At the time of writing, Chomsky is at the forefront of theoretical linguistics and philosophical discussions of language and the mind, and an intellectual figurehead for political activists. He first studied philosophy under **Nelson Goodman** and linguistics under Zellig Harris (1909–92) at the University of Pennsylvania. In the 1950s Chomsky established important mathematical results in the theory of **computable functions**. The work in linguistics for which he became famous began with his development of the theory of **generative grammar**, widely considered the most significant contribution to the science of language to date. A generative grammar is a special system of rules that generates all the sentences of a language. Chomsky argued that generative grammars are a part of the human mind, though not consciously known, that allow us to speak and understand language.

Chomsky became a key figure in the growth of **cognitive science**. This replaced the **behaviorist** approach to **psychology** that was prevalent in the 1960s and was lent philosophical support by **Gilbert Ryle** and **W. V. O. Quine**. The behaviorists thought that language and other mental capacities should be understood in terms of behavioral responses to environmental stimuli. Chomsky argued that the complexity of language has to be understood at a mental or "cognitive" level that underlies human behavior. His theories of the distinctive cognitive principles involved in language became a model for studying other human capacities.

Chomsky was prominent among intellectual critics of the Vietnam War and is now a prolific critic of the political administration, media, and foreign policy of the United States.

Essential philosophy

Cognitivism

Chomsky's 1959 attack on B. F. Skinner's book *Verbal Behavior* (1957) was among the most important factors in the demise of behaviorism. Behaviorists attempted to explain psychological capacities in terms of stimulus and response. They had some success explaining the behavior of rats in simple experiments, where rats were conditioned to press a bar a certain number of times (the response) in order to receive food (the stimulus).

Chomsky made it clear that the behaviorist model was inadequate to the task of explaining human language, for it fails to explain the most basic grammatical facts. Moreover, most of our speech is a matter of choosing to express ourselves rather than reacting to a clearly defined stimulus. To understand language and other highly organized human capacities, we need to understand the cognitive systems that underlie behavior: this view is called **cognitivism**.

Universal grammar

Chomsky was struck by the fact that children grasp their native tongue in only a few years. The languages they acquire work according to complex principles but children pick them up without explicit instruction and irrespective of their general intelligence. The child faces a "poverty of stimulus" for learning its language and yet acquires the language with ease. Chomsky traced the problem of how we can know so much on the basis of so little experience back to **Plato**. To solve "Plato's Problem", Chomsky hypothesized that children have some innate knowledge of languages, a **universal grammar** common to all languages which limits greatly the languages that can be learnt (this is sometimes called the "innateness hypothesis"). The "principles" of universal grammar have a number of open "parameters" – like switches that can be flipped one way or the other by experience – so that children in different speech environments acquire different languages (the "principles and parameters" approach). Chomsky sees universal grammar as a development of **René Descartes'** **innate ideas**. Universal grammar offers the prospect of understanding a distinctive part of human nature in terms of our biological endowment.

The structure of language

In his early works on generative grammar, Chomsky developed the view that sentences have more than one level of structure. They have a "deep structure" that fixes the meaning of a sentence but

Legacy, truth, consequence

■ Chomsky has exerted an influence on contemporary philosophical thought about language and the mind rivalled only by **Ludwig Wittgenstein** among modern thinkers. There are few supporters of the behaviorism he vanquished.

■ Though Chomsky's "innateness hypothesis" is controversial, most linguists and philosophers now agree that our faculty of language is a biologically endowed part of human nature.

■ Chomsky's work on grammar has informed recent **philosophy of language**, uncovering highly intricate structures recognized only by humans, and special principles that generate an infinite number of sentences.

Noam Chomsky became a leading opponent of the Vietnam War.

> ... the faculty mediating human communication appears remarkably different from that of other living creatures ... the human faculty of language appears to be organized like the genetic code – hierarchical, generative, recursive, and virtually limitless with respect to its scope and expression.

Marc D. Hauser, Noam Chomsky and W. Tecumseh Fitch, *The Faculty of Language: What Is It, Who Has It, and How Did It Evolve?* (2002)

also a "surface structure" that is much closer to the sounds which we hear. The rules by which deep structures are mapped onto surface structures, are called "transformations". The different levels of structure are needed to explain the similarity in meaning between sentences like "John kicked the ball", which has an active form, and the passive "The ball was kicked by John". They have the same meaning because they have the same deep structure but they look different (and sound different when uttered) because the deep structure has two different transformations into surface structures.

Chomsky has recently set a new agenda in linguistics, the Minimalist Program, which focuses on economy and efficiency in the design of the linguistic system – jettisoning all but those rules that are absolutely necessary to building linguistic structures. Successes in minimalist theorizing have suggested to Chomsky that the language faculty may be a near to perfectly efficient system.

Power

A central tenet of Chomsky's political thought is that political power must be explicitly justified on rational grounds. Chomsky believes that the onus is always on those who wield power to justify their position, and where they cannot, the power should be given up.

Chomsky is a critic of the power held by "owners" in industry and the "wage slavery" of workers, which he sees as an attack on our integrity and freedom. He has argued since the 1960s that the power the US has in foreign affairs is unjustified because **liberalism** and **democracy** are openly espoused while support is given to and obtained, often secretly, from illiberal and undemocratic states and groups when this suits US objectives. Chomsky sees the media in the US as simply a means of sustaining the power of business and government by "**manufacturing consent**" among the people. Chomsky was heavily influenced by **Bertrand Russell** and aims to bring classical liberal and radical **humanist** ideas into the current industrial, technological context. He believes in a society that is highly organized nevertheless highly democratic.

Bernard Williams

Sir Bernard Williams was one of the most important and interesting moral philosophers of the twentieth century. He rejected both the utilitarian and Kantian theories of morality and attempted to synthesize ideas from a variety of fields, including a study of ancient Greek ethics, to revitalize the tradition of moral philosophy.

Born in a small seaside resort on the southeast coast of England, the son of a civil servant, Bernard Arthur Owen Williams read classics at Oxford University, graduating with a rarely awarded distinction. In 1955 he married his first wife, Shirley Brittain-Catlin (later, Shirley Williams, MP), daughter of English political philosopher George Catlin and the novelist Vera Brittain. They moved to London, where Shirley could follow her political career. Bernard taught at University College London. Their marriage eventually dissolved, and he took up an appointment as a professor of philosophy at the University of Cambridge, where he spent nearly 20 years. In 1988 he moved to America to the University of California, Berkeley, before returning to Oxford University in the UK.

Williams was known for the sharpness of his intellect and was widely respected among his academic peers. He was one of the few philosophers of the **Anglo–American** analytic school to truly appreciate **continental philosophy**, and to unite emotional depth and logical rigor in the same work.

He was also known for his sympathy with the goals of **feminism**, and was Provost of Kings College, Cambridge, when it became one of the first all-male undergraduate colleges to admit women in 1972.

Essential philosophy

Williams was best known for his writing on **ethics** and **moral philosophy**. He found the traditional academic approaches to morality empty and dull, and argued that moral philosophy should not only be of vital interest, but should also relate to other fields such as **psychology**, history, and culture. In trying to ground his moral philosophy, he made a distinction between "thin" and "thick" ethical concepts. He suggested that the broadest terms such as "good" or "wrong" are thin, in that they can be applied universally and do not relate to the specific facts of a situation. Whereas other moral judgements, such as claiming that "lying is sinful" or that "slavery is inhumane", have a meaning that is dependent on the context – they are related to real features of the world and can thus be resolved in an **objective** manner.

He argued that "thick" ethical concepts such as "courage" or "cruelty" have been a fundamental feature of traditional societies, to the point where they could be regarded as knowledge. But the level of introspection in modern theory has meant we have lost the connection to the basics of this knowledge. This was one reason why he tried to make the contrast between modern Christian morality and the very different tropes of ancient Greek ethics, which in some respects he regarded as more robust.

This kind of subtle distinction was characteristic of Williams' thinking – he was able thus to accept elements of both **moral realism** and **moral relativism** in his thinking and to analyze the meaning of both stances. But he was less inclusive in his approach to the two dominant theories of ethics that were pervasive in contemporary academia.

Williams vs utilitarianism and Kantian ethics

His rejection of **utilitarianism** (which basically attempts to measure morality in terms of the happiness or utility produced by an action) was particularly fierce. He focused on several **counterexamples** to the theory. In the best-known one, Jim is faced with a situation where military troops confront him with 20 captured rebels and tell him that if he kills one, the others will be freed, but if he doesn't they will all be killed. Because utilitarianism focuses on consequences, it would suggest Jim should kill one rebel to save the others. But for Williams this was a troubling conclusion, because it removes the individual humanity from the equation, and ignores Jim's status as a moral agent.

Another counterexample was simpler, but still troublesome. He pointed out that utilitarianism would suggest that it was acceptable, for example, to punish a few people who parked in the wrong place by shooting them. Since the long-term results would be to increase a large number of people's utility, the judgement from consequences would seem to justify a few deaths. When opponents argued that **rule utilitarianism** would ask us to analyze the consequences of the general rule of such draconian punishment, rather than the individual act, Williams retorted that it was absurd to even make a calculation to discover whether or not this was a moral act.

- Williams' concept of internal and external reasons has generated much discussion within ethical philosophy, although he complained that it was widely misunderstood.

- He has been criticized on the grounds that he was often most effective at negating past theories rather than proposing new ones. He himself would answer that so much of traditional ethical philosophy has been fatuous, that the whole attempt to frame ethics in a system of moral theory needs to be attacked before progress can be made.

- Like Nietzsche, Williams always opposed system building. He was a philosopher who not only rejected simple solutions, but who embraced the complexity of difficult answers.

A women's rights protest, c.1970. Williams was known for his sympathy with the goals of feminism.

Most moral philosophy at most times has been empty and boring, and the number of great books in the subject ... can be literally counted on the fingers of one hand.

Morality: An Introduction to Ethics (1972)

Williams' rejection of **Immanuel Kant**'s ethics came from a different angle, and one that involved his well-known distinction between "internal" and "external" reasons. The Kantian **categorical imperative** (see pages 100–1) was basically an update of Jesus' "golden rule" in the Christian faith, which claimed that an act could be judged moral if you are acting *"only according to that maxim whereby you can at the same time will that it should become a universal law"*. Williams argued that morality shouldn't expect the individual to act in an impartial manner, claiming not only that this is a bloodless, academic approach to ethics, but that if our values and desires ("internal reasons") are removed from the ethical sphere, we lose our essential humanity.

Internal and external reasons

For Williams, morality had to be about real lives, and had to take account of self-interest. Moral philosophers had traditionally distinguished between motivating reasons for actions and normative (rule-based) reasons. The former are the reasons why we are driven to perform some action from an internal point of view. The latter are the reasons why we "should" act a certain way, from the point of view of society.

One of his most controversial claims was that reasons for action are "internal" rather than "external", that is they come from within the agent's subjective motivational set; indeed, there is no such thing as an external reason for action. He analyzed a range of actions to show that reasons that might on first sight appear to be external were in fact internal, perhaps because we feel empathy with others (as **David Hume** had suggested), because we desire to avoid punishment, or to fit in with society, or whatever. This suggests that there is a degree of **relativism** to morality, although Williams tied this in with an historical contingency to suggest that morality is partly a function of the society in which we live. Later in his career he came to appreciate the writing of **Friedrich Nietzsche**, and there is a similarity between their approaches. Both believed that the will of the individual could not be denied and that morality could only be understood through a close understanding of how moral concepts had evolved ("genealogy").

Williams has sometimes been misinterpreted as a moral and **metaphysical** relativist, but in his last book *Truth and Truthfulness: An Essay in Genealogy* (2002) he went out of his way to reject the idea that truth has no value. For Williams there were no easy answers, but truth and truthfulness were nonetheless worthwhile goals.

Jacques Derrida

Jacques Derrida was an Algerian-born French philosopher, known as the founder of deconstruction. Although Derrida at times expressed regret concerning the fate of the word "deconstruction", its popularity indicates the wide-ranging influence of his thought – in philosophy, literary criticism and theory, art and architectural theory, and in political and cultural studies. His prolific work has had a profound impact upon literary theory and Continental philosophy.

Jacques Derrida was born into a Sephardic Jewish family in 1930 at El Bias in Algeria, which at that time was still French-governed. While young he experienced anti-Semitic discrimination at the hands of the French authorities, which interrupted his schooling.

In 1952 he was admitted to the École Normale Supérieure in Paris, at a time when the establishment was a hothouse of French philosophical innovation. He studied under **Michel Foucault** and Louis Althusser (1918–90), and completed a thesis on **Edmund Husserl**. Graduating in 1956, he then received a grant to study at Harvard University in the US; he married Marguerite Aucouturier in Boston in 1957.

In 1960, two years from the end of the Algerian War of Independence, Derrida took up a teaching post in Paris at the Sorbonne, staying there until 1964. He then went on to teach at the École Normale Supérieure for 20 years, before becoming director of studies at the École des Hautes Études en Sciences Sociales, Paris, where he remained until his death.

Derrida's first book was a prize-winning translation of Husserl's *Origins of Geometry*, which included a 150-page introduction. In 1963 he published "Cogito and the History of Madness", in a critical response to Foucault's *Madness and Civilization* (1961). This caused a rupture between the two philosophers, which would never fully heal.

The year 1967 was to be his most fruitful. Aged 37, he remarkably published three books at once: *Writing and Difference*, *Speech and Phenomena*, and *Of Grammatology*, and it is in these works that the word "deconstruction" first appeared. The word caught on immediately and came to define Derrida's thought.

From the 1970s onwards, Derrida made many annual visits to American universities, where he was more warmly welcomed in literature faculties than he ever was by French institutions. He was most notably attached to Johns Hopkins and Yale universities, and the University of California at Irvine. In Britain, the 1992 award of an honorary doctorate by the University of Cambridge provoked great opposition, with detractors claiming Derrida's work was merely a triumph of style over substance.

Derrida's later writings were more concerned with issues of **ethics** and **politics**. In 2002 he collaborated on the biographical documentary *Derrida*. This was also the year he was diagnosed with pancreatic cancer, which necessitated a reduction in his work commitments. He died two years later.

Essential philosophy

Derrida argued that **Western philosophy** was characterized by a "**metaphysics** of presence" (the privileging of "being" over "appearance") and "logocentrism" (the idea that meanings exist independently of the language used to express them); that Western thought had wrongly privileged speech over writing, treating writing as a mere "supplement"; that what he called "*différance*" (a term combining the meanings of "difference" and "deferral") was a requirement of all writing; and that there was "no escaping from the text", by which he meant that the meaning of a sentence could be given only in other sentences.

Deconstruction

He coined the term "deconstruction" to describe a way of reading that reveals and subverts the assumptions and rules of thought underlying any text. According to Derrida, the idea that a text has a fixed and determinate meaning – indeed, the idea that there can even be such a thing as "meaning" – is based on metaphysical assumptions that can never be substantiated.

Meaning can never be fully "present" in language, but is always deferred endlessly (through *différance*) – as when one may look up a word in a dictionary, only to be given other words, and so on endlessly. While speech gives the illusion of a fixed origin – the presence of the speaker – which can guarantee the meaning of an utterance, writing is more clearly unauthenticated and open to unlicensed interpretation.

One of Derrida's overriding concerns in developing his strategy of deconstruction was to undertake the critical examination of the fundamental conceptual distinctions, or "oppositions", inherent in Western philosophy since the time of the ancient Greeks. These oppositions are characteristically "binary" and "hierarchical",

Legacy, truth, consequence

- The ideas of Derrida helped mark the advance from structuralism through **poststructuralism** to **postmodernism** as the predominant philosophical and critical discourse on the continent and in the US.
- The term "deconstruction" has entered the popular consciousness, even if its meaning is often diluted or divergent from Derrida's original coinage and intention.
- Derrida was an inspirational figure to the Yale School, a group of **sceptical**, **relativistic** literary critics at Yale University, who became known in the 1970s and 1980s for their deconstructionist theories. Its most prominent members were Paul de Man (1919–83) and J. Hillis Miller (b. 1928).
- Among many others, **Noam Chomsky** has expressed the view that Derrida used "pretentious rhetoric" to obscure the simplicity of his ideas. According to Foucault, Derrida practiced the method of *"obscurantisme terroriste"* (terrorism of obscurantism).

Derrida (on the right) meets the Argentinian writer Jorge Luis Borges in 1985. Some of Derrida's detractors decribed his work as an obfuscated recycling of the ideas of Borges.

involving a pair of terms in which one member of the pair is assumed to be primary or fundamental, the other secondary or derivative. Examples include nature and culture, speech and writing, mind and body, literal and metaphorical, and form and meaning, among many others.

To deconstruct an opposition is to explore the tensions and contradictions between the hierarchical ordering, especially those that are indirect or implicit. Such a deconstruction would show that the opposition is not natural or necessary but a product, or "construction", of the text itself. In philosophical terms, deconstruction is a form of **relativist scepticism** in the tradition of **Friedrich Nietzsche**.

Considered by its opponents to be a subversive instrument of **relativism** and **nihilism**, deconstruction was seen by its adherents as a tool for uncovering, by close reading, hidden blind spots and

contradictions (*aporia*) in texts that could serve to transcend conventional readings.

The deconstructive style of textual analysis commonly emphasizes the instabilities of language and meaning through puns, wordplay, and figurative expressions. Derrida's increasing playfulness in his texts, coupled with an opacity of style, led opponents to charge him with employing "obscurantism" to mask a philosophical shallowness.

Key dates

1930	Born at El Biar, Algeria.
1952	Enters the École Normale Supérieure, Paris, France; studies under Foucault and Althusser.
1956	Receives a grant to study at Harvard, US.
1957	Marries Marguerite Aucouturier in Boston.
1960–4	Teaches at the Sorbonne, Paris.
1962	Publishes a translation of Husserl's *The Origins of Geometry*
1964–84	Teaches at the École Normale Supérieure.
1967	Publishes *Writing and Difference*, *Speech and Phenomena*, and *Of Grammatology*
1970s	Begins annual visits to Yale University and Johns Hopkins University, US.
1972	Publication of *Dissemination, Positions, and Margins of Philosophy*, collections of essays, interviews, and lectures.
1976	Publishes *Glas* – a confrontation between **G. W. F. Hegel** and Jean Genet (1910–86).
1978	Publishes *The Truth In Painting* on visual art and the attempts to theorize about it.
1980	Publishes *La Carte Postale* (*The Post Card*).
1983	Contributes to establishment of the Collège International de Philosophie; becomes its first director.
1984	Appointed director of studies at École des Hautes Études en Sciences Sociales, Paris.
1986–2003	Makes annual spring visits to the University of California at Irvine, following move there from Yale of his friend J. Hillis Miller.
1987	Lectures on Martin Heidegger; follows up with *Of Spirit: Heidegger and the Question*, which addresses Heidegger's Nazism.
1992	Accepts honorary doctorate controversially awarded by University of Cambridge, UK.
2002	Takes part in documentary film *Derrida*; diagnosed with cancer of the pancreas.
2004	Dies in Paris.

There is nothing outside of the text.

Of Grammatology (1967)

Richard Rorty

Richard Rorty was an American philosopher who questioned the very foundations of philosophical method. Rorty criticized the foundationalist assumption, that all knowledge is built on unquestionable principles, which he saw at the heart of traditional epistemology (the study of knowledge). Instead he proposed a rather postmodern idea of truth as being no more than the subject of edifying discourse (or "conversation").

Richard Rorty was born in 1931 in New York City. At the age of 14 he enrolled at the University of Chicago, where **Rudolf Carnap** was one of his teachers. In his autobiographical book *Achieving Our Country*, Rorty described how, within his circle of friends at this time, "*American patriotism, redistributionist economics, anti-communism, and Deweyan pragmatism went together easily and naturally.*" He studied for a doctorate at Yale University, and went on to academic posts at Princeton, Virginia, and Stanford. His breakthrough book *Philosophy and the Mirror of Nature* (1979) argued that the general distinction between **objective** and **subjective reality** is meaningless. He began to acquire a reputation as a controversial figure in the philosophy establishment. Among other things he asserted that the whole project of philosophy was less important than it believed itself to be, and that philosophers had spent hundreds of years trying to mark out an academic space in which they could make a claim to unique, **foundational** knowledge. Perhaps unsurprisingly he has attracted many criticisms, but his work nevertheless remains interesting and challenging in the degree to which it embodies an "anti-philosophical" mode of philosophy.

Essential philosophy

Rorty's early work was based on the **analytic philosophy** that was dominant in the **Anglo-American** tradition. He started to revise his position after studying the writing of **John Dewey**, which led him to reconsider how truth works. For Dewey and the **pragmatists** a proposition is true if it helps us understand a problem or choose the right action. Rorty would sometimes call himself a pragmatist, although the label was fiercely disputed by critics (especially Susan Haack, *b.* 1945). In fact Rorty's position on truth took elements of pragmatism, and also elements from **Ludwig Wittgenstein's philosophy of language**, which treated meaning as a product of social interaction.

His 1979 book *Philosophy and the Mirror of Nature* argued against the idea that truth can be measured by some kind of similarity between the objective world that is "out there" and the subjective world in our minds. He argued that sentences or **propositions** do not stand in a relation of correspondence to facts about the world, and that thinking is not a mental mirror of the external world.

Against foundationalism

Rorty drew on the arguments of two contemporaries to construct an argument against the search for the foundations of knowledge ("**foundationalism**"). From **W. V. O. Quine** he adopted criticisms of the distinction between **analytic** propositions (true in virtue of their meaning) and **synthetic** propositions (true because of facts about the world). From Wilfrid Sellars (1912–89), he took a repudiation of the idea that the content of **perception** is a simple, given truth that we can isolate (as the **phenomenologists** had claimed to do with their "bracketing" – see **Edmund Husserl**, pages 134–5).

In Rorty's view, the combination of these two arguments removed any possibility of foundational truths. All we could do to search for the "truth" was to take a pragmatic, scientific approach. He referred to Thomas Kuhn's (1922–96) **philosophy of science** in which periods of normal science (when we proceed on received theory) alternate with periods of abnormal science, when our beliefs suffer a crisis and we look for a new paradigm or resolution.

Rorty wrote that "*we see knowledge as a matter of conversation and of social practice, rather than as an attempt to mirror nature.*" This "conversational" theory of knowledge was treated with some derision by contemporaries, but he meant it to point to Wittgensteinian ideas of the fluidity and social basis of meaning.

The two traditions

Throughout the twentieth century the world of philosophy was divided between the Anglo-American analytic tradition and the **continental tradition**, which encompassed phenomenology, **post-modernism**, and other theories that were generally regarded with suspicion by Anglo-American academics. Rorty was one philosopher who worked hard to unite the two traditions later in his career. He wrote extensively on thinkers such as **Michel Foucault** and **Jacques Derrida**, as well as figures from beyond philosophy such as Marcel Proust and Vladimir Nabokov.

Legacy, truth, consequence

- Rorty's role as an "anti-philosopher" has inevitably provoked some criticism. At times his negative analysis seems more powerful than his solutions, and even some writers who oppose simplistic ideas of truth balk at Rorty's theory of truth as conversation.

- He was a **liberal** thinker, who defended the approach of **John Rawls**, and made a strong philosophical case for recognizing human rights. Nonetheless, some liberal writers have attacked his political work.

- His writing on major figures from Continental and Anglo-American philosophy has been attacked both as elitist (in the idea of "ironism") and as a misappropriation of his heroes. However, Rorty defended himself in *The Historiography of Philosophy: Four Genres* (1984), in which he pointed out that he was reinterpreting these thinkers as a critic might reinterpret a novel. This fits in with Rorty's Nietzschean idea that philosophy can help us to recreate ourselves.

Key dates

1931 Born in New York City, US.

1945–52 Studies at the University of Chicago.

1952–6 Studies for a doctorate at Yale University.

1961 Becomes professor of philosophy at Princeton University, where he stays for 20 years.

1979 *Philosophy and the Mirror of Nature* is published.

1981 Receives a five-year fellowship from the MacArthur Foundation.

1982 Becomes Kenan Professor of Humanities, University of Virginia, marking his growing public status as a philosopher with a reach beyond the usual bounds of his discipline.

1982 *Consequences of Pragmatism* is published.

1989 *Contingency, Irony, and Solidarity* is published.

1991 *Essays on Heidegger and Others: Philosophical Papers* is published.

1998 Takes up an appointment in the Department of Comparative Literature at Stanford University.

1998 *Achieving Our Country: Leftist Thought in Twentieth-Century America* is published.

2007 Dies of pancreatic cancer at his home in California.

Time saving Truth from Envy and Discord, by Nicola Poussin, 1640. Rorty proposed a postmodern idea of truth as being no more than the subject of edifying discourse.

> *Philosophy makes progress not by becoming more rigorous but by becoming more imaginative.*
>
> Truth and Progress: Philosophical Papers (1998)

He identified the idea of "ironism" in opposition to **Platonism**'s belief in eternal facts. By ironism he referred to those writers who attempted to explain the way that meaning works, even while struggling with the essentially unfinished, changeable nature of language and meaning. For Rorty no vocabulary was ever complete, and every philosopher merely identified problems and essayed possible next steps. The ironist understands that they are using an incomplete vocabulary (and one that can never be completed) and that their arguments cannot dispel all doubt.

The role of philosophy

Looking back over philosophical history, Rorty thought that since **René Descartes** philosophers had been responding to the dominance of **empiricism** and science in various ways. **Cartesian doubt** and **scepticism** tried to point out that, while science seemed to be a successful way of acquiring knowledge, doubt could be cast even on its basic assumptions. Meanwhile the empiricists had cast themselves as the foundation of all science and mathematics. In both cases philosophers had been seeking a role in a world where science was the dominant discipline.

He considered writers such as **Bertrand Russell** and **Edmund Husserl** as foundationalists who had sought to create an infallible system through their respective philosophies. Their failure to do so was no reason to condemn their thinking. They had been responding to the problems as they perceived them, as part of the ongoing articulation of new ways to think and live.

This line of thought makes Rorty's views on philosophy notably literary. By insisting on the role of irony, doubt, and conversation, he was democratizing the idea of philosophy, and creating a kind of meta-philosophy, in which he analyzed the motivations and potentialities of philosophers, rather than simply judging their contribution to a "*search for truth*". Sometimes his writing is closer to that of a literary critic than a traditional philosopher, as he draws out the themes and meanings to be found in the writers he admires.

John Searle

John Searle has made major contributions to the philosophy of language and the philosophy of mind, and more recently to social philosophy. His most famous line of reasoning is the Chinese Room Argument, which is widely regarded as a penetrating philosophical critique of artificial intelligence, forcing us to reconsider the fundamental questions about what it is to have a mind and to think.

John Rogers Searle was born in 1932 in Denver, Colorado. His formative philosophical years were spent at Oxford: he arrived as a Rhodes scholar in 1952, stayed for seven years, then became a don at Christ Church, working closely with J. L. Austin (1911–60), H. Paul Grice (1913–88), and **John Rawls**. His first significant philosophical work was published in *Mind* in 1958, focusing on issues in the use of language, and his first book *Speech Acts*, published in 1969, developed a theory of the different ways in which language can be used to communicate. Since then he has published over a dozen books and 200 articles.

In the 1970s Searle made his appearance in the public arena, defending the idea that the things we say and write have fixed and objective meanings, against **Jacques Derrida**'s claim that they are indefinitely interpretable. In 1984 he gave the prestigious Reith Lectures, hammering home an argument, for which he was becoming famous, that understanding the workings of computers does not answer fundamental questions about the nature of the human mind. Around this time he became embroiled in a lawsuit against the Californian Supreme Court to overturn their rent control policy in a case now known as the "Searle Decision".

In addition to developing a theory of consciousness, over the past two decades Searle has begun to build a theory of social reality, first aired at length in his 1995 book, *The Construction of Social Reality*. He has also completed important work on the topics of **perception** and **intentionality**.

Searle's work is famous for its clarity and accessibility, and his commitment to commonsense as a cornerstone of philosophical thought. He is the Slusser Professor of Philosophy at the University of California, Berkeley.

Essential philosophy

The Chinese Room Argument

The question of whether a computer can think is one that exercises science fiction writers, scientists, and philosophers. Searle was influenced by the work of **Alan Turing**, who proposed a test that scientists could develop computers to try and pass, known as the Turing Test. A computer passes the Turing Test if it outputs responses to questions that are indistinguishable to us from the responses that a human being would make. Turing's own attitude to the idea that computers could think was, however, somewhat ambiguous.

Searle's Chinese Room Argument is an argument against the possibility of mere computers being intelligent. Computers, in the relevant sense, include more than just the home computers, laptops, and pocket calculators that we use on a daily basis, extending to any device that processes symbols in a strictly rule-governed way. Searle asks us to imagine a man, who understands English, sitting in a room into which Chinese symbols are fed through a slot. The man is alone in the room with only a book stating rules for manipulating Chinese symbols. The man uses the book to look up the Chinese symbols that are fed into the room and then writes down further Chinese symbols according to what the book tells him to write. These symbols he then passes back to the outside of the room. The man is effectively a computer, computing certain outputs of Chinese symbols from certain inputted symbols, according to fixed rules. Although the symbol manipulation the man carries out in the room determines the right Chinese symbols as outputs given the Chinese symbols as inputs, Searle thought it clear that this is insufficient for the man to have an understanding of Chinese.

But the man in the room does just what a computer does: manipulates symbols according to fixed rules. Hence, if the man in the room fails to understand Chinese, then even when a suitably programmed computer produces the right Chinese outputs given its Chinese inputs, it will fail to understand Chinese, in principle. Computing the right function is, therefore, not enough for understanding language and, by extension, other intelligent behavior. Searle thought that his Chinese Room Argument highlighted that in outputting certain symbols, given certain inputs, computers pay attention only to the syntax (the form or shape) of the symbols but have no access to the semantics (or meaning) of the symbols and so they don't understand what they are doing. By contrast, human minds recognize and

Can the human brain be simulated by a computer? Can machines think? The philosophy of artificial intelligence is an attempt to answer these questions, and an area to which Searle has made important contributions.

■ Early work on speech acts by Searle has been the subject of much philosophical insight into the use of language and has also been developed by scientific linguists.

■ Searle's Chinese Room Argument has connections to an argument by **Gottfried Liebniz** dating from the eighteenth century. Lieniz asked us to imagine a physical system, like a mill, that behaves in such a way that we might suppose it to think and have experiences though when we look inside it we find no such thing.

■ Searle's argument is the most direct and powerful challenge to proponents of **artificial intelligence**. It also presents a challenge to the prevailing **functionalist** orthodoxy in the **philosophy of mind** that treats minds as rule-based information processing systems. No philosophical argument has been more discussed in **cognitive science** in the last 25 years.

The point of the argument is this: if the man in the room does not understand Chinese on the basis of implementing the appropriate program for understanding Chinese then neither does any other digital computer solely on that basis because no computer, qua computer, has anything the man does not have.

"The Chinese Room" in *The MIT Encyclopedia of the Cognitive Sciences* (1999)

understand meanings, but not merely by manipulating symbols without regard to their meaning. While Searle took his argument to show that the human mind computing symbols could not be the full explanation of what it is to be intelligent, he still believed that studying computers might be useful in understanding what minds do.

Social reality
Searle's theory of social reality is that social institutions are constituted by the collective mental states of the populations that participate in them. A good example of Searle's theory in action is the way that the social institution of money is sustained. We all treat pieces of metal and paper, that in themselves are worth very little, as valuable. Searle argues that their value is constituted by the mental states of those that participate in the institution and are prepared to treat them as such. He thinks that this kind of explanation applies to social institutions generally. In particular, he claims that the institution of political power is sustained by the collective attitudes of the population who ascribe certain statuses to political positions and systems.

Key dates

1932	Born in Denver, Colorado, US.
1969	*Speech Acts*, on the uses of language, builds on over a decade's work at Oxford, in the UK, with J. L. Austin and H. Paul Grice.
1980	Publishes "Minds, Brains, and Programs" in the journal *Behavior and Brain Sciences*, which sets out his Chinese Room Argument. It was published along with responses from 27 cognitive scientists and Searle's replies to them.
1984	Gives prestigious Reith Lectures.
1995	Unveils his theory of social reality in *The Construction of Social Reality*.

Robert Nozick

Robert Nozick was the first major American political philosopher to emerge after John Rawls' *A Theory of Justice* was published in 1971. Nozick's *Anarchy, State and Utopia* (1974), a direct response to John Rawls, laid out an alternative libertarian approach to rights and responsibilities in society. Besides political philosophy, he also became known for his work in epistemology and decision theory.

Born in Brooklyn, New York City, in 1938, Robert Nozick was the son of a Jewish businessman from Russia. Nozick became hooked on philosophy after reading **Plato**'s *Republic* at the age of 15, and his interest led him to Princeton University, where he was awarded a doctorate under the supervision of Carl Hempel (1905–97), with a thesis on **decision theory**. In 1969 he became one of the youngest professors in Harvard University's history. Greatly admired for his sharp and wide-ranging intellect, he was also known for his engaging, "thinking out loud" teaching style.

Initially attracted to the left-wing movements of the 1960s, he was later influenced by conservative economists and defenders of **capitalism**, such as Friedrich Hayek (1899–1992), Milton Friedman (1912–2006), Ludwig von Mises (1881–1973), and Ayn Rand (1905–82). This led him to address political theory and, eventually, to produce his first and most famous book, *Anarchy, State, and Utopia* (1974), soon regarded by right-wing thinkers as an exemplary defense of **libertarianism** and an influential philosophical counter-point to **John Rawls**' defense of social-democratic **liberalism**.

A curiously engaging writer who came up with a wide range of memorable thought experiments, including the "utility monster" and the "experience engine", to support his arguments, Nozick was also unusual among philosophers in the degree to which he brought ideas from other disciplines, including psychology and economics, into his work.

Essential philosophy

In *Anarchy, State and Utopia*, Nozick argues for a libertarian viewpoint, in direct opposition to Rawls' vision of a redistributive, liberal **democracy**. Where Rawls promotes the redistribution of wealth to support a welfare state and help the disadvantaged, Nozick argues for the primacy of the rights of the individual, and nothing more than a minimal state. In Nozick's view, justice should be measured by reference to the means through which social policy is enacted, rather than through its consequences, so direct action by the state is rarely warranted. Rawls doesn't count property rights as being part of the primary rights that would be instigated by his imaginary representatives acting behind a "veil of ignorance" (see pages 178–9), whereas Nozick develops a complex theory of entitlement, derived from **John Locke**'s work, to underpin such rights.

Nozick doesn't believe in completely abolishing the state. He pictures a process whereby the minimal state will emerge, as people pay for the services of protection agencies, and economies of scale mean that one dominant protection agency emerges (in other words a state that provides basic policing and military protection to its citizens). He concludes that from an "ultraminimal state" the workings of an "invisible hand" (a phrase that echoes **Adam Smith**'s use of the term, but that Nozick uses in a way that can also be compared to Darwinian "natural selection") will produce a minimal state, which is a more stable solution.

The state of nature

Nozick is unusually open in admitting the assumptions and possible weaknesses in his arguments. In *Anarchy, State and Utopia* he acknowledges that the starting point of a Lockean "state of nature", in which there is no governing state but individuals have rights, can be challenged. However, he defends his starting position with his "entitlement theory", which – following John Locke, **Immanuel Kant**, and Friedrich Hayek – treats humans as ends in themselves, and judges that humans have the right to their property unless they consent to have it redistributed.

One weakness in all such libertarian arguments is that in returning to a "state of nature", they fail to recognize that the concepts of property, money, and the exchange of goods and services are social constructs, and we cannot therefore strip away society and assume that these concepts remain. However, starting from his assumptions, Nozick makes a powerful argument for the idea that no redistributive state can be moral.

The social contract and utilitarianism

Nozick differs from Locke in his rejection of the whole concept of the "**social contract**" (the idea that there is an unspoken contract between the individual and the state which justifies the existence of the state). In Nozick's view, the social contract is a redundant idea. Individuals would naturally group together for self-interested reasons and, guided by the invisible hand, a minimal state would emerge in any case. This is the kind of state the classical liberalism refers to as the "night watchman" state.

Rawls had rejected **utilitarianism**, Nozick rejected it even more forcefully. He put forward two thought experiments against it. The

I know that I am at my desk, even though I don't know that I am not a brain in a vat.

Philosophical Explanations (1981)

Capitalism's social pyramid, a poster from 1911. Nozick advocated private property, but unlike the anarcho-capitalists, still believed in a minimal state.

Legacy, truth, consequence

■ Nozick addressed problems in epistemology and metaphysics, but it is his early work in political theory that has received the greatest attention and will stand as his most significant and lasting contribution.

■ As a former member of the New Left movements, Nozick was never comfortable with his supposed status as theoretician of a national political movement and ideologue of the right. In a 1978 article in *The New York Times Magazine* he said that "*right-wing people like the pro-free-market argument, but don't like the arguments for individual liberty in cases like gay rights – although I view them as an interconnecting whole …*"

Key dates

1938	Born in Brooklyn, New York, US.
1959	Awarded a degree from Columbia College.
1963	Receives a doctorate from Princeton University.
1969	Becomes a professor at Harvard University, where he stays for the remainder of his academic career.
1974	*Anarchy, State, and Utopia* is published.
1981	*Philosophical Explanations* is published.
1982	Cultural advisor to US Delegation to UNESCO Conference on World Cultural Policy.
1987/8	Marries the poet Gjertrud Schnackenberg.
1993	*The Nature of Rationality* is published.
1997	Visiting fellow at St Catherine's College, Oxford University, UK.
2001	*Invariances: The Structure of the Objective World* is published.
2002	Dies after a struggle with cancer, in Cambridge, Massachusetts.

"utility monster" is an individual who gains a great deal of utility by depriving others of theirs. Nozick points out that utilitarianism could suggest that society was best served by this individual taking everyone else's utility. Secondly, to argue against the idea that felt experience is the only thing that matters, he suggested the "experience engine", a device that would give us experiences but no interaction. He points out that we would probably not volunteer to be plugged into the experience engine for life.

The problem of knowledge

In the field of epistemology, twentieth-century **analytic philosophy** had struggled with the old **Platonic** theory that knowledge could be defined as justified true belief. Edmund Gettier (*b.* 1927) put forward some problematic **counterexamples** to this definition. For instance, Farmer Brown believes he sees his cow Daisy in a field. It is true that Daisy is there, but in fact she is out of sight behind a barn, and what Farmer Brown actually saw in the imagined case is another cow or a paper image of Daisy. So far, Brown's belief about Daisy is true and he is justified in his belief because whatever he saw looked just like Daisy, but this isn't a case of knowledge because Brown's belief is based on his seeing something that isn't Daisy and Daisy's presence is entirely coincidental. These Gettier examples seem to show that having a true belief that one is justified in holding is not sufficient to have knowledge.

In his 1981 work *Philosophical Explanations*, Nozick proposed that instead of justification, we should add "truth tracking" to our definition. So if a belief is true the further condition it must meet to qualify as knowledge is this: "*if it were true we would believe it, and if were not true we would not believe it*". This is an external condition – it does not give the subject complete confidence in his knowledge, but it does define a belief that will always track the truth as being knowledge. And it sidesteps the Gettier examples quite effectively – Farmer Brown would have believed the same thing whether Daisy was behind the barn or not, so his belief does not "track the truth". Nozick uses this theory for a limited rejection of **scepticism**. Against the kind of modern sceptical scenarios inspired by **René Descartes**, such as the possibility that I might be merely a brain in a vat having all my experiences induced by a scientist, Nozick argues that I can know many of the things that I ordinarily take myself as knowing without knowing that I am not a brain in a vat. He suggests that I can know a **proposition** if I can track its truth across the closest possible alternative worlds in which it is false or in which it still holds true. But this does not require me to be able to rule out remote sceptical hypotheses. So I can know that I am sitting here now without knowing that I am not a brain in a vat. Nozick's ingenious response to scepticism is still the subject of much scrutiny.

Peter Singer

Peter Singer is a contemporary philosopher, whose utilitarianism follows in the footsteps of Jeremy Bentham and John Stuart Mill. Best known for his writing in areas of applied ethics, his best-selling *Animal Liberation* argues that most treatment meted out to animals is morally intolerable. He has put the ideas and theories of moral philosophy to work in assessing the morality of euthanasia, in vitro fertilization, the distribution of world resources, and many allied topics.

Peter Singer's parents were Viennese Jews who escaped the German annexation of Austria and fled to Australia in 1938. Three of his grandparents, however, were less fortunate, perishing in Nazi concentration camps.

Singer was born in 1946 in Melbourne, Australia, where his father had become a successful importer of tea and coffee. Peter grew up in a prosperous, happy family. After school, he studied law, history, and philosophy at the University of Melbourne, graduating in 1967.

He gained his master's degree in 1969 with a thesis entitled "Why Should I Be Moral?" A subsequent scholarship enabled him to study for a graduate degree at Oxford University in the UK. The resulting thesis on civil disobedience, supervized by the **utilitarian** philosopher R. M. Hare (1919–2002), was published as *Democracy and Disobedience* in 1973.

After spending two years as a Radcliffe lecturer at University College, Oxford, he was visiting professor at New York University 1973-4. During this time he researched and wrote his second book, *Animal Liberation* (1975).

He returned to Australia in 1975, serving first as senior philosophy lecturer at La Trobe University before taking the philosophy chair at Monash University from 1977 to 1999. While at Monash he founded its Centre for Human Bioethics, as well as serving on numerous government committees.

One of his most comprehensive works, *Practical Ethics*, was published in 1979. Since then he has published widely on issues of ethics, animal rights, IVF, euthanasia, disability, the environment and "bioethics". Unafraid to confront difficult questions with utilitarian logic, Singer has inevitably stirred much controversy over the years. His argument that some animals have more sentience, and therefore a greater right to live, than certain human forms of life (such as fetuses or severely disabled children), has attracted particularly virulent criticism.

In 1999 Singer became Ira W. DeCamp Professor of Bioethics at the University Center for Human Values, Princeton University in the US. Since 2005 he has combined that role part-time with a Laureate professorship at the University of Melbourne's Centre for Applied Philosophy and Public Ethics.

Essential philosophy

Singer's work is marked by a strong commitment to **preference utilitarianism** and by a wish to displace the morality of what he terms the "Judaeo-Christian inheritance". He is in many senses a direct descendant of **Jeremy Bentham** and **John Stuart Mill**, who classified the "utility" of an action according to how much pleasure, or how little pain, it brought. However, Singer's utilitarianism measures the desirability of an action according to the preferences of those involved: so, for example, Person A's preference to kill Person B is morally wrong, as it goes against Person B's preference to live. A core tenet of Singer's utilitarianism is that everyone's interests should be considered equally when making decisions:

> "*If I have seen that from an ethical point of view I am just one person among the many in my society, and my interests are no more important, from the point of view of the whole, than the similar interests of others within my society, I am ready to see that, from a still larger point of view, my society is just one among other societies, and the interests of members of my society are no more important, from that larger perspective, than the similar interests of members of*

other societies … Taking the impartial element in ethical reasoning to its logical conclusion means, first, accepting that we ought to have equal concern for all human beings."

> *The Expanding Circle: Ethics and Sociobiology* (1981)

Singer takes sentience – or the capacity to experience pleasure or pain – as a key morally relevant characteristic of a "being" or "person" (note that it is not sufficient on this moral scale to be simply a "human being" – the logic here is that many animal beings have more sentience, or "personhood", than some human beings). Another key characteristic emphasized by Singer is a being's capacity to envisage a past and a future.

Animal Liberation

Published in 1975, *Animal Liberation* was a major formative influence on the animal liberation movement. Singer denotes "animal rights" as derived from utilitarian principles, particularly the principle of minimizing suffering. He argues against what he calls speciesism: discrimination on the grounds that a being belongs

Legacy, truth, consequence

- *Animal Liberation* had a tremendous effect – not only on individuals, bringing many people to vegetarianism, but also on society. It turned the notion of animal liberation into a respectable moral cause.

- *"Peter Singer may be the most controversial philosopher alive; he is certainly among the most influential."* (Assessment by Michael Specter in "The Dangerous Philosopher", New Yorker, Sept 6, 1999).

- Singer's appointment to Princeton University has given him far greater capacity to raise the popular consciousness on matters of ethics. He has commented that *"for one thing, it gave me a platform in the United States … if you have a chair [in the US] you're more likely to get invited to write articles for the New York Times, for example, which are seen then by many millions of readers. This may not be a good thing in itself, but since it exists, I feel that I have a duty to use it to try and get the kind of viewpoints that I think are important for Americans to listen to."* (Peter Singer interview, *Talking Heads*, ABC1, May 28, 2007)

In *Animal Liberation*, Singer condemns animal testing except where the benefit is greater than the harm done to the animal. The picture shows "Ham", a chimpanzee used by NASA to test the Mercury Capsule before launching the astronaut Alan Shepard in May 1961.

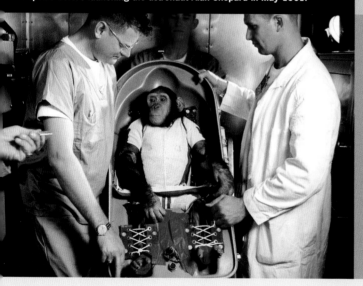

Key dates

1946	Born in Melbourne, Australia.
1967	Graduates from the University of Melbourne.
1971	Gains a graduate degree (B. Phil) from Oxford University, in England, under R. M. Hare's supervision.
1973	Publishes his B. Phil thesis as *Democracy and Disobedience*.
1973–4	Visiting professor of philosophy at New York University.
1975	Publishes *Animal Liberation*.
1977–99	Professor of philosophy at Monash University, Victoria, Australia; founds the Centre for Human Bioethics while at Monash.
1979	Publishes *Practical Ethics*.
1982	Elected fellow of the Academy of the Humanities in Australia.
1989	Elected fellow of the Academy of the Social Sciences in Australia.
1999	Appointed Ira W. DeCamp Professor of Bioethics at Princeton University, US.
2005	Appointed Laureate professor at the Centre for Applied Philosophy and Public Ethics, University of Melbourne.

> *If we can prevent something bad without sacrificing anything of comparable significance, we ought to do it; absolute poverty is bad; there is some poverty we can prevent without sacrificing anything of comparable moral significance; therefore we ought to prevent some absolute poverty.*
>
> Practical Ethics (1979)

to a certain species. He holds the preferences of all beings capable of suffering to be worthy of equal consideration.

Practical Ethics

Singer's most comprehensive work, *Practical Ethics* (1979), analyzes in detail why and how beings' interests should be weighed. His principle of equal consideration of interests does not dictate equal treatment of all those with interests, since different interests warrant different treatment. Not only does his principle justify different treatment for different interests, but it allows different treatment for the same interest when diminishing marginal utility is a factor – favoring, for instance, a starving person's interest in food over the same interest of someone who is only slightly hungry.

Singer holds that a being's preferences should always be weighed according to that being's concrete properties. He favors a "journey" model of life, which is tolerant of some frustrated desires and explains why persons who have embarked on their journeys are not replaceable. Only a personal interest in continuing to live brings the journey model into play. This model also explains the priority that Singer attaches to preferences over trivial desires and pleasures.

Practical Ethics includes arguments for the redistribution of wealth to ameliorate absolute poverty, and for resettling refugees on a large scale in industrialized countries. It also delineates Singer's environmentalism in utilitarian terms: ecological degradation being a profound threat to sentient life.

Select Bibliography and Further Reading

Listed here is a selection of sources that the reader may wish to consult, in addition to the sources noted in the individual entries on philosophers.

Ackrill, J. L., *Aristotle the Philosopher* (Oxford University Press, 1981)

Adams, Marilyn McCord, *William Ockham* (Notre Dame, Ind., 1987)

Aldridge, A. O., *Man Of Reason: The Life Of Thomas Paine* (London: The Cresset Press, 1960)

Altham, J. E. J. & Harrison, Ross, *World, Mind, and Ethics: Essays on the Ethical Philosophy of Bernard Williams* (Cambridge University Press, 1995)

Ames, Roger T., Hall, David L. (trans.), *Laozi, Dao De Jing* (Ballentine, 2003)

Appignanesi, Lisa, *Simone de Beauvoir* (Haus Publishing, 2005)

Arthur Fairbanks (ed. & trans.), *The First Philosophers of Greece* (London: K. Paul, Trench, Trubner, 1898)

Audard, Catherine, *John Rawls* (McGill-Queen's University Press, 2007)

Ayer, A. J., *Voltaire* (Random House, 1986)

Bacon, Michael, *Richard Rorty: Pragmatism and Political Liberalism* (Lexington, 2007)

Baggini, Julian & Stangroom, Jeremy (eds.), *Great Thinkers A–Z* (Continuum, 2004)

Becker, E., *The Structure of Evil* (New York, 1968)

Beiser, Frederick C. (ed.), *The Cambridge Companion to Hegel* (Cambridge University Press, 1993)

Blackburn, Simon, *The Oxford Dictionary of Philosophy* (Oxford University Press, 1996)

Boulton, James T. (ed.), *Edmund Burke: A Philosophical Enquiry into the Origin of our Ideas of the Sublime and Beautiful* (Routledge, 1958)

Bresnan, Patrick S., *Awakening: An Introduction to the History of Eastern Thought* (Pearson Prentice Hall, 3rd edn, 2007)

Briggs, A., *The Age of Improvement* (Longman, 3rd edn, 1983)

Broad, C. D. & Lewy, C., *Leibniz: An Introduction* (Cambridge University Press, 1975)

Bruner, J. S., *Actual Minds, Possible Worlds* (Harvard University Press, 1986)

Buchan, James, *The Authentic Adam Smith: His Life and Ideas* (Norton/Atlas, 2006)

Carman, Taylor & Hansen, Mark B. N., *The Cambridge Companion to Merleau-Ponty,* (Cambridge University Press, 2004)

Cassirer, E., *The Myth of the State* (Yale University Press, 1946)

Cassirer, Ernst; Korner, Stephan; & Haden, James, *Kant's Life and Thought* (Yale University Press, 1986)

Chisolm, R., "The Problem of Empiricism", *The Journal of Philosophy*, 45 (1948)

Collinson, Diané, *Fifty Major Philosophers* (Routledge, 1987)

Cooper, David, *Existentialism* (Oxford, 1990)

Copenhaver, B. P., and Schmitt, C. B., *Renaissance Philosophy* (Oxford University Press, 1992)

Copleston, F., *A History of Philosophy* (Burnes & Oates, 1960)

Cottingham, J., *Descartes* (Oxford University Press, 1986)

Cranston, Maurice, *The Noble Savage: Jean-Jacques Rousseau, 1754–62* (University of Chicago Press, 1991)

Curley, Edwin (ed.), *The Collected Works of Spinoza* (Princeton University Press, 1985)

Danto, Arthur, *Nietzsche as Philosopher* (New York, 1965)

Davidson, A. (ed.), *Foucault and His Interlocutors* (Chicago University Press, 1997)

Dawson, Jr, J. W., *Logical Dilemmas: The Life and Work of Kurt Gödel* (A. K. Peters Ltd, Wellesley, MA, 1997)

Dent, N. J. H., *Rousseau* (Blackwell, 1988)

Dinwiddy, J., *Bentham* (Oxford University Press, 1989)

Dunn, John, *John Locke* (Oxford University Press, 1984)

Fennesey, R. R., *Burke, Paine, and the "Rights of Man"* (The Hague: Martinus Nijhoff, 1963)

Fruchtman, J., *Thomas Paine: Apostle Of Freedom* (New York: Four Walls Eight Windows, 1994)

Galipeau, Claude J., *Isaiah Berlin's Liberalism* (Clarendon Press, 1994)

Gardiner, Patrick L. *Kierkegaard* (Oxford University Press, 1988)

Gardiner, Patrick, *Schopenhauer* (Harmondsworth, 1963)

Gardner, Sebastian, *Routledge Philosophy Guidebook to Kant and the Critique of Pure Reason* (Routledge, 1999)

Garrett, Don (ed.), *The Cambridge Companion to Spinoza* (Cambridge University Press, 1995)

Glover, J., *Causing Death and Saving Lives* (Harmondsworth, 1977)

Graham, A. C., *Chuang-Tzu: The Inner Chapters* (Mandala, 1986)

Grazia, S. de, *Machiavelli in Hell*, (Princeton University Press, 1989)

Grube, G. M. A., *Plato's Thought* (London, 2nd edn, 1980)

Gutting, G. (ed.), *The Cambridge Companion to Foucault* (Cambridge University Press, 1994)

Guyer, Paul (ed.), *The Cambridge Companion to Kant* (Cambridge University Press, 1992)

Haakonssen, Knud (ed.), *The Cambridge History of Eighteenth Century Philosophy*, (Cambridge University Press, 2006)

Hands, Gill, *Marx: A Beginner's Guide* (Hodder & Stoughton, 2000)

Hannay, Alastair & Marino, Gordon Daniel, *The Cambridge Companion to Kierkegaard* (Cambridge University Press, 1997)

Harrison, R., *Bentham* (Routledge & Kegan Paul, 1983)

Hartnack, Justus, *An Introduction to Hegel's Logic* (Hackett, 1998)

Hass, Lawrence, *Merleau-Ponty's Philosophy* (Indiana University Press, 2008)

Hayes, J.R. (ed.), *The Genius of Arab Civilization* (Eurabia, 2nd edn, 1983)

Henry, P., *Voltaire and Camus: The Limits of Reason and the Awareness of Absurdity* (Voltaire Foundation, 1975)

Heywood, Andrew, *Political Ideologies* (Macmillan, 1992)

Honderich, Ted (ed.), *The Oxford Companion to Philosophy* (Oxford University Press, 1995)

Hookway, Christopher, *Peirce* (Routledge, 1992)

Howells, C. (ed.), *The Cambridge Companion to Sartre* (Cambridge, 1992)

Hoy, D. (ed.), *Foucault: A Critical Reader* (London: Fontana, 1986)

Hutchinson, Brian, *G. E. Moore's Ethical Theory: Resistance and Reconciliation* (Cambridge University Press, 2001)

Ignatieff, Michael, *Isaiah Berlin: A Life* (Metropolitan, 1998)

Janaway, Christopher, *The Cambridge Companion to Schopenhauer* (Cambridge University Press, 1999)

Kearney, R., *Modern Movements in European Philosophy* (Manchester, 1986)

Kenny, A. J. P., *Wittgenstein* (London: Allen Lane, 1973)

Kenny, Anthony, *Aquinas* (Oxford University Press, 1980)

Kirk, G. S. , Raven, J. E. & Schofield, M., *The*

Pre-Socratic Philosophers (Cambridge University Press, 2nd edn, 1983)

Klemke, E. D., A Defense of Realism: Reflections on the Metaphysics of G. E. Moore (Humanity, 1999)

Knowles, D., The Evolution of Medieval Thought (London: Longman, 2nd edn, 1988)

Kuklick, Bruce, The Rise of American Philosophy (New Haven, Conn., 1977)

Lilla, Mark; Dworkin, Ronald; & Silvers, Robert B. (eds.), The Legacy of Isaiah Berlin (New York Review Books, 2001)

Lock, Frederick, Edmund Burke (Oxford University Press, 1998)

Long, Herbert S., (ed.), Diogenes Laertius: Lives of Eminent Philosophers, Loeb Classical Library (Harvard University Press, 1972)

Magee, B., Philosophy and the Real World: An Introduction to Karl Popper (Open Court, 1985)

Magee, Bryan, The Great Philosophers (Oxford University Press, 1987)

Magee, Bryan, The Philosophy of Schopenhauer (Clarendon Press, 1997)

Malachowsky, Alan R., Richard Rorty (Princeton University Press, 2002)

McCarney, Joseph, The Routledge Philosophy Guidebook to Hegel on History (Routledge, 2000)

McGinnis, John & Reisman, David C., Classical Arabic Philosophy, An Anthology of Sources (Hackett, 2007)

McLean, Iain & McMillan, Alistair, The Concise Oxford Dictionary of Politics (Oxford, 2003)

Monk, Ray, Ludwig Wittgenstein: The Duty of Genius (Penguin, 1991)

Mossner, E. C., Bishop Butler and the Age of Reason (Macmillan, 1936)

Mossner, E. C., The Life of David Hume (Oxford, 1954)

Needham, Joseph, Science and Civilisation in China (Cambridge University Press, 1954)

Norris, C., Derrida (London: Fontana Press, 1987)

Offord, D., Portraits of Early Russian Liberals (Cambridge University Press, 1985)

Otteson, James, Adam Smith's Marketplace of Life (Cambridge University Press, 2002)

Passmore, John, Recent Philosophers (London, 1985)

Penelhum, Terence, Butler (Routledge & Kegan Paul, 1985)

Perry, Ralph Barton & Haddock Seigfried, Charlene, The Thought and Character of William James (Vanderbilt, 1996)

Pickering, M., Auguste Comte: An Intellectual Biography (Cambridge, 1993)

Powell, J., Derrida: A Biography (Continuum, 2006)

Powell, Jim, Eastern Philosophy for Beginners (Writers and Readers Publishing, 2000)

Putnam, Ruth Anna (ed.), The Cambridge Companion to William James (Cambridge University Press, 1997)

Rachels, J., The End of Life: The Morality of Euthanasia (Oxford University Press, 1986)

Ralph C. S. Walker, Kant (Routledge, 1999)

Rescher, N., Leibniz: An Introduction to His Philosophy (Basil Blackwell, 1979)

Ritzer, G. (ed.), The Blackwell Companion to Major Social Theorists (Blackwell, 2000)

Royle, N., Deconstruction: A User's Guide (Palgrave Macmillan, 2000)

Russell, Bertrand, A History of Western Philosophy (George Allen & Unwin, 1946)

Russell, Kirk, Edmund Burke, A Genius Reconsidered (Intercollegiate Studies Institute, rev. edn 1997)

Sallis, John (ed.), Deconstruction and Philosophy (University of Chicago Press, 1987)

Schaefer, David Lewis, Illiberal Justice: John Rawls Vs. the American Political Tradition (University of Missouri Press, 2007)

Scharff, R. C., Comte After Positivism (Cambridge University Press, 2002)

Schmidtz, David (ed.), Robert Nozick (Cambridge University Press, 2002)

Schrift, A., Twentieth Century French Philosophy: Key Themes and Thinkers (Blackwell Publishing, 2006)

Scott, J. & Marshall, G., A Dictionary of Sociology (Oxford University Press, 2005)

Scruton, Roger, Kant (Oxford University Press, 1983)

Sheridan, A., Foucault: The Will to Truth (London: Tavistock, 1980)

Singer, Peter, Marx, (Oxford University Press, 1980)

Skinner, Q., The Foundations of Modern Political Thought, Vol. I, The Renaissance (Cambridge University Press, 1978)

Skinner, Q., Visions of Politics, Vol. II: Renaissance Virtues (Cambridge University Press, 2002)

Smith, Barry & Smith, David Woodruff (eds.), The Cambridge Companion to Husserl (Cambridge University Press, 1995)

Smith, Vanessa, "The Myth of the Noble Savage", Journal of World History, Vol. 15, Iss. 1 (Honolulu: Mar 2004)

Smullyan, R., Forever Undecided: A Puzzle Guide to Gödel (Oxford University Press, 1988)

Southern, R. W., Saint Anselm: A Portrait in a Landscape (Cambridge University Press, 1990)

Specter, M., "The Dangerous Philosopher", New Yorker (Sept 6, 1999)

Stokes, Philip, Philosophy: The Great Thinkers (London: Arcturus, 2007)

Sykes, N., "Bishop Butler and the Primacy" (Theology, 1936)

Taylor, Charles, Hegel and Modern Society (Cambridge University Press, 1979)

Taylor, Charles, Varieties of Religion Today: William James Revisited (Harvard University Press, 2002)

Thomas, Alan, Bernard Williams (Cambridge University Press, 2007)

Thompson, K. (ed.), Auguste Comte: The Foundation of Sociology (London: Nelson, 1976)

Thompson, Mel, Teach Yourself Philosophy (Hodder & Stoughton Educational, 2003)

Venturi, F., Roots of Revolution: A History of the Populist and Socialist Movements in Nineteenth Century Russia (Weidenfeld & Nicolson, 1960)

Viroli, M., Machiavelli (Oxford University Press, 1998)

Wang, H., A Logical Lourney: From Gödel to Philosophy (MIT Press, 1996)

Wedberg, Anders, History of Philosophy (Oxford, 1984)

Wiener, Philip P., Charles S. Peirce: Selected Writings (Dover, 1980)

Wilson, C., Leibniz's Metaphysics: A Comparative and Historical Study (Manchester University Press, 1989)

Wolff, Jonathan, Robert Nozick: Property, Justice, and the Minimal State (Stanford University Press, 1991)

Wood, David (ed.), Derrida: A Critical Reader (Blackwell, 1994)

Woolhouse, R. S. (ed.), Leibniz: Metaphysics and Philosophy of Science (Oxford University Press, 1981)

Woolhouse, R. S. (ed.), The Empiricists (Oxford University Press, 1981)

Zahavi, Dan, Husserl's Phenomenology (University of Stanford Press, 2003)

Zwemer, Samuel M., A Muslim Seeker After God (Fleming H. Revell Co., 1920)

Glossary

A PRIORI/A POSTERIORI The terms "*a priori*" and "*a posteriori*" refer primarily to how or on what basis a proposition might be known. A proposition is knowable *a priori* if it is knowable independently of experience. A proposition is knowable *a posteriori* if it is knowable on the basis of experience. The *a priori/a posteriori* distinction is **epistemological** and should not be confused with the **metaphysical** distinction between the **necessary** and the **contingent** or the semantical or logical distinction between the **analytic** and the **synthetic**.

ABSOLUTE IDEALISM An early nineteenth-century doctrine according to which "Being" is the **transcendental** expression of thought or reason.

ABSOLUTE KNOWLEDGE A variously employed term that predominantly refers to knowledge of God and divinity or knowledge of indisputable **absolute truths**.

ABSOLUTE TRUTH The view that, within a particular domain, all **propositions** are either absolutely true or absolutely false.

ABSOLUTISM A system of rule according to which the ruling party or individual has absolute, complete power, often without any legally-organized opposition.

AESTHETICS The branch of philosophy concerned with the arts, aesthetic value, and aesthetic experience.

ANALYTIC PHILOSOPHY/TRADITION The twentieth-century movement, initially associated with **Bertrand Russell, G. E. Moore**, and the early thought of **Ludwig Wittgenstein**, and later with philosophy practiced in much of the English-speaking world, which places analysis (in particular, conceptual analysis) at the heart of philosophical methodology and is commonly associated with precision and rigor of argument. This movement is often defined in opposition to **Continental philosophy/tradition**. See also **Anglo-American philosophy**.

ANALYTIC TRUTH/PROPOSITIONS **Propositions** or statements that are true according to the definition of the words in the statement and independently of any

matters of fact. For example, "A square has four sides".

ANCIENT PHILOSOPHY The branch of philosophy concerned with the philosophers and philosophical doctrines of ancient Greece and Rome.

ANGLO-AMERICAN PHILOSOPHY Philosophy practiced in the UK and US, particularly from the twentieth century to the present day. See also **analytic philosophy**.

APHORISM A short profound statement expressing a truism or maxim.

APOLOGISM A **metaphysical** view which states that it is wrong for mankind to alter the conditions of life in the mortal sphere.

APOPHATIC THEOLOGY The belief that God's ineffable essence cannot be described by human beings, and any attempt to do so reduces God to a human level, by applying human terms to Him. Therefore it is only possible to approach an understanding of God by describing what He is not. Only negative statements about God can be true.

ARGUMENT FROM DESIGN An argument for the existence of God, which says that the universe is so complex, it must have been created by an all-powerful, all-knowing being.

ARISTOTELIAN A philosophical school or theory influenced by the philosophical thought of **Aristotle**.

ARISTOTELIAN LOGIC The **syllogistic** logic devised by **Aristotle**, primarily in his works *Prior Analytics* and *De Interpretatione*, and later developed by Boethius in the Middle Ages.

ARTIFICIAL INTELLIGENCE The ability of a machine to imitate human behavior, and an interdisciplinary field, encompassing computer science, neuroscience, philosophy, psychology, robots and linguistics, which aims to reproduce human behavior and human thought in machines. Often known by the acronym AI.

ATOMISM/ATOMIST The broad, variously employed view that a particular phenomenon is composed of indivisible smaller constituent parts or "atoms".

ATOMISTIC MATERIALISM A philosophical position according to which the only elements of reality in the universe are matter and empty space.

AUTHORITARIANISM A form of government or social control according to which the ruler assumes absolute power and enforces control by oppression.

AXIOM A **proposition** that is presumed true in a system or theory and is used to deduce other propositions, which are known as "theorems".

AXIOMATIC A philosophical system or methodology that employs axioms.

BEHAVIORISM In **psychology**, the view that human behavior is to be understood exclusively in terms of patterns of environmental stimulus and responses. This term is defined in opposition to **cognitivism**.

BOURGEOISIE A **Marxist/communist** definition. The social class that owns the means of production (factories) and all the raw materials processed in factories. Often described as **capitalist** or the property-owning middle class, they consume more than they produce.

BRAHMANISM The early Indian philosophy derived from the holy books, the Vedas, and a forerunner of **Hinduism**.

BRAHMIN A Hindu priest or a member of a priestly castle according to the Vedic classification of society. They are the highest class in the Hindu caste system.

BUDDHISM The religion, sometimes called a philosophy, developed in India by Gautama Siddhartha, who became the Buddha or Enlightened One, offering paths to enlightenment or nirvana.

CAPITALISM The economic system based on profit motive, wage labor, and the private ownership of the means of production. Often defined in opposition to **socialism**.

CARTESIAN DOUBT/METHOD A philosophical approach, most commonly associated with the work of **René Descartes**, which employs **scepticism** as a method of enquiry. Descartes used the thought experiment of an evil demon bent on deceiving him in order to ascertain what he could know with genuine certainty.

CARTESIAN DUALISM The theory, defended by **René Descartes**, that the mind and body are two distinct and completely independent things.

CARTESIAN RATIONALISM The **rationalist** philosophy propounded by **René Descartes**.

CATEGORICAL IMPERATIVE The moral principle, defended by **Immanuel Kant**, that the moral value of an act is determined not by its consequences but by an overarching principle that guides our actions (see pages 100–1). Also known as the "moral law".

CAUSATION/CAUSALITY The relation between two items where one is the cause of the other. For example, a relation of causality obtains between A and B if A causes B.

COGNITIVE SCIENCE The interdisciplinary scientific study of the human mind and intelligence.

COGNITIVISM The view that explanations of human behavior require an understanding of the special faculties of the human mind that underlie that behavior. This view is defined in opposition to **behaviorism**.

COMMUNISM An economic and political system closely associated with **Karl Marx** in which property is not privately owned but is held by members of a community. It is often interpreted as the antithesis of **capitalism**.

COMPUTABLE FUNCTIONS In computer science, the basic objects of study in computability theory, the purpose of which is to discover which problems are solvable using different models of computation. Also known as Turing-computable functions after the mathematician Alan Turing (1912–54).

CONCOMITANT VARIATION A method of **inductive logic** suggesting that if a phenomenon changes after an antecedent circumstance changes, then the circumstance is probably the cause of the phenomenon.

CONDITIONALS/CONDITIONALITY Any sentence that depends on a condition, such as those of the form "If A then B" where the occurrence of A is a condition on the occurrence of B.

CONFUCIANISM/CONFUCIAN Chinese philosophy formulated by **Confucius** concerned with creating a moral society.

CONSEQUENTIALIST The view that all actions can be determined as right or wrong by analyzing the value of their consequences.

CONSTRUCTIVIST An exponent of constructivism, who denies the **Platonist** or **realist** view that mathematical objects exist independently of the human mind and argues instead that the existence of mathematical objects is dependent on our construction of them.

CONTINENTAL PHILOSOPHY/TRADITION A philosophical classification commonly employed since World War II to describe the philosophical practices of philosophers in mainland Europe and to distinguish them from the more abstract, technical practices of **Anglo–American** philosophers. Key fields in this tradition have included **existentialism**, **structuralism**, and **critical theory**, as well as their contemporary offshoots. Often defined in opposition to **analytic philosophy/tradition**.

CONTINGENT TRUTH A true **proposition** that is not "**necessarily true**" and thus could be false if the state of affairs that it describes were otherwise.

COSMOLOGY The scientific study of the universe and man's place in it.

COUNTEREXAMPLE An example designed to contradict or disprove an argument or a general rule.

COUNTERFACTUAL A conditional statement whose antecedent is false.

CREATIONIST BELIEFS The belief or beliefs that the universe and all life was created by a deity.

CRITICAL THEORY The examination and critique of literature and society based on knowledge from disciplines in the humanities and social sciences.

CYNICS An influential group of philosophers from the ancient school of cynicism who

argued that the purpose of life was to live virtuously in accordance with nature.

DAOISM A Chinese mystical philosophy suggesting ways to align with nature.

DECISION THEORY In mathematics and statistics, the enterprise of understanding the factors relating to a particular decision and the resulting process of generating the optimal decision.

DECONSTRUCTION The process in philosophy, literary criticism, and the social sciences, most closely associated with the work of **Jacques Derrida**, according to which the meanings of texts are variously interpreted according to incidental features of the text that are purported to subvert the intended meaning or message of the original author.

DECONSTRUCTIONISM/DECONSTRUCTIONIST The critical **postmodernist** philosophy, most closely associated with **Jacques Derrida**, which gains new meaning from old texts by deconstructing them.

DEDUCTION In reasoning, an **inference** in which the conclusion is of no greater generality than the premises and where the premises entail the conclusion.

DEDUCTIVE REASONING/INFERENCE/LOGIC See **deduction**.

DEISM A belief in the existence of God that is founded on natural reason.

DEMOCRACY A predominantly classless and equal state (and also the political circumstances of such a state) that is governed by the citizens or by a fairly elected political party constituted by representatives of those citizens.

DEONTOLOGY An ethical theory that focuses on the rightness or wrongness of actions themselves, as opposed to the rightness or wrongness of the consequences of those actions. Sometimes described as concerned with duties, obligations, and rights because deontologists believe that ethical rules are binding. Deontology is often defined in opposition to **consequentialist** ethical theories, according to which the rightness of an action is determined by its consequences. Deontologists who are also **moral absolutists** believe that some actions are wrong no matter what consequences follow from them.

DESPOTISM Tyrannical authority or behavior, often perpetrated by a political leader.

DETERMINISM The theory that events are causally determined. Strong versions of the theory argue that human beings have no **free will**.

DETERMINISTIC Associated with the doctrine of determinism.

DHARMA In **Buddhism**, usually the ultimate doctrine or ethical principles as taught by the Buddha. It can also mean a phenomenon, or element of reality.

DIALECTIC/DIALECTICAL The debate between two opposing views. In **G. W. F. Hegel**'s philosophy, a method in which contradictions are resolved at a higher level of truth.

DIOGENES LAERTIUS A biographer of the ancient Greek philosophers, writing in the third century CE.

DIVISION OF LABOR The breaking up of a production process into small, specialized and/or repetitive tasks, so that each worker performs a small portion of the overall process, intended to increase the productivity of labor.

DUALISM/DUALITY (of mind and matter and other dualisms) A term, encompassing a broad range of views, that denotes a state of two parts. See, for instance, **Cartesian dualism**.

EASTERN PHILOSOPHY/TRADITION Philosophy that is practiced in the Eastern world. Often defined in opposition to **Western philosophy**.

EGOISM (in ethics) The ethical view adopted by a particular individual that the moral life is the life that maximizes good for that individual.

ELEATIC SCHOOL A group of **Pre-Socratic** philosophers based at Elea, which was founded by **Parmenides** and included **Zeno of Elea**. They rejected the **epistemological** validity of **sense**

experience and instead took clarity and necessity to be the criteria of truth.

EMPIRICAL A general term, which might apply to **propositions**, statements, knowledge etc., which indicates a connection to experience. For example, an item of knowledge is empirical if the way an individual gains that knowledge depends in some way on sensory experience. See also "*a posteriori*".

EMPIRICISM A predominantly **epistemological** movement, closely associated with British philosophers **John Locke**, **George Berkeley**, and **David Hume**, and later with the **Vienna Circle**, which regards the general notion of "experience" gained through the five senses as the central source of human knowledge. Often defined in opposition to **rationalism**.

EMPIRICIST LIBERALISM The view, combined with **liberalism**, that metaphysics and politics cannot mix.

ENLIGHTENMENT The eighteenth-century intellectual movement in Europe that looked to reason and secular **rationalism** to explain and improve the world. It was strongly influenced by the emerging modern **empirical** science.

ENLIGHTENMENT, AGE OF A general term to describe the era of the Enlightenment period. See **Enlightenment**.

EPICUREAN PHILOSOPHY/EPICUREANISM A philosophical school or theory influenced by the philosophical ideas of **Epicurus**, urging the avoidance of pain and rejecting the involvement of the gods in human life.

EPISTEMOLOGY The branch of philosophy, also known as the "theory of knowledge", which studies philosophical issues relating to the acquisition and nature of human knowledge.

ETHICAL EGOISM See **egoism**.

ETHICAL INTUITIONISM The view that human beings can experience an intuitive grasp of the objective facts of morality. Also known as "moral intuitionism".

ETHICAL VALUES Statements of ethical or moral principle.

ETHICS The branch of philosophy concerned with right and wrong conduct and with the nature of the good life.

EXEGESIS Criticism or explanation of a text, particularly a religious book such as the Bible or the Qur'an.

EXISTENTIALISM The philosophy explored by **Jean-Paul Sartre**, **Simone de Beauvoir**, and other European philosophers that is concerned with the experience of human existence.

FALLIBILISM/FALLIBILISTIC The philosophical doctrine that absolute certainty about knowledge is impossible.

FEMINISM The doctrine that advocates equal rights for women.

FORMS (Plato) See **Ideas**.

FOUNDATIONALISM The theory that knowledge of the world rests on a foundation of indubitable beliefs from which further propositions can be inferred to produce a structural system of knowledge.

FREE TRADE The absence of tariffs and regulations designed to curtail or prevent trade among nations.

FREE WILL The power to make unconstrained free choices.

FREE WILL (PROBLEM OF) The variously conceived philosophical problem that considers whether or to what extent human beings possess the power to make unconstrained free choices.

FUNCTIONALISM The view in the **philosophy of mind** that mental states are constituted by their functional role.

GENERATIVE GRAMMAR An explicit description of all the sentences of a language, and the enterprise, most closely associated with **Noam_Chomsky**, which attempts to explain the structure of natural languages.

GEOMANTIC Divination (the art of foretelling future events or revealing occult knowledge) by means of lines and figures or by geographic features.

GESTALT A form, shape, pattern, or structure; a complete pattern or configuration; an organized whole in experience.

HEDONISM The doctrine that the moral value of an act can be defined in terms of the resultant pleasure produced by engaging in that act.

HEGELIAN PHILOSOPHY/HEGELIANISM Philosophical schools or theories influenced by the philosophical ideas of **G. W. F. Hegel**.

HELLENISTIC PHILOSOPHY Philosophical doctrines developed in Hellenic civilization following Aristotle.

HINDUISM A religious tradition originating in the Indian subcontinent whose scriptures include the Vedas and the *Upanishads*.

HISTORICAL DETERMINISM The idea that historical events are predetermined.

HOLISM The broad view according to which the individual parts of any whole cannot be understood independently of their relations with the other parts and thus their relation to the whole.

HUMANIST/HUMANISM An ethical doctrine emphasizing the importance of human life and mankind's place in the world, which is commonly associated with the Renaissance period, beginning at the close of the Middle Ages, when God and religious belief ceased to be man's central interest.

HYPOTHESIS A suggested explanation for a particular phenomenon or an assumption used in an argument.

HYPOTHETICAL SYLLOGISM An argument in classical **logic** claiming that if A implies B, and B implies C, then A also implies C.

IDEALISM The belief that the basic reality is not matter but the mental world; that experience is the sum of **perceptions** and sensations that have registered in the mind.

IDEAS (Plato) In **Plato**'s theory of "Ideas", or "Forms", developed c.427–c.347 BCE in his middle-period dialogues (especially *Phaedo*, *Symposium*, and the *Republic*), Ideas, or Forms, were not meant to be anything in the mind, but were properties or essences of things, treated as non-material abstract entities. They were eternal, changeless, real, and independent of other objects in the world. He treated them as both **universals**, suggesting they were inherent in things, and paradigms (non-material abstract entities serving as a paradigm of objects of the same kind, which are copies of the paradigm), suggesting they were transcendent and themselves had the properties they represented: the Idea blue having itself the color blue. **Aristotle** believed in forms (small f), but not as transcendent objects.

IMPERIALISM The policy or the practice according to which one state imposes its system of rule upon another.

INDIVIDUALISM A social theory or philosophy that emphasizes the importance of the individual above society, advocating individual freedom, rights, and self-expression.

INDUCTION The method of reasoning used in scientific investigation where the premises of the argument offer support for the conclusion but, unlike **deductive reasoning**, do not entail the conclusion.

INDUCTIVE REASONING/LOGIC See **induction**.

INFERENCE The act or process of reasoning employed when drawing a conclusion from a set of premises.

INNATE IDEAS A concept or an item of knowledge that human beings are born possessing, as opposed to concepts or knowledge that are gained through experience.

INTELLECTUALISM A wide range of positions concerned with the development of the intellect and the practice of being an intellectual.

INTENTIONALITY A notion, most commonly associated with Franz Brentano (1838–1917), that highlights the relation between a given mental phenomenon and its content (i.e. the thing the mental phenomenon is "about").

IRREALISM A philosophical position developed by **Nelson Goodman** according to which conflicting doctrines are described as alternative "world-versions" that can both be employed in the correct circumstances.

ISLAMIST The movement to set up Islamic states where religion determines the political organization. Sometimes used generally for Muslim religious fundamentalists.

JAINISM A religion originating in India that has some similarities with **Buddhism**.

JIHAD Literally meaning "struggle", it has come to mean a Muslim holy war waged against non-believers.

KNOWLEDGE, THEORY OF See **epistemology**.

LAISSEZ-FAIRE ECONOMICS A central principle of **capitalism**, this doctrine claims that an economic system should be free from government intervention or moderation and be driven only by market forces.

LEGALISM A Chinese political philosophy advocating a strict rule of law to strengthen the state.

LEIBNIZIAN A philosophical school or theory influenced by the philosophical ideas of **Gottfried Leibniz**.

LEVIATHAN The title of **Thomas Hobbes'** political work comes from chapter 41 of the biblical Book of Job. The Leviathan is a sea monster that "is a king over all the children of pride" (verse 34). The title of Hobbes' work is apposite because the pride of the individual explains why the artificial sate, the Leviathan, must have absolute power.

LIBERALISM Political policies, practices, and opinions in support of progress, reform, and individual freedom.

LIBERTARIANISM The belief that legitimate government should be small and should play only the most minimal possible role in economic, social, and cultural life

LOGIC The study of the formal structure of reasoning and the principles of valid **inference**.

LOGICAL ANALYSIS The analytical process of uncovering the underlying form or structure of statements.

LOGICAL ATOMISM A doctrine that originated in the early twentieth century with the advent of **analytic philosophy** and is most closely associated with the work of

Bertrand Russell according to which the world consists of logical facts or atoms which can be uncovered by analysis.

LOGICAL NECESSITY That which follows from the laws of **logic**. For example, the statement "Either it will rain or it will not rain" expresses a logically **necessary truth** because it is an instance of the law of excluded middle (i.e. it can be deduced from the form of the **proposition** because the "middle" position, that it will neither rain nor not rain, is excluded by logic).

LOGICAL POSITIVISM/LOGICAL POSITIVISTS A movement comprising many scientifically-minded **empiricist** philosophers in early twentieth-century Europe, particularly Austria and Germany, which endorsed the **verification principle** and rejected speculative **metaphysics**. Many of its doctrines laid the foundation for **analytic philosophy** in the second half of the twentieth century, particularly in the US.

LOGICISM A philosophical system that places strong emphasis on **logic**, especially as providing a foundation for a philosophical system.

MANDALA In **Hinduism** and **Buddhism**, a symbolic picture or diagram representing either the cosmos or a deity.

MANUFACTURING CONSENT Noam Chomksy's idea that a major function of the major corporation-led US media is propaganda and that the reports they broadcast and the media outlets that survive are determined by factors like profit and their dependence on government cooperation.

MARXISM/MARXISTS The philosophical, economical, and political school associated with the work of **Karl Marx** and **Friedrich Engels**.

MATERIALISM The broad view that all things are made of matter.

MEDIEVAL PHILOSOPHY The philosophical doctrines propounded in Europe and the Middle East in the Middle Ages.

METAPHYSICAL REALISM See **realism**.

METAPHYSICS The branch of philosophy concerned with the nature of reality,

being, and the world, which goes beyond that provided by the laws of physics. The term "metaphysics" originated as a title given to a work of Aristotle's by Andronicus of Rhodes in the first half of the first century BCE and meant simply the works following those on physics in the library's catalog.

METHOD OF AGREEMENT A method of **inductive logic** to do with the discovery of causal relationships. If a particular circumstance occurs before a phenomenon every time that phenomenon occurs, it may be inferred to be the cause of the phenomenon.

MIND-BODY PROBLEM The problem in the **philosophy of mind** concerned with the relationship between the mind and the brain.

MODAL LOGIC The logic of possibility and necessity.

MODAL SYLLOGISM See **hypothetical syllogism**.

MONISM The doctrine that only one kind of substance exists. This doctrine is the antithesis of **pluralism**.

MONOTHEISM The doctrine that there is only one God.

MORAL ABSOLUTISM The belief that there are absolute standards against which moral questions can be judged, and that certain actions are right or wrong whatever the context of the act. Moral absolutism is often defined in opposition to **moral relativism**.

MORAL PHILOSOPHY See **ethics**.

MORAL REALISM The view that moral beliefs and judgements can be true or false and that there are objective moral properties to which true moral agents must attend.

MORAL RELATIVISM The theory that there are no objective moral properties or truths and that morality can only be defined to cultural, social, historical, or personal circumstances.

MORAL SENSE THEORY A meta-ethical theory according to which morality is grounded in moral sentiments or emotions. Also known as "sentimentalism".

MORAL VALUES Things that are held to be right or wrong, or desirable or undesirable.

MYSTICISM A broad range of views encompassing spiritual belief in or experience of a higher reality.

NAMING, PROBLEM OF A philosophical enterprise that attempts to understand the function and meaning of names, in particular proper names and definite descriptions.

NATURAL PHILOSOPHY The philosophy of nature. A term commonly used to describe the scientific practices, particularly those of physics, before the advent of modern science.

NATURALISM The broad view that everything is natural or that everything there is belongs to the world of nature and can be studied by the **empirical** methods appropriate for studying the natural world.

NECESSARY CONDITION A relation of dependence between two states of affairs. For example, A is a necessary condition for B if B cannot occur without A.

NECESSARY TRUTH A proposition, or truth, that could not possibly be false, or, according to some philosophers such as **Gottfried Leibniz**, is "true in all possible worlds". Such propositions are the opposite of **contingent truths**.

NECESSITY See **logical necessity**.

NEGATIVE THEOLOGY See **apophatic theology**.

NEO-KANTIANISM/NEO-KANTIAN A revival of **Immanuel Kant's** ideas that began in the 1860s, which emphasized **epistemology**, and a scientific interpretation of Kant's thought.

NEO-PLATONISM/NEO-PLATONIC A school of religious or mystical philosophy founded by **Plotinus** in the third century CE which was based on the teachings of **Plato**.

NIHILISM The rejection of values, morality, institutions of authority, and, sometimes, the attack on such concepts.

NOMINALISM The view that **universals** have no objective realities corresponding to them, but are merely names.

Conceptualism, a related doctrine, is the view that universals are concepts and exist only in the mind.

NOMINALIST An exponent of **nominalism** who denies the reality of universals or **Platonic** objects.

NOUMENAL REALM The realm of things as they are in themselves rather than as they appear. According to **Immanuel Kant**, knowledge of this realm is gained by pure reason.

OBJECTIVE TRUTH/KNOWLEDGE/REALITY The property of mind-independence as applied to truths, knowledge, and reality.

OCKHAM'S RAZOR A principle attributed to English logician **William of Ockham**, which advocates that, in any explanation of a particular phenomenon, the simplest explanation of that phenomenon with the fewest assumptions is the best explanation.

ONTOLOGICAL ARGUMENT An *a priori* argument that the concept of God is necessarily instantiated because existence is part of the concept of God. Since we can conceive of the concept of God, He therefore exists.

ONTOLOGY/ONTOLOGICAL The exploration of what type or types of things make up the universe.

OTHER MINDS An **epistemological** problem concerned with how we can know that other individuals possess thoughts and emotions.

PANTHEISM A doctrine that identifies God as identical with the material universe or nature and is therefore present in all things.

PARADOX A statement that appears to be self-contradictory or inherently conflicted and yet cannot be obviously falsified.

PERCEPTION The philosophical study of the processes involved in gaining information about the external world by means of the five senses.

PHENOMENAL REALM Associated with **Immanuel Kant**, the realm of things in the sensible world that are known through sensory experience and can only be experienced as they appear, rather than as they are in themselves.

PHENOMENOLOGY/PHENOMENALISM The study of the way phenomena or things appear to consciousness.

PHILOSOPHES Eighteenth-century European thinkers who emphasized and popularized the ideas of the **Enlightenment** period.

PHILOSOPHY OF LANGUAGE The branch of philosophy concerned with the relationship between human language and the world.

PHILOSOPHY OF MATHEMATICS The branch of philosophy concerned with the **epistemological** and **metaphysical** problems relating to mathematics, in particular questions about the status of mathematical truth, our knowledge of mathematical **propositions**, and the **ontological** nature of mathematical objects.

PHILOSOPHY OF MIND The branch of philosophy that attempts to understand the human mind, the **mind-body problem**, mental **causation**, **intentionality**, and consciousness.

PHYSICALIST/ISM The view that everything that exists is physical, and the denial in the existence of non-physical entities or objects.

PLATONISM/PLATONIC/NEO-PLATONISM A philosophical position or school of thought that endorses the doctrines of **Plato**. In the philosophy of mathematics, a position that endorses a version of Plato's account of the "Forms" or "**Ideas**", a view according to which mathematical objects exist independently of the human mind.

PLURALISM The doctrine that more than one kind of substance exists. This doctrine is the antithesis of **monism**.

POLITICAL PHILOSOPHY The branch of philosophy concerned with political freedom, justice, and rights.

POLYTHEISM The worship or belief in more than one god.

POSITIVISM A theory that theology and **metaphysics** are earlier imperfect modes of knowledge and that positive knowledge is based on natural phenomena and their properties and relations as verified by the **empirical** sciences.

POSTMODERNISM A variously employed term, often describing a range of disciplines which emerged as a reaction to modernism (the range of progressive movements which emerged in Western society in the late nineteenth and twentieth centuries). It is loosely characterized by ambiguity, parody, diversity, and interconnectedness.

POST-STRUCTURALISM School of thought that emerged in the late 1970s that rejects the **structuralist** claims to objectivity and emphasizes the **duality** of meanings.

PRAGMATISM A general philosophical methodology that emphasizes the importance of practical application.

PREDICATE A fundamental concept in first-order **logic**, a formal system of **deductive** logic.

PREFERENCE UTILITARIANISM A strand of utilitarianism according to which the good involved is understood in terms of "preference satisfaction". See also **utilitarianism**.

PRE-SOCRATIC Greek philosophers before the time of **Socrates** who rejected mythological explanations in favor of more rational explanations.

PROLETARIAT A **Marxist/communist** definition. The urban working class; the social class that owns practically nothing, certainly not the means of production, and consumes far less than it actually produces. In order to survive the proletariat has to sell its labor to the **capitalist bourgeoisie** class that owns the means of production.

PROPERTY DUALISM The view that there exists two distinct sorts of properties – physical and mental properties – that adhere in physical substance.

PROPOSITION (PHILOSOPHICAL) The content or meaning of an assertion. Propositions are truth-bearers: they are either true or false. A philosophical proposition is a proposition that makes a claim about philosophy.

PSYCHOANALYSIS The method of studying the mind and treating mental disorders closely identified with the work of Sigmund Freud (1856–1939), which involves uncovering the unconscious mind.

PSYCHOLOGICAL EGOISM The doctrine that human beings are always motivated by rational self interest.

PSYCHOLOGY The study of mental processes and behavior, and the application of such knowledge to issues relating to daily life.

PYTHAGOREAN MYSTICISM The belief in a timeless unchanging world of ideas.

QUANTUM MECHANICS Branch of physics studying the structure and behavior of sub-atomic particles.

RATIONAL SCEPTICISM A scientific philosophical methodology according to which one questions the authenticity of claims that are not supported by empirical evidence. Also known as "scientific scepticism".

RATIONALISM The theory that knowledge is gained through reason. Historically, the rationalist conception of philosophy is most closely identified with the doctrines of **Plato**, **René Descartes**, **Gottfried Leibniz**, and **Baruch Spinoza**.

REALISM In **metaphysics**, after **Plato**, a realist believes that universals are extramental entities. In the theory of knowledge, a version of **empiricism** (where knowledge is acquired through perceptions of the world) in which the characteristics of individuals cause you to know what they are ("direct realism").

REFERENCE, PROBLEM OF The philosophical problem which investigates the relationship between a referring expression and the entity it stands for.

RELATIVISM A term that is variously applied to a range of disciplines but commonly taken to mean that truth (in whatever specified field) is relative and not absolute.

RELATIVIST SCEPTICISM The treatment of moral questions and moral issues as if they were matters of taste.

RHETORIC Grandiose, persuasive, and often public use of language.

ROMANTICISM The literary movement emphasizing passion, emotion, and the beauty of nature that began in the late eighteenth century and dominated British literature and poetry in the nineteenth century. It was in part a backlash against the strictly rational and scientific thought of the earlier Enlightenment.

RULE UTILITARIANISM A branch of utilitarianism which claims that the right moral actions are those that conform to the rules that lead to the greatest possible outcome for the largest number of the community.

SCEPTIC A term that can be employed to varying degrees, from an individual who is dubious about a particular philosophical doctrine to an individual who employs the **Cartesian** methodology of sceptical doubt. See **Cartesian doubt/method**.

SCEPTICISM The philosophical enterprise that attempts to understand cognitive achievements, to challenge the ability to obtain reliable knowledge, and to ascertain the limitations of human knowledge.

SCHOLASTICISM/SCHOLASTICS A tradition in medieval universities associated with the doctrines of **Thomas Aquinas**, **John Duns Scotus**, and **William of Ockham**.

SCIENTISM The view that science has an authority over other alternative methods of explanation.

SCOTISM A philosophical and theological school influenced by the ideas of **John Duns Scotus**.

SENSE EXPERIENCE/PERCEPTION Experience/information gained through the five senses.

SENSE-DATA In the philosophy of **perception**, the information gained through the five senses.

SET THEORY In mathematics, a foundational system in which mathematical concepts can be represented as sets (a set is a collection of distinct objects).

SITUATIONISTS A broadly **Marxist** political group most active in Europe in the 1960s which attempted to make major social and political reforms.

SOCIAL CONTRACT A broadly employed term which describes the philosophical theories that underpin the formation of civilized societies or nations and maintain the social order within such communities.

SOCIAL DARWINISM The application of the evolutionary concept of Darwinism to human development in human society, suggesting that humans, much like animals and plants, compete for survival and the fittest members of a community prevail.

SOCIAL PHILOSOPHY The philosophical study of society and its institutions.

SOCIALISM An economic theory or system according to which the means of production are owned by the community. Often defined in opposition to **capitalism**.

SOLIPSISM A strong form of **scepticism** according to which nothing exists outside the mind of the individual.

SOPHISTS A group of teachers of philosophy and **rhetoric** in ancient Greece. Criticized by **Plato** in his dialogues for being greedy, deceptive, and ambiguous in their use of language, the term has come to mean practitioners of confusing or illogical arguments put forward with the intention of creating a deception, and also it can mean those who engage in the practice of making a business out of such received wisdom.

STOICISM/STOICS A **Hellenistic** tradition founded by **Zeno of Citium**, which placed **ethics** in the context of our understanding of the world as a whole.

STRUCTURALISM A psychological view of French thinkers in the 1950s and 1960s which emphasized studying the elemental structures of consciousness.

SUBJECTIVE REALITY In **epistemology**, especially since **René Descartes**, a realm of experience defined from the first-person perspective.

SUBJECTIVE TRUTH A variously employed idea that refers most commonly to unsupported or unjustified personal feelings or opinions as opposed to knowledge or justified belief.

SUBSTANCE DUALISM A type of dualism, most famously defended by **René Descartes**, according to which there are only two kinds of substance: mental and material.

Sufi A practitioner of **Sufism**.

Sufism The **mystical** and spiritual sect of Islam. Named after the *suf* or coarse wool robe that most Sufis wear. There are several Sufi orders, some stressing abstinence as a way to form a direct relationship with God, others stressing dancing, chanting, or meditation. The whirling dervishes are one order of Sufism.

Sunni Muslim The largest or "orthodox" denomination of Islam.

Sutra A Sanskrit word meaning "thread". In **Hinduism**, a doctrinal saying or text, usually short and clear, meant to be memorized. In **Buddhism**, originally a scripture based on a discourse by the Buddha or his disciples.

Syllogism A deductive inference consisting of two premises and a conclusion.

Symbolism The systematic use of recurrent symbols or images to convey an added level of meaning.

Synthetic truth/propositions A statement that is not analytic (see **analytic truth**) and instead is true in virtue of the facts of the world.

Theory of knowledge See **epistemology**.

Thomism Philosophical school propounding the thought of **Thomas Aquinas**.

Transcendental Often **mystical** or supernatural, a methodology concerned with the intuitive basis of knowledge often taken to be beyond the realm and reach of the senses.

Transcendentality The quality or state of being **transcendental**.

Universal The supposed referents of a general terms like "two" and "red". Understood to differ in kind from physical objects, they are sometimes taken to be abstract or even **Platonic** objects that exist in a non-mental realm outside space and time.

Universal grammar The innate grammatical principles that serve as a basis for acquiring language.

Utilitarianism A philosophical approach to morality, most closely identified with John Stuart Mill and Jeremy Bentham, according to which all actions are to be judged in terms of their utility in producing the best possible outcome for the greatest number of people and therefore to maximize the general level of happiness and welfare.

Value pluralism In **ethics**, the idea that there may be several potentially incompatible value systems that may be equally correct and fundamental. Also known as ethical pluralism or moral pluralism.

Vedanta A philosophical school founded by Badarayana and containing the teachings of the *Upanishads*, it developed out of the Vedic oral traditions and scriptures. It is translated as the "conclusion" of the Vedas.

Vedas Poetic books dating from c.1200 BCE that formed the basis of ancient Indian religion, giving knowledge (Veda) of how to invoke the Vedic gods who were thought to have sprung from the universal essence. From c.800 BCE commentaries were written on the Vedas (*Upanishads*) and the epic poems the *Mahabharata*, containing the *Bhagavad Gita*, and the *Ramayana*, and other important scriptures.

Vedic Ancient Indian **Hindu** philosophy and science that endorsed a **holistic** approach.

Verification principle A principle propounded by members of the **Vienna Circle** which states that the meaning of a statement is the method of its verification and that statements are meaningful only if they are verifiable.

Verificationism The methodological application of the **verification principle**.

Vienna Circle A group of **logical positivist** or logical **empiricist** philosophers based in Vienna in the early twentieth century that emphasized a scientific conception of philosophical methodology and were greatly influenced by the work of the early **Ludwig Wittgenstein**. Notable members included **Rudolf Carnap**, Moritz Schlick (1882–1936), and Friedrich Waisman (1896–1959). Also known as the Wiener Kreis.

Virtue ethics The **ethical** theory that emphasizes character, rather than rules or consequences, as the key element of ethical thinking. It was the prevailing approach to ethical thinking in the ancient and medieval periods, but fell out of favor during the early modern period. In the twentieth century it became one of three dominant approaches to value theory in the West (the other two being **deontology** and **consequentialism**).

Warring States period The last 500 years of the Chou Dynasty in China, a time of cultural fragmentation and civil strife.

Weimar Classicism An interdisciplinary cultural and literary movement in late eighteenth- and early nineteenth-century Europe led by the ideas of Johann Wolfgang von Goethe (1749–1832) and Friedrich Schiller (1759–1805).

Western philosophy/tradition Philosophy that is practiced in the Western world. Often defined in opposition to **Eastern philosophy**.

Yin/yang A traditional Chinese concept of opposing forces creating dynamism in the universe by continuously moving into balance with each other.

Young Hegelians A group of nineteenth-century young German philosophers who were inspired by the **dialectical idealism** of G. W. F. Hegel to spurn church and state, and become radical, republican atheists.

Zen Buddhism A branch of **Buddhism** stressing the possibility of enlightenment through meditation.

Index

About the contributors

Hugh Barker studied philosophy at Clare College Cambridge and has contributed to various titles including a series of guides to philosophy. He is the author of entries on: Philo of Alexandria, Baruch Spinoza, Immanuel Kant, Edmund Burke, Georg Wilhelm Friedrich Hegel, Arthur Schopenhauer, Alexander Herzen, Søren Kierkegaard, Charles Peirce, William James, Edmund Husserl, John Dewey, G. E. Moore, Karl Popper, Nelson Goodman, Maurice Merleau-Ponty, Isaiah Berlin, John Rawls, Bernard Williams, Richard Rorty, and Robert Nozick.

John Bratherton studied philosophy and theology at St John's College Cambridge; his interests are in aesthetics, philosophy of language, and Continental philosophy, and he has lectured on Heidegger and Gadamer. He is the author of entries on: Francis Bacon, Thomas Hobbes, John Locke, George Berkeley, David Hume, John Stuart Mill, and Martin Heidegger.

Dr Dan Cardinal specialized in Continental philosophy and the philosophy of the Enlightenment at the University of Warwick; he is a tutor in philosophy and the co-author of a series of philosophy text books. He is the author of entries on: Thales of Miletus, Pythagoras, Xenophanes of Colophon, Heraclitus of Ephesus, Parmenides of Elea, Anaxagoras, Empedocles, Zeno of Elea, Protagoras, Socrates, Democritus, Plato, Diogenes the Cynic, Aristotle, Pyrrho of Elis, Epicurus, Zeno of Citium, Cicero, Plotinus, and Saint Augustine.

Nicola Chalton studied philosophy at University College London, where she specialized in the philosophy of mind, aesthetics, and ethics; she is the author of Memory Power and the co-author of a history of Europe and a timechart history of revolutions. She is the editor of this book and the author of entries on: Saint Anselm of Canterbury, Peter Abelard, Albert the Great, Saint Thomas Aquinas, Duns Scotus, William of Ockham, Friedrich Nietzsche, Henry Bergson, and Ludwig Wittgenstein. She is also the project editor for *Scientists* in the same series ("They Changed the World").

Gareth Fitzgerald studied philosophy at Oxford University and University College London, where he specialized in the philosophy of language, Wittgenstein, and Quine. For this book he is the consusltant philosopher and the author of entries on: Gottlob Frege, Bertrand Russell, Rudolf Carnap, Gilbert Ryle, William Van Orman Quine, Noam Chomsky, and John Searle.

Meredith MacArdle studied archaeology and anthropology at the University of Cambridge; she is the author of several history books, and has written on a variety of philosophical topics. She is the author of entries on: Confucius, Laozi, Mencius, Zhuangzi, Li Si, Traditional Indian philosophy, Nagarjuna, The Zen Masters, Kukai, Al-Kindi (Alkindus), Avicenna (Ibn Sina), Solomon Ibn Gabirol (Avicebrol), Al-Ghazali (Algazel), Averroës, Maimonides, Moses Mendellssohn, Mary Wollstonecraft, Karl Marx, Friedrich Engels, Nishida Kitaro, José Ortega y Gasset, Sarvepalli Radhakrishnan, Sayyid Abul Ala Maududi, Jean-Paul Sartre, and Simone de Beauvoir. She is also the editor of *Scientists* in the same series ("They Changed the World").

Robert Teed studied English literature at Cambridge University, became an English teacher, and more recently has developed a career as a freelance writer. He is the author of entries on: Niccolò Machiavelli, Gottfried Leibniz, Joseph Butler, Voltaire, Jean-Jacques Rousseau, Adam Smith, Thomas Paine, Jeremy Bentham, Auguste Comte, Kurt Gödel, Michel Foucault, Jacques Derrida, and Peter Singer.